An Autobiography of The Supreme Court

An Autobiography

EDITED AND

WITH AN INTRODUCTION BY

Alan F. Westin

ASSOCIATE PROFESSOR OF PUBLIC LAW AND GOVERNMENT,

COLUMBIA UNIVERSITY;

MEMBER OF THE DISTRICT OF COLUMBIA BAR

# of The Supreme Court

Off-the-Bench Commentary by the Justices

THE MACMILLAN COMPANY, NEW YORK

COLLIER-MACMILLAN LIMITED, LONDON

First Printing

The Macmillan Company, New York
Collier-Macmillan Canada, Ltd., Toronto, Ontario
Divisions of The Crowell-Collier Publishing Company

Printed in the United States of America

Library of Congress catalog card number: 63-10707

Designed by Hermann Strohbach

ACKNOWLEDGMENTS

*The author wishes to give his grateful acknowledgment to the following
publishers and publications for permission to reprint copyrighted material:*

Columbia University Press for the selection from THE SUPREME
COURT OF THE UNITED STATES: ITS FOUNDATIONS, METHODS AND ACHIEVE-
MENTS: AN INTERPRETATION, by Charles Evans Hughes, copyright 1928
by the Columbia University Press; Harper & Row, Publishers, Incorporated, for the selection from ALL IN ONE LIFETIME, by James F. Byrnes,
copyright © 1958 by James F. Byrnes Foundation, reprinted by permission of the publishers; Doubleday & Company, Inc., for the selection
from WE, THE JUDGES, by William O. Douglas, © 1955, 1956 by William
O. Douglas, reprinted by permission of the publishers. Harvard University Press for the selection from THE SUPREME COURT IN THE AMERICAN
SYSTEM OF GOVERNMENT by Robert H. Jackson, copyright 1955 by William Eldred Jackson and G. Bowdoin Craighill, Jr., Executors, reprinted
by permission of the publishers; and for the selection from the address
"John Marshall and the Judicial Function," by Felix Frankfurter, in GOV-
ERNMENT UNDER LAW, A Conference held at Harvard Law School on
the Occasion of the Bicentennial of John Marshall, Chief Justice of the
United States, 1801–1835, edited by Arthur E. Sutherland, copyright
1955, 1956 by The President and Fellows of Harvard College, reprinted
by permission of the publishers.

Proceedings of the American Philosophical Society for the selection
by Felix Frankfurter; *Record of the Association of the Bar of the City*

of New York for the 1947 Benjamin N. Cardozo Lecture by Felix Frankfurter (which appeared in 47 *Columbia Law Review* 527), and for the 1949 Benjamin N. Cardozo Lecture by William O. Douglas; *New York University Law Review* for "Justice Black and the First Amendment—'Absolutes': A Public Interview," copyright © 1962 by the Board of New York University Law Review; for the first James Madison Lecture (1960) by Hugo Black, copyright © 1960 by the Board of New York University Law Review; for the second James Madison Lecture (1961) by William J. Brennan, Jr., copyright © 1961 by the Board of New York University Law Review; and for the third James Madison Lecture (1962) by Earl Warren, copyright © 1962 by the Board of New York University Law Review; *University of Pennsylvania Law Review* for "The Supreme Court in the Mirror of Justices," by Felix Frankfurter, and for "Mr. Justice Roberts," by Felix Frankfurter; *Virginia Law Review* for the "informal talk" by Felix Frankfurter.

Thanks are also due to Chief Justice Earl Warren, Justices Hugo Black, William J. Brennan, Jr., Tom C. Clark, and William O. Douglas, and former Justices James F. Byrnes and Felix Frankfurter for permission to reprint from their speeches and writings. To them, as also to Justices John M. Harlan and Potter Stewart, and former Justices Charles Evans Whittaker and Stanley Reed, the author is indebted for their patience and generosity in supplying manuscript copies and reprints of their out-of-Court commentary. The author is also in the debt of the following secretaries to members of the Supreme Court for their assistance in collecting out-of-Court commentary: Ethel McCall, Elsie Douglas, Frances Lamb, Mary Fowler, Helen E. Dwyer, Jane Pike, Fay Aull, and Alice O'Donnell.

The Introductory Essay first appeared in slightly different form in the *Columbia Law Review*, and is reprinted by permission.

Felix Frankfurter's essay on Oliver Wendell Holmes, Jr., is reprinted from the *Dictionary of American Biography* under special circumstances through the courtesy of Charles Scribner's Sons.

To Mr. Justice Felix Frankfurter —

scholar of the Constitution, wherever he sits

Table of Contents

PART TWO | NINE MEN IN BLACK: COLLEGIAL
           PERSPECTIVES

PART THREE | THE CONTEMPORARY SUPREME COURT

☆☆☆ Roles for the New Constitutionalism

An Autobiography of The Supreme Court

ALAN F. WESTIN

Out-of-Court Commentary by United States Supreme Court Justices, 1790-1962: Of Free Speech and Judicial Lockjaw

Speaking as the guest of honor at the twenty-fifth anniversary dinner of the American Law Institute in 1948, Mr. Justice Frankfurter observed: "How foolish for a Justice of the Supreme Court ever to venture from the bench and accept an invitation to speak. . . . Were I back in Cambridge, I could talk—had I not been down here . . .—on the Chief Justices I have known, the Nine Old Men and the Nine Young Men, and how old men become young, and how young men become old . . . on the bench. I could talk about the judicial process from without and from within. I could talk about what goes into the law reports and what goes into the waste basket. But here," the Justice noted, "I am suffering from what might be called judicial lockjaw." [1]

This theme—that Justices of the Supreme Court should not speak in public about matters of public law and intra-Court affairs—lies close to the heart of the American judicial tradition. It has often been voiced by the Justices themselves, with a variety of complementary reasons assigned for its mandate. Mr. Justice Brennan has written that one explanation is the need for the Court's decisions to be their own exponents:

[1] Frankfurter, *Personal Ambitions of Judges: Should a Judge "Think Beyond the Judicial"?* 34 A.B.A.J. 656, 658 (1948).

I

A great Chief Justice of my home State [New Jersey] was asked by a reporter to tell him what was meant by a passage in an opinion which had excited much lay comment. Replied the Chief Justice, "Sir, we write opinions, we don't explain them." This wasn't arrogance—it was his picturesque, if blunt, way of reminding the reporter that the reasons behind the social policy fostering an independent judiciary also require that the opinions by which judges support decisions must stand on their own merits without embellishment or comment from the judges who write or join them.[2]

Other Justices regard judicial lockjaw as based on the need to avoid discussion of issues that might someday arrive in the Court-room for determination. Mr. Justice Black, formerly a highly vocal United States Senator from Alabama, opened a fully filtered speech to the Missouri Bar Association in 1942 with the almost plaintive comment:

Today . . . the wide range of political subjects which formerly brought me to Missouri are not for me to discuss. And even other sub-jects, wholly non-political, must frequently be approached with caution. . . . One of the interesting features of service as a member of the Su-preme Court is that before us there must eventually come most, if not all, of the problems of the nation. There is no phase of the struggle of society for its own improvement, no aspect of the clashing relations of men to one another that cannot provoke litigation and require judicial settlement. . . . [This] imposes a sharp limitation on . . . [a Justice's] freedom of discussion in his unofficial capacity. The first requisite of a judicial system is that all its judges be fair. Fairness means many things, but above all it means that no issue may be prejudged—that judges must keep open minds upon genuine issues which they may be called upon to determine.[3]

Still another reason for judicial lockjaw was described by Mr. Justice Stone in 1928, addressing the American Bar Association under the pregnant title, "Fifty Years' Work of the United States Supreme Court." His task, Stone explained, was "to make an address not wholly devoid of human interest" and still "avoid making it an arsenal from which counsel may . . . draw ammunition for future conflicts at the Bar." Stone continued:

[2] Address by William J. Brennan, Jr., Student Legal Forum, Charlottesville, Va., Feb. 17, 1959.
[3] Black, *Address*, 13 Mo. B.J. 173 (1942).

In younger and more innocent days, with no premonitions of the future, I took the time from busy days at the Bar to write occasional articles in the law journals on matters of scientific and technical interest, only to experience, in a repentant old age, the unhappy fate of hearing them, on occasion, cited to me in Court in support of both sides of the same question. However much the Judge may become accustomed and reconciled to such startling agility of counsel, it requires a larger judicial experience than mine to prepare one to face with equanimity the varying implications which may be drawn by diligent counsel from his own innocent remarks. So, if what I am about to say should prove to be more dull and uninteresting than even judicial pronouncements are wont to be, I should like to persuade myself that you would attribute it to a newly developed instinct for self-preservation, cautiously applied with an eye to the future.[4]

Finally, the difficulties inherent in making a significant contribution while remaining within the constricting bounds of propriety have led some Justices to say nothing at all about certain aspects of the Court's work. During a student question period at the Harvard Law School in 1960, Mr. Justice Frankfurter was asked to comment on an article by a member of the law faculty concerning the current pressures of casework and their effect on the quality of the Court's decisions. The Justice responded: "How I would love to tell you that part with which I agreed, and that which I would like to cross-examine him on. [But] I do not want to talk about any matters connected with the Supreme Court. I do not like to give mutilated or partial comments. I don't like to comment on things as to which I cannot fully lay bare my mind." [5]

In keeping with these reasons for judicial lockjaw, there have been Justices in the Court's history who, while on the bench, have said nothing, nothing whatever, about the Court's work. Some of these, one may suspect, did not have much in the way of ideas or even attitudes to enlarge upon after the day's packet of opinions had been drafted. Yet others have been silent whose passions were enormous and still others who are counted among the most idea-filled and reflective judges in our national experience. From the day he became a Justice

[4] Stone, *Fifty Years' Work of the United States Supreme Court*, 14 A.B.A.J. 428 (1928).
[5] PROCEEDINGS IN HONOR OF MR. JUSTICE FRANKFURTER (HARVARD LAW SCHOOL OCCASIONAL PAMPHLET NO. 3, 1960) 10.

in 1916, for example, Louis D. Brandeis said nothing in public about Court matters. Although Benjamin N. Cardozo wrote three incisive books on the judicial process and legal theory while serving on the New York Court of Appeals, he spoke and wrote nothing about the judicial process during his six years as a Justice. "[A] member of the Supreme Court must lay upon himself a self-denying ordinance," he once explained,[6] and to a request from a cousin that he deliver a talk to her organization, the Justice wrote this delightful apology:

> My child—for child you are in spirit—I hate to say "no" but really I must. If you knew how I am driven and hounded by requests for speeches, you'd forgive me, I know you would. . . . [Y]ou have no idea of the inhibitions that hedge the soul—the pure undefiled soul—of a Justice of the Supreme Court. He may not talk about events of the day. They may indicate his judgment as to problems that will come before him as a judge! He may not talk about the past. The past is the parent of the present and has given it its shape and mold! He may not talk about the future. The future is what we make it, and is here almost as we speak. . . .
>
> Well, the result is that I don't make speeches anywhere—not even at bar associations. The American Bar Association sent me a letter the day before yesterday threatening extreme displeasure if I put their invitation aside. I defied the haughty monster. The only exceptions I have made have had their origin in the tender from universities of honorary degrees.[7]

(And even in his appearances at such honorary-degree ceremonies, it should be noted at once, Mr. Justice Cardozo would say nothing about the body on which he served or the areas of law in which he toiled.)

Considering the proclamations of self-denial and the examples of silence that have been cited, one might assume that judicial lockjaw has been the dominant tradition among the Justices, or, at least, that most of their addresses embroidering the cloth of public law have been threaded with the safest of generalities. Nothing could be further from the truth. Rather, the basic tradition among the Justices has been one of wide-ranging and frank out-of-court commentary. Several years after making the comment at the American Law Institute dinner in 1948 that has been quoted above, Mr. Justice Frankfurter did deliver an address on "Chief Justices I have Known" (to law students

---

[6] HELLMAN, BENJAMIN N. CARDOZO: AMERICAN JUDGE 271 (1940).
[7] *Id.* at 292.

at the University of Virginia in 1953),[8] and in 1954 he spoke twice on the judicial process, once at the University of Chicago Law School [9] and again at proceedings of the American Philosophical Society.[10] After his witty warnings about the bonds that tie a Justice's tongue, Mr. Justice Brennan has talked about the assumptions of judicial review, the Bill of Rights and the federal system, and Supreme Court review of state court decisions.[11] Justices Robert Jackson and William O. Douglas, as this article will discuss later in some detail,[12] have provided full-dress, book-length statements of their fundamental ideas about the American constitutional system, the Court's place in it, and leading topics of public law.

The reason for this dominant practice of judicial commentary is that most Justices did not accept their commissions with the intention of forsaking the world in quite so drastic a fashion as Cardozo and Brandeis, or Joseph Bradley or Roger Taney. The Justices who have refrained from any discussion of the Court's work have been men whose basic personalities and work habits led them to that policy. An aversion to dinner parties and conventions carries one a long way in establishing a regimen of refusals. Enjoying the company of family and a few select friends or fellow "insiders," and toiling long hours into the night on opinions, make this response still easier. To regard a stray weekend and summers as times for refreshing the mind and spirit, preferably away from civilization, adds another stone to the self-made prison. And such a rigorous respect for judicial proprieties that even the desire for self-justification or advancement of "the Truth" is put aside provides a final personal element that accounts for the near-monastic commitments of the silent Justices.

Most Justices, however, have been simply too gregarious, too accustomed to the dialectical intellectual processes of society, and too committed to their views to be content with an "outside" role limited to asking questions at oral argument and writing opinions. Society is

---

[8] 39 VA. L. REV. 883 (1953).

[9] SOME OBSERVATIONS ON SUPREME COURT LITIGATION AND LEGAL EDUCATION (1954).

[10] *Some Observations on the Nature of the Judicial Process of Supreme Court Litigation*, 98 AMERICAN PHILOSOPHICAL SOC'Y PROCEEDINGS 233 (1954).

[11] See the selected bibliography.

[12] See notes 96–101 *infra* and accompanying text.

ever ready with attractive blandishments: the lectureships at leading
law schools and universities; the annual bar association meetings of
state and nation; the judicial conferences; the naturalization ceremonies; the law review banquets and college commencements; the me-
morials to lawyers, judges, and other public figures of the law; and the
occasions when awards are presented to the Justices themselves, from
honorary degrees to civil-liberties scrolls. Most Justices, if asked why
they do not reject all such invitations, might respond that remaining
at least in part in the society they serve is the best way for a judge to
preserve an awareness of social trends and intellectual currents. They
might also say that broad defenses of the Court's role and general
explanation of the Court's procedures are vital to enlarging public understanding of these matters. Another comment would be that description of the Court's past and its leading figures fosters understanding of traditions that deserve as much presentation to this generation
and its political leaders as possible.

In this, as in so many other matters pertaining to the Supreme Court,
history provides the most revealing (if always partial) clues to understanding. To appreciate the contemporary balance between frank
commentary and judicial lockjaw, the patterns that out-of-court discussion followed during earlier periods of the Court's life must be
surveyed.

I. Pre-Civil War Perspectives and the Struggle for Judicial Status

In the period from 1790 to 1810, an era of proud Presidents, powerful Congresses, and jealous states, the Justices found themselves am-
bivalent members of an ambiguous institution. The Court had not yet
perfected its special tools of judicial-political influence, and many of
the Justices operated freely in the party and administration politics
of the day. With little "tradition" to guide them, the Justices engaged
in far-ranging and free-swinging commentary. Between 1810 and
1860, however, traditions began to develop; there was far less frankly
partisan speech-making and letter writing to the press, and commentaries better suited to advocacy of constitutional principles and
judicial roles became the norm. This 1790–1860 commentary can

most conveniently be analyzed under four headings: campaign and party comments; political talk from the bench; defenses of the Court; and constitutional commentaries.

A. *Campaign and Party Comments*

The line between the judicial and political spheres was quite indistinct in the first days of the young Republic (separation-of-powers theory notwithstanding), and state judges were often open partisans. Supreme Court Justices shared this mode in the first decade or two of the nation. While they were serving on the Supreme Court, Mr. Justice William Cushing ran for Governor of Massachusetts, Mr. Chief Justice John Jay was a gubernatorial candidate in New York, Mr. Justice Samuel Chase stumped for John Adams in the presidential campaign of 1800, and Mr. Justice Bushrod Washington did the same for Charles C. Pinkney in that election.[13] As federal judges were Federalists before 1800, this conduct provoked steady criticism from the anti-Federalist press. One newspaper lamented the spectacle of Justices "mounting the tub at an electioneering meeting . . . and there [exposing] the dignity of the National Judiciary to the coarse jibes and scoffing jokes of every mischievous bystander. . . ."[14] A United States Senator commented acidly in 1800:

What think you, my friends, of our Supreme Judges electioneering at town and county meetings, those grave and solemn characters who ought to be retired from the public eye, who ought never to be seen in numerous assemblies or mingle in their passions and prejudices, and who, with respect to all political questions and characters, ought ever to be deaf and blind to everything except what they hear in evidence? Can a man, brought before such Judges for sentiments expressed at an election [a reference to prosecutions in the federal circuit courts under the Sedition Law] expect a fair trial, particularly if his expressions have been levelled at the candidate those Judges have been electioneering to support? [15]

Election statements by the Justices appear to have reached a high point in 1800; only occasional instances can be found in subsequent

[13] See 1 WARREN, THE SUPREME COURT IN UNITED STATES HISTORY 273–76 (rev. ed. 1947) [hereinafter cited as WARREN]; WHARTON, STATE TRIALS OF THE UNITED STATES 43–48 (1849).
[14] 1 WARREN 274.
[15] *Ibid.*

decades. That party participation was regarded as unusual in the years after 1800 is evident from the "exceptions" that can be examined. Mr. Justice Story's son, in a biographical memoir of his father, commented that "the only instance during his whole judicial life in which he was present at a political meeting, or publicly engaged in the discussion of a political question" was in 1819.[16] A town meeting was held at Salem, Massachusetts, on the proposed Missouri Compromise. Story passionately supported the resolutions calling on Congress to outlaw slavery in the federal territories and to reject new slaveholding territories for statehood unless they adopted abolition. Story's son described the Justice's sentiments as follows: "Involving as it did a question not merely of party politics, but of national policy and constitutional law, striking at the very principles of the government, darkening the whole future of an oppressed race, and drawing after it vast consequences of evil—he felt that his duty to himself, his country, and the world, required him to overstep the limits he had set for himself on ordinary occasions, and to throw the whole weight of his influence and opinions upon the side of liberty and law." [17]

During the 1840's and 1850's, according to Charles Warren, only one Justice "had taken an active part in politics, or . . . had openly expressed his views on crucial political questions. . . ." [18] This was Mr. Justice John McLean of Ohio, appointed in 1829 by Jackson, and a perennial candidate for presidential nomination, on the National Republican, Free Soil, and Republican party tickets. To advance his candidacy, McLean wrote letters to newspapers giving his views on political topics of the day. In 1847 he wrote such a letter condemning the conduct of the Mexican War by the Polk administration. This drew remarks from leading newspapers, which called him a "judicial politician" who was "dragging the ermine in the mire of politics" and displaying "party violence on the bench." [19] A year later, McLean published a letter expounding his views on congressional power to legislate concerning slavery in the federal territories. Sharp congressional and opposition press condemnation followed, as the issue was

[16] 1 LIFE AND LETTERS OF JOSEPH STORY 359–60 (W. Story ed. 1851) [hereinafter cited as STORY].

[17] 1 id. at 360.

[18] 2 WARREN 269. See generally WEISENBURGER, THE LIFE OF JOHN McLEAN: A POLITICIAN ON THE UNITED STATES SUPREME COURT (1937).

[19] 2 WARREN 270 & n.2; WEISENBURGER, op. cit. supra note 18, at 166.

one on which the Court would quite likely rule. Even McLean's supporters thought it necessary to disassociate themselves from his action. Senator Reverdy Johnson commented about the letter: "The judgment of the public, in its almost universal censure of the step, will effectually guard against its repetition. A judge should be separated, not only while he is upon the Bench, but forever, from all the agitating political topics of the day. Once a Judge, he should ever be a Judge." [20] A Philadelphia newspaper man remarked that all the other Justices of the Supreme Court "justly respect the high responsibilities of their position and the notorious feelings of the people, by keeping themselves aloof from the altercations and animosities, the differences and the difficulties of party strife. Justice McLean is an exception." [21]

McLean, unimpressed by this reaction, kept his quill scratching busily across papers addressed to editors. In 1856 he declared his opposition to slavery and drew further criticism, especially from Southern senators, for this "extra-judicial opinion," as Senator James Stewart of Maryland termed it. Senator Stewart noted: "In exciting times like these, when all earthly tribunals, in order to command respect, must be firm, unswerving, and above raving, popular clamor; when, too, the merits of the questions were much involved in a case to come before him as one of the Judges of the last resort—to have made a parade of his opinion, thus intermingling with the partisan debates of a passing hour—cannot certainly commend him to the approval of an intelligent public." [22]

McLean's example indicates that well before the Civil War the practice of avoiding open party participation and topical political comment had become well established on the Supreme Court. Also apparent was the fact that the Court was powerless to force this practice on any Justice who found the stump exhilarating or sought to keep his political prospects alive while serving on the Court. The dilemma was already present, for the nation might want to turn to a Justice (as to generals) at moments when the party leaders seemed soiled or puny men (as with Mr. Justice Charles Evans Hughes in

[20] 2 WARREN 271.
[21] *Ibid.* McLean defended his publication of views, saying that the question of slavery in the territories "had now been settled by several judicial decisions" and could be discussed by a Justice. WEISENBURGER, *op. cit. supra* note 18, at 141.
[22] 2 WARREN 272.

1916). But the goal of nomination always eluded those who pursued it too openly, as the McLeans (and, later, Mr. Chief Justice Salmon Chase) never appreciated.

Actually, the main lines of partisan commentary in the pre-Civil War period were not party orations on the stump or in the press,[23] but a special kind of judicial politics—the political charge to the grand jury.

B. *Political Talk from the Bench*

In providing for division of the new Republic into judicial circuits, to which a Justice of the Supreme Court would travel and hold court, Congress had envisaged promotional as well as legal advantages. As Charles Warren has noted, "It was, in fact, almost entirely through their contact with the Judges sitting in these Circuit Courts that the people of the country became acquainted with this institution, the Federal Judiciary; and it was largely through the charges to the Grand Jury made by these Judges that the fundamental principles of the new Constitution and Government and the provisions of the Federal statutes and definition of the new Federal criminal legislation became known to the people." [24]

Some of the first charges, in the 1790's, such as those by Mr. Chief Justice John Jay and Mr. Justice James Wilson, fulfilled this purpose admirably. (One of Jay's charges in 1790 is reprinted here.) The Justices worked long and diligently on these addresses, which were delivered to sizable audiences. They often took several hours to present, and were generally printed and reprinted in the press.[25]

However, between 1798 and 1803, in the rising bitterness between the Federalists and Jeffersonians, several of the Federalist Justices began to use their charges as hammer blows for the political position

[23] One additional type of political commentary should be mentioned. Several of the Justices served as members of state constitutional conventions in these years—Marshall (Va.), Story (Mass.), and Wayne (Ga.) being prominent examples. In the convention debates, the Justices made speeches and engaged in dialogues about the fundamentals of constitutional government and would often lead the debates on the judiciary provisions.

[24] 1 WARREN 58–59.

[25] 1 *id.* at 58–59, 162–63, 165–66.

of the Adams administration and in attack upon the "Jacobinism" of the anti-Federalists. In June of 1799, for example, Mr. Chief Justice Oliver Ellsworth charged grand juries in South Carolina that those persons "opposing the existence of the National Government or the efficient exercise of its legitimate powers" should and could legally be indicted for subversive activities.[26] This view was adopted by Mr. Justice James Iredell and other members of the Court in what Jeffersonians regarded as a move to institute a common law crime by virtue of which the Justices could punish outspoken critics of the Adams administration.[27]

These charges, at least, could be considered as being within the legitimate scope of a federal judge's interpretation of the criminal law. What set the Jeffersonians to full outcry was that the Justices also lectured grand juries on such political questions as the Jay Treaty, French revolutionary plots against "all religion, and virtue, order and decency," the baneful influence of American "Jacobins" (that is, "anti-Federalists") in fomenting discontent in the nation, the great wisdom of the present administration, and the seditious character of those engaging in denunciation of that administration.[28] These comments usually accompanied the sternest of prosecutions under the hated Sedition Act of 1798.[29] (See the Iredell charge printed here.)

Anti-Federalist feeling mounted rapidly. Thomas Jefferson condemned the conduct of the Justices as "a perversion of the institution of the grand jury from a legal to a political engine." [30] A commentator in the Jeffersonian press denounced the Justices for "itinerating through their Circuits and converting the holy seat of law, reason and equity into a rostrum from which they could harangue the populace under the artful pretense of instructing a grand jury, and excite an alarming fanaticism among them under cover of legal authority." [31] Federalists countered these charges. Congressman James A. Bayard said that the Justices were only replying to critics of the laws they were called upon to enforce on circuit, especially when "enemies of the

26 1 id. at 162.
27 1 id. at 163–64.
28 1 id. at 165–67, 166 n.2.
29 1 Stat. 596.
30 1 WARREN 165.
31 1 id. at 165 n.2.

Administration" had challenged the laws as unconstitutional. The
Justices "have felt themselves called upon to express their judgments
upon that point and the reasons of their opinion." [32]

The most famous political charge was delivered in 1803, when Mr.
Justice Chase addressed a grand jury at an inn in Baltimore, Maryland, his home state and scene of his vigorous campaign for John
Adams in 1800. The charge attacked Republican congressional legislation abolishing the new circuit courts created by the Adams administration and the universal suffrage provisions of a new Maryland
Constitution. The Jeffersonian press reported that in his delivery of
the charge Chase had also attacked President Jefferson's administration as "weak, relaxed and not adequate to a discharge of their functions. . . ." Their goal, Chase stated, was to continue exercising
an "unfairly acquired power." [33] While much of the Federalist press
defended Chase, Republican newspapers went after him with sharp-
ened knives. Wrote the Virginia *Argus:* "Was this man placed in his
high office by the people to become the calumniator of the government of their choice; or was he rather placed there to administer justice conformable to the Constitution of the United States? Is it proper,
is it decent that this man should be forever making political speeches
from the Bench?" [34]

President Jefferson wrote one of his congressional leaders, asking,
rhetorically, "Ought this seditious and official attack on the principles of our Constitution and on the proceedings of the State to go
unpunished?" [35] The Republicans, who had been looking for a Supreme Court Justice to impeach, as a counterattack on the Federalist-
minded judiciary, considered Chase's high-handed conduct in trials
under the Sedition Act, his electioneering for Adams, and his political
charges, and concluded that he was the ideal target. In 1805 the House
of Representatives approved impeachment charges. The eighth article
of the charges read:

And whereas mutual respect and confidence between the government
of the United States and those of the individual states, and between the
people and those governments, respectively, are highly conducive to that

[32] 1 *id.* at 166–67.
[33] 1 *id.* at 276.
[34] 1 *id.* at 277 & n.1.
[35] 1 *id.* at 277.

public harmony, without which there can be no public happiness, yet the said Samuel Chase, disregarding the duties and dignity of his judicial character, did, at a circuit court, for the district of Maryland, held at Baltimore, in the month of May, one thousand eight hundred and three, pervert his official right and duty to address the grand jury then and there assembled, on the matters coming within the province of the said jury, for the purpose of delivering to the said grand jury an intemperate and inflammatory political harangue, with the intent to excite the fears and resentment of the grand jury, and of the good people of Maryland against their state government, and constitution, a conduct highly censurable in any, but peculiarly indecent and unbecoming in a judge of the supreme court of the United States. . . .[36]

The article proceeded to state that Chase had also spoken against the Government of the United States by delivering opinions that, "even if the judiciary were competent to express on a suitable occasion and in a proper manner, were at the time and as delivered highly indecent, extrajudicial, and tending to prostitute the high judicial character with which he was invested and promote the base purposes of an electioneering partisan." [37]

At the trial, Chase's witnesses and his manuscript copy of the charge challenged the allegation that direct accusations had been made against the Jefferson administration, as had been reported in some of the newspapers.[38] The remainder of the charge, however, Chase admitted to be authentic, but contended that it was not a sufficient basis for impeachment. Robert G. Harper argued for Chase:

He contends that according to the custom of this country, subsisting for almost thirty years, without any mark of public disapprobation, he had a right to warn his fellow-citizens, in a charge from the bench, against the political dangers by which he believed them to be threatened; to assist in this manner, in averting impending ruin; in snatching the people of his native state, from the abyss in which he thought them about to plunge. He contends, that for this purpose, and according to this custom, he had a right to point out, what he considered as the pernicious tendency of certain measures of the federal government, in order to shew in a stronger light, the danger of adopting similar measures in the state. This is what he did, and what he supposed himself authorised to do. But he neither claims, nor has exercised, the privilege of abu[s]ing those

[36] 1 SMITH & LLOYD, TRIAL OF SAMUEL CHASE 8 (1805).
[37] Ibid.
[38] 2 id. at 212–26, 293–312.

who have been appointed to administer the government of his country. . . .[39]

Harper further argued that the statements made by Chase were
within his rights as a citizen, even after he became a Justice: "Is it
not lawful for an aged patriot of the revolution to warn his fellow-
citizens of dangers, by which he supposes their liberties and happiness to be threatened? Or will it be contended that a citizen is deprived of these rights, because he is a judge? . . . I trust not. . . ." [40]
Moreover, Chase's defense continued, there was no legal basis for
punishing Chase for his conduct:

In what part of our laws or constitution is it written, that a judge shall
not speak on politics to a grand jury? Shall not advance, in a charge from
the bench, those arguments against a public measure, which it must be
admitted that he might properly employ on any other occasion? Such
conduct may perhaps be ill-judged, indiscreet, or ill-timed. I am ready
to admit that it is so; for I am one of those who have always thought,
that political subjects ought never to be mentioned in courts of justice.
But is it contrary to law? Admitting it to be indecorous and improper,
which I do not admit, is every breach of decorum and propriety a crime?
. . . There is no such law. . . . And will this honorable body, sitting not
in a legislative but a judicial capacity, be called on to make a law, and to
make it for a particular case which has already occurred? [41]

Harper cited examples of political charges by judges before and
after the Revolution, noted that none of their authors had been punished and that no law had been enacted to prohibit them in the future, and demanded that Chase be acquitted on this article. Then, he
concluded, Congress could "resume its legislative character, and pass
a law to restrain the practice in the future." [42]

The managers for the prosecution disputed each of the defense
propositions on the political charges. Representative John Randolph,
asking "whether the prostitution of the bench of justice to the purposes of an hustings is to be tolerated," opened the case on the eighth
article by asserting:

We have nothing to do with the politics of the *man*. Let him speak and
write and publish as he pleases. This is his right in common with his fel-

[39] 2 *id.* at 317–18.
[40] 2 *id.* at 326.
[41] 2 *id.* at 326–27.
[42] 2 *id.* at 328–29.

low citizens. . . . If he must electioneer and abuse the government under which he lives, I know of no law to prevent or punish him, provided he seeks the wonted theatres for his exhibition. But shall a judge declame on these topics from his seat of office? Shall he not put off the political partizan when he ascends the tribune; or shall we have the pure stream of public justice polluted with the venom of party virulence? In short, does it follow that a judge carries all the rights of a private citizen with him upon the bench, and that he may, there, do every act which, as a freeman, he may do elsewhere, without being questioned for his conduct? [43]

Randolph took issue with the contention that "an act to be impeachable, must be indictable," and stated that removal from office was proper for offenses not forbidden by statute.

Representative Caesar A. Rodney replied to Chase's defense that political charges were commonplace and accepted:

The learned counsel, though they acknowledge the conduct of the respondent to have been imprudent, improper and indiscreet, attempt to justify it by the production of charges which wear a political aspect, delivered during the American revolution. I will enter my protest against those, even at so turbulent a season, but none that have been produced furnish any grounds of defense to the respondent. In no instance which has been cited, have they attempted to exclaim against the very government from which they received their commissions. We behold the defendant, a judge of the United States, passing judgment of condemnation on the laws which he was bound to conform to and to execute, and with the policy of which, in his judicial character, he had nothing to do.[44]

Discussing the charge's condemnation of Maryland laws, Rodney also concluded that misbehavior of this kind was clearly impeachable.

It is interesting to observe that, although Chase was not convicted, the largest number of votes to convict—19 out of 34 votes—was cast on the eighth article, the political charge to the grand jury.[45] (The Chase charge appears in this collection in Part One).

Chase's trial and the moderation of partisan intensity after 1804 marked the close of widespread political charging of grand juries by the Justices. In the next decades, the grand jury charge continued to serve as a vehicle for disseminating a Justice's views, but these were

[43] 1 *id.* at 123–24.
[44] 2 *id.* at 447.
[45] 2 *id.* at 492–93.

now confined to constitutional and legal debate, not blatant party and electoral contest.

Mr. Justice Story's practice illustrates the new balance nicely. On the one hand, he rejected political speech-making. Writing to Edward Everett in 1825, after the press had mentioned Story's name in connection with the founding of a political journal in Boston, Story remarked:

Since I have been on the Bench, I have carefully abstained from writing in the newspapers, and have endeavored to avoid mingling in political engagements, so far as I could without a surrender of my own independence. I have done this from the desire that my administration of justice should not be supposed by the public to be connected with political views or attachments; and from a fear that I might insensibly be drawn too much into the vortex of party excitements. I think the public opinion now points out this course to Judges. . . .[46]

On the other hand, Story's antislavery sentiments were so aroused by the clandestine slave trade through New England ports between 1815 and 1820 that he could not treat this offense as just another violation of law. In 1819 he wrote an extended denunciation of the slave trade and delivered it throughout his circuit, district by district from Boston to Providence. The charge was an eloquent and moving attack on the inhumanity of slave trading and, by inescapable logic, of slavery itself.[47] "I make no apology, gentlemen," Story concluded each delivery of the lengthy charge, "for having detained you so long upon this subject. . . . [I]f we tolerate this traffic, our charity is but a name, and our religion little more than a faint and delusive shadow." [48]

Story's charge was not directed at specific grand jury action (although the trade clearly violated federal statutes), but at the influential and prominent New England businessmen who were amassing fortunes from slave trading. These people and their sympathizers were quick to challenge Story's charge as "exaggerated" and to brand as improper Story's use of the bench for this purpose. Much of the New England press echoed this attack; one Boston newspaper said

[46] 1 STORY 363.
[47] 1 *id.* at 336–47.
[48] 1 *id.* at 347.

he should be "hurled from the Bench" for his speech. As Story's son recalled: "This, like all popular clamors, blew by him like the empty wind on a rock. He had made up his mind that it was his duty, judicially and morally, to exert his utmost powers to procure the annihilation of this trade, and nothing availed to check him. He delivered and redelivered this charge. He printed and circulated it, and steadily bore his testimony against the slave trade, as repugnant to law, religion, and humanity." [49]

Story's use of the grand jury charge to promote obedience to a "challenged" law—an appeal to community morality—typified the outermost boundary of this mode of commentary in the 1830's. By this time, some members of the Court had come to regard discursive and comprehensive charges as inappropriate or unnecessary. In 1836 Mr. Chief Justice Taney explained to a grand jury in Maryland that he would "depart from the former practice" of lengthy charges:

There was a time, without doubt, in the days that have gone by, when precise and detailed instructions from the court, to the grand jury, were necessary for the purposes of justice. But in the present enlightened state of the public mind, when education and useful information are not confined to a few, but diffused generally throughout the community, every citizen summoned as a juror, has a general knowledge of the duties he is called there to perform, and of the manner in which it is incumbent on him to discharge them; and in all cases demanding more precise and particular knowledge, you will have the aid of the district attorney. . . .

For this reason, the Chief Justice stated, "it would be a waste of time for the court to engage itself in discussing principles, and enlarging upon topics which are not to lead us to some practical result. . . ." [50]

Writing in 1849, the historian and political commentator Francis Wharton made a perceptive comment about political speeches and grand jury charges in the Federalist era and in the decades of the thirties and forties. In the introduction to his famous work *State Trials of the United States,* Wharton observed:

Since these days [1790–1800], fifty years have now passed, in the first twenty of which the federal judges had to struggle against an administration embittered by their personal onslaughts, and a [national] majority irritated by their political encroachments. When Mr. Jefferson came in,

[49] 1 *id.* at 347–48.
[50] 30 Fed. Cas. 998 (No. 18257) (C.C.D. Md. 1836).

the political consequence of the court seemed over. With its secular dignities destroyed, and its secular possessions confiscated, it was ordered, like a disgraced bishop of feudal days, to betake itself to its own diocese, and no longer to meddle in affairs of state.

As Wharton noted, however, the Court displayed a surprising resiliency:

[T]he court, devoting itself solely to the discharge of its constitutional duties, began to exhibit a power which, in the palmiest days of executive favour it had never shown. Confining itself, under the guidance of the pure and intrepid jurist [John Marshall], who then controlled its course, within its constitutional limits, it soon began to develop those sovereign prerogatives which to it as a co-equal branch of the government, had been entrusted. The judicial veto, the existence of which in its political prosperity it had scarcely hinted, was now applied with equal firmness and vigour to both the executive and legislative departments.

Comparing the troubles of the federal judiciary in the 1790's in securing obedience to federal law with the ease with which the courts conducted comparable trials in 1807 and 1809, Wharton concluded:

This great change is not without its lesson. It has taught us that to the judiciary, as to the church, political consequence is moral peril; and that though, while occupying its own territory, its authority is sovereign and its edicts supreme, the moment it oversteps the boundaries by which that territory is confined—the moment it canvasses for popular honour or executive favours—that moment the magic of its power is gone. . . .[51]

Nothing in the 1850's challenged Wharton's estimate. With the slavery crisis upon the nation, the federal judges used grand jury charges primarily to urge compliance with federal law, including the fugitive rendition statutes. In both northern and southern states, they warned that no person or group had a right to threaten the Union by defying existing legislation. The charge of Justice Samuel Nelson in 1851, printed here, illustrates this commentary.

C. Defenses of the Court

The third major type of judicial commentary developed in the pre-Civil War exploratory decades was the defense of particular de-

[51] WHARTON, *op. cit. supra* note 13, at 48.

cisions or the Court's general reputation and power against both official and public criticism. From the beginning, the Justices usually left Court defenses to the Court's ideological and interest-group supporters at the Bar, in Congress, and in the press. Occasionally, however, criticism was so unfair and unenlightened and a Justice so provoked (each Justice had his own provocation point, of course) that he burst out in refutation. When Mr. Justice William Johnson, a Jefferson appointee, was criticized publicly in 1808 by the Attorney General of the United States for a circuit decision holding invalid an executive instruction under an embargo in a South Carolina port,[52] Johnson addressed a public reply to the South Carolina newspapers.[53] In his sole extrajudicial publication, Mr. Chief Justice John Marshall wrote an anonymous defense of the Court's ruling (and his own opinion) in *McCulloch* v. *Maryland*,[54] in reply to a set of powerful articles by Spenser Roane. Marshall's reply appeared as two letters by "A friend to the Union" in a leading Federalist paper, the Philadelphia *Union*, and are printed here.[55]

To cite one further example, in 1847 abolitionist criticism of the Supreme Court's rulings upholding federal fugitive slave laws led Mr. Justice McLean—himself an outspoken abolitionist—to write a public letter to an abolitionist editor who had denounced the Court as part of the slavery conspiracy. McLean wrote:

It is an easy matter to denounce the action of any Court who may differ from our own views, and thereby endeavor to lessen the public confidence in such Court. But denunciation is not argument, and however well it may be calculated to create prejudice and mislead ignorant minds and thereby promote party purposes, it is not the best mode of attaining a high and honorable object. Had you examined the facts of the cases referred to, I am quite sure you would have been restrained from saying, in effect, that the Court was corrupt and that its decisions were always in favor of slavery.[56]

Noting that one of the opinions criticized had been written by Mr. Justice Story, a firm opponent of slavery, and that the late Justices

[52] Gilchrist *v.* Collector, 10 Fed. Cas. 356 (No. 5420) (C.C.D.S.C. 1808).
[53] 1 WARREN 334.
[54] 17 U.S. (4 Wheat.) 316 (1819).
[55] WARREN 515 & n.1.
[56] 2 *id.* at 157.

Thompson and Baldwin, also foes of slavery, had joined in the decision, McLean lectured the editor on the obligations of a judge:

It is known to every one that Judges are sworn to support the Constitution and laws. They cannot consider slavery in the abstract. If they disregard what they conscientiously believe to be the written law in any case, they act corruptly and are traitors to the country. The Constitution and Act of Congress give to the master of a slave a right to reclaim him in a free State. So plain are the provisions on this subject that no one can mistake them. How is it expected or desired that a Judge shall substitute his own notions for positive law? While this shall become the rule of judicial action, there will be no security for character, property or life.[57]

Again, it is important to note that open defenses of the Court, such as those by Johnson, Marshall, and McLean, were the exception, not the rule. However pained and bitter were their private letters to one another or to confidants about deliberate distortion or misunderstanding of decisions, the Justices normally refrained from public utterance. However, there are several ways to defend the Court and advance its prestige without engaging in public speeches or letters, and one of these methods, the full-scale legal treatise, deserves separate treatment here.

D. Constitutional Commentaries and Judicial Scholarship

One basic tool of the judge is scholarship, and the Justices often employed it extrajudicially. Several members of the Court served as professors or lecturers in law during the pre-Civil War decades; James Wilson was a professor at Philadelphia College, and Joseph Story was Dane Professor of Law at Harvard. Both taught constitutional law as well as private and international law. From this earliest period, anecdotes concerning the Court were to be interspersed in lectures, providing one source of piecemeal but useful bits of information about the life within.

Mr. Justice Story, for example, lectured extemporaneously, letting a case or section of the Constitution, or even a chance remark, lead him to comment. He often spoke of fellow Justices and of Court practices. His son, attending lectures as a law student at Harvard, has

[57] 2 *id.* at 157–58.

provided a useful description of how widely such a lecture might roam:

[He moved] into a glowing discourse upon the principles and objects of the Constitution; the views of the great men of the Revolution, by whom it was drawn; the position of our country; the dangers to which it was exposed; and the duty of every citizen to see that the republic sustained no detriment. He spoke, as he went on, of the hopes for freedom with which America was freighted; of the anxious eyes that watched it in its progress; of the voices that called from land to land to inquire of its welfare; closing in an exhortation to the students to labor for the further-ance of justice and free principles. . . .[58]

Other records describing Story's lectures on constitutional history, on leading jurists, on legislators, and on philosophical approaches to the American constitution, have survived.[59]

In addition to lectures, the Justices developed the practice of writ-ing books and pamphlets about constitutional law, history, politics, and the Court's role in American government. The pre-Civil War commentary included biographies (Marshall's life of Washington[60] and Johnson's life of Greene),[61] articles for encyclopedias and legal treatises on topics of public and private law (Story's contributions on "Congress," the "United States courts," "common law" and many other subjects for Francis Lieber's *Encyclopaedia Americana*), and specialized legal works, such as Iredell's work on pleading and Story's famous commentaries on equity jurisprudence, conflicts, agency, bailments, bills of exchange, partnership, and promissory notes.[62] By far the most significant for our purposes, however, were the general volumes on constitutional law and judicial review. These were ad-dressed not only to lawyers but also to the attentive public of the day, which was substantial. Between 1790 and 1860, there were three

[58] 2 STORY 488–89.

[59] 2 *id.* at 489–507.

[60] MARSHALL, THE LIFE OF GEORGE WASHINGTON (2d ed. 1850).

[61] JOHNSON, SKETCHES OF THE LIFE AND CORRESPONDENCE OF NATHANIEL GREENE (1822).

[62] COMMENTARIES ON THE LAW OF PROMISSORY NOTES (1845); COMMENTARIES ON THE LAW OF BILLS OF EXCHANGE (1843); COMMENTARIES ON THE LAW OF PARTNERSHIP (1841); COMMENTARIES ON THE LAW OF AGENCY (1839); COM-MENTARIES ON EQUITY PLEADINGS (1838); COMMENTARIES ON EQUITY JURIS-PRUDENCE (1836); COMMENTARIES ON THE CONFLICT OF LAWS (1834); COM-MENTARIES ON THE LAW OF BAILMENTS (1832).

such works worth noting: James Wilson's *Works* (1790–92);[63] Joseph Story's *Commentaries on the Constitution;*[64] and Henry Baldwin's *A General View of the Origin and Nature of the Constitution and Government of the United States.*[65] The crucial point is that these commentaries were not narrow and neutral presentations of case law, but broad defenses of the constitutional position of the author-Justice.

Story's work, of course, became the American "Blackstone" and underwent edition after edition, to the dismay of Jacksonian spokesmen. In 1837 a Jackson appointee from Pennsylvania, Henry Baldwin, published a treatise setting out a view opposing Story's and explaining his own votes in four important cases of the 1837 Term of Court. Baldwin claimed that the Constitution was a grant from the people of the states, not from "the people of the United States in the aggregate." After extended argument for this position, Baldwin closed by giving lengthy extracts from Story's work, to expose the views of "eminent persons" whose doctrine Baldwin considered "dangerous, as repugnant to the provisions of the constitution. . . ."[66]

This exchange of volumes, so precursory of later volleys of articles and books between leaders of opposing views within the Court, illustrates how early out-of-court commentary served to provide serious and extended discussions of disputes within the Court for the general public to consider, in addition to what was said in the opinions.

II. Aristocratic Eras and Speeches from the Throne

Following the Civil War, the Court spent at least a decade repairing its prestige after the debacle of the *Dred Scott* case. As if mirroring the Court's lessened status, out-of-court commentary was very sparse and guarded between 1865 and the late 1880's. With the possible exception of some lectures by Mr. Justice Samuel Miller,[67] scholarship in the Wilson-Story tradition was lacking. Charges to grand juries

[63] Works of the Hon. James Wilson (B. Wilson ed. 1804).
[64] Story, Commentaries on the Constitution of the United States (1833).
[65] Baldwin, A General View of the Origin and Nature of the Constitution and Government of the United States (1837).
[66] *Id.* at 107–08.
[67] Miller, The Constitution of the United States (1880).

were tame and apolitical; examples are Mr. Chief Justice Salmon Chase's plea for citizens to pay their taxes,[68] and Mr. Justice Stephen Field's condemnation of the mistreatment of Chinese in California.[69] Newspaper items were few, although one deserves quotation in full. In 1875 friends of Mr. Chief Justice Morrison Waite launched a talking campaign for Waite as the ideal man for the Republican presidential nomination in 1876, when Grant retired after his second term. Waite wrote to his family and friends requesting that he not be considered, and one of these letters was published in a Cincinnati newspaper and widely reprinted, with great editorial praise for its position. Waite wrote:

In my judgment my predecessor detracted from his name by permitting himself to think he wanted the Presidency. Whether true or not, it was said that he permitted his ambitions in that direction to influence his judicial opinions. I am not one of those who believe he did so consciously, but one who occupies this position should keep himself above suspicion. There can't be a doubt that in these days of politico-judicial questions it is dangerous to have a judge who thinks beyond the judicial in his personal ambitions.

He proceeded to say:

The Court is now looked upon as the sheet anchor. Will it be if its Chief Justice is placed in the political whirlpool? The office has come down to me covered with honor. When I accepted it, my duty was not to make it a stepping-stone to something else, but to preserve its purity and make my own name as honorable, if possible, as that of my predecessors. . . .[70]

The sparsity of commentary between 1865 and 1885 was more than compensated for by the explosion of speeches and writing that accompanied the Court's return to heights of authority and prestige in the later 1880's and in the decades immediately following. With Reconstruction ended and the economy booming, a mood of organic, self-congratulatory nationalism swept the nation. Gala national fetes were held between 1876 and 1896 celebrating the centennials of the Declaration of Independence (1876), the promulgation of the Constitution (1889), the organization of the national judiciary (1890), and even the laying of the cornerstone of the Capitol (1896). The

[68] 30 Fed. Cas. 992, 996 (No. 18255) (C.C.D. Cal. 1872).
[69] *Id.* at 996.
[70] TRIMBLE, CHIEF JUSTICE WAITE 141–42 (1938).

oratory on these occasions reflected a popular conception of the Court as the symbol of unity and continuity in the nation, above party and section, a kind of republican Crown. The Justices, keepers of republicanism and orderly progress, were the wise and sternly-loving fathers, instructing people and elected representatives alike in the discipline of constitutional government.

Until the depression of 1929–1933 arrived to shake the notions of inevitable progress, perfected government instruments, and an all-knowing judiciary, the Justices' commentary about the Court resembled royal speeches. For example, at the celebration of the Constitution's centennial in 1889, Mr. Justice Stanley Matthews, responding to a glowing toast to "The Federal Judiciary," suggested that the Court was the central guardian of liberty in America:

Thus was cast upon the Federal Judiciary the burden and the duty, in the due course of judicial determination between litigant parties, of enforcing the supreme law of the land, even though it became essential, in doing so, to declare void acts of Congress and of the legislatures of the States. This is the logical necessity of liberty secured by written constitutions unalterable by ordinary acts of legislation. If the prohibitions and limitations of the charters of government cannot be enforced in favor of individual rights, by the judgments of the judicial tribunals, then there are and can be no barriers against the exactions and despotism of arbitrary power; then there is and can be no guarantee or security for the rights of life, liberty, or property; then everything we hold to be dear and sacred as personal right is at the mercy of a monarch or a mob.[71]

While Mr. Justice Field championed a rigid laissez-faire judicial credo within the Court, its frank exponent in banquet halls, at bar association meetings, and at law school ceremonies across the nation was Field's nephew and fellow conservative, Mr. Justice David J. Brewer, in his day the William O. Douglas of the Right. In a speech at the Yale Law School in 1891 Brewer signaled the new mood within the Court and the battle still being waged. The basic problem of American government, Brewer declared in "Protection to Private Property from Public Attack," [72] was "to secure the rights of the individual against the assaults of the majority," particularly assaults on private and corporate property in the name of state police power.

[71] Matthews, *The Federal Judiciary*, in 2 HISTORY OF THE CELEBRATION OF THE ONE HUNDREDTH ANNIVERSARY OF THE PROMULGATION OF THE CONSTITUTION OF THE UNITED STATES 370 (Carson ed. 1889).
[72] 10 RAILWAY & CORPORATION L.J. 281 (1891).

The danger, Brewer warned, was that "timid judges" might uphold, in the supposed interest of public health, morals, and welfare, state regulation of such matters as utility rates or the use of property, ignoring the fact that these measures of "spoilation" must be struck down. The Court was moving to protect "private capital," but much remained to be done. "[W]e must recast some of our judicial decisions," he said, because "many of those who wrought into the constitution the fourteenth amendment believed that they were placing therein a national guarantee against future state invasion of private rights; but judicial decisions have shorn it of strength, and left it nothing but a figure of speech." [73]

By the mid-1890's and certainly by 1898, although still alarmed by the "coercive" activities of majorities, Brewer was happily content with the position of the Supreme Court. It had fulfilled his hopes and was now "The Nation's Anchor," the title of a Lincoln's Birthday address he delivered in Chicago in 1898. Noting with pleasure recent decisions protecting the rights of capital against income taxation, labor organizations, and other majority measures, he remarked that this was an era in which, "against some local movement, some effort of a few, the Supreme Court calmly lifts its staying hand and says, 'Thus reads the Constitution. . . .' " [74]

Brewer's 1898 speech also serves as an example of the confident defenses of the Court in this period. With sharp attacks mounting against the Court after its spate of conservative rulings in 1895, Brewer spoke of the movement "to displace the courts" and delivered a few smart rebukes against it.

It is part and parcel of the scheme to array the many against the few, the masses against the classes, and this is done under the pretense of realizing a more complete government by the people. The leaders are too adroit to propose their total abolition. The cry is to shear them of jurisdiction and leave them like painted ships on a painted ocean.[75]

Of course, not all the members of the Court shared Brewer's conservatism, though speeches by such Justices as Horace Lurton and Stanley Matthews echoed his themes about judicial omnicompetence.[76] Yet it is interesting to note that little commentary aired the dissent-

[73] *Id.* at 283.
[74] *The Nation's Anchor*, 57 ALB. L.J. 166 (1898).
[75] *Ibid.*
[76] See the selected bibliography.

ing views of John Marshall Harlan, Oliver Wendell Holmes, Jr.,
John H. Clarke, Louis D. Brandeis, and other dissidents between the
1880's and 1920's. Holmes delivered only one or two speeches about
the Court, and these were broadly reflective rather than expositive
of specific issues.[77] Harlan, though fiery in judicial exposition, particularly when dissenting in economic regulation or civil-liberties cases,
did not expound these views in his public speeches, but generally defended the Supreme Court against radical attacks or discussed historical themes. The selections from Holmes and Harlan printed here
were exceptional.

One liberal Justice who challenged the Brewer position from time
to time was Henry Billings Brown. One of his most informal speeches
in this vein was a response at a dinner given to him in 1906, upon his
retirement from the Court.[78] Brown observed in the course of his
remarks:

Speaking for myself, I have left the Bench with a profound reverence
for the Constitution of the United States as a marvelous piece of constructive legislation, and with the conviction that it should be liberally
interpreted—interpreted as if it were intended as the foundation of a
great nation, and not merely a temporary expedient for the united action
of thirteen small States. If it were originally, as said by John Quincy
Adams, "a compromise extorted from the grinding necessities of a reluctant people," it has long since lost that character, and is accepted as
the best possible form of Government for this country,—too sacred to
be trifled with, or even seriously criticized. But like all written Constitutions, there is an underlying danger in its inflexibility. Being practically
unamendable, it can only be adapted to new conditions by construction.
. . . I would disturb little, if anything, that has already been decided, but
I would as new questions arise, adapt the Constitution to them as far as
possible.[79]

Brown then added a glimpse of his uphill struggle within the Court:

My colleagues once poked a good deal of fun at me for saying that the
law was "to a certain extent a progressive science," that restrictions once
necessary were such no longer, and were even detrimental, while in
recent times a vast extension of the police power has been found useful
to the proper protection of the individual and the well-being of society.

[77] See the selected bibliography.
[78] DINNER GIVEN MAY 31, 1906 IN HONOR OF MR. JUSTICE HENRY BILLINGS
BROWN 19 (Bar of the Supreme Court of the United States ed. 1908).
[79] Id. at 20–21.

But I have seen no reason to change my opinion upon that point. I am not frightened at the charge of judicial legislation. . . .[80]

After a discussion of corporations that bore little resemblance to those by Mr. Justice Brewer, Brown offered a description of the role of government and reform movements that must have sent shivers down the spines of the Court's conservatives:

Indeed, I regard all the other achievements of the administration [of President Theodore Roosevelt] in the world of diplomacy and statesmanship as dwarfed by the great wave of reform which it has set in motion, and which is sweeping over the country, carrying everything before it, not only in the Federal Government and the States, but in municipalities and even in private corporations. For once the conscience of the people is aroused, and while injustice may result in particular cases to men who have not done wrong deliberately, the result will not be forgotten. I hope it will lead to a juster appreciation of the proper relations between the State and the individual. True patriotism, instead of looking upon the State as a hostile city to be looted, should regard her as a beneficent mother,—a mother country which protects our lives and guards our interests, and which in return is entitled to our fealty, our affection and above all, to fair and generous treatment.[81]

As for other types of out-of-court commentary, charges to grand juries and partisan comments by Justices still on the Court had vanished by this time. Scholarly commentary was meager. Although several Justices lectured at law schools—Field at the University of California, Harlan at Columbian University in Washington, D.C., and William Strong at Columbian and the University of Pennsylvania—no volumes of commentaries appeared between 1885 and the 1920's. Mr. Justice Harlan had planned to publish a textbook on constitutional law based on his class lectures, but he never found the time to do this while on the Court and could not bring himself to retire and create the leisure. The only book-length work on the Court in these years was written by a former Justice, Charles Evans Hughes. *The Supreme Court of the United States*, published in 1928, was based on six lectures that Hughes, then away from the Court since 1916, delivered at Columbia University.

Between 1920 and 1940, out-of-court commentary on the Court's work and constitutional issues fell to the lowest point in the Court's

[80] *Id.* at 21.
[81] *Id.* at 24–25.

history, before or since. The liberals rarely spoke publicly, and when they did, it was narrow and often technical commentary. Mr. Justice Harlan Fiske Stone's talk on "Fifty Years' Work of the United States Supreme Court," in 1928,[82] was a sluggish recitation of leading case holdings; the policy of silence of Brandeis and Cardozo has already been discussed. Holmes thought it best to keep his gems for opinions, letters, and conversation. Nor were the conservatives outspoken. After one speech in 1924 discussing criticism of the Court by those whose toes were trod upon by constitutional rulings,[83] Mr. Justice George Sutherland did not deliver any further public addresses about the Court during his remaining fourteen years on the bench. Mr. Chief Justice William Howard Taft gave two unpublished talks,[84] in contrast to his frank, published speeches and writings about judicial review between 1891 and 1900, when he was a federal circuit court judge. James McReynolds, Pierce Butler, Willis Van Devanter, Owen Roberts—all spoke infrequently, and in highly limited fashion when they did. The most direct commentary came from a retired Justice, John H. Clarke, who lectured to bar associations in the 1920's on practice before the Supreme Court and gave a radio talk in 1937 supporting the constitutionality of President Roosevelt's Court reform bill.[85]

Why the commentary fell off so strikingly between 1865 and 1885 and again between 1920 and 1940 is difficult to explain. There does not seem to be any relation between the level of commentary and either decisional trends within the Court or the Court's general prestige. Between 1865 and 1885, the Court was moving out of a declined prestige and feeling its way toward a new, assertive, laissez-faire judicial philosophy; between 1920 and 1937 the Court's prestige was extremely high, despite reform and liberal protests, and the majority espoused a full-blown interventionist credo. Yet both periods produced little out-of-court commentary. There was no correlation between public commentary and a Justice's ideological position within the Court, nor was there any strong public conception of judicial propriety that distinguished these two periods. Further, there is no

[82] 14 A.B.A.J. 428 (1928).
[83] 20 UTAH B.A. PROCEEDINGS 55 (1927).
[84] See the selected bibliography.
[85] See the selected bibliography.

evidence to support the notion that the Chief Justices who led the Court during these years had a restraining influence on the Justices greater than that exerted in "normal" periods of more active public expression.[86]

Regardless of whether the final explanation for this dearth lies in the character of the men who happened to be on the Court during these years or in some other factor, the 1920–1940 period was a noticeably lean era for out-of-court commentary. This makes all the more dramatic and worthy of exploration the explosion of frank commentary that characterizes 1940 to the present.

III. COMMENTARY BY THE REAM: EAVESDROPPING ON THE TEMPLE DIALOGUES

Since the arrival of the Franklin Roosevelt appointees, the Justices have produced continuous, revealing, systematic, and far-ranging commentary about the Court and its inner conflicts.[87] The explanations for this new trend are varied but interrelated. The Court now operates in an atmosphere far different from that of an all-embracing popular confidence in the notions of private initiative, limited government, and judicial omnipotence; on the contrary, the nation is presently immersed in the politics of activist government, open group conflict and interaction, and in a psychological climate of introspection typical of a challenged society. The Court itself has made a dramatic shift from a jurisprudence designed to adjust property relations to a jurisprudence especially focused on personal and group

[86] Generally, the Chief Justices themselves have had little to say of significance or in revelation about the Court, even though most Chief Justices have delivered frequent, though vague, ceremonial addresses. The annual report to the American Law Institute, which the Chief Justices began giving in the 1920's, has cited judicial statistics on the Court's work during the preceding term but has focused primarily on the lower federal courts and has featured only infrequent references of any note about the Supreme Court itself. Perhaps the sense of being responsible for "massing the Court," as Mr. Chief Justice Hughes put it, and for promoting internal harmony by avoiding direct advocacy of personal positions except in judicial opinions, accounts for this phenomenon.

[87] Since the contemporary commentary is familiar to readers, and is readily available for examination in the sources listed in the selected bibliography accompanying this article, extensive quotations and doctrinal discussions from this material have not been included in this introductory essay.

rights of status and liberty. Within the Court as well as in public thinking, consideration of judicial review proceeds on assumptions about legal realism and majority rule that make appeals to judicial disinterest and special insight argumentative at best; indeed, many of the men placed on the Court by Presidents since 1939 have contributed powerfully to the stripping away of judicial mystery and claims of omniscience, and they have not found it easy to enunciate a new credo to justify intervention or to support a higher judgment of values by the Court.

The result of these factors has been that articulate Justices accustomed to speaking boldly and frankly about the judicial process before they joined the Court have continued to speak boldly and frankly, though with obvious stopping points, after they have joined the supreme bench. Candor about the Court's internal divisions, about what the Court does, and about the dilemmas of adjusting constitutional limitations to the cold war era has become common, with questions of degree of frankness rather than exceptional Justices being the point of attention.

Within this present mode of commentary, several "styles" have developed.

Mr. Justice Frankfurter has concentrated on judicial biography as his basic technique of expression. While he has spoken at times on the judicial process and on special problems such as statutory interpretation, the great bulk of his out-of-court statements has been about fellow Justices—from Marshall to Fuller, Taft, Holmes, Hughes, Cardozo, Brandeis, Stone, Roberts, and Jackson.[88] Biography serves as Frankfurter's framework for observations about the lessons of history concerning the judiciary's role in American government, about the inner life of the Court, and about the fundamental attributes of disinterest, self-consciousness, and lawyer-like competence and craftsmanship, which represent his concept of judicial greatness.

Though Mr. Justice Frankfurter has been the most prolific writer of judicial biography, this kind of commentary has flowered in the 1940–1960 period. Before 1940, few extended, systematic, and analytical speeches or essays were composed about Justices who had previously been on the Court or had been colleagues and had recently died or retired. The remarks made by Chief Justices or Associate Jus-

[88] See the selected bibliography.

tices at the Court's formal ceremonies on the death of a colleague
tended to be brief appreciations, primarily laudatory, and, if they
dealt with doctrines or judicial personality at all, did so in the manner
of saying good things about the dead. The new biographical literature
is often appreciative and almost never hostile, but it is reflective, discusses the model and variations of ideal judicial conduct, and tends
often to be an argument for the views of the biographizing Justice
as much as for those of the biographee. The black leather chair across
the conference table is an incomparable observation post for the Justice with discrimination and insight. It affords a member of the Court
an opportunity to perceive those qualities—which, as in the case of a
Justice such as Willis Van Devanter, may not be known to the public
—that make a colleague a valuable and sometimes even commanding
influence within the tight ninesome that constitutes the Court.

Another technique, employed by Mr. Justice Harold Burton, has
been that of historical "reconstruction." Burton lectured on the great
cases decided by the Court in earlier periods, such as *Marbury* v.
Madison,[89] the Aaron Burr treason trial,[90] the *Dartmouth College* [91]
case, *Ex parte Milligan*,[92] *Ex parte McCardle*,[93] and the *Legal Tender* [94] cases.[95] While he was not overly explicit in these speeches in
drawing meaningful analogies to the Court's current problems, the
"reconstructions" accomplished this in a light way that Burton found
sufficient for his purposes.

The basic pattern, however, has been discussion of the Court's activities and decisional trends in a more direct fashion than these biographical and historical styles. Many of the Justices have spoken
without self-consciousness about the Court, and without much in the
way of apology for their frankness. To review the Court-years
bibliography of the late Mr. Justice Robert H. Jackson, for example,
is to see a steadily developed edifice of reflections on the Court's
performance—on *stare decisis*, the full faith and credit clause, statu-

---

[89] 5 U.S. (1 Cranch) 137 (1803).
[90] United States *v.* Burr, 25 Fed. Cas. 55 (No. 14693) (C.C.D. Va. 1807).
[91] Trustees of Dartmouth College *v.* Woodward, 17 U.S. (4 Wheat.) 518
(1819).
[92] 71 U.S. (4 Wall.) 2 (1866).
[93] 74 U.S. (7 Wall.) 506 (1868).
[94] 79 U.S. (12 Wall.) 457 (1870).
[95] See the selected bibliography.

tory interpretation, wartime settings and judicial protection of liberty, the relation between civil liberties and property questions, the primacy of political or judicial defense of freedom of expression, and many other topics.[96] These culminated in a full-dress exposition by Jackson of his views on the Court and democratic society in his lectures published as *The Supreme Court in the American System of Government*, issued posthumously in 1955.[97]

A comparable, even more outspoken example from the opposite wing of the Court in the 1940's to 1960's is the commentary of Mr. Justice William O. Douglas. Douglas is the only Justice whose out-of-court literary output comes close to matching his pages of opinions. Wholly apart from his frequent articles, speeches, and books on travel, foreign policy, and the Soviet Union, Douglas has spoken about dissenting opinions, *stare decisis*, due process, criminal procedure, the bar, televising of trials, arrests on suspicion, and a variety of other topics, as well as about the Court's case load, its relations with Congress and administrative agencies, and the role of the Court in civil liberties cases.[98] In addition to these speeches and articles, most of which have been published in law reviews or specialized journals, Mr. Justice Douglas writes frank book reviews and has written for the general public several works on, or including, constitutional themes: his books, *Being an American, An Almanac of Liberty, The Right of the People*, and *America Challenged*, have been popular entries; his treatment of the Court historically and analytically, *We, The Judges*, was also written for the general public.[99] While Mr. Justice Jackson may be said to have confined his frequent commentaries to the issues directly confronting the Court, as has Mr. Justice William J. Brennan, Jr.,[100] Douglas's legal writings have been reformist discussions about law in America that included and also went beyond the judicial function itself.

Douglas has also been distinctive in his frank responses to public comments about the Supreme Court by leading lawyers, professors, and the press. To cite only one example, an article appeared in the August

[96] See the selected bibliography.
[97] See the selected bibliography.
[98] See the selected bibliography.
[99] See the selected bibliography.
[100] See the selected bibliography.

17, 1961 issue of *The Reporter* magazine that described and assessed the splits within the Supreme Court between 1956 and 1961. The author of this article was the correspondent who regularly reports on Supreme Court news and legal affairs for the New York *Times*. Justice Douglas responded with a letter to *The Reporter*, published in its September 14, 1961 issue, that took sharp exception to the article:

I was shocked to read in your issue of August 17, 1961, in Anthony Lewis's "A New Lineup on the Supreme Court," the following:

"As the philosophical division between the four and the five deepens, there is a tendency for each side to suspect the good faith of the other. Extremism breeds extremism."

I have been on the Court for over twenty-two years and I have never known a Justice who suspected the good faith of any associate. The issues involved are not trivia such as one finds on boys' playgrounds. There never has been a Justice who was not dedicated to the free society. It would come as a shock to any who have sat on the Court that the differences between a majority and a minority could ever be cast in terms of a personal equation. In past decades, though not at present, there have been Justices who did not admire one another. But it is inconceivable that anything petty would ever make a difference in a vote on the merits. Statements to the contrary are not worthy of serious students of constitutional history.[101]

Probably only Douglas, among the present Justices, would publish such a letter.

On the recent Court, Justices Douglas, Brennan, and Frankfurter spoke often and in substantively important fashion. Justices Black, Whittaker, and Stewart spoke less often. Justice Clark speaks primarily about the formal internal practices of the Court when he discusses judicial affairs.[102] Justice Harlan speaks occasionally, in sober and guarded fashion.[103] Mr. Chief Justice Warren is a constant speaker, but generally in the tradition of the broad, ceremonial commentator [104] rather than in the Douglas-Brennan-Frankfurter manner.

It should be noted that one can detect a certain amount of low-keyed dissension as to the propriety of judicial commentary in this new manner. What a Justice chooses to say, of course, is his own decision. There is no clearance officer or committee within the

[101] The Reporter, Sept. 14, 1961, p. 8.
[102] See the selected bibliography.
[103] See the selected bibliography.
[104] See the selected bibliography.

Court to pass on speeches before they are delivered or to rate them afterward, as in the sometimes-observed tradition for Pentagon military spokesmen or Cabinet heads. Nor is there any manual of standards, or after-dinner canon of ethics, to which each Justice is required to conform, though he remain master of his conformance. In American society, which has produced many frank memoirs and autobiographies by government leaders, the Justices have tended to mirror the general freedom of expression, but with important limitations based on the secret nature of intra-Court deliberations.

Thus, apart from gentle hints or semihumorous sallies at the luncheon table, there is nothing that the Justices do about a loquacious colleague. When Mr. Justice Brewer was at the peak of his speech-making in the 1890's, the first Justice Harlan and Mr. Chief Justice Fuller lamented his outspoken manner; but they agreed that nothing could be done and they commented that the long illness of Brewer's wife and his need for additional funds helped to explain his speaking on a fee basis.[105] Today, hints of disagreements filter out. Mr. Justice Frankfurter, referring to a Jackson address in 1948 that had preceded his at an American Law Institute affair, told the audience in good humor, but perhaps a little more: "[M]y Brother Jackson . . . has so gayly torn off the shackle of judicial austerity . . . [that he] has preempted the field. . . . I cannot add anything to it. What is more important, I cannot even subtract anything from it." [106] And again, in 1960, Frankfurter seemed to be voicing more than his personal credo when he told a law school audience: "I do not think any member of the Supreme Court should talk about contemporaneous decisions. Because of the nature of the adversary process, an adjudication should be made on the basis of arguments to come before the Court in a particular case. And comments by a member of the Court on these opinions, in public or in private, of what an opinion may mean are, from my point of view, hostile to the full play of the adversary process. . . ." [107]

[105] Harlan Papers, possession of Alan F. Westin (undated memoranda); Fuller Papers, on file in Chicago Historical Soc'y (same).
[106] Frankfurter, *Personal Ambition of Judges: Should a Judge "Think Beyond the Judicial"?* 34 A.B.A.J. 656, 658 (1948).
[107] PROCEEDINGS IN HONOR OF MR. JUSTICE FRANKFURTER (Harvard Law School Occasional Pamphlet No. 3, 1960) 11.

IV. Conclusions: The Meaning of Out-of-Court Commentary

Having surveyed the contemporary pattern of commentary and its historical roots, a few final remarks might be ventured about the practice.

Clearly, the heart of the Supreme Court's function is the decision of concrete cases and the elaboration of constitutional rules for the conduct of American government. The test of every Justice, in his time and as a matter of history, is how well he decides cases and how much illumination his opinions give to his judicial philosophy. Even as a matter of good "institutional public relations," the Court's reputation and status depend primarily on judicial decisions and the reasons formally advanced for them.

Yet, because the Supreme Court does so much of its work in closed-off corridors, behind the locked doors to the conference room, and in the privacy of the Justices' suites, the public can profit from as much explanatory commentary in speeches and books as the Justices can produce without disrupting the sense of corporate privacy and the reputation for impartial judging. A Court that has made judicial review part of the day-to-day operations of law-making in an urban, industrialized, social-welfare state still dedicated to "ordered liberty" can, with these commentaries, aid its appeals to the reason and conscience of the community. And, while so doing, the Justices can provide, as this collection shows, a revealing autobiographical portrait of the unique entity that is the Supreme Court of the United States.

Appendix

A Selected Bibliography of Speeches and Extrajudicial Writings by United States Supreme Court Justices, 1790–1962

This list presents the speeches and extrajudicial writings of the Justices after they joined the Court and secured "the view from inside." Only items with commentary about the Court as an institution, constitutional law issues, and fellow Justices have been included, and memorial remarks are listed only when these did more than review a former colleague's vital statistics and lament his passing. Several charges to federal grand juries are listed from the days when the Justices rode circuit and made general speeches about constitutional issues when opening a trial term. The speeches Chief Justices have made to the American Law Institute since the late 1920's have not been included, as these have contained very little about the Supreme Court as an institution; they can be found in the published *Proceedings* of the Institute. Titles are those assigned by the Justice or the publication in which it appeared. When a speech was published in several journals, a citation to one readily available source has been given. When no citation to a publication is given for an item after 1945, this signifies that a copy of the speech was obtained directly from the Justice or his office and has not been published. The dates beside each Justice's name are his years on the Court.

BALDWIN, HENRY (1830–1844)
    A GENERAL VIEW OF THE ORIGIN AND NATURE OF THE CONSTITUTION AND GOVERNMENT OF THE UNITED STATES (1837).

BLACK, HUGO L. (1937–   )
    Address, 13 Mo. B.J. 173 (1942).
    The Lawyer and Individual Freedom, 21 TENN. L. REV. 461 (1950).
    Mr. Justice Rutledge, 25 IND. L. REV. 541 (1950).
    Mr. Justice Murphy, 48 MICH. L. REV. 739 (1950).
    Commencement Address, Swarthmore College, June 6, 1955.
    Address, Einstein Memorial Meeting, Town Hall, New York City, May 15, 1955.
    The Bill of Rights, 35 N.Y.U.L. REV. 865 (1960).
    Justice Black and the First Amendment—"Absolutes": A Public Interview, 37 N.Y.U.L. Rev. 569 (1962).

BRADLEY, JOSEPH P. (1870–1892)
    Office and Nature of Law as the Basis and Bond of Society, 41 LEGAL INTELLIGENCER 396 (1884).
    MISCELLANEOUS WRITINGS OF THE LATE HON. JOSEPH P. BRADLEY (C. Bradley ed. 1902).

BRENNAN, WILLIAM J., JR. (1956–   )
    Law and Social Sciences Today, Gaston Lecture, Georgetown University, Nov. 25, 1957, in 24 VITAL SPEECHES 143 (1957).
    Address, Student Legal Forum, Charlottesville, Va., Feb. 17, 1959.
    Supreme Court Review of State Court Decisions, 38 Mich. S.B.J., Nov. 1959, p. 14.
    Notes on the Supreme Court, *University of Pennsylvania Law Review* Banquet, March 10, 1960.
    Address, Essex County Bar, Newark, N.J., April 5, 1960.
    State Court Decisions and the Supreme Court, 31 PA. B.A.Q. 393 (1960).
    The Bill of Rights and the States, 36 N.Y.U.L. REV. 761 (1961).

Federal Habeas Corpus and State Prisoners: An Exercise in Federalism, The William H. Leary Lecture, University of Utah, October, 1961.

BREWER, DAVID J. (1889–1910)
Protection to Private Property from Public Attack, 10 RAILWAY & CORPORATION L.J. 281 (1891).
The Nation's Safeguard, 16 N.Y.S.B.A. PROCEEDINGS 37 (1893).
The Federal Judiciary, 12 KAN. S.B.A. PROCEEDINGS 81 (1895).
Government by Injunction, 15 NATIONAL CORPORATION REP. 848 (1896).
The Nation's Anchor, 57 ALB. L.J. 166 (1898).
The Work of the Supreme Court, 1 LAW NOTES 167 (1898).
Address, DINNER GIVEN DEC. 9, 1902 IN HONOR OF MR. JUSTICE JOHN MARSHALL HARLAN 33 (Bar of the Supreme Court of the United States ed. 1902).
Address, 6 COLO. S.B.A. REP. 46 (1903).
The Supreme Court of the United States, 33 SCRIBNER'S 273 (1903).
Organized Wealth and the Judiciary, CHICAGO LEGAL NEWS, Aug. 27, 1904.
Two Periods in the History of the Supreme Court, 19 VA. S.B.A. REP. 133 (1906).

BROWN, HENRY B. (1890–1906)
The Distribution of Property, 16 A.B.A. REP. 213 (1893).
The Judiciary, in ADDRESSES ON THE CELEBRATION OF THE 100TH ANNIVERSARY OF THE LAYING OF THE CORNERSTONE OF THE CAPITOL OF THE UNITED STATES 74 (1896).
Liberty of the Press, 23 N.Y.S.B.A. PROCEEDINGS 133 (1900).
Response, DINNER GIVEN MAY 31, 1906 IN HONOR OF MR. JUSTICE HENRY BILLINGS BROWN 19 (Bar of the Supreme Court of the United States ed. 1908).

BURTON, HAROLD H. (1945–1958)
Address, Judging Is Also Administration, Section on Judicial Administration, ABA, Cleveland, Ohio, Sept. 24, 1947.
The Cornerstone of American Constitutional Law: The Extraordinary Case of Marbury v. Madison, 36 A.B.A.J. 805 (1950).
"Justice the Guardian of Liberty": John Marshall at the Trial of Aaron Burr, 37 A.B.A.J. 735 (1951).
The Dartmouth College Case: A Dramatization, 38 A.B.A.J. 991 (1952).
An Independent Judiciary: The Keystone of Our Freedom, 39 A.B.A.J. 1067 (1953).
Two Significant Decisions: Ex parte Milligan and Ex parte McCardle, 41 A.B.A.J. 121 (1955).
Unsung Services of the Supreme Court of the United States, 24 FORD. L. REV. 169 (1955).
John Marshall—The Man, 104 U. PA. L. REV. 3 (1955).
The Legal Tender Cases: A Celebrated Supreme Court Reversal, 42 A.B.A.J. 231 (1956).
Address, The Independence and Continuity of the Supreme Court of the United States, National Convention of the Phi Alpha Delta Law Fraternity, Cleveland, Ohio, June 22, 1956.

BUTLER, PIERCE (1922–1939)
Some Opportunities and Duties of Lawyers, 9 A.B.A.J. 583 (1923).

BYRNES, JAMES F. (1941–1942)
Address, Preserve Peoples Rights, Conference of Southern Governors, Biloxi, Miss., Nov. 21, 1949, in 16 VITAL SPEECHES 98 (1949).
Address, The Principle of Local Government, South Carolina Democratic Convention, Columbia, S.C., April 16, 1952, in 18 VITAL SPEECHES 450 (1952).
Segregation, 50 VT. B.A. PROCEEDINGS 86 (1956).
Address, The South Respects the Written Constitution: Supreme Court Has No Power to Amend the Constitution, Ill. State Bar Ass'n, Feb. 9, 1957, in 23 VITAL SPEECHES 331 (1957).
ALL IN ONE LIFETIME (1958).
The Supreme Court and States Rights, 20 ALA. LAW. 396 (1959).
Communist Influence, Home and Abroad, 23 TEX. B.J. 416 (1960).

CAMPBELL, JOHN A. (1853–1861)
Address, 6 ALA. S.B.A. PROCEEDINGS 75 (1884).

CHASE, SALMON P. (1864–1873)
Memoranda: Mr. Justice Catron, 70 U.S. (3 Wall.) xiv (1865).
Memoranda: Mr. Justice Wayne, 73 U.S. (6 Wall.) ix (1867).
Resignation of Mr. Justice Grier, 75 U.S. (8 Wall.) viii (1870).

CHASE, SAMUEL (1796–1811)
Address of Justice Chase, Trial of the Northampton Insurgents, May 2, 1800, in WHARTON, STATE TRIALS OF THE UNITED STATES 637 (1849).
Charge to the Grand Jury, Circuit Court, Maryland, Baltimore, May 2, 1803, in 2 SMITH & LLOYD, TRIAL OF SAMUEL CHASE, app. at v (1805).

CLARK, TOM C. (1949–   )
Administrative Law, 18 J.B.A.D.C. 254 (1951).
The Supreme Court Conference, 19 F.R.D. 303 (1956).
Address, University of Texas, Austin, Texas, Dec. 6, 1958.
Address, Some Thoughts on Supreme Court Practice, University of Minn. Law School Alumni Ass'n, Minneapolis, Minn., April 13, 1959.
The Internal Operation of the United States Supreme Court, 43 J. AM. JUD. SOC'Y 45 (1959).
The Supreme Court as a Protector of Liberty Under the Rule of Law, 43 MARQ. L. REV. 11 (1959).
Remarks on the Supreme Court of the United States, 31 PA. B.A.Q. 430 (1960).
Constitutional Adjudication and the Supreme Court, 9 DRAKE L. REV. 59 (1960).
Address, Behind Scenes at the Supreme Court, Sept. 16, 1960.
Address, Forth Worth, Tarrant County, Texas Bar Ass'n, May 1, 1961.

CLARKE, JOHN H. (1916–1922)
Practice Before the Supreme Court, 8 VA. L. REV. 241 (1922).
Methods of Work of the United States Supreme Court Judges, 9 A.B.A.J. 80 (1923).

The "New Federalist Series": Judicial Power to Declare Legislation Un-constitutional, 9 A.B.A.J. 689 (1923).

Reminiscences of the Courts and the Law, 5 CAL. S.B.A. PROCEEDINGS 20 (1932).

The Naked Question of the Constitutionality of the Court Proposal, in 3 VITAL SPEECHES 369 (1937).

CLIFFORD, NATHAN (1858–1881)

Memoranda: Death of Chief Justice Chase, 84 U.S. (17 Wall.) viii (1873).

CURTIS, BENJAMIN R. (1851–1857)

Charge to Grand Jury—Neutrality Laws and Treason, 30 Fed. Cas. 1024 (No. 18269) (C.C.D. Mass. 1851).

EXECUTIVE POWER (1862).

Address, Character and Public Services of Chief Justice Taney, Boston Bar, Oct. 15, 1864, in 2 A MEMOIR OF BENJAMIN R. CURTIS 336 (Curtis ed. 1879).

Lectures on the Jurisdiction and Practice of the Federal Courts, Harvard Law School, 1872–73, in JURISDICTION, PRACTICE, AND PECULIAR JURIS-PRUDENCE OF THE COURTS OF THE UNITED STATES (1880).

DAVIS, DAVID (1862–1877)

Addresses in the Senate on Relief for the Supreme Court, 13 CONG. REC. 3464–66, 3869–70, and other pages cited in the index for that volume (1882).

DOUGLAS, WILLIAM O. (1939–   )

Democratic Government, 1 TEXAS L. REV. (Bar No.) 81 (1940).

The Lasting Influence of Mr. Justice Brandeis, 19 TEMP. L. Q. 361 (1946).

Chief Justice Stone, 46 COLUM. L. REV. 693 (1946).

BEING AN AMERICAN (1948).

The Dissent: A Safeguard of Democracy, 32 J. AM. JUD. SOC'Y 104 (1948).

Procedural Safeguards in the Bill of Rights, 31 J. AM. JUD. SOC'Y 166 (1948).

Stare Decisis, 49 COLUM. L. REV. 735 (1949).

Recent Trends in Constitutional Law, 30 ORE. L. REV. 279 (1951).

Some Antecedents of Due Process of Law, 39 A.B.A.J. 871 (1953).

AN ALMANAC OF LIBERTY (1954).

WE THE JUDGES: STUDIES IN AMERICAN AND INDIAN CONSTITUTIONAL LAW FROM MARSHALL TO MUKHERJEA (1956).

Interposition and the Peters Case 1778–1809, 9 STAN. L. REV. 3 (1956).

Mr. Justice Black, 65 YALE L.J. 449 (1956).

THE RIGHT OF THE PEOPLE (1958).

Address, Legal Institutions in America, Columbia University Law School, Nov. 8, 1958; printed in Paulson (ed.) LEGAL INSTITUTIONS TODAY AND TOMORROW (1959) 274.

The Means and the End, 1959 WASH. U.L.Q. 103.

In Forma Pauperis Practice in the United States, 2 N.H.B.J. 5 (1959).

The Role of the Lawyer, 12 OKLA. L. REV. 1 (1959).

On Misconception of the Judicial Function and the Responsibility of the Bar, 59 COLUM. L. REV. 227 (1959).

Address, The Public Trial and the Free Press, University of Colorado, May 10, 1960.
Address, Vagrancy and Arrest on Suspicion, University of New Mexico Law School, March 15, 1960.
Mr. Justice Cardozo, 58 MICH. L. REV. 549 (1960).
The Supreme Court and Its Case Load, 45 CORNELL L.Q. 401 (1960).
AMERICA CHALLENGED (1960).

ELLSWORTH, OLIVER (1796–1800)
Charge to the Grand Jury, Circuit of Georgia, April 25, 1796, in 2 FLANDERS, LIVES AND TIMES OF THE CHIEF JUSTICES 189 (1858).
Charge to the Grand Jury, Circuit of South Carolina, 1799, in Independent Chronicle, June 13, 1799.

FIELD, STEPHEN J. (1863–1899)
Charge to Grand Jury, 30 Fed. Cas. 992 (No. 18255) (C.C.D. Cal. 1872).
The Late Chief Justice Chase, 11 OVERLAND MONTHLY 305 (1873).
Address, The Supreme Court of the United States, Centennial Celebration of the Organization of the Federal Judiciary, New York, N.Y., Feb. 4, 1890, 134 U.S. 729 (1890).
Farewell to Supreme Court, 5 AMERICAN LAW. 537 (1897).

FRANKFURTER, FELIX (1939–1962)
Mr. Justice Brandeis, 55 HARV. L. REV. 181 (1941).
Oliver Wendell Holmes, Jr., 21 DICTIONARY OF AMERICAN BIOGRAPHY 417 (Supp. 1, 1944).
Harlan Fiske Stone, 1946 AMERICAN PHILOSOPHICAL SOC'Y YEAR BOOK 334.
Some Reflections on the Reading of Statutes, 47 COLUM. L. REV. 527 (1947).
Personal Ambitions of Judges: Should a Judge "Think Beyond the Judicial"? 34 A.B.A.J. 656 (1948).
"The Administrative Side" of Chief Justice Hughes, 63 HARV. L. REV. 1 (1949).
Benjamin Nathan Cardozo, 22 DICTIONARY OF AMERICAN BIOGRAPHY 93 (Supp. 2, 1949).
A Symposium on Statutory Construction—Foreward, 3 VAND. L. REV. 365 (1950).
Chief Justices I Have Known, 39 VA. L. REV. 883 (1953).
The Job of a Supreme Court Justice, N.Y. Times, Nov. 28, 1954, § 6 (Magazine), p. 14.
SOME OBSERVATIONS ON SUPREME COURT LITIGATION AND LEGAL EDUCATION (1954).
Some Observations on the Nature of the Judicial Process of Supreme Court Litigation, 98 AMERICAN PHILOSOPHICAL SOC'Y PROCEEDINGS 233 (1954).
Mr. Justice Roberts, 104 U. PA. L. REV. 311 (1955).
Mr. Justice Jackson, 68 HARV. L. REV. 937 (1955); 55 COLUM. L. REV. 435 (1955).
John Marshall and the Judicial Function, 69 HARV. L. REV. 217 (1955).
"Moral Grandeur" of Mr. Justice Brandeis, N.Y. Times, Nov. 11, 1956, § 6 (Magazine), p. 26.
OF LAW AND MEN: PAPERS AND ADDRESSES, 1939–1956 (Elman ed. 1956).
The Supreme Court in the Mirror of the Justices, 105 U. PA. L. REV. 781 (1957).

PROCEEDINGS IN HONOR OF MR. JUSTICE FRANKFURTER (Harvard Law School
Occasional Pamphlet No. 3, 1960).

FULLER, MELVILLE W. (1888–1910)
In Memoriam: Mr. Justice Matthews, 131 U.S. 456 (1889).
Centennial of the Constitution of the United States, 21 CHICAGO LEGAL
NEWS 303 (1889).
In Memoriam: Mr. Justice Miller, 137 U.S. 706 (1890).
In Memoriam: Mr. Justice Bradley, 143 U.S. 708 (1892).
In Memoriam: Mr. Justice Lamar, 148 U.S. 710 (1893).
In Memoriam: Mr. Justice Blatchford, 150 U.S. 710 (1893).
In Memoriam: Mr. Justice Howell Jackson, 159 U.S. 706 (1895).
Retirement of Mr. Justice Field, 168 U.S. 717 (1897).
Centennial of Chief Justice Marshall's Appointment, 180 U.S. 645 (1901).
In Memoriam: Mr. Justice Gray, 187 U.S. xxxvii (1903).
Proceeding on the Death of Mr. Justice Peckham, 215 U.S. ix (1909).
Proceeding on the Death of Mr. Justice Brewer, 218 U.S. xv (1910).

GRAY, HORACE (1881–1902)
An Address on the Life, Character and Influence of Chief Justice Marshall,
14 VA. S.B.A. REP. 365 (1901).

HARLAN, JOHN M. (1877–1911)
Address, Washington and the Constitution, Union League Club, Chicago,
Ill., 1887, in Harlan Papers, possession of Alan F. Westin.
The Supreme Court of the United States, 20 CHICAGO LEGAL NEWS 208
(1888).
Centennial of the Adoption of the Constitution, 21 CHICAGO LEGAL NEWS
301 (1889).
The Supreme Court of the United States, Centennial Celebration of the
Organization of the Federal Judiciary, 134 U.S. 751 (1890).
The Supreme Court of the United States and Its Work, 30 AM. L. REV. 900
(1896).
Lectures on Constitutional Law, Transcript of Law Lectures for 1897–1898,
Columbia Law School, collection of Justice John M. Harlan, Wash.,
D.C.
James Wilson and the Formation of the Constitution, 34 AM. L. REV. 481
(1900).
Address, DINNER GIVEN DEC. 9, 1902 IN HONOR OF MR. JUSTICE JOHN
MARSHALL HARLAN 23 (Bar of the Supreme Court of the United States
ed. 1902).
The Courts in the American System of Government, 37 CHICAGO LEGAL
NEWS 271 (1905).
Address, Banquet Given by "The Kentuckians," New York, N.Y., Dec. 23,
1907, in Harlan Papers, possession of Alan F. Westin.
Government Under the Constitution, 11 LAW NOTES 206 (1908).

HARLAN, JOHN M. (1955–   )
Address, What Part Does the Oral Argument Play in the Conduct of an
Appeal? Judicial Conference, 4th Circuit, Asheville, N.C., June 24,
1955.

Address, Some Aspects of Handling a Case in the United States Supreme
Court, N.Y. State Bar Ass'n, New York, N.Y., Jan. 26, 1957.
Manning the Dikes, 13 RECORD OF N.Y.C.B.A. 541 (1958).
Some Fiftieth Anniversary Remarks, 50th Anniversary Dinner, N.Y.C.
Lawyers Ass'n, Nov. 25, 1958.
*Some Aspects of the Judicial Process in the Supreme Court of the United
States*, 33 AUSTL. L.J. 108 (1959).

HOLMES, OLIVER WENDELL (1902–1932)
COLLECTED LEGAL PAPERS (1921).
SPEECHES (1934).
Law and the Court, in THE MIND AND FAITH OF JUSTICE HOLMES 387 (Lerner
ed. 1943).
John Marshall, in *id.* at 382.
Law and Social Reform, in *id.* at 399.

HUGHES, CHARLES EVANS (1910–1916, 1930–1941)
Some Aspects in the Development of American Law, 48 CHICAGO LEGAL
NEWS 198 (1916).
War Powers Under the Constitution, 2 MASS. L.Q. 575 (1917).
Liberty and Law, 1925 A.B.A. PROCEEDINGS 183.
THE SUPREME COURT OF THE UNITED STATES (1928).
The Obligation of the Bar, 3 CAL. S.B.J. 223 (1929).
Address, ABA, Aug. 21, 1931, in Hughes Papers, on file in Library of
Congress.
Retirement of Mr. Justice Holmes, 284 U.S. at v (1932).
Proceeding in Memory of Chief Justice Taft, 285 U.S. xxviii (1931).
Mr. Justice Holmes, 44 HARV. L. REV. 677 (1931).
Roger Brooke Taney, 17 A.B.A.J. 785 (1931).
Address, Federal Bar Ass'n, Feb. 12, 1931, in Hughes Papers, on file in
Library of Congress.
Address at Judicial Conference, 18 A.B.A.J. 445 (1932).
The Social Thought of Mr. Justice Brandeis, in MR. JUSTICE BRANDEIS 1
(Frankfurter ed. 1932).
Proceeding in Memory of Mr. Justice Cardozo, 305 U.S. xxii (1938).
Address, Making Democracy Workable, 150th Anniversary of the First
Meeting of Congress, Wash., D.C., March 4, 1939, in 5 VITAL SPEECHES
327 (1939).
150th Anniversary of the Supreme Court, 309 U.S. xii (1940).
In Memory of Mr. Justice Butler, 310 U.S. xv (1940).
Address, Justice Our Anchor, 150th Anniversary of the First Sitting of the
Supreme Court, Wash., D.C., Feb. 1, 1940, in 6 VITAL SPEECHES 259
(1940).
An Imperishable Ideal of Liberty Under Law, 25 J. AM. JUD. SOC'Y 99
(1941).
Address, Ass'n of Bar of City of N.Y., March 16, 1946, in Hughes Papers,
on file in Library of Congress.

IREDELL, JAMES (1790–1799)
Charge to the Grand Jury, Trial of the Northampton Insurgents, April 11,
1799, in WHARTON, STATE TRIALS OF THE UNITED STATES 458 (1849).

JACKSON, ROBERT H. (1941–1954)
Address, Our American Legal Philosophy, N.Y. State Bar Ass'n, Jan. 24, 1942 in 8 VITAL SPEECHES 356 (1942).
Address, Brandeis Memorial Colony Dinner, June 24, 1943, in 9 VITAL SPEECHES 664 (1943).
Decisional Law and Stare Decisis, 30 A.B.A.J. 334 (1944).
American Courts, 67 N.Y.S.B.A. PROCEEDINGS 429 (1944).
Decline of Stare Decisis Is Due to Volume of Opinions, 28 J. AM. JUD. SOC'Y 6 (1944).
Full Faith and Credit—The Lawyer's Clause of the Constitution, 45 COLUM. L. REV. 1 (1945).
Address, The Constitutional System of the United States, Dinner in Honor of Justice Jackson, given by the Lawyers of the Ministry of Justice, Paris, France, April 3, 1946.
Lawyers Today: The Legal Profession in a World of Paradox, 33 A.B.A.J. 24 (1947).
The Meaning of Statutes: What Congress Says or What the Court Says, 34 A.B.A.J. 535 (1948).
Foreword to RAMASWAMY, THE COMMERCE CLAUSE IN THE CONSTITUTION OF THE UNITED STATES (1948).
The Advocate: Guardian of Our Traditional Liberties, 36 A.B.A.J. 607 (1950).
Advocacy Before the Supreme Court: Suggestions for Effective Case Presentations, 37 A.B.A.J. 801 (1951).
Wartime Security and Liberty Under Law, James McCormick Mitchell Lecture, University of Buffalo School of Law, May 9, 1951.
The Task of Maintaining Our Liberties: The Role of the Judiciary, 39 A.B.A.J. 961 (1953).
THE SUPREME COURT IN THE AMERICAN SYSTEM OF GOVERNMENT (1955).

JAY, JOHN (1789–1795)
Charge to the Grand Juries on the Eastern Circuit at the Circuit Courts of N.Y., Conn., Mass., and N.H., April 4–May 20, 1790, in 3 THE CORRESPONDENCE AND PUBLIC PAPERS OF JOHN JAY 387–95 (Johnston ed. 1893).
Charge to the Grand Jury, Trial of Gideon Henfield, May 22, 1793, in WHARTON, STATE TRIALS OF THE UNITED STATES 49 (1849).

JOHNSON, WILLIAM (1804–1834)
Remarks on the Publication of the Attorney General's letter to the President, on the Subject of the Mandamus Issued by the Circuit Court of South Carolina to the Collector, in the Case of the Resource, 10 Fed. Cas. 359 (No. 5420) (C.C.D.S.C. 1808).

LURTON, HORACE (1900–1914)
A Government of Law or a Government of Men? 193 NORTH AMERICAN REV. 9 (1911).

MCLEAN, JOHN (1829–1861)
Charge to the Grand Jury—Neutrality Laws, 30 Fed. Cas. 1018 (No. 18265) (C.C.D. Ohio 1838).

Charge to the Grand Jury—Neutrality Laws, 30 Fed. Cas. 1021 (No. 18267) (C.C.D. Ohio 1851).

MCREYNOLDS, JAMES (1914–1941)
Remarks, 42 TENN. B.A. PROCEEDINGS 121 (1923).
Speech, 45 *id.* at 132 (1926).
Address, 54 *id.* at 65 (1935).

MARSHALL, JOHN (1801–1835)
Bank of the United States, a Defense of the Supreme Court, under the nom de plume, A Friend to the Union, in the Philadelphia Union: United States Gazette and True American for the Country, April 28, 1819, and May 1, 1819.

MATTHEWS, STANLEY (1900–1914)
Address, The Judicial Power of the United States, Yale Law School, June 26, 1888, on file in Yale Law Library.
The Federal Judiciary, in 2 HISTORY OF THE CELEBRATION OF THE ONE HUNDREDTH ANNIVERSARY OF THE PROMULGATION OF THE CONSTITUTION OF THE UNITED STATES 370 (Carson ed. 1889).

MILLER, SAMUEL F. (1862–1890)
The Study and Practice of the Law in the United States, 48 LAW TIMES 171 (1870).
Judicial Reform, 6 WESTERN JURIST 49 (1872).
THE AMERICAN JUDICIARY, INTRODUCTION TO THE SUPREME COURT OF THE UNITED STATES: A SERIES OF BIOGRAPHIES (1877).
Introduction to Constitutional Law, 4 SCOT. L. REV. (n.s.) 79 (1878).
Legislation in This Country As It Affects the Administration of Justice, 2 N.Y.S.B.A. PROCEEDINGS 31 (1879).
Address, 13 WESTERN JURIST 6 (1879).
The Removal of Judges and the Jury System, 8 CENT. L.J. 35 (1879).
THE CONSTITUTION OF THE UNITED STATES (1880).
The Weight of Authorities, 10 VA. L.J. 582 (1886).
The System of Trial by Jury, 21 AM. L. REV. 859 (1887).
In Memoriam: Chief Justice Waite, 126 U.S. 610 (1888).
Oration, in HISTORY OF THE CELEBRATION OF THE ONE HUNDREDTH ANNIVERSARY OF THE PROMULGATION OF THE CONSTITUTION OF THE UNITED STATES 262 (Carson ed. 1889).
ADDRESSES: THE CONSTITUTION AND THE SUPREME COURT OF THE UNITED STATES (1889).
The Use and Value of Authorities, 23 AM. L. REV. 165 (1889).
LECTURES ON THE CONSTITUTION OF THE UNITED STATES (1891).

NELSON, SAMUEL (1845–1872)
Charge to Grand Jury—Fugitive Slave Law, 30 Fed. Cas. 1007 (No. 18261) (C.C.S.D.N.Y. 1851).
Charge to Grand Jury—Treason, 30 Fed. Cas. 1034 (No. 18271) (C.C.S.D.-N.Y. 1861).

PATERSON, WILLIAM (1793–1806)
Charge to the Grand Jury, Portsmouth, N.H., reported May 24, 1800, Oracle of the Day (Portsmouth, N.H.).

REED, STANLEY (1938–1957)
   Address, Dedication of the Birthplace of Chief Justice Stone, Chesterfield,
      N.H., Aug. 25, 1948, in Stone Papers, on file in Library of Congress.
   Law and Society: Fixed Principles and Changing Applications, Morrison
      Lecture, State Bar of California, Monterey, Cal., Oct. 3, 1957.
   *Our Constitutional Philosophy: Concerning the Significance of Judicial
      Review in the Evolution of American Democracy*, 21 KY. S.B.J. 136
      (1957).
   Address, The Living Law, Columbia University Law School, Nov. 8, 1958.

ROBERTS, OWEN J. (1930–1945)
   Memorial Address to Chief Justice Hughes, before the N.Y. State Bar Ass'n
      Committee, Dec. 12, 1948.
   Now Is the Time: Fortifying the Supreme Court's Independence, 35
      A.B.A.J. 1 (1949).
   THE COURT AND THE CONSTITUTION (1951).
   American Constitutional Government: The Blueprint and Structure, in
      GASPAR G. BACON LECTURES ON THE CONSTITUTION OF THE UNITED
      STATES, 1940–1950, at 379 (1953).

RUTLEDGE, WILEY B. (1943–1949)
   Foreword to A Symposium on Constitutional Rights During Wartime, 29
      IOWA L. REV. 379 (1944).
   A DECLARATION OF LEGAL FAITH (1947).

STEWART, POTTER (1958–   )
   Address, First Impressions, ABA Convention, Miami Beach, Fla., Aug. 24,
      1959.
   Justice Stewart Discusses Right to Counsel, 18 BRIEF CASE 91 (1960).

STONE, HARLAN F. (1925–1941, 1941–1946)
   Address, 1926 N.Y. COUNTY LAW. A. YEARBOOK 261.
   Fifty Years' Work of the United States Supreme Court, 14 A.B.A.J. 428
      (1928).
   The Public Influence of the Bar, 48 HARV. L. REV. 1 (1934).
   The Chief Justice, 27 A.B.A.J. 407 (1941).
   Proceedings in Memory of Mr. Justice van Devanter, 316 U.S. xxxviii
      (1942).
   Dissenting Opinions Are Not Without Value, 26 J. AM. JUD. SOC'Y 78
      (1942).
   Note on Sutherland, 317 U.S. at v (1942).
   Proceedings in Memory of Mr. Justice Brandeis, 317 U.S. xlii (1942).
   Address, Judicial Conference 4th Circuit, Asheville, N.C., June 21, 1944, in
      Stone Papers, on file in Library of Congress.
   In Memory of Mr. Justice Sutherland, 323 U.S. xvi (1944).

STORY, JOSEPH (1811–1845)
   Charge to the Grand Jury, Slave Trade, 1819, in MISCELLANEOUS WRITINGS
      OF JOSEPH STORY 122 (Story ed. 1852).
   COMMENTARIES ON THE CONSTITUTION OF THE UNITED STATES (1833).
   THE CONSTITUTIONAL CLASS BOOK (1833).

Obituary: John Marshall, Chief Justice of the United States Supreme Court, 35 U.S. (10 Pet.) iii (1836).

A FAMILIAR EXPOSITION OF THE CONSTITUTION OF THE UNITED STATES (1842).

Charge to the Grand Jury—Treason, 30 Fed. Cas. 1046 (No. 18275) (C.C.D.R.I. 1842).

Life, Character and Services of Chief Justice Marshall, in MISCELLANEOUS WRITINGS OF JOSEPH STORY 639 (Story ed. 1852).

Sketch of:

> *Mr. Justice Robert Trimble,* in *id.* at 801.
> *Mr. Justice Bushrod Washington,* in *id.* at 808.
> *Mr. Justice John Todd,* in *id.* at 817.
> *Mr. Justice Philip P. Barbour,* in *id.* at 825.

STRONG, WILLIAM (1870–1880)

The Needs of the Supreme Court, 132 NORTH AMERICAN REV. 437 (1881).

Relief for the Supreme Court, 151 NORTH AMERICAN REV. 567 (1890).

SUTHERLAND, GEORGE (1922–1938)

Address, 20 UTAH B.A. PROCEEDINGS 55 (1924)

TAFT, WILLIAM H. (1921–1930)

Address to the Chicago Bar, Dec. 27, 1921, in Taft Papers, on file in Library of Congress.

Proceedings on the Death of Chief Justice White, 257 U.S. xxiv (1921).

Address, 1922 N.Y. COUNTY LAW. A. PROCEEDINGS 198.

Retirement of Mr. Justice Pitney, 261 U.S. at v (1922).

Retirement of Mr. Justice Day, 260 U.S. ix (1922).

Address to Yale Alumni, New Haven, Conn., June 20, 1923, in Taft Papers, on file in Library of Congress.

Salmon P. Chase Memorial, 9 A.B.A.J. 348 (1923).

The Jurisdiction of the Supreme Court Under the Act of February 13, 1925, 35 YALE L.J. 1 (1925).

TANEY, ROGER B. (1836–1864)

Charge to the Grand Jury, 30 Fed. Cas. 998 (No. 18257) (C.C.D. Md. 1836).

Obituary: Mr. Justice Barbour, 40 U.S. (15 Pet.) v (1841).

The Death of Judge Story, 45 U.S. (4 How.) vii (1846).

Death of Judge McKinley, 55 U.S. (14 How.) v (1852).

Death of Mr. Justice Daniel, 65 U.S. (24 How.) v (1860).

Obituary: Judge McLean, 66 U.S. (1 Black) 12 (1861).

VINSON, FRED M. (1946–1953)

An Observation Anent Judge Stone's Judicial Life, 16 U. KAN. CITY L. REV. 1 (1947).

In Memory of Mr. Chief Justice Stone, 333 U.S. xx (1948).

In Memory of Mr. Justice McReynolds, 334 U.S. xx (1948).

In Memory of Mr. Chief Justice Hughes, 338 U.S. xxiv (1948).

The Work of the United States Supreme Court, 12 TEXAS B.J. 551 (1948).

The Supreme Court's Work: Opinion and Dissents, 20 OKLA. B.A.J. 1296 (1949).

Our Enduring Constitution, 6 WASH. & LEE L. REV. 1 (1949).

In Memory of Mr. Justice Murphy, 340 U.S. xx (1950).

In Memory of Mr. Justice Rutledge, 341 U.S. xxii (1950).
Mr. Justice Murphy, 48 MICH. L. REV. 738 (1950).

WAITE, MORRISON R. (1874–1888)
Memoranda: Retirement of Mr. Justice Strong, 103 U.S. xi (1880).
Memoranda: Mr. Justice Clifford, 104 U.S. xii (1881).
Proceedings at the Unveiling of the Statue of Chief Justice Marshall, 112
    U.S. 745 (1884).
The Supreme Court of the United States, 36 ALB. L.J. 318 (1887).

WARREN, EARL (1953–   )
In Memory of Mr. Chief Justice Vinson, 349 U.S. xxi (1954).
In Memory of Mr. Justice Jackson, 349 U.S. xlviii (1954).
The Law and the Future, Fortune, November 1955, p. 106.
Chief Justice Taney, 41 A.B.A.J. 504 (1955).
Chief Justice Marshall, 41 A.B.A.J. 1008 (1955).
The Blessings of Liberty, 1955 WASH. U.L.Q. 105.
Retirement of Mr. Justice Reed, 352 U.S. xiii (1957).
Foreword to CHIEF JUSTICE JOHN MARSHALL: A REAPPRAISAL (Jones ed.
    1956)
Retirement of Mr. Justice Minton, 352 U.S. vii (1956).
Chief Justice William Howard Taft, 67 YALE L.J. 353 (1958).
Address, Supreme Court of Civil and Criminal Judicature, Karlsruhe, Ger-
    many, Aug. 25, 1959.
THE PUBLIC PAPERS OF CHIEF JUSTICE EARL WARREN (Christman ed.
    1959).
Address, The Declaration of Independence, University of Judaism, Los
    Angeles, Cal., July 4, 1961.
The Bill of Rights and the Military, 37 N.Y.U.L. Rev. 181 (1962).

WAYNE, JAMES M. (1835–1867)
Charge to the Grand Jury—Slave Trade, 30 Fed. Cas. 1026 (No. 18269a)
    (C.C.D. Ga. 1859).
Memoranda: The Hon. Roger Brooke Taney, 69 U.S. (2 Wall.) x (1864).

WHITE, EDWARD D. (1894–1921)
Proceedings on the Death of Mr. Chief Justice Fuller, 219 U.S. xv (1911).
Proceedings on the Death of Mr. Justice Harlan, 222 U.S. xxv (1911).
Proceedings on the Death of Mr. Justice Lurton, 237 U.S. xxi (1915).
Proceedings on the Death of Mr. Justice Lamar, 241 U.S. xvi (1916).
The Supreme Court of the United States, 7 A.B.A.J. 341 (1921).

WHITTAKER, CHARLES E. (1957–1962)
Address, Judicial Discretion, Ill. Division of the Fed. Bar Ass'n, Chicago,
    Ill., Sept. 17, 1960.

WILSON, JAMES (1789–1798)
Charge to the Grand Jury, Pennsylvania District, July 22, 1793, in WHARTON,
    STATE TRIALS OF THE UNITED STATES 59 (1849).
WORKS OF THE HON. JAMES WILSON (B. Wilson ed. 1804).

WOODBURY, LEVI (1845–1851)
WRITINGS OF LEVI WOODBURY, POLITICAL, JUDICIAL AND LITERARY (1852).

THE
SUPREME
COURT OF
HISTORY

PART
ONE

THE
SUPREME
COURT OF
HISTORY

☆ ☆ ☆ The Experimental Court and Its Formative Decades, 1790-1860

CHIEF JUSTICE JOHN JAY
The New Judicial Department

John Jay, Chief Justice from the Supreme Court's organization in 1790 until he resigned in 1795 to become Governor of New York, was one of the "Renaissance men" produced in the American revolutionary period. A graduate of King's College (now Columbia University), he became President of the Continental Congress; served as Minister to Spain, Peace Commissioner in Europe, and Secretary of Foreign Affairs under the Articles of Confederation; collaborated with Hamilton and Madison in writing the *Federalist Papers*; negotiated the famous Jay Treaty with Great Britain (while serving as Chief Justice); and functioned as party leader and Governor of New York between 1795 and 1801 after leaving the Court.

In this selection, Jay addressed the federal grand juries at meetings of the circuit courts in New York, Connecticut, Massachusetts, and New Hampshire, during April and May of 1790. The charges Jay delivered were well received in the press, and he does not seem to have waxed in political style during his five years on circuit.

While Jay argued here for popular support of the federal judiciary, he later became pessimistic about the possibilities and prospects of the Supreme Court. In 1800, refusing to be considered for reappointment as Chief Justice, he commented that he thought the Supreme Court lacked "the energy, weight, and dignity which are essential to its affording due support to the national Government."

SOURCE: Henry P. Johnston (ed.), *The Correspondence and Public Papers of John Jay* (N.Y. and London: G. P. Putnam's Sons, 1890–1893), III, 387–395.

Whether any people can long govern themselves in an equal, uniform, and orderly manner, is a question which the advocates for free government justly consider as being exceedingly important to the cause of liberty. This question, like others whose solution depends on facts, can only be determined by experience. It is a question on which many think some room for doubt still remains. Men have had very few fair opportunities of making the experiment; and this is one reason why less progress has been made in the science of government than in almost any other. The far greater number of the constitutions and governments of which we are informed have originated in force or in fraud, having been either imposed by improper exertions of power, or introduced by the arts of designing individuals, whose apparent zeal for liberty and the public good enabled them to take advantage of the credulity and misplaced confidence of their fellow-citizens.

Providence has been pleased to bless the people of this country with more perfect opportunities of choosing, and more effectual means of establishing their own government, than any other nation has hitherto enjoyed; and for the use we may make of these opportunities and of these means we shall be highly responsible to that Providence, as well as to mankind in general, and to our own posterity in particular. Our deliberations and proceedings being unawed and uninfluenced by power or corruption, domestic or foreign, are perfectly free; our citizens are generally and greatly enlightened, and our country is so extensive that the personal influence of popular individuals can rarely embrace large portions of it. The institution of general and State governments, their respective conveniences and defects in practice, and the subsequent alterations made in some of them, have operated as useful experiments, and conspired to promote our advancement in this interesting science. It is pleasing to observe that the present national government already affords advantages which the preceding one proved too feeble and ill-constructed to produce. How far it may be still distant from the degree of perfection to which it may possibly be carried, time only can decide. It is a consolation to reflect that the good-sense of the people will be enabled by experience to discover and correct its imperfections, especially while they continue to retain a proper confidence in themselves, and avoid those jealousies and dissensions which, often springing from the worst designs, frequently frustrate the best measures.

Wise and virtuous men have thought and reasoned very differently respecting government, but in this they have at length very unanimously agreed, viz., that its powers should be divided into three distinct, independent departments—the executive, legislative and judicial. But how to constitute and balance them in such a manner as best to guard against abuse and fluctuation, and preserve the Constitution from encroachments, are points on which there continues to be a great diversity of opinions, and on which we have all as yet much to learn. The Constitution of the United States has accordingly instituted these three departments, and much pains have been taken so to form and define them as that they may operate as checks one upon the other, and keep each within its proper limits; it being universally agreed to be of the last importance to a free people, that they who are vested with executive, legislative, and judicial powers should rest satisfied with their respective portions of power, and neither encroach on the provinces of each other, nor suffer themselves to intermeddle with the rights reserved by the Constitution to the people. If, then, so much depends on our rightly improving the before-mentioned opportunities, if the most discerning and enlightened minds may be mistaken relative to theories unconfirmed by practice, if on such difficult questions men may differ in opinion and yet be patriots, and if the merits of our opinions can only be ascertained by experience, let us patiently abide the trial, and unite our endeavours to render it a fair and an impartial one.

These remarks may not appear very pertinent to the present occasion, and yet it will be readily admitted that occasions of promoting good-will, and good-temper, and the progress of useful truths among our fellow-citizens should not be omitted. These motives urge me further to observe, that a variety of local and other circumstances rendered the formation of the judicial department particularly difficult.

We had become a nation. As such we were responsible to others for the observance of the *Laws of Nations;* and as our national concerns were to be regulated by *national laws,* national tribunals became necessary for the interpretation and execution of them both. No tribunals of the like kind and extent had heretofore existed in this country. From such, therefore, no light of experience nor facilities of usage and habit were to be derived. Our jurisprudence varied in almost every State, and was accommodated to local, not general convenience; to partial, not national policy. This convenience and this policy were nevertheless to be regarded and tenderly treated. A judicial control, general and final, was indispensable; the manner of establishing it with powers neither too extensive nor too limited, rendering it properly independent, and yet properly amenable, involved questions of no little intricacy.

The expediency of carrying justice, as it were, to every man's door, was obvious; but how to do it in an expedient manner was far from being apparent. To provide against discord between national and State jurisdictions, to render them auxiliary instead of hostile to each other, and so to connect both as to leave each sufficiently independent, and yet sufficiently combined, was and will be arduous.

Institutions formed under such circumstances should therefore be received with candour and tried with temper and prudence. It was under these embarrassing circumstances that the articles in the Constitution on this subject, as well as the act of Congress for establishing the judicial courts of the United States were made and passed. Under the authority of that act, this court now sits. Its jurisdiction is twofold, *civil and criminal.* To the exercise of the *latter* you, gentlemen, are necessary, and for that purpose are now convened.

The most perfect constitutions, the best governments, and the wisest laws are vain, unless well administered and well obeyed. Virtuous citizens will observe them from a sense of duty, but those of an opposite description can be restrained only by fear of disgrace and punishment. Such being the state of things, it is essential to the welfare of society, and to the protection of each member of it in the peaceable enjoyment of his rights, that offenders be punished. The end of punishment, however, is not to expiate for offences, but by the terror of example to deter men from the commission of them. To render these examples useful, policy as well as morality requires not only that punishment be proportionate to guilt, but that all proceedings against persons accused or suspected, should be accompanied by the reflection *that they may be innocent*. Hence, therefore, it is proper that dispassionate and careful inquiry should precede these rigours which justice exacts, and which should always be tempered with as much humanity and benevolence as the nature of such cases may admit. Warm, partial, and precipitate prosecutions, and cruel and abominable executions, such as racks, embowelling, drawing, quartering, burning and the like, are no less impolitic than inhuman; they infuse into the public mind disgust at the barbarous severity of government, and fill it with pity and partiality for the sufferers. On the contrary, when offenders are prosecuted with temper and decency, when they are convicted after impartial trials, and punished in a manner becoming the dignity of public justice to prescribe, the feelings and sentiments of men will be on the side of government; and however disposed they may and ought to be, to regard suffering offenders with compassion, yet that compassion will never be unmixed with a due degree of indignation. We are happy that the genius of our laws is mild, and we have abundant reason to rejoice in possessing one of the best institutions that ever was devised for bringing offenders to justice without endangering the peace and security of the innocent. I mean that of Grand Juries. Greatly does it tend to promote order and good government that in every district there should frequently be assembled a number of the most discreet and respectable citizens in it, who on their oaths are bound to inquire into and present all offences committed against the laws in such districts, and greatly does it tend to the quiet and safety of good and peaceful citizens, that no man can be put in jeopardy for imputed crimes without such previous inquiry and presentment.

It cannot be too strongly impressed on the minds of us all how greatly our individual prosperity depends on our national prosperity, and how greatly our national prosperity depends on a well organized,

vigorous government, ruling by wise and equal laws, faithfully executed; nor is such a government unfriendly to liberty—to that liberty
which is really inestimable; on the contrary, nothing but a strong
government of laws irresistibly bearing down arbitrary power and
licentiousness can defend it against those two formidable enemies.
Let it be remembered that civil liberty consists not in a right to
every man to do just what he pleases, but it consists in an equal right
to all the citizens to have, enjoy, and to do, in peace, security, and
without molestation, whatever the equal and constitutional laws of
the country admit to be consistent with the public good. It is the
duty and the interest, therefore, of all good citizens, in their several
stations, to support the laws and the government which thus protect their rights and liberties.

JUSTICE JAMES IREDELL

Liberty and Sedition in the New Republic

Iredell, Associate Justice from 1790 to 1799, had been a distinguished lawyer and judge in North Carolina. As counsel and as a pamphleteer, he had advanced the idea of judicial review of legislation in the famous North Carolina case, *Bayard* v. *Singleton*, 1 Martin 42 (1787). A Federalist with some States' rights leanings, he was thirty-eight years old when Washington placed him on the Court.

The selection which follows was Iredell's charge to the grand jury at the circuit court in Philadelphia on April 11, 1799, at the trial of the "Northampton Insurgents." Congress in 1798 had provided for the counting and measuring of windows in all houses as part of the federal "house tax." Popular outcry arose in several Pennsylvania counties, with one newspaper noting that a woman had "poured a shower of hot water" on the head of a federal window measurer and that the assessors were being "intimidated from pursuing" the count. When federal marshals arrested several persons for such interference, "a body of the people, some on horseback and others on foot," demanded their release. These protestors were later arrested and tried for sedition and treason, in one of the "political trials" which pitted Federalist judges and juries against Republican lawyers and local public opinion.

After Justice Iredell delivered the charge, the grand jury wrote him in praise of the address. "At a time like the present,"

57

they wrote, "when false philosophy and the most dangerous and wicked principles are spreading with rapidity, under the imposing garb of Liberty, over the fairest countries of the Old World—they are convinced, that the publication of a Charge, fraught with such clear and just observations on the nature and operation of the Constitution and laws of the United States, will be highly beneficial to the citizens thereof. . . ." Iredell "readily" consented to publication, adding that he had "seen with astonishment and regret, attempts made in the pursuit of visionary chimeras, to subvert or undermine so glorious a fabric [as the Constitution]. . . ."

SOURCE: Francis Wharton, *State Trials of the United States During the Administrations of Washington and Adams* (Philadelphia: Carey and Hart, 1849), 458–481.

If ever any people had reason to be thankful for a long and happy enjoyment of peace, liberty and safety, the people of these states surely have. While every other country almost has been convulsed with foreign or domestic war, and some of the finest countries on the globe have been the scene of every species of vice and disorder, where no life was safe, no property was secure, no innocence had protection, and nothing but the basest crimes gave any chance for momentary preservation; no citizen of the United States could truly say that in his own country any oppression had been permitted with impunity, or that he had any grievance to complain of, but that he was required to obey those laws which his own representatives had made, and under a government which the people themselves had chosen. But in the midst of this envied situation, we have heard the government as grossly abused as if it had been guilty of the vilest tyranny; as if common sense or common virtue had fled from our country; and those pure principles of republicanism, which have so strongly characterized its councils, could only be found in the happy soil of France, where the sacred fire is preserved by five Directors on ordinary occasions, and three on extraordinary ones—who, with the aid of a republican army, secure its purity from violation by the legislative representatives of the people. The external conduct of that government is upon a par with its internal. Liberty, like the religion of Mahomet, is propagated by the sword. Nations are not only compelled to be free, but to be free on the French model, and placed under French guardianship. French arsenals are the repository of their arms, French treasuries of their money, the city of Paris of their curiosities; and they are honoured with the constant support of French enterprises in any other part of the world. Such is the progress of a power which began by declarations that it abhorred all conquests for itself, and sought no other felicity but to emancipate the world from tyrants, and leave each nation free to choose a government of its own. Those who take no warning by such an awful example, may have deeply to lament the consequences of neglecting it.

The situation in which we now stand with that country is peculiarly critical. Conscious of giving no real cause of offence, but irritated with injuries, and full of resentment for insults; desirous of peace, if it can be preserved with honour and safety, but disdaining a security equally fallacious and ignominious at the expense of either; still holding the rejected olive branch in one hand, but a sword in the other—we now remain in a sort of middle path between peace and war, where one false step may lead to the most ruinous consequences, and nothing can be safely relied on but unceasing vigilance, and persevering firmness in what we think right, leaving the event to Heaven, which seldom suffers the destruction of nations, without some capital fault of their own.

Among other measures of defence and precaution which the exigency of the crisis, and the magnitude of the danger suggested to those to whom the people have entrusted all authority in such cases, were certain acts of the legislature of the United States, not only highly important in themselves, but deserving of the most particular attention, on account of the great discontent which has been excited against them, and especially as some of the State legislatures have publicly pronounced them to be in violation of the Constitution of the United States. I deem it my duty, therefore, on this occasion, to state to you the nature of those laws which have been so grossly misrepresented, and to deliver my deliberate opinion as a judge, in regard to the objections arising from the Constitution.

The acts to which I refer, you will readily suppose to be what are commonly called the Alien and Sedition acts. I shall speak of each separately, so far as no common circumstances belonging to them may make a joint discussion proper. . . .

[Discussion of the Alien Laws is omitted.]

Having said what I thought material as to the alien laws, upon the particular objections to them, I now proceed to discuss the objections which have been made to what is called the Sedition Act, one of which equally applies to the alien laws as well as to this. . . .

With regard to the first objection, I readily acknowledge, that soon after the Constitution was proposed, and when I had taken a much more superficial view of it than I was sensible of at the time, I did think Congress could not provide for the punishment of any crimes but such as are specifically designated in the particular powers enumerated. I delivered that opinion in the convention at North Carolina, in the year 1788, with a perfect conviction, at the time, that it was well founded. But I have since been convinced it was an erroneous opinion, and my reasons for changing it I shall state to you as clearly as I am able.

It is in vain to make any law unless some sanction be annexed to it, to prevent or punish its violation. A law without it might be equivalent to a good moral sermon; but mad members of society would be as little influenced by one as the other. It is, therefore, necessary and proper, for instance, under the constitution of the United States, to secure the effect of all laws which impose a duty on some particular persons, by providing some penalty or punishment if they disobey. The authority to provide such is conveyed by the following general words in the Constitution, at the end of the objects of legislation particularly specified: "To make all laws which shall be necessary and proper for carrying into execution the foregoing powers, and all other powers vested by this Constitution in the government of the United States, or in any department or officer thereof." A penalty alone would not in every case be sufficient, for the offender might be rich and disregard it, or poor, though a wilful offender, and unable to pay it. A fine, therefore, will not always answer the purpose, but imprisonment must be in many cases added, though a wise and humane legislature will always dispense with this, where the importance of the case does not require it. But if it does, from the very nature of the punishment, it becomes a *criminal*, and not a *civil* offense; the grand jury must indict, before the offender can be convicted. . . .

In further illustration of this subject, I shall state a case which was determined in this court—The United States against Worrell, published in Mr. Dallas' reports, p. 384,—where there was an indictment against the defendant for attempting to bribe Mr. Coxe, the Commissioner of the Revenue. The defendant was found guilty, and afterwards a motion was made in arrest of judgment, assigning, together with some technical objections, this general one, that the Court had no cognizance of the offence, because no act of Congress had passed creating the offence and prescribing the punishment, but it was solely on the foot of the common law. . . .

Judge Chase, who on that occasion differed from Judge Peters as to the common law jurisdiction of the Court, held, that under the 8th section of the first article, which I am now considering, although bribery is not among the crimes and offences specially mentioned, it is certainly included in that general provision; and Congress might have passed a law on the subject which would have given the Court cognizance of the offence. Judge Peters was of opinion, that the defendant was punishable at common law; but that it was competent for Congress to pass a legislative act on the subject.

I conclude, therefore, that the first objection is not maintainable.

With regard to the second objection, which is, that this law is not warranted by that clause of the Constitution authorizing Congress to pass all laws which shall be necessary and proper for carrying into execution the powers specially enumerated, and all other powers vested by the Constitution in the government of the United States, or in any department or officer thereof; because, it is not necessary and proper to pass any such law, in order to carry into execution any of those powers—it is to be observed, that, from the very nature of the power, it is, and must be, discretionary. What is necessary and proper, in regard to any particular subject, cannot, before an occasion arises, be logically defined; but must depend upon various extensive views of a case, which no human foresight can reach. What is necessary and proper in a time of confusion and general disorder, would not, perhaps, be necessary and proper in a time of tranquillity and order. These are considerations of policy, not questions of law, and upon which the legislature is bound to decide according to its real opinion of the necessity and propriety of any act particularly in contemplation. It is, however, alleged, that the necessity and propriety of passing collateral laws for the support of others are confined to cases where the powers are delegated, and do not extend to cases which have a reference to general danger only. The words are general, "for carrying into execution the special powers previously enumerated, and all other powers vested by the Constitution in the government of the United States, or any department or officer thereof." If, therefore, there be anything necessary and proper for carrying into execution any or all of those powers, I presume that may be constitutionally enacted. Two objects are aimed at by every rational government, more especially by free ones: 1. That the people may understand the laws, and voluntarily obey them. 2. That if this be not done by any individual, he shall be compelled to obey them, or punished for disobedience. The first object is undoubtedly the most momentous; for, as the legitimate object of every government is the happiness of the people committed to its care, nothing can tend more to promote this than that, by a voluntary obedience to the laws of the country, they should render punishments unnecessary. This can never be the case in any country but a country of slaves, where gross misrepresentation prevails, and any large body of people can be induced to believe that laws are made either without authority, or for the purpose of oppression. Ask the great body of the people who were deluded into an insurrection in the western parts of Pennsylvania, what gave rise to it? They will not hesitate to say, that the government had been vilely misrepresented, and made to appear to them in a character directly the reverse of what they deserved. In consequence of such misrepresentations, a civil war had nearly desolated our country, and a certain expense of near two millions of dollars was actually incurred, which might be deemed the price of libels, and among other causes made necessary a judicious and moderate land tax, which no man denies to be constitutional, but is now made the pretext of another insurrection. The liberty of the press is, indeed, valuable—long may it preserve its lustre! It has converted barbarous nations into civilized ones—taught science to rear its head—enlarged the capacity—increased the comforts of private life—and, leading the banners of freedom, has extended her sway where her very name was unknown. But, as every human blessing is attended with imperfection, as what produces, by a right use, the greatest good, is productive of the greatest evil in its abuse, so this, one of the greatest blessings ever bestowed by Providence on his creatures, is capable of producing the greatest good or the greatest mischief. A pen, in the hands of an able and virtuous man, may enlighten a whole nation, and by observations of real wisdom, grounded on pure morality, may lead it to the path of honour and happiness. The same pen, in the hands of a man equally able, but with vices as great as the other's virtues, may, by arts of sophistry easily attainable, and inflaming the passions of weak minds, delude many into opinions the most dangerous, and conduct them to actions the most criminal. Men who are at a distance from the source of information must rely almost altogether on the accounts they receive from others. If their accounts are founded in truth, their heads or hearts must be to blame, if they think or act wrongly. But, if their accounts are false, the best head and the best heart cannot be proof against their influence; nor is it possible to calculate the combined effect of innumerable artifices, either by direct falsehood, or invidious insinuations, told day by day, upon minds both able and virtuous. Such being unquestionably the case, can it be tolerated in any civilized society that any should be permitted with impunity to tell falsehoods to the people, with an express intention to deceive them, and lead them into discontent, if not into insurrection, which is so apt to follow? It is believed no government in the world ever was without such a power. It is unquestionably possessed by all the State governments, and probably has been exercised in all of them: sure I am, it has in some. If necessary and proper for them, why not equally so, at least, for the government of the United States, naturally an object of more jealousy and alarm, because it has greater concerns to provide for? Combinations to defeat a particular law are admitted to be punishable. Falsehoods, in order to produce such combinations, I should presume, would come within the same principle, as being the first step to the mischief intended to be prevented; and if such falsehoods, with regard to one particular law, are dangerous, and therefore ought not to be permitted without punishment—why should such which are intended to destroy confidence in government altogether, and thus induce disobedience to every act of it? It is said, libels may be rightly punishable in monarchies, but there is not the same necessity in a republic. The necessity, in the latter case, I conceive greater, because in a republic more is dependent on the good opinion of the people for its support, as they are, directly or indirectly, the origin of all authority, which of course must receive its bias from them. Take away from a republic the confidence of the people, and the whole fabric crumbles into dust.

I have only to add, under this head, that, in order to obviate any probable ill use of this large and discretionary power, the Constitution, and certain amendments to it, have prohibited, in express words, the exercise of some particular authorities, which otherwise might be supposed to be comprehended within them. Of this nature is the prohibitory clause relating to the present object, which I am to consider under the next objection.

4. That objection is, that the act is in violation of this amendment of the Constitution.

"Congress shall make no law respecting an establishment of religion, or prohibiting the free exercise thereof; or abridging the freedom of speech, or of the press, or the right of the people peaceably to assemble, and to petition the government for a redress of grievances."

The question then is, whether this law has abridged the freedom of the press?

Here is a remarkable difference in expressions as to the different objects in the same clause. They are to make no law *respecting* an establishment of religion, or prohibiting the free exercise thereof, or *abridging* the freedom of speech, or of the press. When, as to one object, they entirely prohibit any act whatever, and, as to another object, only limit the exercise of the power, they must, in reason, be supposed to mean different things. I presume, therefore, that Congress may make a law *respecting* the press, provided the law be such as not to *abridge its freedom.* What might be deemed the freedom of the press, if it had been a new subject, and never before in discussion, might indeed admit of some controversy. But, so far as precedent, habit, laws, and practices are concerned, there can scarcely be a more definite meaning than that which all these have affixed to the term in question.

It is believed that, in every State in the Union, the common law principles concerning libels apply; and in some of the States words similar to the words of the Amendment are used in the Constitution itself, or a contemporary Bill of Rights, of equal authority, without ever being supposed to exclude any law being passed on the subject.

So that there is the strongest proof that can be of a universal concurrence in America on this point, that the freedom of the press does not require that libellers shall be protected from punishment.

But, in some respects, the Act of Congress is much more restrictive than the principles of the common law, or than, perhaps, the principles of any State in the Union. For, under the law of the United States, the truth of the matter may be given in evidence, which at common law, in criminal prosecutions, was held not to be admissible; and the punishment of fine and imprisonment, which at common law was discretionary, is limited in point of severity, though not of lenity. It is to be observed, too, that by the express words of the act, both malice and falsehood must combine in the publication, with the seditious intent particularly described. So that if the writing be false, yet not malicious, or malicious and not false, no conviction can take place. This, therefore, fully provides for any publication arising from inadvertency, mistake, false confidence, or anything short of a wilful and atrocious falsehood. And none surely will contend, that the publication of such a falsehood is among the indefeasible rights of men, for that would be to make the freedom of liars greater than that of men of truth and integrity. . . .

Long, gentlemen, as I have detained you, for which the great importance of the occasion, I trust, is a just apology, it will be useful to recollect that, ever since the first formation of the present government, every act which any extraordinary difficulty has occasioned, has been uniformly opposed before its adoption, and every art practiced to make the people discontented after it; without any allowance for the necessity which dictated it, some seem to have taken it for granted that credit could be obtained without justice, money without taxes, and the honor and safety of the United States only preserved by a disgraceful foreign dependence. But, notwithstanding all the efforts made to vilify and undermine the government, it has uniformly risen in the esteem and confidence of the people. Time has disproved arrogant predictions; a true knowledge of the principles and conduct of the government has rectified many gross misrepresentations; credit has risen from its ashes; the country has been found full of resources, which have been drawn without oppression, and faithfully applied to the purposes to which they were appropriated: justice is impartially administered; and the only crime which is fairly imputable is, that the minority have not been suffered to govern the majority, to which they had as little pretension upon the ground of superiority of talents, patriotism, or general probity, as upon the principles of republicanism, the perpetual theme of their declamation. If you suffer this government to be destroyed, what chance have you for any other? A scene of the most dreadful confusion must ensue. Anarchy will ride triumphant, and all lovers of order, decency, truth and justice be trampled under foot. May that God, whose peculiar providence seems often to have interposed to save these United States from destruction, preserve us from this worst of all evils! And may the inhabitants of this happy country deserve his care and protection by a conduct best calculated to obtain them!

Federalist Politics from the Bench

Chase protrudes in American constitutional history as the only Justice ever impeached, even if unsuccessfully. A Maryland lawyer and leader in the movement for independence, he had opposed the adoption of the Constitution but had later become a passionate Federalist. His hatred of Jefferson and the anti-Federalists was openly proclaimed, particularly during the sedition trials or in his whiplashing of Republican lawyers. As noted in the "Introduction," the charge printed here was delivered on May 2, 1803, and was one count in Chase's Impeachment trial. After his acquittal, he remained as an Associate Justice until his death in 1811. Francis Wharton wrote of Chase: 'He had that singular instinct for tumult which scents it at a distance from whence it is imperceptible to other eyes and irresistibly impels a participation in it."

SOURCE: Samuel Smith and Thomas Lloyd, *Trial of Samuel Chase* (Washington: Samuel Smith, 1805), II, Appendix, v.

Before you retire, Gentlemen, to your chamber to consider such matters as may be brought before you, I will take the liberty to make a few observations, which I hope you will receive as flowing only from my regard to the welfare and prosperity of our common country.

It is essentially necessary at all times, but more particularly at the present, that the public mind should be more truly informed; and that our citizens should entertain correct principles of government, and fixed ideas of their social rights. It is a very easy task to deceive or mislead the great body of the people by propagating plausible, but false doctrines; for the bulk of mankind are governed by their passions and not by reason.

Falsehood can be more readily disseminated than truth, and the latter is heard with reluctance if repugnant to popular prejudice. From the year 1776, I have been a decided and avowed advocate for a representative or republican form of government, as since established by our state and national constitutions. It is my sincere wish that freemen should be governed by their representatives, fairly and freely elected by that class of citizens described in our [Maryland] bill of rights, "who have property in, a common interest with, and an attachment to, the community."

The purposes of civil society are best answered by those governments, where the public safety, happiness and prosperity are best secured; whatever may be the constitution and form of government; but the history of mankind in ancient and modern times informs us "that a monarchy may be free, and that a republic may be a tyranny." The true test of liberty is in the practical enjoyment of protection to the person and the property of the citizen, from all enquiry. Where the same laws govern the whole society without any distinction, and there is no power to dispense with the execution of the laws; where justice is impartially and speedily administered, and the poorest man in the community may obtain redress against the most wealthy and powerful, and riches afford no protection to violence, and where the person and property of every man are secure from insult and injury; in that country the people are free. This is our present situation. Where law is uncertain, partial or arbitrary; where justice is not administered to all; where property is insecure, and the person is liable to insult and violence without redress by law, the people are *not free*, whatever may be their form of government. To this situation, I greatly fear we are fast approaching!

You know, gentlemen, that our state and national institutions were framed to secure to every member of our society, equal liberty and equal rights; but the late alteration of the federal judiciary by the abolition of the office of the fifteen circuit judges, and the recent change in our state constitution by the establishing of universal suffrage, and the further alteration that is contemplated in our state judiciary will, in my judgment, take away all security for property and personal liberty. The independence of the national judiciary is already shaken to its foundation, and the virtue of the people alone can restore it. The independence of the judges of this state will be entirely destroyed, if the bill for the abolition of the two supreme courts should be ratified by the next general assembly. The change of the state constitution, by allowing universal suffrage, will, in my opinion, certainly and rapidly destroy all protection to property, and all security to personal liberty; and our republican constitution will sink into a mobocracy, the worst of all possible governments. . . .

The declarations respecting the natural rights of man, which originated from the claim of the British parliament to make laws to bind America in all cases whatever; the publications since that period, of visionary and theoretical writers, asserting that men in a state of society, are entitled to exercise rights which they possessed in a state of nature; and the modern doctrines by our late reformers, that all men in a state of society, are entitled to enjoy equal liberty and equal rights, have brought this mighty mischief upon us; and I fear that it will rapidly progress, until peace and order, freedom and property shall be destroyed. . . .

It appears to me that the institution of government is really no sacrifice made, as some writers contend, to natural liberty, for I think that previous to the formation of some species of government, a state of liberty could not exist. It seems to me that personal *liberty* and *rights* can be acquired only by becoming a member of a community, which gives the protection of the whole to every individual. . . . From hence I conclude that liberty and rights (and also property) must spring out of civil society, and must be forever subject to the modification of particular governments. . . . I understand by equality of liberty and rights, only this, that every citizen, without respect to property or station, should enjoy an equal share of civil liberty; an equal protection of the laws, and an equal security for his person and property. . . . I will ask only two questions. Will justice be impartially administered by judges dependant on the legislature for their continuance in office, and also for their support? Will liberty or property be protected or secured, by laws made by representatives chosen by electors, who have no property in, a common interest with, or attachment to the community?

WILLIAM JOHNSON
A Jeffersonian Defense of the Federal Courts

Johnson, who served as a Justice from 1804 to 1835, was put on the Court as Jefferson's first appointee because he was a Republican with firm "political principles." His pre-Court career had been in South Carolina as a state legislator and judge. While Johnson and Jefferson remained on cordial personal terms, they disagreed repeatedly over judicial policies after Johnson's appointment to the Court, particularly Johnson's failure to register dissents in cases disliked by the Jeffersonians.

The selection here grew out of an interpretation of the Embargo Act. Under instructions from President Jefferson, the Port Collector of Charleston had refused to issue clearance papers to coastal vessels he suspected of intention to evade the Embargo. Johnson granted a petition for mandamus ordering the Collector to issue the clearances and holding the Executive instruction illegal, *Ex parte Gilchrist*, 5 Hughes 1 (1808). Johnson added: "The officers of our government, from the highest to the lowest, are equally subjected to legal restraint; and it is confidently believed that all of them feel themselves equally incapable, as well from law as inclination, to attempt an unsanctioned encroachment upon individual liberty." Jefferson regarded this as an attack upon himself and the Embargo, and had Attorney General Caesar Rodney issue an opinion contesting Justice Johnson's position. Johnson replied with the statement printed here. Rodney noted it in a fascinating letter

71

to the President deploring the "judicial power" being used to promulgate "*high-church* doctrines. . . ." He added, speaking of Johnson, "You can scarcely elevate a man to a seat in a Court of Justice before he catches the leprosy of the Bench." Johnson was not really that much of a turncoat, though he never satisfied Jeffersonian hopes as a counterweight to Marshall.

SOURCE: *Charleston Courier*, Oct. 15, 17, 18, 1808; 10 *Fed. Cas.* 359 (No. 5420).

EDGEFIELD DISTRICT, 26th August, 1808.
In a Charleston paper, received by the last mail, I have perused a letter addressed by the attorney general of the United States to the president, relative to the proceedings of the circuit court of South Carolina, in the case of The Resource. That the president should have consulted that officer upon a legal subject, is perfectly consistent with the relation subsisting between their respective stations; and as long as the result of that consultation was confined to the cabinet, there had occurred nothing inconsistent with the relation between the executive and judicial departments. But when that opinion is published to the world, under the sanction of the president, an act so unprecedented in the history of executive conduct could be intended for no other purpose than to secure the public opinion on the side of the executive and in opposition to the judiciary. Under this impression I feel myself compelled, as the presiding judge of the court, whose decision is the subject of the attorney general's animadversions, to attempt a vindication of, or at least an apology for that decision. So long as its merits were the subject of mere newspaper discussion, I felt myself under no concern about the opinion that the public might form of it. The official acts of men in office are proper subjects for newspaper remarks. The opinion that cannot withstand a free and candid investigation must be erroneous. It is true that a judge may, without vanity, entertain a doubt of the competency of some of the editors of newspapers to discuss a difficult legal question; yet no editorial or anonymous animadversions, however they may have been characterized by illiberality or ignorance, should ever have induced me to intrude these observations upon the public. But when a bias is attempted to be given to public opinion by the overbearing

influence of high office, and the reputation of ability and information, the ground is changed; and to be silent could only result from being borne down by weight of reasoning or awed by power. I should regret exceedingly should I err in attributing to the president the publication of the attorney general's letter. I do so because, from the nature of the case, it is impossible to think otherwise. There is no reason to suppose that the attorney general would have published it at all; or at least not without the command or permission of the president. . . .

The jurisdiction of the court, as is properly observed by the attorney general, must depend upon the constitution and laws of the United States. We disclaim all pretensions to any other origin of our jurisdiction, especially the unpopular grounds of prerogative and analogy to the king's bench. That judicial power, which the constitution vests in the United States, and the United States in its courts, is all that its courts pretend to exercise. In the constitution it is laid down, that "the judicial power of the United States shall extend to all cases in law or equity, arising under this constitution and laws of the United States, and treaties made, or which shall be made," &c. The term "judicial power" conveys the idea, both of exercising the faculty of judging and of applying physical force to give effect to a decision. The term "power" could with no propriety be applied, nor could the judiciary be denominated a department of government, without the means of enforcing its decrees. In a country where laws govern, courts of justice necessarily are the medium of action and reaction between the government and the governed. The basis of individual security and the bond of union between the ruler and the citizen must ever be found in a judiciary sufficiently independent to disregard the will of power, and sufficiently energetic to secure to the citizen the full enjoyment of his rights. To establish such a one was evidently the object of the constitution. But to what purpose establish a judiciary, with power to take cognizance of certain questions of right, but not power to afford such redress as the case evidently requires? Suppose congress had vested in the circuit court a certain jurisdiction, without prescribing by what forms that jurisdiction should be exercised; would it not follow that the court must itself adopt a mode of proceeding adapted to the exigency of each case? It must do so, or refuse to act. One thing, at least, cannot be denied: that the power

of congress was competent to authorize the circuit court to issue the
writ of mandamus. From this it would follow, that issuing that writ
is a mere incident to the judicial power, and not in itself a distinct
branch of jurisdiction; for the constitution nowhere expressly vests
in the United States the power to issue that writ, or any other. And
if a mere incident, I see no reason why it should not follow with the
principal jurisdiction, when vested by congress in its courts. . . .

Some other observations of the attorney general remain to be noticed, viz. that in giving redress by the process of mandamus, the
courts may extend their claim to jurisdiction, to a general usurpation
of power over the ministerial officers in the executive department;
that it is a mode of proceeding which takes away from the government the benefit of appeal, and interferes with the responsibility to
which officers of government are subject by impeachment. With
regard to the first of these observations, it is evident that the attorney
general mistakes the object against which his complaint should be
directed. The courts do not pretend to impose any restraint upon any
officer of government, but what results from a just construction of
the laws of the United States. Of these laws the courts are the constitutional expositors; and every department of government must submit to their exposition; for laws have no legal meaning but what is
given them by the courts to whose exposition they are submitted.
It is against the law, therefore, and not the courts, that the executive
should urge the charge of usurpation and restraint: a restraint which
may at times be productive of inconveniences, but which is certainly
very consistent with the nature of our government: one which it is
very possible the president may have deserved the plaudits of his
country for having transcended, in ordering detentions not within
the embargo acts, but which notwithstanding it is the duty of our
courts to encounter the odium of imposing. Let us take this argument together with that which relates to the liability of officers to
impeachment, and some others which are used by the attorney general, into one view; and to what conclusions do they lead us? The
president is liable to impeachment; he is therefore not to be restrained
by the courts. The collector and every other officer, with equal propriety, who holds his office at the will of the president, are his agents,
mere ministers of his will; therefore they are not to be restrained by
the process of the courts. The power given to them is power given

to him; in subordination to his will they must exercise it. He is charged with the general execution of the laws; and the security of the citizen lies in his liability to impeachment, or in an action for damages against the collector. This would indeed be an improvement on presidential patronage. It would be organizing a band, which in the hands of an unprincipled and intrepid president (and we may have the misfortune to see such a one elevated to that post) could be directed with an effect, but once paralleled in history. If these arguments have any force at all, as directed against the correctness of the circuit court's issuing the writ of mandamus, they would have equal weight to prove the impropriety of permitting them to issue the writ of habeas corpus; which is but an analogous protection to another class of individual rights, and might be urged to show that the whole executive department, in all its ramifications, civil, military and naval, should be left absolutely at large, in their conduct to individuals. What benefit results to the ruined citizen from the impeachment of the president, could we suppose it in the power of any individual to effect it? or what security from an action against a public officer whose circumstances may be desperate? But such is not the genius of our constitution. The law assigns every one his duty and his rights; and for enforcing the one and maintaining the other, courts of justice are instituted.

I will dismiss this subject with two additional remarks. The courts of the United States never have laid claim to a controlling power over officers vested by law with an absolute discretion, not inconsistent with the constitution; for in such a case, the officer is himself the paramount judge and arbiter of his own actions. Nor would they, for the same reason, undertake to control the acts of an officer who is a mere agent of the executive or any other department, in the performance of whatever may be constitutionally, and is by law, submitted to the discretion of that department; for in that case, the process of the court should be directed to the head of the department, or it should not issue at all. In such cases there is an evident propriety in leaving an injured individual to his action for damages; as it is only upon evidence of express malice or daring disregard to propriety, that this action could be maintained. In such a case, the authority to act is complete; but the motive is censurable. The courts will not interfere to prevent the act; because the law authorizes it. But as the law did not authorize it for individual oppression, they will give damages to the individual who suffers by the wanton exercise of a legal power. . . .

It is very possible that the court may have erred in their decision. It is enough, however, and all that a judge, who has understanding enough to be conscious of his own fallibility, can pretend to, that there existed grounds at least specious for the issuing of the mandamus. Though the laws had not vested the power, the submission of the officers of government would, at least, excuse the act of the court. There never existed a stronger case for calling forth the powers of a court; and whatever censure the executive sanction may draw upon us, nothing can deprive us of the consciousness of having acted with firmness, impartiality and an honest intention to discharge our duty.

JOHN MARSHALL

A Friend to the Union

"The great Chief Justice" spoke out only once publicly about the work of his Court during his thirty-four years on the bench. In 1819, he announced the Court's unanimous ruling in the national bank case, *McCulloch* v. *Maryland*, 4 Wheaton 316 (1819) which upheld Congress' right to charter a national bank as within the "necessary and proper" power and struck down a Maryland tax on the bank as a state charge upon a national instrument. States Rights spokesmen were furious at the ruling and a leading Republican jurist, Spenser Roane, Chief Justice of the Virginia Court of Appeals, wrote a series of articles under the pseudonyms of "Hampden" and "Amphictyon" attacking the decision. These spread to newspapers throughout the country. At first, Marshall suffered in silence, writing his ideological compatriot, Justice Story, on May 27, 1819, "[T]he opinion has been grossly misrepresented, and where its argument has been truly stated it has been met by principles one would think too palpably absurd for intelligent men." Before long, though, seemingly stung beyond endurance, Marshall took up his pen and wrote a reply to Roane's attacks. Then he arranged for Justice Bushrod Washington to have these published in the Philadelphia *Union*, under the signature "A Friend to the Union."

Once the articles appeared, Marshall had second thoughts about them. He told Story that he did not want them reprinted in New England; he felt that the meaning had been distorted by the printer (who had rearranged some parts), so that the argument was now "mangled and unclear." Marshall was also

77

worried about the articles being traced back to him, and refused to allow them to be published by Henry Wheaton, the Reporter of the Court's decisions, in the Appendix to the official volume of the year's opinions.

Marshall's biographer, Albert J. Beveridge, found the letters "peevish" and "wordy"; reading them today, he said, was "exhausting." Their publication, Beveridge remarked, provides that little touch of "human frailty" which showed Marshall to be less than divine; he was, far from being arrogant, "sensitive in the extreme; in reality, thirsting for approval, hurt by criticism." Yet these letters reprinted here for the first time since their original appearance in 1819, provide us with those attitudes of Marshall that were filtered out of his opinion in *McCulloch*, and such an additional window into his mind deserves to be opened.

Source: Philadelphia *Union*, April 28, May 1, 1819; New-York Historical Library Collection.

Mr. Editor, My attention has been a good deal attracted by some essays which have appeared lately in one of the Virginia papers which seem to have for their object the infliction of deep wounds on the constitution through a misrepresentation of the opinion lately delivered by the Supreme Court on the constitutionality of the act incorporating the bank of the United States. I have bestowed a few leisure moments on the refutation of some of the mischievous errours contained in these essays; and, if you think what I have written worth publishing you will give this answer to Amphyction a place in your useful paper.

A spirit which was supposed to have been tranquillized by a long possession of the government, appears to be resuming its original activity in Virginia. The decision of the Supreme Court in the case of McCullough against the state of Maryland has been seized as a fair occasion for once more agitating the publick mind, and reviving those unfounded jealousies by whose blind aid ambition climbs the ladder of power.

The bill for incorporating the bank of the United States had become a law, without exciting a single murmur. The reason is obvious. Those who fill the legislative and executive departments are elected by the people, and are of course popular. In addition, they possess great power and great patronage. Had they been unjustly attacked, champions would have arisen on every side, who would with equal zeal and ability have presented the truth to a publick not unwilling to perceive it. But the Judges of the Supreme Court, separated from the people by the tenure of office, by age, and by the nature of their duties, are viewed with respect, unmingled with affection, or interest. They possess neither power nor patronage. They have no sops to give; and every coffeehouse furnishes a Cerberus, hoping some reward for that watchfulness which his bark proclaims; and restrained by no apprehension that any can be stimulated by personal considerations to expose the injustice of his attacks. We ought not, therefore, to be surprized if it should be deemed criminal in the judicial department to sustain a measure, which was adopted by the legislature, and by the executive with impunity. Hostility to the Union, must cease to be guided by its usual skill, when it fails to select the weakest department as that through which a breach may be effected.

The Inquirer, the leading paper of Virginia, abounds with hostile attacks on this opinion. That which is written with most talent, most system, and most design, appears under the signature of Amphyction. The Editor assures his readers that it contains "a most satisfactory exposition" "of the alarming errours of the Supreme Court of the United States" in their interpretation of the constitution; and Amphyction himself does not leave his object to conjecture. "Most ardently" does he "hope that this decision of the Supreme Court will attract the attention of the state legislatures, and that Virginia will, as heretofore, do her duty."

The avowed object being of so serious a nature, it behooves not only the friends of the Bank, but the friends of the constitution, the friends of Union, to examine well the principles which are denounced as heretical; and those which are supported as orthodox.

The objections of Amphyction are to that part of the opinion which declares the act incorporating the bank to be constitutional. He introduces them with expressing his disapprobation of that mode of transacting their official duties which the Supreme Court has adopted. He would prefer seriatim opinions, to the combined opinion of the bench delivered by a single Judge.

On the justness of this criticism in general, or on its peculiar application to this particular case, I shall make no observation; because the principles expressed in this single opinion are neither more nor less vulnerable than they would have been if expressed in six separate opinions. But the criticism was made for the purpose of conveying an insinuation which marks the spirit in which the discussion is conducted. "We are not," says Amphyction, "informed whether the whole court united in the course of reasoning adopted by the Chief Justice, nor whether they all accorded in the various positions and principles he advanced."

Now I humbly conceive this is a subject on which we are informed. The opinion is delivered, not in the name of the chief justice, but in the name of the whole court. This observation applies to the "reasoning adopted," and "to the various positions and principles which were advanced" as entirely as to the conclusions drawn from "those positions and principles." Throughout the whole opinion, the chief justice never speaks in the singular number, or in his own person, but as the mere organ of the court. In the presence of all the judges, and in their names he advances certain propositions as their propositions and certain reasoning as their reasoning. I appeal to Amphyction himself, I appeal to every man accustomed to judicial proceedings, to determine whether the judges of the Supreme Court, men of high and respectable character, would sit by in silence, while great constitutional principles of which they disapproved, were advanced in their name, and as their principles. I appeal to the usage of the Supreme Court itself. Their decisions are reported, and are in possession of the publick. It has often happened that a judge concurring in the opinion of the court, but on reasons peculiar to himself, has stated his own reasoning. The great case of the Nereid is one among many examples, of this course of proceeding. In some instances too it has occurred, that the judge delivering the opinion of the court, has stated the contrariety of reasoning on which the opinion was formed. Of this, the case of Olivera v. the Union Ensurance Co. is an example. The course of every tribunal must necessarily be, that the opinion which is to be delivered as the opinion of the court, is previously submitted to the consideration of all the judges; and, if any part of the reasoning be disapproved, it must be so modified as to receive the approbation of all, before it can be delivered as the opinion of all. Amphyction himself thinks so; for he says: "We are driven, however reluctantly, to the conclusion that each judge approves of each argument and position advanced by the chief justice."

Why then has he suggested a contrary idea? He leaves us in no uncertainty for the answer to this question.

After stating that the subject is one "which has employed his (the chief justice's) thoughts, his tongue, and his pen, as a politician and as an historian for more than thirty years," he adds that it "is one which has, perhaps more than any other, heretofore drawn a broad line of distinction between the two great parties in this country, in which line no one has taken a more distinguished and decided rank than the judge who has thus expounded the supreme law of the land."

The chief justice then is a federalist; who was a politician of some note before he was a judge; and who with his tongue and his pen, supported the opinions he avowed. To expose the reasoning of the court to still greater odium, if it be possible, we are told that "the liberal and latitudinous construction" he has attached to a term in the constitution, had been attached to it, before him, "by Mr. Secretary Hamilton." The reasoning, then, of the court is, dexterously enough, ascribed to Mr. Secretary Hamilton and the chief justice, two inveterate federalists. This question cannot be trusted, by Amphyction, to his exposition of the constitution unless the spirit of party be introduced into the cause, and made its judge. How favourable this spirit is to truth, and to a fair exercise of the human judgment, Amphyction well knows. Had he admitted this opinion, including the reasoning, to be what it professes to be,—what it must be,—the opinion and the reasoning of all the judges,—four of whom have no political sin upon their heads;—who in addition to being eminent lawyers, have the still greater advantage of being sound republicans; of having been selected certainly not for their federalism, by Mr. Jefferson, and Mr. Madison, for the high stations they so properly fill, his argument would have been stripped of one powerful recommendation, and must have depended rather more on its intrinsick merit. We need not then be surprised that this improbable suggestion is made, although a sense of propriety has compelled the writer to abandon it as soon as its effect was produced.

Having thus prepared his readers for the dangerous errors contained in the opinion of the Supreme Court, Amphyction proceeds to inform them what those errors are.

"The first is the denial that the powers of the federal government were delegated by the states; and the second is that the grant of powers to that government, and particularly the grant of powers necessary and proper to carry the other powers into effect, ought to be construed in a liberal rather than a restricted sense."

But before Amphyction can permit himself to enter on his first point, he deems it necessary to cast a little more odium on the opinion he is about to examine. "For what purpose," he asks, "did the federal court decide that question?" After stating that it was totally unnecessary, that the opinion on it "is obiter and extrajudicial;" he adds that "whether the powers of the federal government were delegated to it by the states in their sovereign capacity, or by the people, can make but little difference in the extent of those powers. In either case it is still true that the powers of that government are limited by the charter that called it into existence." &c

I shall not controvert the proposition that the constitution ought to receive the same construction, whether its powers were delegated by the people or the states. That Amphyction entertains the same opinion, is brought into some doubt by the extreme importance he attaches to his theory.

If the powers of the general government were to be in no degree affected by the source from which they were derived, it is not easy to comprehend how the liberty of the American people can depend on the adoption of the one opinion or of the other. The origin of the government would seem to be the fair sense of the words used in the constitution, and a restricted sense. The opinion professes to found itself on the fair interpretation. Amphyction professes to condemn that opinion because it ought to have adopted the restricted interpretation.

The counsel for the state of Maryland had contended that the clause authorizing Congress "to pass all laws necessary and proper to carry into execution" the various powers vested in the government, restrained the power which Congress would otherwise have possessed; and the reasoning of Amphyction would seem to support the same proposition.

This question is of real importance to the people of the United States. If the rule contended for would not absolutely arrest the progress of the government, it would certainly deny to those who administer it the means of executing its acknowledged powers in the manner most advantageous to those for whose benefit they were conferred.

To determine whether the one course or the other be most consistent with the constitution, and with the publick good, let the principles laid down by the counsel for the state of Maryland, as stated in the opinion of the court, and the principles of Amphyction as stated by himself, be examined, and compared with the reasoning which has been so bitterly execrated.

The counsel for the state of Maryland, as we are informed, contended that the word "necessary" limits the right of Congress to pass laws for the execution of the specifick powers granted by the constitution "to such as are indispensable, and without which the power would be nugatory, that it excludes the choice of means, and leaves to Congress in each case that only which is most direct and simple."

Amphyction contends that necessary means "are those means without which the end could not be obtained." "When a law is about to pass, the inquiry," he says "which ought to be made by Congress is, does the constitution expressly grant the power? If not, then, is this law one without which some power cannot be executed? If it is not, then it is a power reserved to the states, or to the people, and we may not use the means, nor pass the law."

With some variety of expression, the position maintained in the argument of the cause, and that maintained by Amphyction, are the same. Both contend that Congress can pass no laws to carry into execution their specifick power, but such as are indispensably necessary; that they can employ no means but those without which the end could not be obtained.

Let us apply this rule to some of the powers relegated to the government.

Congress has power to lay and collect taxes.

According to the opinion of the Supreme Court, Congress may exercise this power in the manner most beneficial to the people, and may adopt those regulations which are adapted to the object, and will best accomplish it. But according to Amphyction, the inquiry must always be, whether the particular regulation be one without which the power could not be executed. If the power could be executed in any other way, the law is, in his opinion, unconstitutional.

Look at our tax laws. Observe their complex and multifarious regulations. All of them, no doubt, useful and conducing directly to the end;—all of them essential to the beneficial exercise of the power. But how many may be indispensably necessary;—how many may be such that without them the tax could not be collected, it is probable that neither Amphyction nor myself can say. In some of the laws imposing internal taxes, the collector is directed to advertise certain places of meeting, at which certain acts are to be performed; and those who do not attend and perform those acts, are subject to an increased tax. Is this regulation indispensable to the collection of the tax? It is certainly proper and convenient; but who will deny that the tax may be collected without it?

In almost every conceivable case, there is more than one mode of accomplishing the end. Which, or is either, indispensable to that end? Congress, for example, may raise armies; but we are told they can execute this power only by those means which are indispensably necessary; those without which the army could not be raised. Is a bounty proposed? Congress must inquire whether a bounty be absolutely necessary? Whether it be possible to raise an army without it? If it be possible, the bounty, on this theory, is unconstitutional.

Undoubtedly there are other means for raising an army. Men may enlist without a bounty; and if they will not they may be drafted. A bounty, then, according to Amphyction, is unconstitutional, because the power may be executed by a draft; and a draft is unconstitutional because the power may be executed by a bounty.

So too, Congress may provide for calling out the militia; and this power may be executed by requisitions on the governours, by direct requisitions on the militia, or, perhaps, by receiving volunteers. According to the reasoning of Amphyction, no one of these modes can be constitutional, because no one of them is indispensably necessary.

Every case presents a choice of means. Every end may be attained by different means. Of no one of these means can it be truly said, that, "without it, the end could not be attained."

The rule then laid down by Amphyction is an impracticable, and consequently an erroneous rule.

If we examine the example he has adduced for its illustration, we shall find that, instead of sustaining, it disproves his proposition. The example is this: "Where lands are let by one man to another at the will of the lessor, and the lessor sows the land, and the lessee, after it is sown and before the corn is ripe, put him out, yet the lessor shall have the corn, and shall have free entry ingress, and regress, to cut, and carry away the corn."

The right to the crop growing on the land when the lessor determines the estate, is an incident which the law, with much justice, annexes to a tenancy at will, but is not indispensable to its existence. To this right is annexed as a necessary incident, the power of carrying away the crop. The transportation of the crop then becomes the end for which entry into the land is allowed, and the mode of transportation, the means by which that end is to be accomplished—Has the tenant the choice of means, or can he use that mode of conveyance only without which the crop cannot be carried away? A crop may be removed by employing men only, by employing men and horses, by employing horses and carts, or by employing wagons. In some instances it may be removed by land or by water. Has the person entitled to the crop, and exercising this power of conveyance, his choice of means? or may the landlord say to him, whatever mode of conveyance he may adopt, this is not indispensably necessary; you might have conveyed away the crop by other means? Undoubtedly the person allowed to carry away his crop, would not be permitted to throw down the fences, trample the enclosed fields, and trespass at will on the landholder. But he has the choice of "appropriate" means for the removal of his property, and may use that which he thinks best.

This example then might very well have been put by the court, as an apt illustration of the rule avowed in their opinion.

The rule which Amphyction gives us, for the construction of the constitution, being obviously erroneous, let us examine that which is laid down by the Supreme Court.

The Court concludes a long course of reasoning which completely demonstrates the fallacy of the construction made by the counsel for the state of Maryland, and now adopted by Amphyction, by stating its own opinion in these words: "We think the sound construction of the constitution must allow to the national legislature that discretion with respect to the means by which the powers it confers are to be carried into execution, which will enable that body to perform the high duties assigned to it, in the manner most beneficial to the people. Let the end be legitimate, let it be within the scope of the constitution, and all means which are appropriate, which are plainly adapted to that end, which are not prohibited, but consist with the letter and spirit of the constitution, are constitutional."

To this rule of construction, unless it be itself grossly misconstrued, I can perceive no objection. I think, as the Supreme Court has thought, that it would be the proper rule, were the grant which has been the subject of so much discussion, expunged from the constitution.

It is a palpable misrepresentation of the opinion of the court to say, or to insinuate that it considers the grant of a power "to pass all laws necessary and proper for carrying into execution" the powers vested in the government, as augmenting those powers, and as one which is to be construed "latitudinously," or even "liberally."

It is to be recollected that the counsel for the state of Maryland had contended that this clause was to be construed as restraining and limiting that choice of means which the national legislature would otherwise possess. The reasoning of the court is opposed to this argument, and is concluded with this observation: "The result of the most careful and attentive consideration bestowed upon this clause is, that, if it does not enlarge, it cannot be construed to restrain the powers of congress, or to impair the rights of the legislature to exercise its best judgment in the selection of measures to carry into execution the constitutional powers of the government. If no other motive for its insertion can be suggested, a sufficient one is found in the desire to remove all doubt respecting the right to legislate on that vast mass of incidental powers which must be involved in the constitution, if that instrument be not a splendid bauble."

The court then has not contended that this grant enlarges, but that it does not restrain the powers of Congress; and I believe every man who reads the opinion will admit that the demonstration of this proposition is complete. It is so complete that Amphyction himself does not venture directly to controvert the conclusion, although the whole course of his reasoning seems intended to weaken the principles from which it is drawn. His whole argument appears to be intended to prove that this clause does restrain congress in the execution of all the powers conferred by the constitution, to those "means without which the end could not be obtained." Thus converting an apparent grant of power into a limitation of power.

The court has said, and I repeat it, that the constitution and laws of the United States abound with evidence demonstrating the errour of this construction. I have already stated some instances in which this rule must be discarded; and I will now refer to others which were selected by the court, the aptness of which Amphyction denies.

I will pass over the acts requiring an oath of office because Amphyction seems half disposed to admit there is something in that particular example, and will proceed to some of those which he pronounces totally inapplicable.

Congress possesses power "to establish post offices, and post roads." Amphyction says that the right to carry the mail, and to punish those who rob it, are necessary incidents to this power. I admit it. But who does not perceive that, in making this assertion, he abandons his own interpretation of the word "necessary" and adopts that of the supreme court? Let us apply his rule to the case. Let us suppose a bill before congress to punish those who rob the mail. The inquiry is, he says: "Does the constitution expressly grant the power?" The answer must be in the negative. There is no express power to carry the mail, nor to punish those who rob it. The member is next to ask: "Is this law one without which the power cannot be executed?"—That is, can a post office and a post road be established, without an act of Congress for the punishment of those who rob the mail? The plain common sense of every man will answer this question in the affirmative. These powers were divided under the confederation. Then the conclusion of the member must be, this right to punish those who rob the mail "is a power reserved to the states, or to the people, and we may not use the means, nor pass the law. Then the state legislature may pass laws to punish those who rob the mail, but congress cannot. Post offices and post roads may be established without such a law, and therefore the power to pass it is reserved to the states." Adopt the construction of Amphyction, and this conclusion is inevitable.

Let the question be on the right of Congress to pass an act for the punishment of those who falsify a record.

The power is to ordain and establish inferiour courts, the judges of which shall hold their offices during good behaviour, and receive as a compensation for their services, salaries which shall not be diminished during their continuance in office. The second section defines the extent of the judicial power.

Is a law to punish those who falsify a record, one without which a court cannot be established, or one without which a court cannot exercise its functions? We know that under the confederation Congress had the power to establish, and did establish certain courts, and, had not the power to pass laws for the punishment of those who should falsify its records.—Unquestionably such a law is "needful," "requisite," "essential," "conducive to," the due administration of justice; but no man can say it is one without which courts cannot decide causes, or without which it is physically impossible for them to perform their functions. According to the rule of Amphyction then, such a law cannot be enacted by Congress, but may be enacted by the state legislatures.

It would be tedious to go through all the examples put by the supreme court. They are all of the same character, and show, conclusively, that the principles maintained by the counsel for the state of Maryland, and by Amphyction, would essentially change the constitution, render the government of the Union incompetent to the objects for which it was instituted, and place all its powers under the control of the state legislatures. It would, in a great measure, reinstate the old confederation.

It cannot escape any attentive observer that Amphyction's strictures on the opinion of the supreme court, are founded on a total and obvious perversion of the plain meaning of that opinion, as well as on a misconstruction of the constitution. He occasionally substitutes words not used by the court, and employs others, neither in the connexion, nor in the sense, in which they are employed by the court, so as to ascribe to the opinion sentiments which it does not merely not contain, but which it excludes. The court does not say that the word "necessary" means whatever may be "convenient," or "useful." And when it uses "conducive to," that word is associated with others plainly showing that no remote [end, lacking?] no distinct conduciveness to the object was in the mind of the court.

With as little remorse as the Procrustes of ancient fable stretched and lopped limbs in order to fit travellers to his bed, does Amphyction extend and contract the meaning of words in the constitution, and in the opinion of the court, in order to accommodate those papers to his strictures. Thus, he says, if Congress should impose a tax on Land, "it would be extremely convenient, and a very appropriate measure and very conducive to their purpose of collecting this tax speedily, and promptly, if the state governments could be prohibited during the same year, from laying & collecting a land tax. Were they to pass such a law and thereby directly encroach on one of the most undoubted rights of the states, the present liberal and sweeping construction of the clause by the Supreme court would justify the measure."

Now I deny that a law prohibiting the state legislatures from imposing a land tax would be an "appropriate" means, or any means whatever, to be employed in collecting the tax of the United States. It is not an instrument to be so employed. It is not a means "plainly adapted," or "conducive to" the end. The passage of such an act would be an attempt on the part of Congress, "under the pretext of executing its powers, to pass laws for the accomplishment of objects, not intrusted to the government." So far is the construction given to this clause by the supreme court from being so "liberal & sweeping" as to "justify the measure" that the opinion expressly rejects it. Let its language be quoted. "That the power of taxation is one of vital importance; that it is retained by the states; that it is to be concurrently exercised by the two governments, are truths," says the opinion, "which have never been denied." The court afterwards quotes a passage from the Federalist in which this construction is urged vehemently as an objection to the constitution itself, and obviously approves the argument against it.

Many laborious criticisms would be avoided; if those who are disposed to condemn a paper, would take the trouble to read, with a disposition to understand, it.

I shall not notice the various imaginary and loose opinions which Amphyction has collected, or suggested, because they are not imputable to the supreme court. I content myself with exposing some of his errours in construing the constitution, and in ascribing to the opinion he condemns, doctrines which it does not contain.

I cannot however avoid remarking that Amphyction himself, as soon as he has closed his stricture on the supreme court, seems to desert his own construction and take up theirs. "I think it clear," he says, "that the intention of the constitution was to confer on Congress the power of resorting to such means as are incidental to the express powers; to such means as directly and necessarily tend to produce the desired effect."

How much more, let me ask, has been said by the supreme court?

That court has said: "Let the end be legitimate, let it be within the scope of the constitution, and all means which are appropriate, which are plainly adapted to that end, which are not prohibited," "are constitutional." The word "appropriate," if Johnson be authority, means "peculiar," "consigned to some particular use or person,"—"belonging peculiarly."

Let the constructive words used by the supreme court, in this their acknowledged sense, be applied to any of the powers of Congress. Take for example, that of raising armies. The court has said that "all means which are peculiar" to raising armies, which are "consigned to that particular use," which "belong peculiarly" to it, all means which are, "plainly adapted" to the end, are constitutional.

If Amphyction is better pleased with his own language, I shall not contest its right to the preference; but what essential difference is there between "means which directly and necessarily tend to produce the desired effect," and means which "belong peculiarly" to the production of that effect? I acknowledge that I perceive none. Means which are "appropriate," which are "plainly adapted" to the end, must "directly and necessarily tend to produce" it. The difference however between these means, and those without which the effect cannot be produced, must be discerned by the most careless observer.

Let us apply these different definitions of the words, to any of the most common affairs of human life. A leases to B a mill for a number of years on a contract that A shall receive half the profits, and shall pay half the expenses of all the machinery which B may erect therein, and which shall be "necessary and proper" for the manufacture of flower [sic]. Pending this lease, the elevator and hopper boy are invented, and applied, with great advantage, to the manufacture of flower. B erects them in his mill. A is very well satisfied with receiving the increased profits, but is unwilling to pay half the expense of the machinery, because, as he alleges, it was not "necessary" to the manufacture of flower. All will admit that this machinery is "appropriate, and plainly adapted to the end"; or, in the words of Amphyction, that it "directly and necessarily tends to produce the desired effect." But none can think it so indispensably necessary that the end cannot be produced without it. The end was produced, flower was manufactured, before the elevator and hopper boy were invented.

The same may be observed of the cotton machine of the south, of the use of Gypsum on a farm, of many things which occur in the ordinary transactions of human life.

It will be readily perceived in every case, that this rule of construction, which seems to have escaped Amphyction in a moment when the particular object of his essay was out of view, and that contained in the opinion he condemns, are precisely the same; and are both in direct opposition to that other restricted rule by which he tries the reasoning of the supreme court.

If, as I think all will admit, that construction of the words in which Amphyction and the court concur, furnish the true rule for construing the words "necessary and proper" in a contract between man & man, how much more certainly must it be the true rule for construing a constitution,—an instrument the nature of which excludes the possibility of inserting in it an enumeration of the means for executing its specifick powers. If this rule be applicable to the relations between individuals, how much more applicable must it be to the relations between people and their representatives, who are elected for the very purpose of selecting the best means of executing the powers of the government they are chosen to administer.

This fact is stated in the opinion of the court; and the inference drawn from it is completely refuted by the observation that the constitution, when it came from the hands of that convention, was a mere proposal without any obligation. Its whole obligation is derived from the assent and ratification of the people afterwards assembled in state conventions. Had Amphyction confined himself to the assertion that the constitution was proposed to the people by delegates appointed by the state legislatures, he would have accorded with the Supreme Court, and would have asserted a fact which I believe no person is disposed to deny.

His second proposition is: "That the constitution was submitted to conventions elected by the people of the several states; that is to say, to the states themselves in their highest political and sovereign authority; by those separate conventions, representing, not the whole mass of the people of the United States, but the people only within the limits of the respective sovereign states, the constitution was adopted and brought into existence. The individuality of the several states was still kept up, &c."

It surely cannot escape Amphyction himself, that these positions accord precisely with the opinion he pronounces so mischievously erroneous. He admits in terms the whole subject in controversy. He admits that the powers of the general government were not delegated by the state governments, but by the people of the respective states. This is the very proposition advanced by the Supreme Court, and advanced in terms too plain to be mistaken. The argument on the part of the state of Maryland was, as we learn from the opinion, that the constitution did not emanate from the people, but was the act of sovereign and independent states; clearly using the term "states" in a sense distinct from the term "people." It is this argument which is denied by the court; and in discussing it, after stating that the constitution was submitted to conventions of the people in their respective states, the opinion adds: "From these conventions the constitution derives its whole authority."

Were it possible to render the views of the court on this subject more clear, it is done in that part of the opinion which controverts the proposition advanced by the counsel for the state of Maryland, "that the people had already surrendered all their power to the state sovereignties and had nothing more to give," and which, in opposition to this doctrine, maintains that the legitimacy of the general government would be much more questionable had it been created by the states. It is impossible to read that paragraph and retain a single doubt, if indeed a doubt could ever have been created, of the clear understanding of the court that the term "people" was used as designating the people of the states, and the term "states" as designating their government.

Amphyction adds, that those conventions represented "not the whole mass of the people of the United States, but the people only within the limits of the respective sovereign states." "The individuality of the several states was still kept up, &c."

And who has ever advanced the contrary opinion? Who has ever said that the convention of Pennsylvania represented the people of any other state, or decided for any other state than itself? who has ever been so absurd as to deny that "the individuality of the several states was still kept up?" Not the Supreme Court certainly. Such opinions may be imputed to the judges, by those who, finding nothing to censure in what is actually said, and being predetermined to censure, create odious phantoms which may be very proper objects of detestation, but which bear no resemblance to anything that has proceeded from the court.

Nothing can be more obvious than that in every part of the opinion, the terms "state" and "state sovereignties" are used in reference to the state governments, as contradistinguished from the people of the states. The words of the federal convention, requesting that the constitution might "be submitted to a convention of delegates chosen in each state by the people thereof," are quoted; and it is added, "This mode of proceeding was adopted; and by the convention, by congress, and by the state legislatures, the instrument was submitted to the people." That is, to the people of the respective states; for that is the mode of proceeding said to have been recommended by the convention, and to have been adopted.—After noticing that they assembled in their respective states, the opinion adds: "And where else should that have assembled? No political dreamer was ever wild enough to think of breaking down the lines which separate the states, and of compounding the American people into one mass."

Yet Amphyction affects to be controverting the reasoning of the supreme court when he says that the convention of our state did not represent all the people of the United States, that "the individuality of the several states was still kept up." Disregarding altogether the language of the court, he ascribes to the judges an opinion which they "say no political dreamer was ever wild enough to think of."

The next proposition advanced by Amphyction is that "the President is elected by persons who are, as to numbers, partly chosen on the federal principle"; and that the senators are chosen by the state legislatures.

If these facts are alleged for the purpose of proving that the powers of the general government were delegated by the state legislatures, he has not shown us, and I confess I do not perceive, their bearing on that point. If they are alleged to prove the separate existence of the states, he has very gravely demonstrated what every body knows, & what nobody denies. He would be about as usefully employed in convincing us that we see with our eyes & hear with our ears.

The last fact on which the argument of Amphyction is founded is, that the constitution is to be amended by the legislatures of three fourths of the states, or by conventions of the same number of states, in the manner provided by the 5th article.

It is not true that the legislatures of the states can of themselves amend the constitution. They can only decide on those amendments which have previously been recommended to them by Congress. Or they may require Congress to call a convention of the people to propose amendments, which shall, at the discretion of Congress, be submitted to the state legislatures, or to conventions to be assembled in the respective states.

Were it untrue that the constitution confers on the state legislatures the power of making amendments, that would not prove that this power was delegated to them by themselves. The amendments would indeed be the act of the states, but the original would still be the act of the people.

I have now reviewed the first number of Amphyction; and will only add my regrets that a gentleman whose claims to our respect appear to be by no means inconsiderable should manifest such excessive hostility to the powers necessary for the preservation of the Union, as to arraign with such bitterness the opinion of the supreme court on an interesting constitutional question, either for doctrines not to be found in it, or on principles totally repugnant to the words of the constitution, and to the recorded facts respecting its adoption.

A Friend to the Union.

Mr. Editor,

The second errour supposed by Amphyction to be contained in the opinion of the Supreme Court is: "That the grant of powers to Congress which may be necessary and proper to carry into execution, the other powers granted to them or to any department of the government, ought to be construed in a liberal rather than a restricted sense."

For the sake of accuracy I will observe that the Supreme Court has not said that this grant ought to be construed in a "liberal sense;" although it has certainly denied that it ought to be construed in that "restricted sense" for which Amphyction contends. If by the term "liberal sense" is intended an extension of the grant beyond the fair and usual import of the words, the principle is not to be found in the opinion we are examining.

There is certainly a medium between that restricted sense which confines the meaning of words to narrower limits than the common understanding of the world affixes to them, and that extended sense which would stretch them beyond their obvious import. There is a fair construction which gives to language the sense in which it is used, and interprets an instrument according to its true intention. It is this medium, this fair construction that the Supreme Court has taken for its guide. No passage can, I think, be extracted from the opinion, which recognises a different rule; and the passages are numerous which recognise this. In commenting on the omission of the word "expressly" in the 10th amendment, the court says: "Thus leaving the question whether the particular power which may become the subject of contest, has been delegated to the one government or prohibited to the other, to depend on a fair construction of the whole instrument." So too, in all the reasoning on the word "necessary," the court does not, in a single instance, claim the aid of a "latitudinous," or "liberal" construction; but relies, decidedly and confidently, on its true meaning, "taking into view the subject, the context, and the intention of the framers of the constitution."

Ought any other rule to have been adopted?

Amphyction answers this question in the affirmative. This word, he contends, and indeed all the words of the constitution, ought to be understood in a restricted sense; and for not adopting his rule, the Supreme Court has drawn upon itself his heaviest censure.

The contest, then, so far as profession goes, is between a mere historical fact, which it would be desirable to settle correctly, but for the settlement of which it could scarcely be necessary to call on the legislatures of the respective states, or to express so earnest a hope that "Virginia would, as usual, do her duty." If it be possible for Amphyction to persuade himself that the right of the state legislatures "to canvass" or "remonstrate against the publick measures of the Congress or of the President," depended on their having delegated to the general government all its powers, it would prove only with what facility the most intelligent mind may impose on itself, when pursuing a favourite and dominant idea. Surely nothing can be more obvious, nothing better established, than that the right to canvass the measures of government, or to remonstrate against the abuse of power, must reside in all who are affected by those measures, or over whom that power is exercised, whether it was delegated by them or not. Were this allegation of Amphyction true, it would follow that the people have no right to canvass the measures of government, or to remonstrate against them. The right to canvass and remonstrate resides, according to his argument, in those only who have delegated the powers of the government. Those powers were delegated, not by the people, but by the states in their sovereign capacity. It follows that the states in their sovereign capacity, not the people, have the right to canvass publick measures. If this conclusion be false, as it must be, the premises are false also; and that a man of Amphyction's intelligence should have advanced them, only proves that he is too little accustomed to political opposition, and is too confident of the prejudices he addresses, to be very attentive to the correctness of his positions, or to the accuracy of his reasoning.

But if Amphyction had not been more anxious to throw obloquy on the court than to ascertain its justice, he might have spared this unnecessary charge of travelling out of the case for the purpose of delivering, extrajudicially, a doctrine so dangerous as he represents this to be. The principles he now maintains, appear to have been advanced, and relied on at the bar. "The counsel for the state of Maryland," we are told in the opinion, "have deemed it of some importance in the construction of the constitution to consider that instrument, not as emanating from the people; but, as the act of sovereign and independent states. The powers of the general government, it has been said, are delegated by the states who alone are truly sovereign, and must be exercised in subordination to the states, who alone possess supreme dominion." It is in consequence of this argument that the subject is introduced into the opinion.

His eagerness to censure must be much stronger than his sense of justice, who will criminate a court for noticing an argument advanced by eminent counsel, as one of leading importance in the cause.

But waiving any further discussion of these incidental observations, I will proceed to consider the first objection made to the opinion of the Supreme Court. It is stated to be "the denial that the powers of the federal government were delegated by the states."

This assertion is not literally true.—The court has not, in terms, denied "that the powers of the federal government were delegated by the states," but has asserted affirmatively that it "is emphatically and truly a government of the people," that it, "in form and in substance emanates from them."

If Amphyction chuses to construe the affirmative assertion made by the court into a negative assertion that "the powers of the government were not delegated by the states," I shall not contest the point with him, unless he uses the word "states" in a different sense from that which [a] great part of his argument imports. In what sense, let me ask, does he use the word? Does he mean the people inhabiting that territory which constitutes a state? Or does he mean the government of that territory? If the former, the controversy is at an end. He concurs with the opinion he arraigns. The Supreme Court cannot be mistaken. It has said, not indeed in the same words, but in substance, precisely what he says. The powers of the government were delegated, according to that opinion, by the people assembled in convention in their respective states, and deciding, as all admit, for their respective states.

If Amphyction means to assert, as I suppose he does, that the powers of the general government were delegated by the state legislatures, then I say that his assertion is contradicted by the words of the constitution, and by the fact; and is not supported even by that report, on which he so confidently relies.

The words of an instrument, unless there be some sinister design which shuns the light, will always represent the intention of those who frame it. An instrument intended to be the act of the people, will purport to be the act of the people. An instrument intended to be the act of the states, will purport to be the act of the states. Let us then examine those words of the constitution, which designate the source whence its powers are derived. They are: "We the people of the United States, in order to form a more perfect union, &c, do ordain and establish this constitution for the United States of America."

The constitution then proceeds in the name of the people to define the powers of that government which they were about to create.

This language cannot be misunderstood. It cannot be construed to mean, "We the states, &c."

If still more complete demonstration on this point could be required, it will be furnished by a comparison of the words just recited from the constitution, with those used in the articles of confederation.

The confederation was intended to be the act of the states, and was drawn in language comporting with that intention. The style is: "Articles of confederation and perpetual union between the states of New Hampshire, Massachusetts Bay, &c." The 3d article is completely descriptive of the character of the instrument. It is in these words: "The said states hereby severally enter into a firm league of friendship with each other for their common defence, the security of their liberties, and their mutual and general welfare; binding themselves to assist each other against all force offered to, or attacks made upon them, or any of them, on account of religion, sovereignty, trade, or any other pretence whatever."

The confederation was a mere alliance offensive and defensive, and purports to be, what it was intended to be,—the act of sovereign states. The constitution is a government acting on the people, and purports to be, what it was intended to be,—the act of the people.

The fact itself is in perfect consonance with the language of the instrument. It was not intended to submit the constitution to the decision of the state legislatures, nor was it submitted to their decision. It was referred to conventions of the people "for their assent or ratification," whose decision thereon was not to be reported to the state legislatures but to Congress. Had the legislature of every state in the Union been hostile to the constitution, it would still have gone into operation, if assented to and ratified by the conventions of the people. With what propriety, then, can it be denied to be the act of the people?

On this part of the question also, a comparison with the mode of proceeding for the adoption of the constitution, which was the act of the people, with that observed in adopting the confederation, which was the act of the states, may not be altogether useless.

We have seen that the constitution was submitted to the people themselves assembled in convention.

The confederation was submitted to the state legislatures, who adopted or rejected it; and who expressed their adoption by empowering their members in Congress, who were their ministers plenipotentiary, to subscribe it in their behalf.

I cannot be mistaken when I say that no political proposition was ever more fully demonstrated than that maintained by the Supreme Court of the United States, respecting the source from which the government of the Union derives its powers.

I will now show that the very report cited by Amphyction admits the proposition contained in the opinion he reprobates.

Certain resolutions he informs us had been adopted by the legislature of Virginia in 1798, one of which contained the assertion that the assembly viewed "the powers of the federal government as resulting from the compact to which the states are parties." "Those resolutions," he says, "having been disapproved of by most of the other state legislatures, became the subject of examination at the succeeding session, and produced that remarkable commentary which has generally been known by the name of Madison's report." The language of this commentary on this part of the resolution is; "It is indeed true that the term 'states,' is sometimes used in a vague sense and sometimes in different senses, according to the subject to which it is applied. Thus it sometimes means the separate sections of territory occupied by the political societies within each; sometimes the particular governments established by those societies; sometimes those societies as organized into those particular governments; and lastly, it means the people in their highest sovereign capacity."

In which of these senses does the committee assert that the states are parties to the constitution or compact? In that sense in which the term is used to designate the government established by the particular society within the territory? No. The chairman of that committee had too much self respect, too much respect for the opinions of intelligent men out of Virginia as well as in it, to advance a proposition so totally untrue. The report continues: "Whatever different constructions of the term 'states' in the resolution may have been entertained, all will at least concur in that last mentioned" (the people composing those political societies in their highest sovereign capacity) "because," the report proceeds, "in that sense the constitution was submitted to the 'states.' In that sense the states ratified it; and in that sense they are consequently parties to the compact from which the powers of the federal government result."

This celebrated report, then, concurs exactly with the Supreme court, in the opinion that the constitution is the act of the people.

I will now examine the facts on which those arguments are founded, with which Amphyction attempts to support his most extraordinary dogma.

The first is that "the federal convention of 1787, was composed of delegates appointed by the respective state legislatures."

I have confined my observations to the reasoning of the Supreme Court, and have taken no notice of the conclusion drawn from it, because the essays I am reviewing make no objections to the latter, but denounce the former as false and dangerous. I think, on the contrary, I hazard nothing when I assert that the reasoning is less doubtful than the conclusion. I myself concur in the conclusion; but I do not fear contradiction from any fair minded and intelligent man when I say that the principles laid down by the court for the construction of the constitution may all be sound, and yet the act for incorporating the Bank be unconstitutional. But if the act, be constitutional, the principles laid down by the court must be sound. I defy Amphyction, I defy any man, to furnish an argument which shall, at the same time, prove the Bank to be constitutional, and the reasoning of the courts to be erroneous. Why, then is Amphyction so delicate on the constitutionality of the law, while he is vehement and strenuous in his exertions to rouse the nation against the court? If we do not account for this by saying that the court is less popular, and therefore more vulnerable, than the executive and legislature, how shall we account for it?

Before I conclude let me ask this gentleman and those who think with him, what train of reasoning would have satisfied him and them? The court did not volunteer in this business. The question was brought before them, and they could not escape it. What course then does Amphyction think they ought to have adopted? Does he think they ought to have declared the law unconstitutional and void? He does not say so; and we are not permitted to draw this inference from what he does say. After lamenting that seriatim opinions were not delivered, he supposes what might have been the opinions of Judges, concurring in the decision, but dissenting from the reasoning, delivered by the Chief Justice. "Some of them," he says, "may have believed that it was for Congress to have judged of that necessity and propriety, and having exercised their undoubted functions in so deciding, that it was not consistent with judicial modesty to say there was no such necessity, and thus to arrogate to themselves a right of putting their veto upon a law."

Again, he says: "It may however be asked, whether I can at this day pretend to argue against the constitutionality of a bank established by Congress? In answer, I reply that it is not my intention by these remarks to bring that subject into discussion. I am willing to acquiesce in this particular case, so long as the charter continues without being violated—because it has been repeatedly argued before Congress, and not only in 1791 but in 1815, was solemnly decided in favour of the measure."

Let us suppose that the court had supported its decision by the reasoning which Amphyction conjectures may have influenced some of the Judges whom he does not appear inclined to censure, or by that which he adopts for himself. Suppose the court had said: "Congress has judged of the necessity and propriety of this measure, and having exercised their undoubted functions in so deciding, it is not consistent with judicial modesty to say there is no such necessity, and thus to arrogate to ourselves the right of putting our veto upon a law."

Or suppose the court, after hearing a most elaborate and able argument on the constitutionality of the law, had said: "It is not our intention to bring that subject into discussion. We are willing to acquiesce in this particular case so long as the charter continues without being violated—because it has been repeatedly argued before Congress, and not only in 1791, but in 1815, was solemnly decided against the measure."

Would this reasoning have satisfied, or ought it to have satisfied the publick? Would Amphyction himself be content with the declaration of the Supreme Court that, on any question concerning the constitutionality of an act, it is enough to say "it is not consistent with judicial modesty" to contradict the opinion of Congress, and "thus to arrogate to themselves the right of putting their veto upon a law" or that "they are willing to acquiesce" in the particular act, because it has been repeatedly argued before congress, and not only in 1791, but in 1815," or at some other time since 1801, "was solemnly decided in favour of the measure?"

But if, as we must believe was the fact in this case, because it is so stated by the Judges, the court should be "unanimously and decidedly of opinion that the law is constitutional," would it comport with their honour, with their duty, or with truth, to insinuate an opinion that Congress had violated the constitution? If it would not, then was it incumbent on the court in this case, to pursue, not the course marked by Amphyction but that which he censures. It was incumbent on them to state their real opinion and their reasons for it. Those reasons, I am persuaded, require only to be read with fairness and with attention to be approved.

A FRIEND TO THE UNION

JOSEPH STORY

Why Republics Need an Independent Judiciary

Story, the Massachusetts Republican who became Marshall's brilliant and useful supporter in Federalist doctrine, was a Harvard graduate who had served in Congress and was appointed to the Court by President Madison at the age of thirty-two. His enormous output of incisive writing has been discussed in the "Introduction." The selection here is from his *Commentaries on the Constitution*, which first appeared in 1833. Always gloomy about attacks on the Court and its ability to survive the blows of the Jeffersonians and the Jacksonians, Story ended the work with passages worrying that the constitutional order as he knew it was about to be washed away by the tides of democracy and States' rights. Marshall, to whom the volume was dedicated, commented to Story that the concluding admonitions "will not, I fear, avail as they ought to avail against this popular frenzy." Ironically, Marshall and Story feared the flood in the midst of their completion of a seawall of constitutional doctrine which stood, almost without leakage, for a century.

SOURCE: Joseph Story, *Commentaries on the Constitution of the United States* (Boston: Little, Brown & Co., 1833), Chapter XXXVIII.

[E] very government must, in its essence, be unsafe and unfit for a free people, where [a judicial] department does not exist, with powers coextensive with those of the legislative department. Where there is no judicial department to interpret, pronounce, and execute the law, to decide controversies, and to enforce rights, the government must either perish by its own imbecility, or the other departments of government must usurp powers, for the purpose of commanding obedience, to the destruction of liberty. The will of those, who govern, will become, under such circumstances, absolute and despotic; and it is wholly immaterial, whether power is vested in a single tyrant, or in an assembly of tyrants. . . .

Two ends, then, of paramount importance, and fundamental to a free government, are proposed to be attained by the establishment of a national judiciary. The first is a due execution of the powers of the government; and the second is a uniformity in the interpretation and operation of those powers, and of the laws enacted in pursuance of them. The power of interpreting the laws involves necessarily the function to ascertain, whether they are conformable to the constitution, or not; and if not so conformable, to declare them void and inoperative. As the constitution is the supreme law of the land, in a conflict between that and the laws, either of congress, or of the states, it becomes the duty of the judiciary to follow that only which is of paramount obligation. This results from the very theory of a republican constitution of government; for otherwise the acts of the legislature and executive would in effect become supreme and uncontrollable, notwithstanding any prohibitions or limitations contained in the constitution; and usurpations of the most unequivocal and dangerous character might be assumed, without any remedy within the reach of the citizens. The people would thus be at the mercy of their rulers, in the state and national governments; and an omnipotence would practically exist, like that claimed for the British Parliament. The universal sense of America has decided that, in the last resort, the judiciary must decide upon the constitutionality of the acts and laws of the general and state governments, so far as they are capable of being made the subject of judicial controversy. It follows, that when they are subjected to the cognizance of the judiciary, its judgments must be conclusive; for otherwise they may be disregarded, and the acts of the legislature and executive enjoy a secure and irresistible triumph. To the people at large, therefore, such an institution is peculiarly valuable; and it ought to be eminently cherished by them. On its firm and independent structure they may repose with safety, while they perceive in it a faculty, which is only set in motion, when applied to; but which, when thus brought into action, must proceed with competent power, if required to correct the error, or subdue the oppression of the other branches of the government. Fortunately too for the people, the function of the judiciary, in deciding on constitutional questions, is not one, which it is at liberty to decline. While it is bound not to take jurisdiction, if it should not, it is equally true, that it must take jurisdiction, if it should. It cannot, as the legislature may, avoid a measure, because it approaches the confines of the constitution. It cannot pass it by, because it is doubtful. With whatever doubt, with whatever difficulties a case may be attended, it must decide it, when it arises in judgment. It has no more right to decline the exercise of a jurisdiction which is given, than to usurp that which is not given. The one or the other would be treason to the constitution. . . .

It has sometimes been suggested that, though in monarchical governments the independence of the judiciary is essential to guard the rights of subjects from the injustice and oppression of the crown; yet that the same reasons do not apply to a republic, where the popular will is sufficiently known, and ought always to be obeyed. A little consideration of the subject will satisfy us that, so far from this being true, the reasons in favor of the independence of the judiciary apply with augmented force to republics; and especially to such as possess a written constitution, with defined powers and limited rights.

In the first place, factions and parties are quite as common and quite as violent in republics as in monarchies; and the same safeguards are as indispensable in the one as in the other, against the encroachments of party spirit, and the tyranny of factions. Laws, however wholesome or necessary, are frequently the objects of temporary aversion and popular odium, and sometimes of popular resistance. Nothing is more facile in republics than for demagogues, under artful pretences, to stir up combinations against the regular exercise of authority. Their selfish purposes are too often interrupted by the firmness and independence of upright magistrates, not to make them at all times hostile to a power which rebukes, and an impartiality which condemns them. The judiciary, as the weakest point in the constitution on which to make an attack, is therefore constantly that to which they direct their assaults; and a triumph here, aided by any momentary popular encouragement, achieves a lasting victory over the constitution itself. Hence, in republics, those who are to profit by public commotions or the prevalence of faction, are always the enemies of a regular and independent administration of justice. They spread all sorts of delusion, in order to mislead the public mind and excite the public prejudices. . . . It is obvious that, under such circumstances, if the tenure of office of the judges is not permanent, they will soon be rendered odious, not because they do wrong, but because they refuse to do wrong; and they will be made to give way to others, who shall become more pliant tools of the leading demagogues of the day. There can be no security for the minority in a free government, except through the judicial department. In a monarchy, the sympathies of the people are naturally enlisted against the mediated oppressions of their ruler; and they screen his victims from his vengeance. His is the cause of one against the community. But in free governments, where the majority who obtain power for the moment, are supposed to represent the will of the people, persecution, especially of a political nature, becomes the cause of the community against one. It is the more violent and unrelenting, because it is deemed indispensable to attain power, or to enjoy the fruits of victory. . . .

It has been observed with great sagacity, that power is perpetually stealing from the many to the few; and the tendency of the legislative department to absorb all the other powers of the government has always been dwelt upon by statesmen and patriots as a general truth, confirmed by all human experience. If the judges are appointed at short intervals, either by the legislative or executive department, they will naturally, and, indeed, almost necessarily become mere dependents upon the appointing power. If they have any desire to obtain, or to hold office, they will at all times evince a desire to follow and obey the will of the predominant power in the state. Justice will be administered with a faltering and feeble hand. It will secure nothing but its own place; and the approbation of those who value, because they control it. It will decree what best suits the opinions of the day, and it will forget that the precepts of the law rest on eternal foundations

. . . and thus the fundamental maxim of a republic, that it is a government of laws and not of men, will be silently disproved or openly abandoned. . . .

The argument of those who contend for a short period of office of judges, is founded upon the necessity of a conformity to the will of the people. But the argument proceeds upon a fallacy, in supposing that the will of the rulers and the will of the people are the same. Now they not only may be, but often actually are in direct variance to each other. No man in a republican government can doubt, that the will of the people is, and ought to be supreme. But it is the deliberate will of the people, evinced by their solemn acts, and not the momentary ebullitions of those who act for the majority, for a day, or a month, or a year. The constitution is the will, the deliberate will, of the people. They have declared under what circumstances, and in what manner it shall be amended and altered; and until a change is effected in the manner prescribed, it is declared that it shall be the supreme law of the land, to which all persons, rulers, as well as citizens, must bow in obedience. When it is constitutionally altered, and not until then, are the judges at liberty to disregard its original injunctions. . . . If the constitution is to be expounded, not by its written text, but by the opinions of the rulers for the time being, whose opinions are to prevail, the first or the last? When, therefore, it is said that the judges ought to be subjected to the will of the people, and to conform to their interpretation of the constitution, the practical meaning must be that they should be subjected to the control of the representatives of the people in the executive and legislative departments, and should interpret the constitution as the latter may from time to time deem correct.

But it is obvious that elections can rarely, if ever, furnish any sufficient proofs, what is deliberately the will of the people, as to any constitutional or legal doctrines. Representatives and rulers must be ordinarily chosen for very different purposes, and in many instances, their opinions upon constitutional questions must be unknown to their constituents. The only means known to the constitution, by which to ascertain the will of the people upon a constitutional question, is in the shape of an affirmative or negative proposition by way of amendment, offered for their adoption in the mode prescribed by the constitution. . . .

If, then, the judges were appointed for two, or four, or six years, instead of during good behavior, the only security which the people would have for a due administration of public justice and a firm support of the constitution would be, that being dependent upon the executive for their appointment during their brief period of office, they might, and would represent more fully, for the time being, the constitutional opinion of each successive executive, and thus carry into effect his system of government. Would this be more wise, or more safe, more for the permanence of the constitution, or the preservation of the liberties of the people, than the present system? . . .[1]

FOOTNOTE

[1] Mr. Jefferson, during the latter years of his life, and indeed from the time when he became president of the United States, was a most strenuous advocate of the plan of making the judges hold their offices for a limited term of years only. He proposed that their appointments should be for *four* or *six* years, renewable by the president and senate. It is not my purpose to bring his opinions into review, or to comment on the terms in which they are expressed. It is impossible not to perceive that he entertained a decided hostility to the judicial department; and that he allowed himself in language of insinuation against the conduct of judges, which is little calculated to add weight to his opinions. He wrote on this subject apparently with the feelings of a partisan, and under influences which his best friends will most regret. . . .

The truth is, that even with the most secure tenure of office during good behavior, the danger is not that the judges will be too firm in resisting public opinion, and in defence of private rights or public liberties; but that they will be too ready to yield themselves to the passions, and politics, and prejudices of the day. In a monarchy, the judges, in the performance of their duties with uprightness and impartiality, will always have the support of some of the departments of the government, or at least of the people. In republics, they may sometimes find the other departments combined in hostility against the judicial; and even the people for a while, under the influence of party spirit and turbulent factions, ready to abandon them to their fate. Few men possess the firmness to resist the torrent of popular opinion; or are content to sacrifice present ease and public favor in order to earn the slow rewards of a conscientious discharge of duty; the sure, but distant gratitude of the people; and the severe but enlightened award of posterity. . . . The framers of the constitution, with profound wisdom, laid the cornerstone of our national republic in the permanent independence of the judicial establishment.

☆☆☆ The Confident Court in a Gilded Age, 1880-1920

SAMUEL F. MILLER
The Weakest Branch

Miller, a Kentuckian who originally had practiced medicine, became a member of the Kentucky Bar in 1847. When the Whig party cracked apart on the slavery issue, Miller, a vigorous opponent of slavery, left for Iowa and opened law practice there. He was active in forming the state Republican party, and President Lincoln named him to the Supreme Court in 1862. Though almost unknown at the time of his appointment, Miller would probably be on anyone's list of the Court's dozen greatest members. As a Justice without Field's and Brewer's love for the New Capitalism, with strong sympathies for national power, careful about individual liberties, and committed to a role of balanced restraint for the judiciary, Miller was something of a lonely Justice in his later years on the Court, after the transition years under Chief Justice Morrison Waite (1874–1888) gave way to the period of judicial muscle flexing under Chief Justice Melville Fuller. The selection printed here was part of a series of law lectures which Justice Miller delivered in Washington, D.C., in February of 1880.

SOURCE: *Lectures on the Constitution* (Washington: Morrison, 1880), 24–29.

The judicial branch of the government is, of all others, the weakest branch. It has no army; it has no navy; it has no press; it has no officers except its marshals, and they are appointed by the President and confirmed by the Senate; and the marshals that we send our processes to cannot be removed by us, but they may be removed any day by the executive. The clerks whom they permit us in some form or other to appoint, have salaries and compensations regulated by the legislature; and a clerk who gets $20,000 in fees, pays all but $3,500 into the Treasury of the United States. We are, then, so far as the ordinary forms of power are concerned, by far the feeblest branch or department of the government. We have to rely—I beg pardon for using the personal pronoun in this discussion—but the judiciary have to rely on the confidence and respect of the public for their weight and influence in the government; and I am happy to say that the country, the people, and the other branches of the government have never been found wanting in that respect and in that confidence. It is one of the best tributes to the American nation—a tribute which it deserves above all others even of the Anglo-Saxon race—a tribute which can be paid to no other race like the Anglo-Saxon race—that they submit to the law as expounded by the judiciary.

Under all the excitement of wealth; of money; of the contest of railroads; of political existence—everything which can be got before the court—everything which can come fairly within judicial cognizance—our people seem to think is safe. And whatever may be said or felt about the recent trouble in the State of Maine, there is no grander phenomenon to be found in the history of this country than a body calling itself a legal legislature and government quietly laying down its functions and dispersing at the mere opinion of a court that they were not the proper government.

Of course, gentlemen, there are nice questions between these various departments of the government as to the lines of demarkation; and it has always been an anxious question, and always must be one, where there is a conflict in the claims of these branches of the government. While it is the duty of the court to construe the great instrument, the Constitution, whenever it shall come before it in a fair judicial proceeding, and it can construe it in no other way,—for it is a delusion, it is a mistake, the idea that the Supreme Court of the United States was created with one of its special functions to interpret and construe that instrument,—I say while, however, it is the special function of the courts to construe the Constitution in a judicial proceeding, with parties properly before them, it is equally the duty of each member of Congress and of the executive to make that construction for himself when he is called to act within the sphere of his duty. And I think myself I have changed one of my beliefs of early life, when I used to think that when a Marshall and his compeers had decided that the Bank of the United States was a financial institution authorized by the Constitution of the United States, the legislative and executive branches should also concede that fact. I am prepared to admit, that while they are bound to consider that in that particular—that is, its execution of the law as between the parties—all the other branches of the government must yield, yet when it comes to the conscience of any member of Congress or any executive to say, "Can I sign a bill?" or "Can I vote for a measure?" it is for him to decide, on the best lights he has, whether the act he is going to do is within the constitutional power of the body of which he is a member. Therefore you see the difficulty in getting a settled construction of this instrument. And since every branch of the government, when called on to act originally, is bound to act on the judgment it forms of its own powers, you can understand the reason that for eighty or ninety years the question of the relations of the States to the Federal government should remain an open and undecided question.

We are, however, getting a body of decisions of recognized principles. The instrument is being construed by the judicial branch more than the others, but largely by all others, in the light of the events which have arisen to test it. The construction which was put upon the Constitution during the recent insurrection—the powers that could be exercised in such an emergency by the President, by the War Department, by the Legislature, by the Judiciary, all have been tested—all have undergone investigation; and while no man can say that all the decisions have been correct, because they have been varying, it must, in the light of any impartial mind, be clear that we are completing a construction and are deciding a great many things that will remain forever, with regard to the Constitution.

It is very desirable that it should be so. All loose construction of

authority is dangerous; all construction of authority too limited to
serve the purpose for which it is given is injurious. You must look
at that instrument in the light of the purposes which it was intended
to answer; in the light of the evils it was intended to remedy; in the
light of the fact that we were a dissolving people, and the instrument
was intended to bind us anew forever; in the light of the fact that
the government was going to pieces for want of power to protect itself, and we must consider that one of the purposes of the Constitution was to give the government that power; in the light of the
fact that the Confederacy—the government under the Articles of
Confederation—could only request the States to do a great deal that
was necessary to carry on the Federal government, and it was desirable
to give the new government the power of operating directly upon the
people without going through the instrumentality of the States, and
that instead of laws which before that Constitution was made were
intended to have effect through the State legislatures, the government
should now have direct effect through the legislation of Congress—
the action of the legislative branch—and the judiciary, upon the people
themselves, without the consent, and even against the wishes, of the
States, if it were necessary.

In all these ways, when you come to construe this instrument like
a remedial statute, like a contract between individuals, it must be construed in the light of the times in which it was made—of the evils to
be remedied, of the good to be effected, and, above all, in the light of
the idea that it was made to create a perpetual government of the
people, among the people, and by the people.

STEPHEN J. FIELD

Our Power to Declare Laws Unconstitutional

Field was raised in an aristocratic New England family, had an adventurous and stormy career in young California after the gold rush of 1849, and brought to the Court a flowing beard and stern features which matched perfectly his moral righteousness and judicial absolutism. He arrived on the Court as a Lincoln appointee from the West in 1863 and retired in 1897. Always hopeful that the Democratic party might turn to him as its presidential candidate in the 1860's, or 1870's, or 1880's, or 1890's, Field wrote fierce letters within the Court and to friends about the Court's work, and his opinions were hammer blows at those who failed to see Truth. Yet he made few public speeches. The selection here was a rare address by Field at the official celebration of the Court's centenary. When the time came for Field to release his seat, he wrote a letter to his colleagues (published in the Court's Reports) which reviewed his judicial career and concluded with some observations about the Court's role: "Now and then we hear it spoken of as an aristocratic feature of a republican government. But it is the most democratic of all. Senators represent their states and representatives their constituents, but this court stands for the whole country, and as such it is truly 'of the people, by the people, and for the people.' It has, indeed, no power to legislate. It cannot appropriate a dollar of money. It carries neither the purse nor the sword. But it possesses the power of declaring the law, and in that is found the safeguard which keeps the whole mighty fabric of government from rushing to destruction. This negative power, the power of resistance, is the only safety of a popular government. . . ." 42 L. Ed. 1219, 1221 (1897).

SOURCE: "Address at the Centennial Celebration of the Organization of the Federal Judiciary," New York, N.Y., February 4, 1890, 134 U.S. App. VI (1890).

The power of the court to pass upon the conformity with the Constitution of an Act of Congress, or of a State, and thus to declare its validity or invalidity, or limit its application, follows from the nature of the Constitution itself, as the supreme law of the land— the separation of the three departments of government into legislative, executive and judicial—the order of the Constitution—each independent in its sphere, and the specific restraints upon the exercise of legislative powers contained in that instrument. In all other countries, except perhaps Canada under the government of the Dominion, the judgment of the legislature as to the compatibility of a law passed by it with the constitution of the country has been considered as superior to the judgment of the courts. But under the Constitution of the United States, the Supreme Court is independent of other departments in all judicial matters, and the compatibility between the Constitution and a statute, whether of Congress or of a State, is a judicial and not a political question, and therefore is to be determined by the court whenever a litigant asserts a right or claim under the disputed Act for judicial decision.

This power of that court is sometimes characterized by foreign writers and jurists as a unique provision of a disturbing and dangerous character, tending to defeat the popular will as expressed by the legislature. In thus characterizing it they look at the power as one that may be exercised by way of supervision over the general legislation of Congress, determining the validity of an enactment in advance of its being contested. But a declaration of the unconstitutionality of an Act of Congress or of the States cannot be made in that way by the Judicial Department. The unconstitutionality of an Act cannot be pronounced except as required for the determination of contested litigation. No such authority as supposed would be tolerated in this country. It would make the Supreme Court a third house of Congress, and its conclusions would be subject to all the infirmities of general legislation.

The limitations upon legislative power, arising from the nature of the Constitution and its specific restraints in favor of private rights, cannot be disregarded without conceding that the legislature can change at will the form of our government from one of limited to one of unlimited powers. Whenever, therefore, any court, called upon to construe an enactment of Congress or of a State, the validity of which is assailed, finds its provisions inconsistent with the Constitution, it must give effect to the latter, because it is the fundamental law of the whole people, and, as such, superior to any law of Congress or any law of a State. Otherwise the limitations upon legislative power expressed in the Constitution or implied by it must be considered as vain attempts to control a power which is in its nature uncontrollable.

This unique power, as it is termed, is therefore not only not a disturbing or dangerous force, but is a necessary consequence of our form of government. Its exercise is necessary to keep the administration of the government, both of the United States and of the States, in all their branches, within the limits assigned to them by the Constitution of the United States, and thus secure justice to the people against the unrestrained legislative will of either—the reign of law against the sway of arbitrary power.

As to the decisions of the Supreme Court respecting the constitutionality of Acts of Congress or of the States, they have, as a general rule, been recognized as furthering the great purposes of the Constitution,—as where, in *Gibbons* v. *Ogden*, the court declared the freedom of the navigable waters of New York to all vessels, against a claim of an exclusive right to navigate them by steam vessels under a grant of the State to particular individuals;—or where, as in *Dartmouth College* v. *Woodward*, the court enforced the prohibition of the Constitution against the impairment by the Legislation of a State of the obligation of a contract, declaring void an Act of New Hampshire which altered the character of the college in essential particulars, and holding that the charter granted to the trustees of the college was a contract within the meaning of the Constitution and protected by it, and that the college was a private charitable institution—not under the control of the Legislature;—or where, as in *Brown* v. *Maryland*, the court declared that commerce with foreign nations could not, under a law of the State, be burdened with a tax upon goods imported, before they were broken in bulk, though the tax was imposed in the form of a license to sell;—or where, as in *Weston* v. *Charleston*, the court declared that the bonds and securities of the United States could not be subjected to taxation by the States, and thus the credit of the United States be impaired;—or where, as in *McCulloch* v. *Maryland*, and *Osborn* v. *Bank of the United States*, the court denied the authority of the States, by taxation or otherwise, to impede, burden, or in any manner control the means or measures adopted by the government for the execution of its powers;—or where, as in *Hall* v. *DeCuir, The Wabash Railway Co.* v. *Illinois, The Philadelphia* and *Southern Steamship Co.* v. *Pennsylvania*, and other cases determined in the last quarter of a century, the court has removed barriers to interstate and foreign commerce interposed by state legislation.

And so, in the great majority of cases in which the validity of an Act of Congress or of a State has been called in question, its decisions have been in the same direction, to uphold and carry out the provisions of the Constitution. In some instances the court, in the exercise of its powers in this respect, may have made mistakes. The judges would be more than human if this were not so. They have never claimed infalibility; they have often differed among themselves. All they have ever asserted is, that they have striven to the utmost of their abilities to be right, and to perform the functions with which they are clothed to the advancement of justice and the good of the country.

In respect to their liability to err in their conclusions this may be said—that in addition to the desire which must be ascribed to them to be just—the conditions under which they perform their duties, the publicity of their proceedings, the discussions before them, and the public attention which is drawn to all decisions of general interest, tend to prevent any grave departure from the purposes of the Constitution. And, further, there is this corrective of error in every such departure; it will not fit harmoniously with other rulings; it will collide with them, and thus compel explanations and qualifications until the error is eliminated. Like all other error it is bound to die; truth alone is immortal, and in the end will assert its rightful supremacy. . . .

Furthermore, I hardly need say that, to retain the respect and confidence conceded in the past, the court, whilst cautiously abstaining from assuming powers granted by the Constitution to other departments of the government, must unhesitatingly and to the best of its ability enforce, as heretofore, not only all the limitations of the Constitution upon the federal and state governments, but also all the guaranties it contains of the private rights of the citizen, both of person and of property. As population and wealth increase; as the inequalities in the conditions of men become more and more marked and disturbing; as the enormous aggregation of wealth possessed by power should become dominating in the legislation of the country, and thus encroach upon the rights or crush out the business of individuals of small means; as population in some quarters presses upon the means of subsistence, and angry menaces against order find vent in loud denunciations,—it becomes more and more the imperative duty of the court to enforce with a firm hand all the guaranties of the Constitution. Every decision weakening their restraining power is a blow to the peace of society and to its progress and improvement. It should never be forgotten that protection to property and to persons cannot be separated. Where property is insecure, the rights of persons are unsafe. Protection to the one goes with protection to the other; and there can be neither prosperity nor progress where either is uncertain.

That the Justices of the Supreme Court must possess the ability and learning required by the duties of their office, and a character for purity and integrity beyond reproach, need not be said. But it is not sufficient for the performance of his judicial duty that a judge should act honestly in all that he does. He must be ready to act in all cases presented for his judicial determination with absolute fearlessness. Timidity, hesitation and cowardice in any public officer excite and deserve only contempt, but infinitely more in a judge than in any other, because he is appointed to discharge a public trust of the most sacred character. To decide against his conviction of the law or judgment as to the evidence, whether moved by prejudice, or passion, or the clamor of the crowd, is to assent to a robbery as infamous in morals and as deserving of punishment as that of the highwayman or the burglar; and to hesitate or refuse to act when duty calls is hardly less the subject of just reproach. If he is influenced by apprehensions that his character will be attacked, or his motives impugned, or that his judgment will be attributed to the influence of particular classes, cliques or associations, rather than to his own convictions of the law, he will fail lamentably in his high office.

To the intelligent and learned bar of the country the judges must look for their most effective and substantial support. Its members appreciate more than any other class the difficulties and labors and responsibilities of the judicial office; and whilst the most severe and unsparing of critics, they are in the end the most just in their judgments. If they entertain for the judges respect and confidence, if they accord to them learning, integrity and courage, the general public will not be slow in accepting their appreciation as the true estimate of the judges' character. Sustained by this professional and public confidence, the Supreme Court may hope to still further strengthen the hearts of all in love, admiration and reverence for the Constitution of the United States—the noblest inheritance ever possessed by a free people.

JOHN MARSHALL HARLAN

Our Duty to Respect Legislative Enactments

Harlan, a towering, jovial, tobacco-chewing product of the great days of Kentucky, came to the Court in 1877, on the eve of the nation's love affair with capitalism. He died, in judicial harness, in 1911, when the progressive movement was in full voice. Symbolically, Harlan was a link between the progressive tradition of the 1850's and that of 1896–1912. He was a liberal in economic affairs, antimonopolist, mildly prolabor, and pro-taxation of incomes, as well as staunchly pro-Negro and an advocate of maximal fairness in criminal procedure. Yet he was also a defender of liberty of contract, of strict enforcement of bond obligations, and of property rights. While these themes are not easily balanced, Harlan kept them all aloft during his thirty-four years on the Court, constantly stating that his colleagues were engaging in judicial legislation when they differed from his position. The selection here is a response by Harlan to a toast, "The Supreme Court of the United States and Its Work," at a bar dinner in Cincinnati, Ohio, in 1896.

SOURCE: 30 *American Law Review* 900 (1896).

The toast just read relates to the court of which I have the honor to be a member. It has not escaped observation that that tribunal is now the subject of frequent mention, both in the public prints and on the hustings. Some have expressed the belief that there is a purpose to have the Supreme Court reconstructed so as to accomplish certain objects of a political character. Whether any such purpose exists, I do not at this time affirm or deny. I could not do either without seeming to enter the field of political discussion. But this I may say, that the Supreme Court of the United States is safe in the hands of the People of the United States. That tribunal will, as heretofore, go forward in the path marked out by its own sense of duty. And the People will see to it that nothing is done that will impair its usefulness or cripple its just authority. When Washington invited John Jay to become the Chief Justice of the United States he said that the Judicial Department of the National Government was the keystone of our political fabric. If that seemed to be true at the organization of the General Government, before the Federal judicial system had been tried, how much more is it true, at this day, after the experience of more than a century. The American judicial system is now the wonder and admiration of enlightened statesmen throughout the world. When our government was organized, some Europeans ridiculed the idea that any government could be safely administered under a written constitution that established judicial tribunals and invested them with authority to enforce its sanctions and provisions against all. But wise statesmen in other lands are beginning to see and to admit that such tribunals must exist, if the exercise of arbitrary power is to be checked, and if the rights of life, liberty and property are to be adequately protected, as well against illegal action by government as against the lawlessness of mere majorities. We proceed in this country upon the idea, which crowned heads, claiming to rule by divine right, do not understand or appreciate, that liberty is safe only when it is regulated by a fundamental law, binding equally upon the People and upon those whom they commission to carry out the objects for which government is established. Eliminate from our governmental system an independent judiciary invested with authority to protect the rights both of the public and of individuals against illegal acts by whomsoever committed, and our free institutions will disappear, and in their stead will be established a government resting upon mere force, and not, as now, on the consent of the governed, as manifested by a written constitution.

The Supreme Court of the United States has, now and then, been compelled to pass upon questions more or less connected with political matters. It has sometimes given a construction to the Constitution or to acts of Congress, or to State enactments alleged to be in violation of the supreme law of the land, that was displeasing to those who had reached different conclusions. But to the honor of the American People, its decisions have been respected, so far, at least, that no attempt has been made to overturn them by indirection, or in any mode not authorized by the Constitution.

Here I may be permitted to say that there is a tendency in some quarters to look to the Supreme Court of the United States for relief against legislation which is admittedly free from constitutional objection, and which therefore is not liable to criticism except upon grounds of public policy. But that court has itself said that the judiciary has nothing to do with the expediency of legislation, and cannot, with safety to our institutions, entrench upon the domain of another Department of the Government. The remedy for evils arising from impolitic and unjust legislation, not in conflict with the fundamental law, is with the people at the ballot-box. If we should ever come to that condition of things when the courts, acting simply upon their own view as to the wisdom of legislation, habitually interfere with the due course of public affairs, as ordained by the representatives of the people, we may look for the downfall of our Government, and the substitution of a government of men in the place of a government of laws. No more imperative or sacred duty rests upon the Judiciary than to sustain in its integrity the fundamental law of the land. An act of legislation inconsistent with that law cannot be regarded as binding; otherwise, as Chief Justice Marshall has declared, written constitutions are absurd attempts, on the part of the people, to limit a power in its nature illimitable. But equally imperative and equally sacred is its duty to respect legislative enactments, except where their incompatibility with the Constitution is so manifest that a contrary view cannot for a moment be entertained. If an act of legislation, whether of Congress or of the States, be of doubtful constitutionality, let the will of the people, as expressed by their legislative department, have full operation until the people themselves, in the designated mode, shall otherwise ordain. No line of public policy can be long maintained in this country against the will of those who established, and who can change, the Constitution.

DAVID J. BREWER

The Nation's Safeguard

Brewer, a Yale man and the only Supreme Court Justice to be born in Asia Minor, was a nephew of Stephen J. Field. He had settled in Kansas and served on the state and federal bench there from 1861 until his appointment to the Court by Harrison in 1889. A conservative whose ideological bark was a bit worse than his decisional bite, Brewer was unquestionably the rostrum celebrity of his day on the Court. A witty, polished, sometimes florid speaker, he orated on the Supreme Court, constitutional law issues, woman's suffrage (he was for it), anti-imperialism, restricting immigration, and fostering international peace, among other topics. Bar associations were a steady engagement for him, and the selection which follows is from an address to the New York State Bar Association in 1893.

SOURCE: *Proceedings of the New York State Bar Association,* 16th Annual Meeting (1893), 37–47.

I am not here this evening to defend the eighth commandment, or to denounce its grosser violators. I do not propose to discuss the foot-pad or the burglar; they are vulgar and brutal criminals, in whose behalf there has as yet been organized no political party. I wish rather to notice that movement of "coercion," and which by the mere force of numbers seeks to diminish protection to private property. It is a movement which in spirit, if not in letter, violates both the eighth and tenth commandments; a movement, which seeing that which a man has attempts to wrest it from him and transfer it to those who have not. It is the unvarying law, that the wealth of a community will be in the hands of a few; and the greater the general wealth, the greater the individual accumulations. The large majority of men are unwilling to endure that long self-denial and saving which makes accumulation possible; they have not the business tact and sagacity which brings about large combinations and great financial results; and hence it always has been, and until human nature is re-modeled always will be true, that the wealth of a nation is in the hands of a few, while the many subsist upon the proceeds of their daily toil. But security is the chief end of government; and other things being equal, that government is best which protects to the fullest extent each individual, rich or poor, high or low, in the possession of his property and the pursuit of his business. It was the boast of our ancestors in the old country, that they were able to wrest from the power of the king so much security for life, liberty and property. Indeed, English history is the long story of a struggle therefor. The greatest of English orators opposing a bill which seemed to give power to the government to enter the homes of the individual, broke forth in this most eloquent eulogy of that protection and security which surrounded an English home, even against the king: "The poorest man in his cottage may bid de-fiance to all the forces of the crown. It may be frail; its roof may shake; the wind may blow through it; the storm may enter it, but the king of England cannot enter it. All his power dares not cross the threshold of that ruined tenement!"

Here, there is no monarch threatening trespass upon the individual. The danger is from the multitudes—the majority, with whom is the power; and if the passage quoted is the grandest tribute to the liberty which existed in England, I would thus paraphrase it to describe that which should prevail under this government by the people: The property of a great railroad corporation stretches far away from the domicile of its owner, through State after State, from ocean to ocean; the rain and the snow may cover it; the winds and the storms may wreck it; but no man or multitude dare touch a car or move a rail. It stands as secure in the eye and in the custody of the law, as the purposes of justice in the thought of God.

This movement expresses itself in two ways: First, in the improper use of labor organizations to destroy the freedom of the laborer, and control the uses of capital. I do not care to stop to discuss such wrongs as these—preventing one from becoming a skilled laborer, by forbidding employers to take more than a named number of apprentices; compelling equal wages for unequal skill and labor; forbidding extra hours of labor to one who would accumulate more than the regular stipend. That which I particularly notice, is the assumption of control over the employer's property, and blocking the access of laborers to it. The common rule as to strikes is this: Not merely do the employees quit the employment, and thus handicap the employer in the use of his property, and perhaps in the discharge of duties which he owes to the public; but they also forcibly prevent others from taking their places. It is useless to say that they only advise—no man is misled. When a thousand laborers gather around a railroad track, and say to those who seek employment that they had better not, and when that advice is supplemented every little while by a terrible assault on one who disregards it, every one knows that something more than advice is attended. It is coercion, force; it is the effort of the many, by the mere weight of numbers, to compel the one to do their bidding. It is a proceeding outside of the law, in defiance of the law; and in spirit and effect an attempt to strip from one that has, that which of right belongs to him—the full and undisturbed use and enjoyment of his own. It is not to be wondered at, that deeds of violence and cruelty attend such demonstrations as these; nor will it do to pretend that the wrong-doers are not the striking laborers, but lawless strangers who gather to look on. Were they strangers who made the history of the "Homestead" strike one of awful horror? Were they women from afar who so maltreated the surrendered guards; or were they the very ones who sought to compel the owners of that property to do their bidding? Even if it be true that at such places the lawless will gather,—who is responsible for their gathering? Weihe, the head of a reputable labor organization may only open the door to lawlessness; but Beekman, the anarchist and assassin, will be the first to pass through; and thus it will be always and everywhere.

In the State of Pennsylvania, only last year, to such an extent was this attempt of an organization to control both employee and employer carried, that there is now pending in the courts of the State, upon the concurrent advice of all the justices of its supreme court, an inquiry as to whether this disturbance of social order did not amount to treason. And this is but one type of multitudes of cases all over the land. This is the struggle of irresponsible persons and organizations to control labor. It is not in the interest of liberty—it is not in the interest of individual or personal rights. It is the attempt to give to the many a control over the few—a step toward despotism. Let the movement succeed, let it once be known that the individual is not free to contract for his personal services, that labor is to be farmed out by organizations, as today by the Chinese companies, and the next step will be a direct effort on the part of the many to seize the property of the few.

The other form of this movement assumes the guise of a regulation of the charges for the use of property subjected, or supposed to be, to a public use. This acts in two directions: One by extending the list of those things, charges for whose use the government may prescribe; until now we hear it affirmed that whenever property is devoted to a use in which the public has an interest, charges for that use may be fixed by law. And if there be any property in the use of which the public or some portion of it has no interest, I hardly know what it is or where to find it. And second, in so reducing charges for the use of property, which in fact is subjected to a public use, that no compensation or income is received by those who have so invested their property. By the one it subjects all property and its uses to the will of the majority; by the other it robs property of its value. Statutes and decisions both disclose that this movement, with just these results, has a present and alarming existence. A switching company in Minneapolis had for eight years been operating under charges of $1.50 a car. With such charges it had not during that time paid off a floating debt incurred in construction, nor a dollar of interest or dividend to those who had invested in its stock or bonds. Without a hearing before any tribunal, the State of Minnesota, through its railroad commission, reduced these charges to $1 a car. Of what value would the ownership of that property be to its owners; and how soon would all semblance of title be swept away under foreclosure by the unpaid bondholders? Sometimes there is an appeal from a majority, and that effort at confiscation failed. And yet that the effort was made and that it did receive some judicial sanction is but a revelation of the spirit which lies behind and prompts the movement, and of the extent to which it has taken hold of the public mind.

There are today ten thousand million of dollars invested in railroad property, whose owners in this country number less than two million persons. Can it be that whether that immense sum shall earn a dollar, or bring the slightest recompense to those who have invested perhaps their all in that business, and are thus aiding in the development of the country, depends wholly upon the whim and greed of that great majority of sixty millions who do not own a dollar. It may be said that that majority will not be so foolish, selfish and cruel as to strip that property of its earning capacity. I say that so long as constitutional guarantees lift on American soil their buttresses and bulwarks against wrong, and so long as the American judiciary breathes the free air of courage, it cannot.

It must not be supposed that the forms in which this movement expresses itself are in themselves bad. Indeed the great danger is in the fact that there is so much of good in them. . . . But the great body of judges are as well versed in the affairs of life as any, and they who unravel all the mysteries of accounting between partners, settle the business of the largest corporations and extract all the truth from the mass of scholastic verbiage that falls from the lips of expert witnesses in patent cases, will have no difficulty in determining what is right and wrong between employer and employees, and whether proposed rates of freight and fare are reasonable as between the public and the owners; while as for speed, is there any thing quicker than a writ of injunction?

But the real objection lies deeper. Somehow or other men always link the idea of justice with that of judge. It matters not that an arbitrator or commissioner may perform the same function, there is not the same respect for the office nor the same feeling that justice only can be invoked to control the decision. The arbitrator and commission will be approached with freedom by many with suggestions that the public or the party, or certain interests demand or will be profited by a decision in one way; but who thus comes near to the court or offers those suggestions to the judge? There is the tacit but universal feeling that justice, as he sees it, alone controls the decision. It is a good thing that this is so; that in the common thought the idea of justice goes hand in hand with that of judge; and that when anything is to be wrought out which it is feared may not harmonize with eternal principles of right and wrong, the cry is for arbitration or commission, or something else whose name is not symbolical or suggestive. I would have it always kept so, and kept so by the very force of the work and life of him who is a judge. It is an Anglo-Saxon demand that he who holds that office shall so bear himself as to be worthy of respect.

So it is that the mischief-makers in this movement ever strive to get away from courts and judges, and to place the power of decision in the hands of those who will the more readily and freely yield to the pressure of numbers, that so-called demand of the majority. But the common idea of justice is that the judge should be indifferent between the litigants—as free as possible from the influence of either; and no temporary arbitrator or political commission can ever equal in these respects the established courts and regular judges.

And so it is, that because of the growth of this movement, of its development in many directions and the activity of those who are in it, and especially because of the further fact that, carrying votes in its hand, it ever appeals to the trimming politician and time-serving demagogue and thus enters into so much of legislation, arises the urgent need of giving to the judiciary the utmost vigor and efficiency. Now, if ever in the history of this country, must there be somewhere and somehow a controlling force which speaks for justice and for justice only. Let this movement sweep on with obvious right and conceded wrong, the triumph of the former would be sure and speedy. Labor organizations are the needed and proper complement of capital organizations. They often work wholesome restraints on the greed, the unscrupulous rapacity which dominates much of capital; and the fact that they bring together a multitude of tiny forces, each helpless in a solitary struggle with capital, enables labor to secure its just rights. So also, in regulating the charges of property which is appropriated to a public use, the public is but exercising a legitimate function, and one which is often necessary to prevent extortion in respect to public uses. Within limits of law and justice labor organizations and State regulation of charges for the use of property which is in fact devoted to public uses are commendable. But with respect to the proposition that the public may rightfully regulate the charges for the use of any property in whose use it has an interest, I am like the lawyer who, when declared guilty of contempt, responded promptly that he had shown no contempt, but on the contrary had carefully concealed his feelings.

Now conceding that there is this basis of wisdom and justice, and that within these limits the movement in both directions will work good to society, the question is how can its excesses, those excesses which mean peril to the nation, be stayed? Will the many who find in its progress temporary and apparent advantages, so clearly discern the ultimate ruin which flows from injustice as voluntarily to desist; or must there be some force, some tribunal, outside, so far as possible, to lift the restraining hand? The answer is obvious. Power always chafes at but needs restraint. This is true whether that power be in a single monarch or in a majority. All history attests the former. We are making that which proves the latter. The triple subdivision of governmental powers into legislative, executive and judicial, recognizes the truth, and has provided in this last co-ordinate department of government the restraining force. And the question which now arises is whether, in view of this exigency, the functions of the judiciary should be strengthened and enlarged, or weakened and restricted. As might be expected, they who wish to push this movement to the extreme, who would brook no restraint on aught that seems to make for their gain, are unanimous in crying out against judicial interference, and are constantly seeking to minimize the power of the courts. Hence the demand for arbitrators to settle all disputes between employer and employees, for commissions to fix all tariffs for common carriers. The argument is that judges are not adapted by their education and training to settle such matters as these; that they lack acquaintance with affairs and are tied to precedents; that the procedure in the courts is too slow and that no action could be had therein until long after the need of action has passed. It would be folly to assert that this argument is barren of force. There are judges who never move a step beyond what has been; who would never adjudge the validity of the plan of salvation without a prior decision of the Master of the Rolls or the Queen's Bench in favor of the doctrine of no restraining force, and it is the rule of all such movements that, unchecked they grow in violence . . .

What, then, ought to be done? My reply is, strengthen the judiciary. How? Permanent tenure of office accomplishes this. If a judge

is to go out of office in a few months the litigant will be more willing
to disobey and take the chances of finally escaping punishment by
delaying the proceedings until a new judge shall take the place—one
whom his vote may select and from whom, therefore, he will expect
slight if any punishment; while if the incumbent holds office for life,
the duration of that life being uncertain, whether one or thirty years,
no litigant wants to take the risk of disobedience with a strong probability that a punishment, though it may be delayed, will come and
come with a severity equal to the wrong of the disobedience. A striking illustration of the truth of this is found in the troubles that followed the election of 1876. The three States in which arose contests
for the possession of the State government were Florida, Louisiana
and South Carolina. In each of them an application was made to the
highest court of the State and a decision announced by such court.
In Florida the decision was accepted without question and the control of the State government passed safely in accordance therewith.
In each of the other States it was an insignificant and disregarded
factor in the strife. In Florida the judges held office for life; in the
other States, for only short terms. The party having or believing it
had a majority was willing in these States to risk a contest with judges
whose term of office would soon expire, for it hoped to place its own
friends on the bench and thus be secured from all consequences of
disobedience; but in the former State there was little safety in entering upon a contest with those who might remain in office for a generation and who could be disturbed in their position by nothing short of
a revolution. So if you would give the most force and effect to the
decisions of your courts, you must give to the judges a permanent
tenure of office.

Again, it will give greater independence of action. Judges are but
human. If one must soon go before the people for re-election, how
loath to rule squarely against public sentiment! There is no need of
imputing conscious dishonesty; but the inevitable shrinking from
antagonizing popular feeling or the wishes or interests of some prominent leader or leaders tends to delay or modify the due decision,
while the judge who knows nothing can disturb his position does not
hesitate promptly and clearly to "lay judgment to the line and righteousness to the plummet." "Let the jury determine," is the motto of
one tribunal; "The court must decide," is the rule of the other. Cases

at law and a jury are favored in the one; equity and its singleness of responsibility is the delight of the other. Far be it from me to intimate aught against the character or ability of that larger number of elective judges in this country who secure continuation in office only through the well-earned confidence of the people. The bulk of my judicial life has been spent in such tribunals and under such experiences, and I know the worth and prize the friendship of these men. I am simply comparing system with system. It is a significant fact that some of the older States which have the elective system are lengthening the terms of judicial office. The judges of your highest court hold office for fourteen years, and in the sister State of Pennsylvania for twenty-one years. And this is almost equivalent to a life tenure, for it will be found that the term of office of a justice of the supreme court of the United States (taking all who have held that office, including the present incumbents), averages less than fifteen years.

It is said that the will of the people would often be delayed or thwarted, and that this is against the essential idea of government of and by the people. But for what are written constitutions? They exist, not simply to prescribe modes of action, but because of the restraints and prohibitions they contain. Popular government may imply, generally speaking, that the present will of the majority should be carried into effect; but this is true in no absolute or arbitrary sense, and the limitations and checks which are found in all written constitutions are placed there to secure the rights of the minority. Constitutions are generally, and ought always to be, formed in times free from excitement. They represent the deliberate judgment of the people as to the provisions and restraints which, firmly and fully enforced, will secure to each citizen the greatest liberty and utmost protection. They are rules prescribed by Philip sober to control Philip drunk. When difficulties arise, when the measures and laws framed by a majority are challenged as a violation of these rules and a trespass upon the rights of the minority, common justice demands that the tribunal to determine the question shall be as little under the influence of either as is possible. Burke says: "Society requires not only that the possessions of individuals should be subjected, but that even in the mass and body, as well as in the individuals, the inclinations of men should be thwarted, their wills controlled and their passions brought into subjection. This can only be done by a power out of themselves and not in the exercise of its functions subject to that will and those passions which it is his office to bridle and subdue. In this sense the restraints on men, as well as their liberties, are to be reckoned among their rights." And surely, if the judges hold office by a life tenure and with a salary which cannot be disturbed, it would seem as though we had a tribunal as far removed from disturbing influences as possible. Though if I were to perfect the judiciary system I would add a provision that they should also be ineligible to political office and to that extent free from political ambition.

It may be said that this is practically substituting government by the judges for government by the people, and thus turning back the currents of history. The world has seen government by chiefs, by kings and emperors, by priests and by nobles. All have failed, and now government by the people is on trial. Shall we abandon that and try government by judges? But this involves a total misunderstanding of the relations of judges to government. There is nothing in this power of the judiciary detracting in the least from the idea of government of and by the people. The courts hold neither purse nor sword; they cannot corrupt nor arbitrarily control. They make no laws, they establish no policy, they never enter into the domain of popular action. They do not govern. Their functions in relation to the State are limited to seeing that popular action does not trespass upon right and justice as it exists in written constitutions and natural law. So it is that the utmost power of the courts and judges works no interference with true liberty, no trespass on the fullest and highest development of government of and by the people, it only means security to personal rights—the inalienable rights, life, liberty, and the pursuit of happiness; it simply nails the Declaration of Independence, like Luther's theses against indulgences upon the doors of the Wittenburg church of human rights and dares the anarchist, the socialist and every other assassin of liberty to blot out a single word.

While preparing this address I had a dream. I dreamt that I was reading before an association an article which had been prepared by another. When I had nearly finished I came to a page which was written in shorthand. Unable to decipher that, I was forced to extemporize a little. When I awoke from my sleep and thought of this address, I saw that that dream was not wholly a dream. I realize full well that this subject is old and stale and that I have added nothing new to what has been so often and so well said; but things may be stale and yet not flat and unprofitable. The tale of love is as old as Adam and as new and sweet as today's blushing girl of sixteen. All of Christianity is found in "the old, old story of Jesus and His love"; and so it has seemed to me that this threadbare story is, as always in a free country and today in this country more than ever, of living and pressing importance. Who does not see the wide unrest that fills the land; who does not feel that vast social changes are impending, and realize that those changes must be guided in justice to safety and peace or they will culminate in revolution? Who does not perceive that the mere fact of numbers is beginning to assert itself? Who does not hear the old demagogic cry, "*Vox populi vox Dei*" (paraphrased today, "the majority are always right"), constantly invoked to justify disregard of those guaranties which have hitherto been deemed sufficient to give protection to private property?

"To him that hath shall be given," is the voice of Scripture. "From him that hath shall be taken," is the watchword of a not inconsiderable, and through the influx of foreign population, a growing portion of our voters. In such a time as this the inquiry may well be, what factor in our national life speaks most emphatically for stability and justice, and how may that factor be given the greatest efficiency? Magnifying, like the apostle of old, my office, I am firmly persuaded that the salvation of the nation, the permanence of government of and by the people, rests upon the independence and vigor of the judiciary. To stay the waves of popular feeling, to restrain the greedy hand of the many from filching from the few that which they have honestly acquired, and to protect in every man's possession and enjoyment, be he rich or poor, that which he hath, demands a tribunal as strong as is consistent with the freedom of human action and as free from all influences and suggestions other than is compassed in the thought of justice, as can be created out of the infirmities of human nature. To that end the courts exist, and for that let all the judges be put beyond the reach of political office and all fear of losing position or compensation during good behavior. It may be that this is not popular doctrine today and that the drift is found in such declarations as these—that the employee has a right to remain on his employer's property and be paid wages, whether the employer wishes him or no; that the rights of the one who uses are more sacred than of him who owns property; and that the Dartmouth College case, though once believed to be good in morals and sound in law, is today an anachronism and a political outrage. The black flag of anarchism, flaunting destruction to property, and therefore relapse of society to barbarism; the red flag of socialism, inviting a redistribution of property which, in order to secure the vaunted equality, must be repeated again and again at constantly decreasing intervals, and that colorless piece of baby-cloth, which suggests that the State take all property and direct all the life and work of individuals as if they were little children, may seem to fill the air with their flutter. But as against these schemes, or any other plot or vagary of fiend, fool or fanatic, the eager and earnest protest and cry of the Anglo-Saxon is for individual freedom and absolute protection of all his rights of person and property; and it is the cry which, reverberating over this country from ocean to ocean, thank God, will not go unheeded. That personal independence which is the lofty characteristic of our race will assert itself, and no matter what may stand in the way or who may oppose, or how much of temporary miscarriage or disappointment there may be, it will finally so assert itself in this land that no man or masses shall dare to say to a laborer he must or must not work, or for whom or for how much he shall toil; and that no honest possessor of property shall live in fear of the slightest trespass upon his possessions. And to help and strengthen that good time, we shall yet see in every State an independent judiciary, made as independent of all outside influences as is possible, and to that end given a permanent tenure of office and an unchangeable salary; and above them that court, created by the fathers, supreme in fact as in name, holding all, individuals and masses, corporations and States—even the great Nation itself—unswervingly true to the mandates of justice; that justice which is the silver sheen and the golden band in the jewelled diadem of Him to whom all Nations bow and all worlds owe allegiance.

OLIVER WENDELL HOLMES, JR.

Law and the Court

Holmes, who came to the Supreme Court in 1902 after twenty years on the Massachusetts Supreme Judicial Court, is known today and was known between 1902 and his retirement in 1932 for his flashing opinions. So many of these, particularly his dissents, were diamonds of logic and literature, and short at that, that they circulated in the press and magazines as though they had been speeches expounding ideas for the general public. Holmes, like Story and many others, wrote revealing letters to friends about the Court and himself, but he spoke publicly about his institution on only a handful of occasions. The speech printed below was delivered at a dinner of the Harvard Law School Association of New York on February 15, 1913. It was reprinted as a United States Senate Document and widely quoted in the press.

SOURCE: Max Lerner (ed.), *The Mind and Faith of Justice Holmes* (New York: Halcyon House, 1943), 387–391.

Vanity is the most philosophical of those feelings that we are taught to despise. For vanity recognizes that if a man is in a minority of one we lock him up, and therefore longs for an assurance from others that one's work has not been in vain. If a man's ambition is the thirst for a power that comes not from office but from within, he never can be sure that any happiness is not a fool's paradise

—he never can be sure that he sits on that other bench reserved for the masters of those who know. Then too, at least until one draws near to seventy, one is less likely to hear the trumpets than the rolling fire of the front. I have passed that age, but I still am on the firing line, and it is only in rare moments like this that there comes a pause and for half an hour one feels a trembling hope. They are the rewards of a lifetime's work.

But let me turn to more palpable realities—to that other visible Court to which for ten now accomplished years it has been my opportunity to belong. We are very quiet there, but it is the quiet of a storm centre, as we all know. Science has taught the world scepticism and has made it legitimate to put everything to the test of proof. Many beautiful and noble reverences are impaired, but in these days no one can complain if any institution, system, or belief is called on to justify its continuance in life. Of course we are not excepted and have not escaped. Doubts are expressed that go to our very being. Not only are we told that when Marshall pronounced an Act of Congress unconstitutional he usurped a power that the Constitution did not give, but we are told that we are the representatives of a class— a tool of the money power. I get letters, not always anonymous, intimating that we are corrupt. Well, gentlemen, I admit that it makes my heart ache. It is very painful, when one spends all the energies of one's soul in trying to do good work, with no thought but that of solving a problem according to the rules by which one is bound, to know that many see sinister motives and would be glad of evidence that one was consciously bad. But we must take such things philosophically and try to see what we can learn from hatred and distrust and whether behind them there may not be some germ of inarticulate truth.

The attacks upon the Court are merely an expression of the unrest that seems to wonder vaguely whether law and order pay. When the ignorant are taught to doubt they do not know what they safely may believe. And it seems to me that at this time we need education in the obvious more than investigation of the obscure. I do not see so much immediate use in committees on the high cost of living and inquiries how far it is due to the increased production of gold, how far to the narrowing of cattle ranges and the growth of population, how far to the bugaboo, as I do in bringing home to people a few social and economic truths. Most men think dramatically, not quantitatively, a fact that the rich would be wise to remember more than they do. We are apt to contrast the palace with the hovel, the dinner at Sherry's with the working man's pail, and never ask how much or realize how little is withdrawn to make the prizes of success (subordinate prizes —since the only prize much cared for by the powerful is power. The prize of the general is not a bigger tent, but command). We are apt to think of ownership as a terminus, not as a gateway, and not to realize that except for the tax levied for personal consumption large ownership means investment, and investment means the direction of labor towards the production of the greatest returns—returns that so far as they are great show by that very fact that they are consumed by the many, not alone by the few. If I may ride a hobby for an instant, I should say we need to think things instead of words—to drop ownership, money, etc., and to think of the stream of products; of wheat and cloth and railway travel. When we do, it is obvious that the many consume them; that they now as truly have substantially all there is, as if the title were in the United States; that the great body of property is socially administered now, and that the function of private ownership is to divine in advance the equilibrium of social desires—which socialism equally would have to divine, but which, under the illusion of self-seeking, is more poignantly and shrewdly foreseen.

I should like to see it brought home to the public that the question of fair prices is due to the fact that none of us can have as much as we want of all the things we want; that as less will be produced than the public wants, the question is how much of each product it will have and how much go without; that thus the final competition is between the objects of desire, and therefore between the producers of those objects; that when we oppose labor and capital, labor means the group that is selling its product and capital all the other groups that are buying it. The hated capitalist is simply the mediator, the prophet, the adjuster according to his divination of the future desire. If you could get that believed, the body of the people would have no doubt as to the worth of law.

That is my outside thought on the present discontents. As to the truth embodied in them, in part it cannot be helped. It cannot be helped, it is as it should be, that the law is behind the times. I told a labor leader once that what they asked was favor, and if a decision was against them they called it wicked. The same might be said of their opponents. It means that the law is growing. As law embodies beliefs that have triumphed in the battle of ideas and then have translated themselves into action, while there still is doubt, while opposite convictions still keep a battle front against each other, the time for law has not come; the notion destined to prevail is not yet entitled to the field. It is a misfortune if a judge reads his conscious or unconscious sympathy with one side or the other prematurely into the law, and forgets that what seem to him to be first principles are believed by half his fellow men to be wrong. I think that we have suffered from this misfortune, in State courts at least, and that this is another and very important truth to be extracted from the popular discontent. When twenty years ago a vague terror went over the earth and the word socialism began to be heard, I thought and still think that fear was translated into doctrines that had no proper place in the Constitution or the common law. Judges are apt to be naïf, simple-minded men, and they need something of Mephistopheles. We too need education in the obvious—to learn to transcend our own convictions and to leave room for much that we hold dear to be done away with short of revolution by the orderly change of law.

I have no belief in panaceas and almost none in sudden ruin. I believe with Montesquieu that if the chance of a battle—I may add, the passage of a law—has ruined a state, there was a general cause at work that made the state ready to perish by a single battle or a law. Hence I am not much interested one way or the other in the nostrums now so strenuously urged. I do not think the United States would come to an end if we lost our power to declare an Act of Congress void. I do think the Union would be imperiled if we could not make that declaration as to the laws of the several States. For one in my place sees how often a local policy prevails with those who are not trained to national views and how often action is taken that embodies what the Commerce Clause was meant to end. But I am not aware that there is any serious desire to limit the Court's power in this regard. For most of the things that properly can be called evils in the present state of the law I think the main remedy, as for the evils of public opinion, is for us to grow more civilized.

If I am right it will be a slow business for our people to reach rational views, assuming that we are allowed to work peaceably to that end. But as I grow older I grow calm. If I feel what are perhaps an old man's apprehensions, that competition from new races will cut deeper than working men's disputes and will test whether we can hang together and can fight; if I fear that we are running through the world's resources at a pace that we cannot keep; I do not lose my hopes. I do not pin my dreams for the future to my country or even to my race. I think it probable that civilization somehow will last as long as I care to look ahead—perhaps with smaller numbers, but perhaps also bred to greatness and splendor by science. I think it not improbable that man, like the grub that prepares a chamber for the winged thing it never has seen but is to be—that man may have cosmic destinies that he does not understand. And so beyond the vision of battling races and an impoverished earth I catch a dreaming glimpse of peace.

The other day my dream was pictured to my mind. It was evening. I was walking homeward on Pennsylvania Avenue near the Treasury, and as I looked beyond Sherman's Statue to the west the sky was aflame with scarlet and crimson from the setting sun. But, like the note of downfall in Wagner's opera, below the sky line there came from little globes the pallid discord of the electric lights. And I thought to myself the Götterdämmerung will end, and from those globes clustered like evil eggs will come the new masters of the sky. It is like the time in which we live. But then I remembered the faith that I partly have expressed, faith in a universe not measured by our fears, a universe that has thought and more than thought inside of it, and as I gazed, after the sunset and above the electric lights there shone the stars.

☆☆☆ The "Old" and "New" Court in Industrial America, 1920-1941

CHARLES EVANS HUGHES
Self-Inflicted Wounds and Popular Prescriptions

Like John Jay, Hughes moved effortlessly across an astounding variety of legal and political career lines—leader at the corporate bar, full professor at Cornell University Law School at twenty-nine, Governor of New York, Associate Justice of the Supreme Court from 1910 to 1916, private citizen and presidential candidate of the Republican party in 1916, Secretary of State, 1921 to 1925, a member of the Hague Tribunal and a Judge of the Permanent Court of International Justice, and then Chief Justice of the United States from 1930 until 1941. In 1927, while back in private practice, he delivered six lectures at Columbia University on the Supreme Court, which were published in book form in 1928. "My endeavor," he wrote at the opening of the volume, "will be simply to aid to some extent in the interpretation of an institution which despite its constant and unique service is a mystery, I fear, to most of our people. . . . Even with this limitation, much that I should like to say must be omitted." The book was very well received by reviewers, and remains a skillful tour through the Court's history and assumptions.

SOURCE: Charles Evans Hughes, *The Supreme Court of the United States: Its Foundations, Methods and Achievements: An Interpretation* (New York: Columbia University Press, 1928), pp. 50–55, 236–242.

Putting aside the long course of criticism of the Court, bitter and unrelenting, neither the occasion nor the grounds of which I can take time to review, with respect to which the Court has either been vindicated in public opinion or the criticism has had but slight effect upon the general reputation of the Court, it remains true that in three notable instances the Court has suffered severely from self-inflicted wounds. The first of these was the *Dred Scott* case.[1] Von Holst said that it had been the systematic and conscious aim of the South to make the Supreme Court the citadel of slaveocracy and that the *Dred Scott* decision was a witness of the success of their efforts. There the Supreme Court decided that Dred Scott, a negro, not being a citizen could not sue in the United States Courts and the Congress could not prohibit slavery in the territories. Assuming the sincerity of the judges who took this view, the grave injury that the Court sustained through its decision has been universally recognized. Its action was a public calamity. The decision was greeted by the anti-slavery papers in the North with derision and contempt. There were not lacking more conservative expressions and there was support from strong Democratic papers, but the widespread and bitter attacks upon the judges who joined in the decision undermined confidence in the Court. False and scurrilous comments upon the traits and character of the judges supplemented hostile analysis of Chief Justice Taney's opinion. Lincoln riddled the decision in his speeches, but he gave due respect to the judicial institution. He said in the course of his debate with Douglas: "We believe as much as Judge Douglas (perhaps more) in obedience to and respect for the judicial department of government. We think its decisions on constitutional questions, when fully settled, should control, not only the particular cases decided, but the general policy of the country, subject to be disturbed only by amendments of the Constitution as provided in that instrument itself. More than this would be revolution. But we think the *Dred Scott* decision is erroneous. We know the court that made it has often overruled its own decisions, and we shall do what we can to have it overrule this. We offer no resistance to it." [2] It was many years before the Court, even under new judges, was able to retrieve its reputation.

It was during this period, while the Court was still suffering from lack of a satisfactory measure of public confidence, that another decision was rendered which brought the Court into disesteem. I refer to the legal tender cases decided in 1870. It has repeatedly been sought to use for political purposes the power of Congress to fix the number of justices. In 1866, Congress had provided for a reduction in the number in order to deprive President Johnson of the opportunity to make appointments and, after that danger was passed and Grant had become President, the number of the justices was increased to nine. While there were two vacancies on the Court, the case of *Hepburn* v. *Griswold* [3] involving the validity of the legal tender act passed during the Civil War was decided, the Court holding the act to be unconstitutional as to contracts made before its passage and indicating in the reasoning of its opinion that the act was also invalid as to contracts subsequently made. The decision was by a bench of seven, and three Justices dissented. On the day that the opinion was delivered by Chief Justice Chase, President Grant nominated William Strong of Pennsylvania and Joseph P. Bradley of New Jersey to fill the two vacancies. The action of the Court, taken soon after their confirmation, in ordering a reargument of the constitutional question and then deciding that the legal tender act was constitutional,[4] the two new judges joining with the three judges, who had dissented in the *Hepburn* case, to make a majority, caused widespread criticism. From the standpoint of the effect on public opinion, there can be no doubt that the reopening of the case was a serious mistake and the overruling in such a short time, and by one vote, of the previous decision shook popular respect for the Court. There was no ground for attacking the honesty of the judges or for the suggestion that President Grant had attempted to pack the Court. Both the new judges were able and honest men, Justice Bradley being one of the strongest men who have sat on the bench. President Grant stated that he knew nothing of the decision of the Court at the time of the appointment, and it has well been said that in view of the fact that every prominent Republican lawyer apparently considered the legal tender act to be constitutional and practically every State Court had so held it would have been difficult for the President to find any qualified men of his own party who had any other opinion. The Court alone was responsible for the unfortunate effect of its change of front and for its action in reopening the case which might well have been considered closed. The argument for reopening was strongly presented in view of the great importance of the question, but the effect of such a sudden reversal of judgment might easily have been foreseen. Stability in judicial opinions is of no little importance in maintaining respect for the Court's work.

Twenty-five years later, when the Court had recovered its prestige, its action in the income tax cases gave occasion for a bitter assault. Here again, there was not the slightest ground for criticism of the integrity of the judges who participated in the decision. Nor did the actual decision against the validity of the tax furnish basis for anything more than the conflict, even of expert opinion, which attaches to the determination of difficult constitutional questions. The circumstance which caught the public imagination and which ever since has furnished occasion for disparaging comment, was that after the question of the validity of the income tax with respect to income from personal property as such, and the question whether the provision held void with respect to income from real estate as a direct and unapportioned tax invalidated the whole act, had been reserved owing to an equal division of the Court,[5] a reargument was ordered and in the second decision the act was held to be unconstitutional by a majority of one.[6] Justice Jackson was ill at the time of the first argument but took part in the final decision, voting in favor of the validity of the statute.[7] It was evident that the result was brought about by a change in the vote of one of the judges who had participated in the first decision. There can be no objection to a conscientious judge changing his vote, but the decision of such an important question by a majority of one after one judge had changed his vote aroused a criticism of the Court which has never been entirely stilled. At the time, the most bitter attacks were made upon Justice Shiras, who was popularly supposed to have been the one who changed his vote. He bore the criticism with a calm dignity, but there is good reason to believe that the charge was without foundation and that he was not the member of the Court whose views were altered on the reargument. The demand for a federal income tax culminated in the adoption of the Sixteenth Amendment authorizing a federal income tax without apportionment.

When, however, we consider the hundred and thirty-six years of the Court's activities, the thousands of its determinations, the difficult questions with which it has dealt, and the fact that it has come out of its conflicts with its wounds healed, with its integrity universally recognized, with its ability giving it a rank second to none among the judicial tribunals of the world, and that today no institution of our government stands higher in public confidence, we must realize that this is due, whatever may be thought as to the necessity of the function it performs, to the impartial manner in which the Court addresses itself to its never-ending task, to the unsullied honor, the freedom from political entanglements and the expertness of the judges who are bearing the heaviest burden of severe and continuous intellectual work that our country knows.

Much of the criticism of the Court deals with what is occasional rather than typical. In looking to the future the fundamental questions are these: Are we ready to give up a written constitution with its definition of powers? Do we desire to abandon our dual system and to confer upon a single legislature the supreme authority of the people through a completely centralized government? If we maintain our dual system and a written constitution, with the limitations essential to such a plan, do we wish to attempt to define more specifically in the Constitution the division of authority as, for example, in relation to interstate commerce? Is it likely that we could make a success of such a plan? If we prefer to retain the dual system and limited governmental powers, are we ready to give to Congress the final determination whether the States exceed the powers retained by them or whether Congress transcends the limitations of its own powers? If not, what substitute is there to suggest for the Supreme Court? Do we desire constitutional questions, if such there are to be, to be determined by political assemblies and by partisan divisions? Is there any better plan, whatever imperfections our present one may have, for securing a reasonably continuous, non-partisan and philosophical exposition of the Constitution than by regarding it as the supreme law of the land to be applied in actual cases and controversies through the exercise of the judicial power? These are the questions which must be considered in discussing the value of the work of the Supreme Court, which in a practical and systematic way enables us to draw upon our resources of reason in maintaining the balance of rights which is characteristic of the Republic.

Proposals for changes in the organization and the exercise of the jurisdiction of the Supreme Court have been of two sorts; those suggested for the purpose of promoting its efficiency and those which have been sought to curb the exertion of the judicial power. Relief from the laborious duty at Circuit became absolutely necessary if the Justices were properly to attend to the work of the Supreme Court. The establishment of Circuit Courts of Appeals, as intermediate appellate tribunals, was a most important improvement in the Federal judicial system. It has been said that "perhaps the decisive factor in the history of the Supreme Court is its progressive contraction of jurisdiction." But the limitation of the scope of review, as a matter of right on the part of litigants, has been accompanied by the preservation of the judicial authority to review in the cases deemed appropriate for its exercise. The selection of such cases, in an increasing degree, has been left with the Supreme Court itself. Efforts further to increase the number of judges have failed. After the number of associate justices had been enlarged to eight in 1837, Justice Story wrote: "You may ask how the Judges got along together? We made very slow progress, and did less in the same time than I ever knew. The addition to our numbers has most sensibly affected our facility as well as rapidity of doing business. 'Many men of many minds' require a great deal of discussion to compel them to come to definite results; and we found ourselves often involved in long and very tedious debates. I verily believe, if there were twelve Judges, we should do no business at all, or at least very little." Doubtless, a rhetorical exaggeration to emphasize a strong point! Everyone who has worked in a group knows the necessity of limiting size to obtain efficiency. And this is peculiarly true of a judicial body. It is too much to say that the Supreme Court could not do its work if two more members were added, but I think that the consensus of competent opinion is that it is now large enough. Happily, suggestions for an increased number and for two divisions of the Court have not been favored because of their impracticality in view of the character of the Court's most important function.

A certain plausibility has attached to the proposal that legislation should not be held to be unconstitutional by a bare majority of the judges, but that the concurrence of six, or even of seven, judges should be required. Difficulties at once suggest themselves. If, for example, a lower Federal Court, or a State Court has held legislation to be unconstitutional, is the decision to be reversed by a minority of the Supreme Court who believe it to be constitutional? It is often said, when a decision of the Court is by a vote of five to four, that one judge determines the result. This is more striking than accurate, for the actual decision is that of five judges. But if the concurrence of six judges were required, then if there were four judges of the opinion that the statute was constitutional they would in effect outvote the five and it could still be said that the vote of one judge had made the result possible, as otherwise there might have been the required six votes. If seven votes were necessary to hold a statute invalid, then three judges would outweigh six on a judicial question, and still a change of one vote might be determinative.

It is urged that as legislation should be held to be repugnant to the Constitution only in clear cases, and as this is recognized as a principle of decision, a division in the Court should be regarded as enough to show reasonable doubt. Plainly, that suggestion cannot be carried to its logical limit. If it were, the action of a single judge in the court of first instance, holding an act to be constitutional would be conclusive, for is he not a reasonable man? Or, if that judge decided the act to be unconstitutional, and in the Circuit Court of Appeals two judges agreed with him, but the third dissented, should not the majority bow to his dissent as sufficiently indicating doubt? We have similar considerations with respect to State court decisions. Why have any review by the Supreme Court in such cases, unless the courts under review, whether Federal or State, should hold legislation to be unconstitutional? And, then, on the view suggested, their unanimous opinions to this effect might be overthrown, and the legislation still be sustained, if a minority of the Supreme Court considered it to be valid, as a vote of the majority of the Supreme Court would not be sufficient to render a contrary decision.

In truth, judges will have their convictions, and it is of the essence of the appropriate exercise of judicial power that these should be independently expressed. Divisions on close questions cannot be prevented. The unpopularity of a decision against the constitutionality of a legislative act is sometimes too readily assumed by those who propose changes. It has already been observed that our history shows serious complaint in certain important cases where acts of Congress have been sustained. If the object is to create public content with the result, it would not likely be obtained if a statute highly obnoxious to many, as interfering with cherished liberty of action, were made effective by a minority of the highest court. It must also be remembered that we are considering the exercise of the judicial power which the Constitution places in one Supreme Court and the lower Federal courts. The Supreme Court has appellate jurisdiction with such exceptions and under such regulations as are made by Congress. But making allowance for such exceptions and giving effect to such regulations as Congress may appropriately provide with respect to the cases in which the appellate jurisdiction shall be exercised, when the appellate jurisdiction attaches to a case the judicial power extends to it, and it is doubtful to say the least if Congress would have the constitutional authority to fetter the exercise of the judicial power by giving the control of it to the minority of the Court. In a small group, the action of any one may be of decisive effect, no matter what rule may be adopted, and the method that best accords with our traditions and is most likely to have public favor in the long run is that of decision by the majority.

In our system, the individual finds security in his rights because he is entitled to the protection of tribunals that represent the capacity of the community for impartial judgment as free as possible from the passion of the moment and the demands of interest or prejudice. The ends of social justice are achieved through a process by which every step is examined in the light of the principles which are our inheritance as a free people. The spirit of the work of the Supreme Court permeates every legislative assembly and every important discussion of reforms by legislative action. We largely subject our political thinking to the conception of law, not as an arbitrary edict of power, but as governed by the fundamental conceptions of justice. No one is above the law. The officer of government, the State itself, is subject to the fundamental law that the humblest may invoke. Our relations to each other, to the society of which we are a part, to the governments, Federal and State, which are the organs of that society, come to the judicial test, as far removed from the intrusions of artifice, selfishness and caprice as any test can be. The Supreme Court is the embodiment of this conception of our law, the exemplar of its application, and the assurance that in the complexities of an extraordinarily expanded life, we have not forgotten the ancient faith by which we have pledged ourselves to render to each one his due,—a faith which alone makes it possible to look to the coming years with confidence as well as hope.

FOOTNOTES

[1] *Scott* v. *Sandford,* 19 Howard, 393.
[2] June 26, 1857; *Abraham Lincoln, Complete Works,* Nicolay and Hay, Vol. I, 228.
[3] 8 Wallace, 603.
[4] *Knox* v. *Lee,* 12 Wallace, 457.
[5] *Pollock* v. *Farmers' Loan & Trust Co.,* 157 U.S. 429, 586.
[6] *Id.,* 158 U.S. 601.
[7] *Id.,* 158 U.S. 696.

JOHN H. CLARKE

History and the 1937 Court Proposal

John H. Clarke was a progressive from Ohio, a Wilson appointee to the Federal District Court in 1914, and Wilson's choice for the Supreme Court in 1916. A voting partner of Justice Louis D. Brandeis, and much more in the Wilson tradition than the President's other appointee, Justice James Mc-Reynolds, Clarke stayed on the Court for only six years. He resigned in 1922 to devote his full time to world peace, as President of the League of Nations Non-Partisan Association and a trustee of the World Peace Foundation. During the 1920's he spoke a few times in public about the Supreme Court, particularly to bar associations, urging lawyers to cease wasting the Court's time with frivolous appeals and baseless arguments. In 1937, with most leaders of the bar and conservatives openly attacking President Franklin Roosevelt's proposal to enlarge the Court (by adding a new Justice for each Justice over seventy who had not voluntarily resigned), Clarke decided to speak out against one major argument of the critics. On March 22, 1937, he made the following radio address over the National Broadcasting Company network.

SOURCE: "The Naked Question of the Constitutionality of the Court Proposal," 3 *Vital Speeches* 369 (1937).

For a month I have steadfastly refused many requests for a public expression of my views on the President's program for judiciary reform. This for the reason that the obvious proprieties forbid that one who has served six years as a member of the Supreme Court should publicly criticize either the contemporary decisions of that court or the political principles or policies of the President of the United States.

However, it has become so widely asserted that the President's proposal with respect to the Supreme Court is unconstitutional that I have concluded it to be not improper, but my duty as a citizen, to publicly state my views as to this purely legal question, the decision of which may be so fateful to our country.

The case that is clearly stated is more than half argued, and therefore let it be known that I yield to no man in my confidence in and estimate of the great value of the Supreme Court as a department of our government and that in what I have to say I shall not criticize in any manner either any of its recent decisions, or the proposals of the President, but shall confine myself to the naked legal question, "would a conditional increase of the number of judges of the Supreme Court by act of Congress, as recommended by the President, be constitutional or not?" That is the question.

No rule of law is better established than that great weight must always be given by the courts to early, contemporaneous construction of the Constitution by the legislative or executive departments of the government, especially when such construction has been repeated, acted upon and long accepted by the country. Let us apply this rule to the history of the action of Congress and of many Presidents with respect to our subject.

The government under the Constitution was organized in April, 1789, and five months later, in September, by act of Congress approved by President Washington, provision was made for the organization of the Supreme Court, and the number of judges was fixed at six. This action of Congress was accepted by the country as obviously constitutional, the judges were appointed by President Washington and proceeded to act under it.

The number of judges remained at six for eleven years, until in 1801, when Congress reduced the number to five by an act approved by John Adams, our second President. The number of five judges continued for only one year when, by act of Congress approved by President Jefferson, our third President, the number of judges was restored to the original six.

With this number of six judges the court continued for five years, when again by act of Congress, also approved by Jefferson, the number was increased to seven. With this number of seven judges the court continued in the discharge of its high duties for thirty years, when the growth of the country and of the business of the court led Congress to add two more associate judges in an act approved by President Andrew Jackson, thus, with the Chief Justice, making the number nine. With this number the court continued for twenty-six years, until in 1863, when the number was increased from nine to ten by act of Congress approved by President Lincoln.

This fifth change to ten continued for only three years, when in 1866, shortly after the death of President Lincoln, again by act of Congress it was provided, "that no vacancy in the office of associate justice of the Supreme Court shall be filled by appointment until the number of associate justices shall be reduced to six," making seven with the Chief Justice.

This potential reduction of the total number of judges from ten to seven also lasted only three years, when, General Grant being elected President, by act of Congress approved by him in 1869, the number of associate justices was restored to nine, at which number it has continued to our day.

Thus in eighty years of our history, the number of judges of the Supreme Court was first determined by act of Congress, twice the number has been reduced and five times it has been increased, always by act of Congress and never before has the power of Congress under the Constitution to thus legislate been questioned, certainly not in the courts.

It is confidently believed that few, if any, other important powers of Congress have been so early and so often exercised with the entire approval of our country, our Presidents and our courts, as this of determining the number of judges of the Supreme Court.

This history alone, were there no other reason, would warrant the courts, indeed would compel any court to approve as constitutional such exercise of power by Congress as the President proposes.

Consider now for a moment the specific provisions of the Constitution on which this long line of congressional and executive action which we have recalled has been based. They are only two, and they are very short.

First. The Constitution declares "the judicial power of the United States shall be vested in one Supreme Court, and in such inferior courts as Congress may from time to time ordain and establish."

Second. After providing a very limited original jurisdiction for the Supreme Court, the Constitution declares, "in all other cases before mentioned the Supreme Court shall have appellate jurisdiction—with such exceptions and under such regulations as the Congress shall make," and that is all.

While the Constitution thus declared we shall have a Supreme Court, no provision whatever was made for its organization, and it was at once apparent that the only department of government which could provide for such organization was the Congress, and accordingly the long course of Congressional action with regard to the membership of the court, which we have just recalled, was promptly entered upon, was accepted, and by acting under it approved, by the court and the country.

But, in addition to this, in the provisions of the Constitution quoted, the Congress also found obvious warrant for regulating in all respects the appellate jurisdiction of the court, and this power of Congress over the Supreme Court has also been frequently exercised—always with the approval of all three branches of the government. . . .

The wise men who framed our Constitution may have had more confidence in the wisdom and patriotism of the Congresses and the Presidents which were to come after them, and less confidence in courts than some seem to have today.

Whether or not they were wise in entrusting to the Congress and to the President such extensive powers over the courts as we have found they possess and have long exercised is not now before us. The single question I am considering is, would a conditional increase of the number of judges of the Supreme Court by act of Congress, as recommended by the President, be constitutional or not—and for the reasons thus briefly stated I think that the answer to that question should be—must be—that such an act would plainly be within the powers granted to the Congress and therefore clearly constitutional.

JAMES F. BYRNES

A Year in the New Court

The year which James Brynes spent as an Associate Justice of
the United States Supreme Court, 1941–1942, came midway
in a career at the center of national political influence. A lawyer
and prosecuting attorney in Aiken, South Carolina, Byrnes had
been a Congressman (1911–1925), then a powerful figure in
the Senate (1930–1941). From June of 1941 until October of
1942, he served as Franklin Roosevelt's sixth appointee to the
Supreme Court. He resigned in 1942 to become Director of
Economic Stabilization, then head of the War Mobilization
Board. In 1945 he became Secretary of State, resigning in 1947
after policy disagreements with President Truman. A key
Southern political leader since 1947, with service as Governor
of South Carolina, Byrnes has been continually outspoken in
criticism of the Supreme Court for its decisions in the fields
of segregation and internal security. The following selection
is from Chapter Nine of his autobiography.

Source: *All in One Lifetime* (New York: Harper &
Brothers, 1958), 135–144.

My transfer from the familiar Capitol Building, around
which for over twenty years my Washington activities had centered, to the splendors of the new Supreme
Court Building represented a great change. The classic
structure, and in particular its core, the Court Room itself,

reflected a dignified strength and even aloofness far removed from the organized confusion of the Hill. The justices are seated upon a dais; in front of them is a desk the full width of the dais; and behind them are red velvet curtains, which the public may think are a part of the decorative scheme, but which in fact have a utilitarian purpose, for they are hung principally to improve the acoustics. . . .

Each justice has a suite of three offices, one of which is used by his law clerk, another by his secretary; the quarters of the Chief Justice are somewhat larger than the rest. The offices are furnished in American oak with open fireplaces, and as an additional luxury each suite has a shower bath. I was told that Justice McReynolds used to have a fire in his fireplace, often eating his lunch before it, but I never heard of others making use of theirs. The shower certainly seemed an extravagance.

There is a large conference room where the members assemble before each court session or for deliberation. They lunch together in a room on the second floor; guests are not invited. Each justice has his messenger serve him a lunch brought from the dining room on the first floor, which is open to the public, or from some other nearby restaurant. Chief Justice Stone, I remember, was a lover of cheese and often his lunch consisted of a "collection" of cheeses brought from his home. Discussion at lunch was stimulating and entertaining, with only one subject barred—the work of the Court.

According to political writers, the Court of which I was a member was one of the youngest—the average age being around fifty-seven— and one of the friendliest. I never had time to check these calculations of the ages of my colleagues, but I can testify to their general good humor. Contrary to popular impression, justices are very human, and during my service, at least, they were very sociable. I recall a dinner at my home for the justices and their wives, when their spirited singing of old songs prompted me to comment that there was more harmony in their singing than in their decisions.

There is one term of court annually, commencing on the first Monday in October and lasting until the final week in May. During this period, sessions are not continuous but last about two weeks, with a free period intervening. While I served, conferences were held at twelve noon on Saturday, though since then the time has been changed to eleven o'clock each Friday. When arguments have been heard, cases are usually decided at that week's conference, which, in order to assure complete secrecy, is attended only by the justices themselves.

When members gather for a conference or for a session of court, it has been the custom for more than half a century that upon entering the room each should shake hands with all his colleagues, who are referred to as "brethren." On my first day I regarded this as rather superfluous, for I had greeted each of the brethren elsewhere that morning. Later there were times when it reminded me of the usual instruction of the referee in the prize ring, "Shake hands, go to your corner and come out fighting." But I soon realized that it was a useful reminder of the courtesy and mutual respect that the justices seek to preserve no matter how heated their debates. As a rule, conferences continued for five or six hours, the Chief Justice seated at the head of the table, his senior colleague opposite him. The Chief Justice presents the issues of each case and expresses his opinion first. He is followed by the justices in order of seniority, and at the conclusion a vote is taken. At this time it is the junior justice who votes first. It has been said that this arrangement was adopted to avoid any question of senior members influencing their juniors. This explanation did not impress me, for surely any justice, having already expressed his views, would ordinarily vote in harmony with them.

During periods of recess the justices are occupied with writing opinions. That task is assigned to a member by the Chief Justice, provided the decision is unanimous or the Chief Justice has voted with the majority. When the Chief Justice is with the minority, the task of assigning the writing of the opinion falls to the senior justice among the majority. The Court has the services of its own printers, and elaborate precautions are taken in this department also to insure essential secrecy. The author of an opinion circulates the proof to the other justices in order that each may approve it as an appropriate expression of the Court's view of the case. If a justice is impressed with the opinion, frequently he will amplify the customary "I agree." In fact, when recently I looked over some of my opinions, with the notations by the justices, I was considerably amused. One notation is "Neat and complete. I verily believe that you say more by saying less—and what you say is truly good." Another, and this is from the Chief Justice, "I agree. It makes the stump speech of your opponent seem quite unnecessary." A decision will not be announced until the language used is agreed upon by all the concurring justices. Thus it is evident that the opinion in a case represents not only the view of the author but also that of the majority of the Court responsible for the decision. If there is dissent, the senior justice of the minority either writes the dissenting view himself or designates a colleague to prepare it. This too is circulated and perhaps changed several times in order to meet the views of other dissenters. Any one of the justices may contribute a separate dissenting opinion if he desires to.

I had known all the members of the Court before my appointment; most of them I knew intimately, and they quickly made me feel at home. I was agreeably surprised that it was not very difficult for me to adjust my thinking to this new field. In the Senate I had enjoyed the friendship of senators on the Republican side because they knew I had no violent prejudices. The truth is, I had schooled myself to consider the point of view of the other man.

In thinking of the role of the Supreme Court, I felt strongly that its function was to interpret the laws and not to make laws; that where there was doubt about the meaning of the language of a statute, the Court should seek to ascertain the intent of the legislature by referring to the reports of the legislative committees and the statements made at the time by those in charge of the bill; and that a judge should not substitute his personal views for the intent of the Congress and the President who approved the bill.

While I believed it to be the supreme test of judicial statesmanship to preserve the balance between the powers of the federal government and the powers of the states, I realized that the preservation of that balance was difficult and called for the exercise of wise discretion, free of personal prejudices. It is commonplace that the Constitution expresses great principles in language that permits the application of those principles to entirely new conditions. This is perhaps most clearly demonstrated in the application of the Commerce Clause to methods of transportation and communication hardly dreamed of in the days of the Founding Fathers. This philosophy was to be subjected to severe tests in the cases decided by the Court during my service, but I tried to adhere to it.

Of the fifteen or sixteen decisions announced by me, several were of more than routine interest. The first opinion I wrote was that of

Edwards v. *The State of California.*[1] Following the depression, thousands of people migrated to that state—not entirely because of the mild climate, but because of its liberal allowances for relief. In this situation the state legislature enacted a law making it a misdemeanor for anyone to bring, or assist in bringing, into California a nonresident, knowing him to be indigent. In December, 1939, Edwards, who lived in Marysville, California, went to Texas in order to bring back with him his wife's unemployed brother. Edwards was subsequently prosecuted and, upon admitting the facts, was convicted and sentenced to six months' imprisonment. On appeal, the state supreme court had affirmed the lower court.

When this case came to the United States Supreme Court, a majority decided to reverse the state court. We differed, however, about whether the Court's opinion should be based on the Commerce Clause of the Constitution or on the ground that the right to move freely from one state to another is an incident of national citizenship. Writing the opinion, I based reversal on the Commerce Clause, which had been frequently construed by the Court as protecting the interstate travel of persons as well as commodities. The social phenomenon of large-scale migration of citizens did not admit of diverse treatment by the several states; for if one state could deny admission to a person regarded as indigent, others would surely adopt retaliatory measures.

In another case from Texas,[2] I wrote an opinion in which the Court reversed the judgment of the state court that the defendant was guilty of "murder without malice." The appellant was an ignorant Negro who, it was charged, in an altercation with a white man, had grabbed him by the throat, choked him to death, and then fled. The Negro had been sentenced to three years' imprisonment. Here the record disclosed a clear case of an extorted confession. It also occurred to me, from my knowledge of Texas, that the jury must have entertained some doubt about the defendant's guilt, else the verdict would never have been "murder without malice," nor would any judge have imposed so light a sentence. The Supreme Court reversed the state court and subsequently the petitioner was acquitted.

Other cases were not so easy of solution.

While on the Court I felt a dissenting opinion should not be written unless a justice felt strongly on the subject. The value of dissent was, however, demonstrated in a case brought by the Wages and

Hours Division of the United States Department of Labor against the A. H. Belo Corporation.[3] This company published the Dallas *Morning News* and also owned a radio station there. The question involved was a complicated one—it suffices that it concerned an effort of the Department to prevent the corporation from paying a certain wage scale which was allegedly in violation of the Fair Labor Standards Act.

In our conference the Court divided five to four in sustaining the Department's position, the majority including Justice Robert Jackson, who, though absent, had asked to be so recorded. It fell to me to write the dissenting opinion for the minority, and Justice Reed wrote the majority opinion. When the two opinions were circulated, Justice Jackson visited me and said that after reading the dissent he regretted not having been present when the decision was reached. After some discussion he decided that his first thoughts about the case were erroneous, and he notified Justice Reed that he wished to change his vote. Bob Jackson had that sort of courage. Subsequently, Justice Reed and I met and made the changes necessary to make mine the majority opinion and his the dissenting opinion.

My belief that it is the duty of a judge to declare what is the law and not what he thinks the law should be was severely tested in the case of the United States against the International Brotherhood of Teamsters *et al.*[4] This arose from the following circumstances. Quantities of merchandise regularly entered New York from other states in trucks owned by farmers or by various companies, driven by their own employees. Members of the Teamsters' Union insisted on their right to drive the vehicles within the state or at least to unload them. When truckers balked at using union drivers, there were some instances of violence to force them to do so or to pay a fixed charge representing the day's hire of a union member. There was adequate state law to punish such acts of violence or extortion, but, instead, the union men had been prosecuted and convicted in the United States District Court under what is known as the "Anti-Racketeering Act" of 1934. The Court of Appeals for the Second Circuit, in an opinion written by Judge Learned Hand, one of the ablest judges ever to have served on any court in the United States, reversed these convictions on the ground that the district judge had inaccurately interpreted the language of the act. With five other members of the Supreme Court,

I voted to sustain that decision of the Court of Appeals. When given the task of writing the opinion, I did not welcome the assignment, for I heartily disapproved the action of the union drivers. But Justice Black and I had been members of the Senate at the time the Anti-Racketeering Act was passed, and we knew the act was not intended to apply to the facts of this case.

In the opinion, I emphasized that where there was doubt about the proper interpretation of a statute, the Court should look to the legislative intent. Referring to the *Congressional Record,* I showed that Congress did not pass the bill until it had been redrafted by the Department of Justice, following conferences with the president of the American Federation of Labor, and after a proviso had been added "preserving the rights of bona fide labor organizations." Even so, the House would not consider it until Attorney General Cummings wrote a letter stating that the bill was approved by the Federation of Labor and that it would apply only to activities affecting interstate commerce in connection "with price fixing and economic extortion directed by professional gangsters." Before the bill received the President's signature, Senator Copeland, on behalf of the Senate committee, had submitted to the Senate a report saying that the essential purpose of the legislation was to "close gaps in existing federal laws and to render more difficult the activities of predatory criminal gangs of the Kelly and Dillinger types." At the time I talked with Copeland, who said that the report was made for the deliberate purpose of preventing any future misunderstanding of the intent of the Congress. The accuracy of his statement of the intention of the Congress was not questioned.

On the evening before the Court conference at which the majority opinion was finally agreed upon, Chief Justice Stone, the sole dissenter, told me that after reading the opinion I had submitted, he was thinking of changing his position. The next morning he said that though he had some doubts because of the evidence bearing on the intent of Congress, the conduct of the union truckers was so outrageous that he was going to resolve his doubts against them and write a dissent. Because of my great admiration for him as a judge and affection for him personally, I regretted his decision, but I knew our course was in accord with his own philosophy. This view was confirmed a few years later when, just before he was mortally stricken while on the bench, he declared in an opinion, "It is not the function of this Court to disregard the will of the Congress in the exercise of its constitutional power."

The opinion in the teamster case hinted that if Congress wished to broaden the application of the law, it should legislate to that effect. Congressman Hobbs of Alabama, an able member of the House Judiciary Committee, introduced a bill repealing the provision of the law exempting labor activities, but a year later told me it was impossible to get Congress seriously to consider his bill, its opponents contending that the evils complained of were already punishable or could be made punishable by state laws. Nor has Congress acted since, which seems to be ample evidence that the Court correctly interpreted the intent of the Congress.

FOOTNOTES

[1] 314 U.S. 160.
[2] *The State of Texas* v. *Ward*, 316 U.S. 547.
[3] *Walling, Admr.* v. *A. H. Belo Corp.*, 316 U.S. 624.
[4] 315 U.S. 521.

NINE
MEN IN BLACK:
COLLEGIAL
PERSPECTIVES

FELIX FRANKFURTER

The Supreme Court in the Mirror
of Justices

During the 1950's, several leading conservative congressmen and columnists advanced the idea that prior judicial experience should be required for appointment to the Court. This was, in part, an indirect slap at the "liberals" on the Court, especially in its implication that those with previous judicial experience would have a greater awareness of the values of consistency and predictability than nominees drawn from political posts, the bar, or law schools. In this selection, the first Owen J. Roberts Memorial Lecture at the University of Pennsylvania Law School, Justice Felix Frankfurter, whose pre-Court career had been primarily that of a law professor and political adviser, took up the "judicial experience" argument. "To so learned a legal audience," Frankfurter noted, in explanation of his title, "I need hardly confess that my title is a plagiarism. . . . [M]y motive, if I know it, is the antithesis of that thirteenth century author, Andrew Horn . . . [who] wrote to expose the judges of his day. . . . My purpose is to attest my devotion to an institution for which I have a feeling akin to reverence and to do so, as becomes an old teacher, by contributing to whatever small extent to a better understanding of the nature of its functions and of the qualifications for their exercise."

SOURCE: "The Supreme Court in the Mirror of Justices," 105 *University of Pennsylvania Law Review*, 781–796 (1957).

During the one hundred and sixty-seven years since the day appointed for its first session, ninety Justices have sat on the Supreme Court. The number of men over so long a period would seem to be sufficient to afford some light on the kind of experience or qualifications that may be deemed appropriate for service on the Court. Indeed, the actualities about the men who were appointed to the Court may well be wiser guides than abstract notions about the kind of men who should be named. Of the ninety Justices I shall consider seventy-five, omitting contemporary and relatively recent occupants of the Court. And my concern is not with the substantive views of these Justices—neither their conception of the nature of the judicial process generally nor of that process in the specialized context of Supreme Court business. I am dealing with externally ascertainable factors. One of these has been intermittently urged and, in recent years, revived in an extreme form. I refer to the suggestion, indeed the assumption that, since the Supreme Court is the highest judicial tribunal, prior "judicial service" is not only a desirable, but an indispensable, qualification.

What is the teaching of history on this? Of the seventy-five Justices, twenty-eight had not a day's prior judicial service. Seven more had sat on some bench from a few months to not more than two years. Nine sat six years or less. Measures have been proposed that would require "judicial service" of not less than five years in a lower federal court or as a member of the highest court of a State; some bills demand ten years of such service. A five-year requirement would have ruled out at least thirty-five of the seventy-five judges (in fact more, because several of the Justices who had had judicial experience did not sit on a federal bench or on the highest court of a State), and the ten-year requirement would have barred certainly forty-five of our seventy-five Justices.

Who were these Justices who came on the Supreme Court without any "judicial service," without even the judicial experience of an Iredell, who at the age of twenty-six sat on the Superior Court of his State, North Carolina, only long enough—six months—to resign.[1] They begin with your own James Wilson and include Bushrod Washington, Marshall, Story, Taney, Curtis, Campbell, Miller, Chase,

Bradley, Waite, Fuller, Moody, Hughes, Brandeis, Stone and Roberts. Of the twelve Chief Justices within our period, five had not had any judicial experience at the time of their appointment as Chief Justice and two more had had none when they first came on the Court.

Apart from the significance of a Chief Justice as the administrative head of the Court [2] what of the quality of judicial service of the men who came on the Court totally devoid of judicial experience? Assessment of distinction in the realm of the mind and spirit cannot exclude subjective factors. Yet it is as true of judges as of poets or philosophers that whatever may be the fluctuations in what is called the verdict of history, varying and conflicting views finally come to rest and there arises a consensus of informed judgment. It would indeed be a surprising judgment that would exclude Marshall, William Johnson, Story, Taney, Miller, Field, Bradley, White (despite his question-begging verbosities), Holmes, Hughes, Brandeis and Cardozo in the roster of distinction among our seventy-five. I myself would add Curtis, Campbell, Matthews and Moody. (Some might prefer the first Harlan or Brewer or Brown.) Of the first twelve, five had had judicial experience and seven none before coming on the Court; of the others only Matthews can be counted a judge, for a brief period, before he came to Washington. Of the sixteen Justices whom I deem pre-eminent, only six came to the Court with previous judicial experience, however limited. It would require discernment more than daring, it would demand complete indifference to the elusive and intractable factors in tracking down causes, in short, it would be capricious, to attribute acknowledged greatness in the Court's history either to the fact that a Justice had had judicial experience or that he had been without it.

Greatness in the law is not a standardized quality, nor are the elements that combine to attain it. To speak only of Justices near enough to one's own time, greatness may manifest itself through the power of penetrating analysis exerted by a trenchant mind, as in the case of Bradley; it may be due to persistence in a point of view forcefully expressed over a long judicial stretch, as shown by Field; it may derive from a coherent judicial philosophy, expressed with pungency and brilliance, reinforced by the *Zeitgeist*, which in good part was itself a reflection of that philosophy, as was true of Holmes; it may be achieved by the resourceful deployment of vast experience and an originating mind, as illustrated by Brandeis; it may result from the influence of a singularly endearing personality in the service of sweet reason, as Cardozo proves; it may come through the kind of vigor that exerts moral authority over others, as embodied in Hughes.

The roll-call of pre-eminent members of the Supreme Court who had had no judicial experience in itself establishes, one would suppose, that judicial experience is not a prerequisite for that Court. It would be hard to gainsay that this galaxy outshines even the distinguished group that came to the Court with prior experience on state courts, though these judges included the great names of Holmes and Cardozo. It has been suggested that the appearance on the Court of Marshall, Story, Taney, Curtis, Campbell, Miller, Bradley, Hughes and Brandeis, all without prior judicial experience, is "a curious accident." But this accident has been thrown up by history over a period of one hundred and fifty years. After all, these men were not self-appointed. They must have been found by, or suggested to, the various and very different Presidents who named them. In at least one instance a lawyer without prior judicial experience was urged on a President by the Court itself—John A. Campbell, whose prior judicial experience was his refusal, twice, to go on the Supreme Court of Alabama.[3] (It would indeed be interesting to ascertain what men were recommended for appointment when the Executive invited suggestions from the Court.)

The notion that prior judicial experience is a prerequisite for the Supreme Court, whether made a formal statutory requirement or acted upon as an accepted assumption, deserves closer scrutiny than its *ad hominem* refutation. Apart from meaning that a man had sat on some court for some time, "judicial service" tells nothing that is relevant about the qualifications for the functions exercised by the Supreme Court. While it seems to carry meaning, it misleads. To an uncritical mind it carries emanations of relevance in that it implies that a man who sat on a lower court has qualifications for sitting on a higher court, or, conversely, that a man has not the qualifications for sitting on a higher court unless he has had the experience of having sat on a lower court, just as a man presumably cannot run a mile in less than four minutes unless he had already run it in six, or a player has not the aptitude or experience for a major league unless he has played in a minor league.

Need I say that judicial experience is not like that at all? For someone to have been a judge on some court for some time, having some kind of business resulting in some kind of experience, may have some abstract relation to the Supreme Court conceived of as an abstract judicial tribunal. The Supreme Court is a very special kind of court. "Judicial service" as such has no significant relation to the kinds of litigation that come before the Supreme Court, to the types of issues they raise, to qualities that these actualities require for wise decision.

To begin with, one must consider the differences in the staple business of different courts and the different experiences to which different judicial business gives rise, and the bearing of different experiences so generated on the demands of the business of the Supreme Court. Thus, there is a vital difference, so far as substantive training is afforded, between the experience gained on state courts and on the lower federal courts. There are the so-called federal specialties whose importance for the Supreme Court has copiously receded since the Evarts Act of 1891,[4] but is still relevant to its work. One would suppose that if prior judicial experience would especially commend itself for Supreme Court appointments, the federal courts would furnish most materials for promotion. History falsifies such expectation. Of the forty-seven Justices who had had some kind of prior judicial experience, no matter how short, fifteen came from the federal courts—Trimble, Barbour, Daniel, Woods, Blatchford, Brewer, Brown, Howell E. Jackson, McKenna, Day, Lurton, Taft, Sanford, Van Devanter and John H. Clarke—whereas thirty-two had only experience on state courts.

How meagerly the experience on a state court, even if of long duration, prepares one for work on the Supreme Court is strikingly borne out by the testimony of the two Justices who are indubitably the two most outstanding of those who came to the Supreme Court from state courts. After having spent twenty years on the Supreme Judicial Court of Massachusetts, part of it as Chief Justice, in the course of which he wrote more than a thousand opinions on every conceivable subject, Mr. Justice Holmes found himself not at all at home on coming to the Supreme Court. Listen to what he wrote to his friend Pollock after a month in his new judicial habitat:

"Yes—here I am—and more absorbed, interested and impressed than ever I had dreamed I might be. The work of the past seems a finished book—locked up far away, and a new and solemn volume opens. The variety and novelty to me of the questions, the remote spaces from which they come, the amount of work they require, all help the effect. I have written on the constitutionality of part of the Constitution of California, on the powers of the Railroad Commissioners of Arkansas, on the question whether a law of Wisconsin impairs the obligation of the plaintiff's contract. I have to consider a question between a grant of the U.S. in aid of a military road and an Indian reservation on the Pacific coast. I have heard conflicting mining claims in Arizona and whether a granite quarry is 'Minerals' within an exception in a Railway land grant and fifty other things as remote from each other as these." [5]

Nor did Cardozo, after eighteen years on the New York Court of Appeals, five of them as Chief Judge, in the course of which he gained the acclaim of the whole common-law world, find that his transplantation from Albany to Washington was a natural step in judicial progression. On more than one occasion he complained to friends (sometimes as bitterly as that gentle soul could) that he should not have been taken from judicial labors with which he was familiar and which were congenial to him, to types of controversies to which his past experience bore little relation and to which, though these were the main concern of the Supreme Court, he was not especially drawn.

To be sure, by the time that Holmes and Cardozo came to the Supreme Bench, the heavy stream of commercial and common-law litigation that reached the Supreme Court in its earlier periods had been diverted to the courts of appeals and largely stopped there. But even when a good deal of the business of the Court consisted of litigation related to what loosely may be called common-law litigation, the transition from a state court to the Supreme Court was not in a straight line of experience. Thus, although on the bench in Connecticut Ellsworth's opinions sustained "his reputation as a good lawyer and a just and able judge" [6] and in the Senate he had been the chief architect of the First Judiciary Act, on his appointment by Washington as Chief Justice, he "undertook a severe course of study and reading." [7] And when Monroe offered a place on the Court to his Secretary of the Navy, Smith Thompson, who had been a New York judge for seventeen years and for nearly five Kent's successor as Chief Justice,

Thompson hesitated to accept, in part because of his lack of judicial experience outside the common law.[8]

But, it may be suggested, if experience on a state court does not adequately prepare even the greatest of judges for the problems that are the main and certainly the most important business of the Supreme Court, judicial experience intrinsically fosters certain habits of mind and attitudes, serves to train the faculties of detachment, begets habits of aloofness from daily influences, in short, educates and reinforces those moral qualities—disinterestedness and deep humility—which are indeed preconditions for the wise exercise of the judicial function on the Supreme Bench. Unhappily, history again disappoints such expectation. What is more inimical for good work on the Court than for a Justice to cherish political, and more particularly Presidential, ambition? Who will disagree with Mr. Justice Holmes's observation, "I think a judge should extinguish such thoughts when he goes on the Bench." [9] Sad and strange as it may be, the most numerous and in many ways the worst offenders in this regard have been men who came to the Court from the state courts, in some instances with long service on such courts. Their temperamental partisanship and ambition were stronger than the disciplining sway supposedly exercised by the judiciary. To be sure, there have been instances of such political ambition by those who came on the Court without judicial experience. Salmon P. Chase, of course, is a conspicuous example. But I think it is fair to say that fewer Justices who had had no prior judicial experience dallied with political ambition while on the Court than those who came there with it. And it deserves to be noted that the most vigorous, indeed aggressive hostility to availability of a member of the Court for a Presidential nomination came from one who had no prior judicial experience, Chief Justice Waite,[10] and from another whose name ought not to go unmentioned on this occasion—Mr. Justice Roberts.

Even though the history of the Court may demonstrate that judicial experience whether on state or federal bench ought not to be deemed a prerequisite, what of the lower courts as a training ground for the Supreme Bench? The fact is that not one so trained emerges over a century and a half among the few towering figures of the Court. Oblivion has overtaken almost all of them. Probably the most intellectually powerful of the lot, Mr. Justice Brewer, does not owe the weight of the strength that he exerted on the Court to his five years on the circuit court after his long service on Kansas courts. Surely it is safe to attribute it to the native endowment that the famous Field strain gave him. Mr. Justice Van Devanter was undoubtedly a very influential member of the so-called Taft Court. But he was that essentially on the procedural aspect of the Court's business and by virtue of the extent to which Chief Justice Taft leaned on him. It was characteristic of Taft's genial candor that he spoke of Van Devanter outside the purlieus of the Supreme Court as "my chancellor."

One is not unappreciative of Chief Justice Taft by saying that his significance in the Court's history is not that of an intellectual leader but as the effective force in modernizing the federal judiciary and in promoting jurisdictional changes to enable the Court to be capable of discharging its role in our federal scheme. Moreover, it was not Taft's eight years of service on the Sixth Circuit, highly esteemed as it was, that led President Harding to make him Chief Justice White's successor after Taft's twenty years of separation from active concern with law. . . .

More immediately relevant to our subject is the fact that even Justices who have come to the Supreme Court fresh from a longish and conspicuously competent tenure on the lower federal courts do not find the demands of their new task familiar. Their lower court experience does not make the transition an easy one. Thus Philip Barbour, despite the deserved reputation that he brought to the Supreme Court from his years on the United States district court, felt it necessary to fit himself by "conscientious study" for his duties on the Supreme Court.[11] A recent striking example of how hard the sledding can be for a judge who also made an exceptional record over long years on the district court and was an uncommonly cultivated man, was Mr. Justice Sanford. Thus it has been as true of capable Justices who came to Washington from lower federal courts as of those who came to the Court richly endowed but without judicial experience, that they actively set about educating themselves for the work of the Court and were educated by it.

Mr. Justice Moody, who had had exceptional preparation for the Court's work as lawyer, legislator, and member of the Cabinet, including forensic activity as Attorney General, on his appointment to the Court turned to his classmate, Professor Eugene Wambaugh of the

Harvard Law School, for guidance in the study of constitutional law and the jurisdiction of the Supreme Court as eagerly as any avid neophyte. Again, Mr. Justice Brandeis who brought not only as well-stocked a mind for the substantive issues with which he had to deal as a Justice as any member of the Court but also a reputation second to none as an advocate before it, used to say that no one can have the right kind of feel regarding the distinctive jurisdictional and procedural problems touching the Court's business in less than three or four Terms of actual service on the Court. He set about to acquire mastery of this essential aspect of the Court's business by studying the Reports, from Dallas down. Nor did he limit his systematic study of the Court's business to these aspects. Thus, he spent one whole summer in familiarizing himself with all the decisions of the Court pertaining to criminal law. These modern instances are recognition of the truth discerned from the beginning of the Court, that membership on it involves functions and calls for faculties as different from those called for by other judicial positions as those called for by private practice or non-judicial public service.

In response to an inquiry by the House of Representatives into the federal judicial system that had just been set up, Attorney General Edmund Randolph, addressing himself more particularly to the undesirability of the circuit duties with which the Justices were charged, wrote the following:

"Those who pronounce the law of the land without appeal, ought to be pre-eminent in most endowments of the mind. Survey the functions of a judge of the Supreme Court. He must be a master of the common law in all its divisions, a chancellor, a civilian, a federal jurist, and skilled in the laws of each State. To expect that in future times this assemblage of talents will be ready, without further study, for the national service, is to confide too largely in the public fortune. Most vacancies on the bench will be supplied by professional men, who, perhaps, have been too much animated by the contentions of the bar deliberately to explore this extensive range of science. In a great measure, then, the supreme judges will form themselves after their nomination. But what leisure remains from their itinerant dispensation of justice? Sum up all the fragments of their time, hold their fatigue

at naught, and let them bid adieu to all domestic concerns, still
the average term of a life, already advanced, will be too short for
any important proficiency." [12]

Circuit-riding ceased long before members of the Court were statutorily relieved of it, and the establishment of the circuit courts of appeals in 1891 freed the Court of the vast mass of what roughly may be
called private litigation that used to come to it by way of diversity
jurisdiction and the federal specialties. And the Judiciary Act of
1925 [13] has made the Court the master of its docket so that it now may
be free to concern itself only with cases that have a substantial public
interest. Yet it is still true today as it was when Randolph wrote in
1790 that "in a great measure . . . the supreme judges will form
themselves after their nomination." This is true as we have seen even
of men of the highest capacity, men who had had wide professional
experience with the federal courts before they came on the Supreme
Court as well as of judges with long service on the federal bench.

In addition to all other considerations, this is so because the practical workings of the Supreme Court, not only in our governmental
scheme but in the influences it exerts on our national life, to no small
extent are determined by the effective administration of the appellate
jurisdiction allotted to the Court, the manner in which it conceives
what issues are open on review, and how it deals with them—raising
not only unique problems in the wise articulation of its jurisdiction
with that of the lower federal courts and the state courts but often
involving perplexities in the successful operation of our federal system.
These are subtle matters carrying deep implications that do not lie on
the surface. Partly because of their seemingly technical nature and
partly because they have few dramatic ingredients, they are hardly
appreciated by the laity and all too little by the profession at large.
The proper treatment of these problems has far-reaching consequences, but they do not bulk big in the work of lower courts and
therefore do not become part of the experience of judges either on
the state courts or on the lower federal courts.

Not only is the framework within which the judicial process of
the Supreme Court operates drastically different from the jurisdictional
and procedural concern of other courts but the cases that now come
before the Court, and will increasingly in the future, present issues that

make irrelevant considerations in the choice of Justices that at former periods had pertinence. Mastery of the federal specialties by some members of the Court was an obvious need of the Court in days when a substantial part of the Court's business related to such specialties. Thus, when maritime and patent cases appeared frequently enough on the Court's docket, it was highly desirable to have a judge so experienced in these fields as was Judge Blatchford when he was named to the Court. The extent of the Court's maritime litigation naturally brought Henry Billings Brown, an outstanding admiralty judge, to the Court. And since the business that came to the Court in times past reflected to no small degree sectionally different economic interests, geographic considerations had their relevance. Thus, when the western circuit, consisting of Ohio, Kentucky and Tennessee, was established, at a time when litigation dealing with land title and other local property questions was important, the selection of one conversant with these problems was clearly indicated. Therefore, on the recommendation of the representatives in Congress from the interested states, Jefferson named Thomas Todd, the then Chief Justice of the Kentucky Court of Appeals. Still later, when California opened up not only a new world for gold-rushers but also a new world of litigation for the Supreme Court, it was inevitable that a judge as knowledgeable about western land and mineral law as was Stephen J. Field should be named to the Court.

All this has changed. Not only in the course of a hundred years but in the course of fifty years. Today there is a totally different flow of business to the Court from what it was a hundred years ago; it is predominantly different from what it was fifty years ago.

An examination of the Reports in these three periods demonstrates the great changes that have taken place. Analysis of the written opinions of the Court a hundred years ago, in the 1854 and 1855 Terms (17 and 18 How.) discloses that, aside from questions of Supreme Court practice and procedure, four major categories of litigation, comprising two-thirds of the cases decided by written opinion, occupied the Court's time. The four categories were (1) estates and trusts, (2) admiralty, (3) real property, and (4) contracts and commercial law. With one partial exception, common-law questions comprised the major categories of the litigation coming before the Court. The exception is that perhaps one-third to one-half of the real property cases involved, directly or indirectly, questions of federal land law. The remaining third of the litigation that occupied the Court one hundred years ago involved a variety of issues: a number of constitutional cases, a few patent, tariff, corporation, tort, and bankruptcy cases, and the rest scattered.

Fifty years later, in the 1904 and 1905 Terms (195–203 U.S.), not only had the volume of the Court's work increased greatly but its nature had changed considerably, especially because of the fourteenth amendment, the Judiciary Act of 1875,[14] and the Circuit Court of Appeals Act of 1891.[15] Constitutional law had become by far the major item of the Court's business, involving approximately one-third of the cases decided by written opinion. And questions under the fourteenth amendment comprised one-half of all the constitutional cases. These apart, the Court's business was almost equally divided between questions of public and private law. Real property law was the next largest class of cases after constitutional law, with federal land law comprising almost the entire category. The remaining principal types of litigation included federal jurisdiction, bankruptcy, corporations, estates and trusts, commercial law and contracts, and torts. Admiralty litigation, which had formed a major portion of the Court's work fifty years previous, was negligible. Significant as indicating the increasing industrialization of the country was the dual increase in corporate and tort law cases. Significant also for the number of pages in the Reports and perhaps also as a portent for the future were several antitrust and Interstate Commerce Commission cases.

Examination of the work of the two most recent Terms (348–351 U.S.) indicates how complete the reversal of the character of the Supreme Court's business has been. Whereas a hundred years ago, private common-law litigation represented the major part of the Court's business, and fifty years ago, constitutional cases apart, public and private law business was equally divided, today private litigation has become virtually negligible. Constitutional law and cases with constitutional undertones are of course still very important, with almost one-fourth of the cases in which written opinions were filed involving such questions. Review of administrative action, mainly reflecting enforcement of federal regulatory statutes, constitutes the largest category of the Court's work, comprising one-third of the total cases decided on the merits. The remaining significant categories of litigation

—federal criminal law, federal jurisdiction, immigration and nationality law, federal taxation—all involve largely public law questions.

The Court was of course from the beginning the interpreter of the Constitution and thereby, for all practical purposes, the adjuster of governmental powers in our complicated federal system. But the summary of the contemporaneous business before the Court that is reflected in written opinions statistically establishes these constitutional adjudications and kindred public law issues as constituting almost the whole of Supreme Court litigation. It is essentially accurate to say that the Court's preoccupation today is with the application of rather fundamental aspirations and what Judge Learned Hand calls "moods," embodied in provisions like the due process clauses, which were designed not to be precise and positive directions for rules of action. The judicial process in applying them involves a judgment on the processes of government. The Court sits in judgment, that is, on the views of the direct representatives of the people in meeting the needs of society, on the views of Presidents and Governors, and by their construction of the will of legislatures the Court breathes life, feeble or strong, into the inert pages of the Constitution and the statute books.

Such functions surely call for capacious minds and reliable powers for disinterested and fair-minded judgment. It demands the habit of curbing any tendency to reach results agreeable to desire or to embrace the solution of a problem before exhausting its comprehensive analysis. One in whose keeping may be the decision of the Court must have a disposition to be detached and withdrawn. To be sure, these moral qualities, for such they are, are desirable in all judges, but they are indispensable for the Supreme Court. Its task is to seize the permanent, more or less, from the feelings and fluctuations of the transient. Therefore it demands the kind of equipment that Doctor Johnson rather grandiloquently called "genius," namely, "a mind of large general powers accidentally determined to some particular direction as against a particular designation of mind and propensity for some essential employment."

For those wielding ultimate power it is easy to be either wilful or wooden: wilful, in the sense of enforcing individual views instead of speaking humbly as the voice of law by which society presumably consents to be ruled, without too much friction in attributing such consent; wooden, in uncritically resting on formulas, in assuming the familiar to be the necessary, in not realizing that any problem can be solved if only one principle is involved but that unfortunately all controversies of importance involve if not a conflict at least an interplay of principles.

If these commonplaces regarding the reach of the powers of the Supreme Court and the majesty of the functions entrusted to nine mere mortals give anyone the impression that a Justice of the Court is left at large to exercise his private wisdom, let me hasten to say as quickly and as emphatically as I can that no one could possibly be more hostile to such a notion than I am. These men are judges, bound by the restrictions of the judicial function, and all the more so bound because the nature of the controversies that they adjudicate inevitably leaves more scope for insight, imagination, and prophetic responsibility than the types of litigation that come before other courts. It was the least mentally musclebound and the most creative mind among Justices, Mr. Justice Holmes, who, with characteristic pithiness, described his task as "that of solving a problem according to the rules by which one is bound." [16] Some years later, Chief Justice Hughes spelled out Holmes's thought. "We do not write on a blank sheet. The Court has its jurisprudence, the helpful repository of the deliberate and expressed convictions of generations of sincere minds addressing themselves to exposition and decision, not with the freedom of casual critics or even of studious commentators, but under the pressure and within the limits of a definite official responsibility." [17]

This is not abstract or self-deceiving talk. The great men in the Court's history give proof of its truth. Will anyone deny that the four most distinguished minds of the latter part of the period under review were Holmes, Hughes, Brandeis, and Cardozo? All four had the largeness of view so essential for adjudicating the great issues before the Court. But is it just a coincidence that all four were to a superlative degree technically equipped lawyers? They built on that equipment for the larger tasks of the Court; they were not confined by it. Again, is it mere coincidence that all four were widely read and deeply cultivated men whose reading and cultivation gave breadth and depth to their understanding of legal problems and infused their opinions?

I have now come to the end of my story with its self-evident moral. Since the functions of the Supreme Court are what they are and demand the intellectual and moral qualities that they do, inevitably touching interests not less than those of the Nation, does it require an explicit statement that in choosing men for this task no artificial or irrelevant consideration should restrict choice?

The search should be made among those men, inevitably very few at any time, who give the best promise of satisfying the intrinsic needs of the Court, no matter where they may be found, no matter in what professional way they have manifested the needed qualities. Of course these needs do not exclude prior judicial experience, but, no less surely, they do not call for judicial experience. One is entitled to say without qualification that the correlation between prior judicial experience and fitness for the functions of the Supreme Court is zero. The significance of the greatest among the Justices who had had such experience, Holmes and Cardozo, derived not from that judicial experience but from the fact that they were Holmes and Cardozo. They were thinkers, and more particularly legal philosophers. The seminal ideas of Holmes, by which to so large an extent he changed the whole atmosphere of legal thinking, were formulated by him before he ever was a judge in Massachusetts. And while the Court of Appeals gave Cardozo an opportunity to express his ideas in opinions, Cardozo was Cardozo before he became a judge. On the other side, Bradley and Brandeis had the pre-eminent qualities they had and brought to the Court, without any training that judicial experience could have given them.

There is another irrelevance, regard for which may lead to a narrower choice than that to which the country is entitled—geographic considerations. The claims of uncritical tradition led President Hoover, who had the most impressive recommendations for naming Cardozo as Holmes's successor, to hesitate because there were at the time already two New Yorkers on the Court. When the President urged this difficulty on Senator Borah, the latter, to the President's astonishment, said that Cardozo was no New Yorker. When asked to explain, the Senator replied that Cardozo belonged as much to Idaho as to New York. Those of sufficient stature for the Court in its modern responsibilities should not be sought among men who have professionally a merely parochial significance and choice of them should not be restricted to a confined area. From the point of view of intrinsic need, any geographical consideration has long since become irrelevant. The pride of a region in having one of its own on the Court does not outweigh the loss to the Court and the country in so narrowing the search for the most qualified.

Perhaps a word should be said on the bearing of political affiliations that men had before coming on the Court to their work on it. The fact is that past party ties as such tell next to nothing about future Justices. The Democratic President Wilson put two Democrats from the bar on the Court; but what notions about law and life, about their conception of their functions as Justices, did James C. McReynolds and Louis D. Brandeis share? President Harding was commended for his broad-mindedness in selecting the Democrat Pierce Butler for the Court [18] at the time that he named his former Republican senatorial colleague, George Sutherland, a Justice much cherished by brethren most in disagreement with him. It would not be inaccurate to say that Butler, the Democrat, and Sutherland, the Republican, were judicial twins. But when Harlan F. Stone came on the Court, the stout Republicanism that Sutherland and Stone had shared was not at all reflected in a shared outlook as Justices. A matter that is kindred to looking for party ties as an index to the behavior of future Justices is the expectation of Presidents regarding the outlook of their appointees on matters of great moment that may come before the Court. There can be little doubt that Lincoln would have been as surprised and perhaps as displeased by his Secretary of the Treasury's attitude towards the Legal Tender Act, when Chase, as Chief Justice, passed on its constitutionality,[19] as was President Theodore Roosevelt by Holmes's dissent in the *Northern Securities* case.[20] The upshot of the matter is that only by disregard of all these irrelevancies in the appointment of Justices will the Court adequately meet its august responsibilities.

Selection wholly on the basis of functional fitness not only affords the greatest assurance that the Court will best fulfill its functions. It also will, by the quality of such performance, most solidly establish the Court in the confidence of the people, and the confidence of the people is the ultimate reliance of the Court as an institution.

FOOTNOTES

[1] 1 McREE, LIFE AND CORRESPONDENCE OF JAMES IREDELL 367, 395 (1857).

[2] See KING, MELVILLE WESTON FULLER 334–335 (1950) (statement by Mr. Justice Holmes).

[3] CONNOR, JOHN A. CAMPBELL 16–17 (1920); 87 U.S. (20 Wall.) ix (1873).

[4] Act of March 3, 1891, c. 517, 26 Stat. 826 (codified in scattered sections of 28 U.S.C.)

[5] 1 HOLMES-POLLOCK LETTERS 109–110 (Howe ed. 1941).

[6] BROWN, THE LIFE OF OLIVER ELLSWORTH 109 (1905).

[7] *Id.* at 242.

[8] 18 DICTIONARY OF AMERICAN BIOGRAPHY 472 (Malone ed. 1936).

[9] 1 HOLMES-POLLOCK LETTERS 192 (Howe ed. 1941).

[10] TRIMBLE, CHIEF JUSTICE WAITE: DEFENDER OF THE PUBLIC INTEREST 141 (1938).

[11] 1 DICTIONARY OF AMERICAN BIOGRAPHY 596 (Johnson ed. 1928).

[12] 1 AMERICAN STATE PAPERS 23–24 (1834) (report of the Attorney General on the judiciary system, read in the House of Representatives, Dec. 31, 1790).

[13] Act of Feb. 13, 1925, c. 229, § 237, 43 STAT. 937.

[14] Act of March 3, 1875, c. 137, 18 STAT. 470.

[15] Act of March 3, 1891, c. 517, 26 STAT. 826 (codified in scattered sections of 28 U.S.C.).

[16] SPEECHES BY OLIVER WENDELL HOLMES 99 (Holmes ed. 1934).

[17] 309 U.S. xiv (1940) (statement by Chief Justice Hughes on the occasion of the 150th anniversary of the Court).

[18] For a vivid delineation of this strong-minded judge, see 310 U.S. xiii (1940) (address by Attorney General Jackson to the Court).

[19] Legal Tender Cases, 79 U.S. (12 Wall.) 457, 570 (1870) (dissenting opinion).

[20] Northern Securities Co. *v.* United States, 193 U.S. 197, 400 (1904).

JOSEPH STORY

John Marshall as Chief Justice

Story, as noted earlier, was a fervent admirer and ideological compatriot of Chief Justice Marshall. Story's son said that his father's feeling for Marshall "fell little short of reverence, and he looked forward to his death with gloomy forebodings, as an irreparable loss to himself personally, and as removing one great pillar from the support of the Constitution." Marshall died on July 6, 1835. A meeting of the Suffolk Bar was held in Boston, and Story was formally invited to deliver "a discourse" commemorating the Chief Justice. Story wrote Harriet Martineau on October 8, 1835: "Of late I have been much engaged in writing a sketch of a discourse upon the life of Chief Justice Marshall, which is to be delivered on the 15th of October. It is (strange as it may seem) at once a delightful and painful subject; delightful, as I am in love with his character, positively in love; painful, as I never hope to look upon his like again." The portion of Story's discourse dealing with Marshall's characteristics as Chief Justice is printed here.

SOURCE: "Life, Character, and Services of Chief Justice Marshall," in William W. Story, *Miscellaneous Writing of Joseph Story* (Boston: Little, Brown & Co., 1852), 639.

The Chief Justiceship of the United States is a station full of perplexing duties, and delicate responsibilities, and requiring qualities so various, as well as so high, that no man, conscious of human infirmity, can fail to approach it with extreme diffidence and distrust of his own competency. It is the very post, where weakness, and ignorance, and timidity must instantly betray themselves, and sink to their natural level. It is difficult even for the profession at large fully to appreciate the extent of the labors, the various attainments, the consummate learning, and the exquisite combination of moral qualities, which are demanded to fill it worthily.

There is nothing in the jurisprudence of the States, which affords any parallel or measure of the labors of the national courts [to guide the Supreme Court Justice]. The jurisprudence of each state is homogeneous in its materials. It deals with institutions of a uniform character. It discusses questions of a nature familiar to the thoughts and employments of the whole profession. The learned advocate, who finds himself transferred, by public favor or superior ability, from the state bar to the state bench, finds the duties neither new nor embarrassing in their elements or details. He passes over ground, where the pathways are known and measured; and he finds pleasure in retracing their windings and their passages.

How different is the case in the national courts! With whatever affluence of learning a judge may come there, he finds himself at once in a scene full of distressing novelties and varieties of thought. Instead of the jurisprudence of a single state, in which he has been educated and trained, he is at once plunged into the jurisprudence of twenty-four States, essentially differing in habits, laws, institutions, and principles of decision. He is compelled to become a student of doctrines, to which he has hitherto been an entire stranger. . . . The words seem to belong to the dialect of his native language; but other meanings are attached to them, either so new, or so qualified, that he is embarrassed at every step of his progress. Nay; he is required in some measure to forget in one cause, what he has learned in another, from its inapplicability or local impropriety; and new statutes, perpetually accumulating on every side, seem to snatch from his grasp the principles of local law, at the moment when he is beginning to congratulate himself upon the possession of them. Independent of this complicated intermixture of state jurisprudence, he is compelled to master the whole extent of Admiralty and Prize Law; the public and private law of nations; and the varieties of English and American Equity jurisprudence. To these confessedly herculean labors he must now add some reasonable knowledge of the Civil Law, and of the jurisprudence of France and Spain, as they break upon him from the sunny regions of the farthest South. Nor is this all . . . he must gather up the positive regulations of the statutes and treaties of the national government, and the silent and implied results of its sovereignty and action. He must finally fully expand his studies to that most important branch of national jurisprudence, the exposition of constitutional law, demanding, as it does, a comprehensiveness of thought, a calmness of judgment, and a diligence of research (not to speak of other qualities), which cannot be contemplated without the most anxious apprehensions of failure.

These, however, are but a part of the qualifications required of the man, who holds the office of Chief Justice. He must also possess other rare accomplishments, which are required of one who, as the head of the Court, is to preside over its public deliberations, and its private confidential conferences. Patience, moderation, candor, urbanity, quickness of perception, dignity of deportment, gentleness of manners, genius, which commands respect, and learning which justifies confidence;—These seem indispensable qualifications to fill up the outlines of the character.

[John Marshall], this great and good man, was all that we could ask, or even desire for the station. He seemed the very personification of Justice itself, as he ministered at its altars. . . . Enter but that hall, and you saw him listening with a quiet, easy dignity to the discussions at the bar; silent, serious, searching; with a keenness of thought, which sophistry could not mislead, or error confuse, or ingenuity delude; with a benignity of aspect, which invited the modest to move on with confidence; with a conscious firmness of purpose, which repressed arrogance, and overawed declamation. You heard him pronounce the opinion of the Court in a low but modulated voice, unfolding in luminous order every topic of argument, trying its strength, and measuring its value, until you felt yourself in the presence of the very oracle of the law.

Follow him into the conference room, a scene of not less difficult or delicate duties, and you would observe the same presiding genius, the same kindness, attentiveness, and deference; and yet, when the occasion required, the same power of illustration, the same minuteness of research, the same severity of logic, and the same untiring accuracy in facts and principles.

It may truly be said of him, as it was of Lord Mansfield, that he excelled in the statement of a case; so much so, that it was almost of itself an argument. If it did not at once lead the hearer to the proper conclusion, it prepared him to assent to it, as soon as it was announced. Nay, more; it persuaded him, that it must be right, however repugnant it might be to his preconceived notions. Perhaps no Judge ever excelled him in the capacity to hold a legal proposition before the eyes of others in such various forms and colors. It seemed a pleasure to him to cast the darkest shades of objection over it, that he might show how they could be dissipated by a single glance of light. He would by the most subtle analysis resolve every argument into its ultimate principles, and then with a marvelous facility apply them to the decision of the cause.

That he possessed an uncommon share of juridical learning, would naturally be presumed, from his large experience and inexhaustible diligence. Yet it is due to truth, as well as to his memory to declare, that his juridical learning was not equal to that of many of the great masters in the profession, living or dead, at home or abroad. He yielded at once to their superiority of knowledge, as well in the modern as in the ancient law. He adopted the notion of Lord Bacon, that "studies serve for delight, for ornament, and for ability,"—"in the judgment and disposition of business." The latter was his favorite object. Hence he "read not to contradict and confute; nor to believe and take for granted; nor to find talk and discourse; but to weigh and consider." And he followed another suggestion of that great man, that "Judges ought to be more learned than witty; more reverend than plausible; and more advised than confident." The original bias, as well as the choice of his mind was to general principles, and comprehensive views, rather than to technical, or recondite learning. . . . He was solicitous to hear arguments; and not to decide causes without them. And no judge ever profited more by them. No matter, whether the subject was new or old; familiar to his thoughts, or remote from them; buried under a mass of obsolete learning, or developed for the first time yesterday; whatever was its nature, he courted argument, nay, he demanded it. It was [a] matter of surprise to see how easily he grasped the leading principles of a case, and cleared it of all its accidental incumbrances; how readily he evolved the true points of the controversy, even when it was manifest that he never before had caught even a glimpse of the learning on which it depended. He seized, as it were by intuition, the very spirit of juridical doctrines, though cased up in the armor of centuries; and he discussed authorities, as if the very minds of the Judges themselves stood disembodied before him.

But his peculiar triumph was in the exposition of constitutional law. It was here, that he stood confessedly without a rival, whether we regard his thorough knowledge of our civil and political history, his admirable powers of illustration and generalization, his scrupulous integrity and exactness in interpretation, or his consummate skill in moulding his own genius into its elements, as if they had constituted the exclusive study of his life. His proudest epitaph may be written in a single line—Here lies the Expounder of the Constitution of the United States.

BENJAMIN R. CURTIS

The Disciplined Passion of Chief Justice Taney

Curtis, Associate Justice from 1851–1857, was educated at Harvard College and Harvard Law School, and became a skilled constitutional law specialist at the Boston Bar. After serving in the Massachusetts legislature, he was appointed to the Supreme Court by President Fillmore through the influence of Daniel Webster. This eulogy, delivered at a meeting of the Boston Bar (the bar of the First Federal Circuit) on October 15, 1864, was particularly meaningful because Curtis and Taney had parted (at the time of Curtis's resignation in 1857) with angry words. Their disagreement had been over the printing of Curtis's dissent in the *Dred Scott* case by the newspapers before the opinion of Taney for the Court had been released.

SOURCE: 30 *Fed. Cas.* 1341.

May it please the court: I have been requested to second the resolutions which Mr. Attorney has presented. I suppose the reason for this request is, that for six years I was in such official connection with the late chief justice as enabled me to know him better than the other members of this bar. My intimate association with him began in the autumn of 1851. He was then seventy-three years old;

185

a period of life when, the Scripture admonishes us, and the experience of mankind proves, it is best for most men to seek the repose which belongs to old age. But it was not best for him. I observe that it has been recently said, by one who had known him upwards of forty years, that during all those years there had never been a time when his death might not reasonably have been anticipated within the next six months. Such was the impression produced on me, when I first knew him. His tall, thin form, not much bent with the weight of years, but exhibiting in his carriage and motions great muscular weakness, the apparent feebleness of his vital powers, the constant and rigid care necessary to guard what little health he had, strongly impressed casual observers with the belief that the remainder of his days must be short. But a more intimate acquaintance soon produced the conviction that his was no ordinary case, because he was no ordinary man. An accurate knowledge of his own physical condition and its necessities: an unyielding will, which, while it conformed everything to those necessities, braced and vivified the springs of life; a temper which long discipline had made calm and cheerful; and the consciousness that he occupied and continued usefully to fill a great and difficult office, whose duties were congenial to him, gave assurance, which the event has justified, that his life would be prolonged much beyond the allotted years of man. In respect to his mental powers, there was not then nor at any time while I knew him intimately, any infirmity or failure whatever. I believe the memory is that faculty which first feels the stiffness of old age. His memory was and continued to be as alert and true, as that of any man I ever knew. In consultation with his brethren he could, and habitually did, state the facts of a voluminous and complicated case, with every important detail of names and dates, with extraordinary accuracy, and I may add with extraordinary clearness and skill. And his recollection of principles of law and of the decisions of the court over which he presided was as ready as his memory of facts. He had none of the querulousness which too often accompanies old age. There can be no doubt that his was a vehement and passionate nature; but he had subdued it. I have seen him sorely tried, when the only observable effects of the trial were silence and a flushed cheek. So long as he lived, he preserved that quietness of temper and that consideration for the feelings and wishes of others which were as far as possible removed from weak and selfish querulousness. And I believe it may truly be said, that though the increasing burden of years had somewhat diminished his bodily strength, yet down to the close of the last term of the supreme court, his presence was felt to be as important as at any period of his life. I have been long enough at the bar to remember Mr. Taney's appointment; and I believe it was then the general impression, in this part of the country, that he was neither a learned nor a profound lawyer. This was certainly a mistake. His mind was thoroughly imbued with the rules of the common law and of equity law; and, whatever may have been true at the time of his appointment, when I first knew him, he was master of all that peculiar jurisprudence which it is the special province of the courts of the United States to administer and apply. His skill in applying it was of the highest order. His power of subtle analysis exceeded that of any man I ever knew; a power not without its dangers to a judge as well as to a lawyer; but in his case, it was balanced and checked by excellent common sense and by great experience in practical business, both public and private. His physical infirmities disqualified him from making those learned researches, with the results of which other great judges have illustrated and strengthened their written judgments; but it can be truly said of him that he rarely felt the need of them. The same cause prevented him from writing so large a proportion of the opinions of the court as his eminent predecessor; and it has seemed to me probable, that for this reason his real importance in the court may not have been fully appreciated, even by the bar of his own time. For it is certainly true, and I am happy to be able to bear direct testimony to it, that the surpassing ability of the chief justice, and all his great qualities of character and mind, were more fully and constantly exhibited in the consultation-room, while presiding over and assisting the deliberations of his brethren, than the public knew, or can ever justly appreciate. There, his dignity, his love of order, his gentleness, his caution, his accuracy, his discrimination, were of incalculable importance. The real intrinsic character of the tribunal was greatly influenced by them, and always for the better. How he presided over the public sessions of the court some who hear me know. The blandness of his manner, the promptness, precision, and firmness which made every word he said weighty, and made very few words necessary, and the unflagging attention which he fixed on everyone who addressed the court, will be remembered by all. But all may not know that he had some other attainments and qualities important to the prompt, orderly, and safe despatch of business. In the time of his predecessor the practice of the court is understood to have been somewhat loosely administered. The amount of business in the court was then comparatively so small, that this occasioned no real detriment, probably no considerable inconvenience. But when the docket became crowded with causes, and heavy arrears were accumulated, it would have been quite otherwise. The chief justice made himself entirely familiar with the rules of practice of the court and with the circumstances out of which they had arisen. He had a natural aptitude to understand, and so far as was needed, to reform the system. It was almost a necessity of his character to have it practically complete. It was a necessity of his character to administer it with unyielding firmness. I have not looked back to the reports to verify the fact, but I have no doubt it may be found there, that even when so infirm that he could not write other opinions, he uniformly wrote the opinions of the court upon new points of its practice. He had no more than a just estimate of their importance. The business of the supreme court came thither from nearly the whole of a continent. It arose out of many systems of laws, differing from each other in important particulars. It was conducted by counsel who travelled long distances to attend the court. It included the most diverse cases, tried in the lower courts in many different modes of procedure. Some according to the course of the common law; some under the pleadings and practice of the courts of chancery in England; some under forms borrowed from the French law; many under special laws of the United States framed for the execution of treaties; and many more so anomalous that it would not be easy to reduce them to any classification. And the tribunal itself, though it was absolutely supreme within the limits of its powers, was bounded and circumscribed in its jurisdiction by the constitution and by acts of congress, which it was necessary constantly to regard. Let it be remembered also, for just now we may be in some danger of forgetting it, that questions of jurisdiction were questions of power as between the United States and the several states. The practice of the court therefore involved, not merely the orderly and convenient conduct of this vastly diversified business, drawn from a territory so vast, but questions of constitutional law, running deep into the frame-work of our complicated political system. Upon this entire subject the chief justice was vigilant, steady, and thoroughly informed. Doubt-less it would be the tendency of most second-rate minds, and of not a few first-rate minds, to press such a jurisdiction out to its extremest limits, and occasionally beyond them; while for timid men, or for those who might come to that bench with formed prejudices, the opposite danger would be imminent. Perhaps I may be permitted to say, that though on the only important occasions on which I had the misfortune to differ with the chief justice on such points, I thought he and they who agreed with him carried the powers of the court too far, yet, speaking for myself, I am quite sure he fell into neither of these extremes. The great powers intrusted to the court by the con-stitution and laws of his country he steadily and firmly upheld and administered; and, so far as I know, he showed no disposition to ex-ceed them.

I have already adverted to the fact that his physical infirmities ren-dered it difficult for him to write a large proportion of the opinions of the court. But my own impression is that this was not the only reason why he was thus abstinent. He was as absolutely free from the slightest trace of vanity and self-conceit as any man I ever knew. He was aware that many of his associates were ambitious of doing this conspicuous part of their joint labor. The preservation of the harmony of the members of the court, and of their good-will to himself, was always in his mind. And I have not the least doubt that these considerations often influenced him to request others to prepare opinions, which he could and otherwise would have written. As it was, he has recorded many which are important, some of which are very important. This does not seem to me to be the occasion to spec-ify, still less to criticise them. They are all characterized by that purity of style and clearness of thought which marked whatever he wrote or spoke; and some of them must always be known and recurred to as masterly discussions of their subjects. It is one of the favors which the Providence of God has bestowed on our once happy country, that for the period of sixty-three years this great office has been filled by only two persons, each of whom has retained, to extreme old age, his great and useful qualities and powers. The stability, uniformity, and completeness of our national jurisprudence are in no small degree attributable to this fact. The last of them has now gone. God grant that there may be found a successor true to the constitution, able to expound and willing to apply it to the portentous questions which the passions of men have made.

DAVID J. BREWER

Bible and Constitution:
Mr. Justice Harlan

Brewer and Harlan were warm friends on the Supreme Court, sharing (among other things) a taste for Southern anecdotes and Washington political stories. On December 9, 1902, the Bar of the Supreme Court gave Justice Harlan a dinner in celebration of his twenty-fifth year on the Court. President Theodore Roosevelt was there to open the dinner and "do homage to a career which has honored America." He spent most of his time extolling Harlan the "fearless" warrior for the Union during the Civil War. Chief Justice Melville Fuller, mentioning his fourteen-year rule against after-dinner speeches, made a short after-dinner speech to honor Harlan, then called on Justice Brewer to deliver the main response from the Court, part of which appears here.

SOURCE: *Dinner Given by the Bar of the Supreme Court of the United States to Mr. Justice John Marshall Harlan* (Washington, 1902), 33–36.

It is a difficult task to speak for a body like the Supreme Court, each one of whose members is so conscious of his ability to speak for himself, as you will readily perceive should you come to the court-room on a Monday morning and listen to his attempted explanation of his own opinion. It is also very embarrassing to speak in lieu of the Chief

Justice, whom we should all delight to hear. And yet I cannot decline to say a few words in honor of one with whom for thirteen years I have had my earnest controversies over the Constitution and the law, yet never a harsh or unkindly word. The brevity of the notice, given me only this morning, is an assurance that my talk will not be long— no longer than one of Brother Harlan's dissents, and perhaps no better.

James A. Garfield said that to sit at one end of a log with Mark Hopkins at the other was of itself a liberal education. So, to sit in the conference room of the Supreme Court and struggle with Mr. Justice Harlan in the consideration of the various cases presented, is of itself a legal education, at least to any one capable of receiving such an education. I regret that my juvenile brethren seem to have profited so little by this and other instruction.

All men are said to have their hobbies, and Justices of the Supreme Court are no exception. Mr. Justice Harlan has a hobby—a judicial hobby—and that is the Constitution of the United States. He has read and studied it so assiduously that I think he can repeat it from one end to the other, forward and backward, and perhaps with equal comprehension either way. I regret that he does not always fully comprehend it, for he has never yet been able to perceive that it expresses no difference between oleomargarine and butter, and he has always labored under the delusion that the only Original Package protected by its commerce clause is a package as large as himself and as compactly put together. They who know his persuasive ways and words appreciate the fact that he is largely responsible for the decisions of the Supreme Court, and any future Ingersoll, conning the judicial errors of that Court during the last quarter of a century, will catalogue them, not among the Mistakes of Moses, but as the Errors of John. But all men make mistakes; even Jupiter nods; and occasional traces of mental aberration may easily be pardoned in one brought up in Kentucky, where, as we have been told this evening, there are things which have a disturbing influence on both mind and body.

Some mistakes a man may never regret. Brother Harlan made a mistake in holding that the Civil Rights Bill was constitutional. The Court said so; and in our governmental system the Supreme Court, on constitutional questions, is infallible, though, as every one knows, no one of its members ever comes within sight or sound of infallibility. But it was a mistake on the side of equal rights, and no act done or

word said in behalf of liberty and equality ever fails to touch humanity with inspiring, prophetic thrill. John Brown of Ossawatomie made
a mistake and was hung for it. As our Kansas poet has said:

"He dared begin. He lost, but losing won."

And although to-day his body is mouldering in the grave, his inspiring
soul will march triumphantly on through all the coming ages.

Mr. Justice Harlan has done something else than make an occasional
constitutional mistake. He has not been a judicial blunderer. He believes implicitly in the Constitution. He goes to bed every night with
one hand on the Constitution and the other on the Bible, and so sleeps
the sweet sleep of justice and righteousness. He believes in the Constitution as it was written; that the Constitution as it was must be the
Constitution as it is, and the Constitution as it shall be, unless and
until the American people shall, in the way they have appointed,
amend its provisions. To him it is no rope of sand to be broken by
every legislative mandate, nor cord of rubber to be stretched by any
tension of popular feeing, but a strong cable, binding this Government in all its movements and activities to those eternal principles of
justice, liberty, and equality without which the fathers believed that
no free republic could ever endure and prosper. He believes that the
Constitution and the flag, like liberty and the Union, "are now and
forever one and inseparable"; that there is no place over which Old
Glory flies in dominion which is beyond the reach of the protecting
guarantees of the Constitution.

We boast, and rightly, of the marvellous growth of this nation in
population, wealth, power, and moral grandeur. Not three centuries
have passed since the first settlement of civilized life within its territory, and it is only one hundred and twenty-six years since the
nation began to be. Rejoicing in all that has been accomplished, there
is no true patriot who does not look forward with hope and faith
to a richer and more marvellous growth and development and along
the same great lines of population, wealth, power, and moral grandeur.
And he who through twenty-five years of judicial life has been holding the nation within the safe courses prescribed by the Constitution,
will certainly stand high in the great future among the honored heroes
of the nation.

FELIX FRANKFURTER

The Court Years of Oliver
Wendell Holmes, Jr.

Frankfurter was one of the young men who were drawn into
the magnetic inner circle of Justice Holmes's life. Conversation
ranged across history, politics, jurisprudence, and—though
Holmes chewed it less enthusiastically—economics and sociology. Along with Harold Laski, Frankfurter shared the
special affection of Holmes for brilliant young men. For Mr.
Justice Frankfurter to note that Holmes took such-and-such
a view of a legal issue was, later, almost to put a burden of proof
on the opposite position. Since Frankfurter, as a professor in
1938, had published a penetrating study of Holmes's judicial
philosophy, *Mr. Justice Holmes and the Supreme Court* (Cambridge: Harvard University Press, 1938), it was natural for the
Dictionary of American Biography to approach Justice Frankfurter when it commissioned the article on Oliver Wendell
Holmes, Jr. If ever there were a labor of love, in the Story-
Marshall manner, this must have been one for Justice Frankfurter. The selection which follows, about half of the full article, opens with Holmes's move from Massachusetts to the
Supreme Court in 1902.

SOURCE: 21 *Dictionary of American Biography*, 417,
(Supplement One, 1944, "Oliver Wendell Holmes, Jr.")

Holmes took his seat on Dec. 8, 1902. He came to the Court at a time when vigorous legislative activity reflected changing social conceptions, which in turn were stimulated by vast technological development. What was in the air is well epitomized by the observation that Theodore Roosevelt "was the first President of the United States who openly proposed to use the powers of political government for the purpose of affecting the distribution of wealth in the interest of the golden mean" (C. A. and Mary R. Beard, *The Rise of American Civilization*, 1927, II, 597).

Though formally the product of ordinary lawsuits, constitutional law differs profoundly from ordinary law. For constitutional law is the body of doctrines by which the Supreme Court marks the boundaries between national and state action and by means of which it mediates between citizen and government. The Court thus exercises functions that determine vital arrangements in the government of the American people. These adjustments are based, for the most part, on very broad provisions of the Constitution. Words like "liberty" and phrases like "due process of law" and "regulate Commerce . . . among the several States," furnish the text for judgment upon the validity of governmental action directed toward the infinite variety of social and economic facts. But these are words and phrases of "convenient vagueness." They unavoidably give wide judicial latitude in determining the undefined and ever-shifting boundaries between state and nation, between freedom and authority. Even as to these broad provisions of the Constitution distinctions must be observed. In a federated nation, especially one as vast in its territory and varied in its interests as the United States, the power must be somewhere to make the necessary accommodation between the central government and the states. "I do not think the United States would come to an end," said Mr. Justice Holmes, "if we lost our power to declare an Act of Congress void. I do think the Union would be imperilled if we could not make that declaration as to the laws of the several states. For one in my place sees how often a local policy prevails with those who are not trained to national views and how often action is taken that embodies what the Commerce Clause was meant to end" (*Collected Legal Papers*, pp. 295–296). The agency, moreover, must be one not subject to the vicissitudes and pressures under which the political branches of government rest. The Supreme Court is that ultimate arbiter.

Two major issues affecting the whole scheme of government have been the dominant concern of the Supreme Court throughout its history. The Court has had to decide in the most variegated situations from what lawmaking the states are excluded and what legislative domain Congress may enter. And as to both state and national authority it rests with the Court to determine under what circumstances society may intervene and when the individual is to be left unrestricted. But while the Supreme Court thus moves in the perilous sphere of government it does not itself carry the burdens of governing. The Court is merely the brake on other men's actions. Determination of policy—what taxes to impose, how to regulate business, when to restrict freedom—rests with legislatures and executives. The nature of the Court's task thus raises a crucial problem in our constitutional system in that its successful working calls for rare intellectual detachment and penetration, lest limitations in personal experience are transmuted into limitations of the Constitution.

His profound analysis of the sources of our law before he became a judge left in Holmes an abiding awareness of the limited validity of legal principles. He never forgot that circumstances had shaped the law in the past, and that the shaping of future law is primarily the business of legislatures. He was therefore keenly sensitive to the subtle forces that are involved in the process of reviewing the judgment of others not as to its wisdom but as to the reasonableness of their belief in its wisdom. As society became more and more complicated and individual experience correspondingly narrower, tolerance and humility in passing judgment on the experience and beliefs expressed by those entrusted with the duty of legislating, emerge as the decisive factors in constitutional adjudication. No judge could be more aware than Holmes of these subtle aspects of the business of deciding constitutional cases. He read omnivorously to "multiply my scepticisms" (unpublished letter). His imagination and humility, rigorously cultivated, enabled him to transcend the narrowness of his immediate experience. Probably no man who ever sat on the Court was by temperament and discipline freer from emotional commitments compelling him to translate his own economic or social views into constitutional commands. He did not read merely his own mind to discover the powers that may be exercised by a great nation. His personal views often ran counter to legislation which came before him for judgment. He privately distrusted attempts at improving society by what he deemed futile if not mischievous economic tinkering. But that was not his business. It was not for him to prescribe for society or to deny it the right of experimentation within very wide limits. That was to be left for contest by the political forces in the state. The duty of the Court was to keep the ring free. He reached the democratic result by the philosophic route of scepticism—by his disbelief in ultimate answers to social questions. Thereby he exhibited the judicial function at its purest.

He gave such ample scope to legislative judgment on economic policy because he knew so well to what great extent social arrangements are conditioned by time and circumstances. He also knew that we have "few scientifically certain criteria of legislation, and as it often is difficult to mark the line where what is called the police power of the States is limited by the Constitution of the United States, judges should be slow to read into the latter a *nolumnus mutare* as against the law-making power" (*Noble State Bank* v. *Haskell*, 219 U.S. 104, 110). But social development is an effective process of trial and error only if there is the fullest possible opportunity for the free play of the mind. He therefore attributed very different legal significance to those liberties which history has attested as the indispensable conditions of a free society from that which he attached to liberties which derived merely from shifting economic arrangements. Even freedom of speech, however, he did not erect into a dogma of absolute validity nor did he enforce it to doctrinaire limits.

For him the Constitution was not a literary document but an instrument of government. As such it was to be regarded not as an occasion for juggling with words but as a means for ordering the life of a people. It had its roots in the past—"historic continuity with the past," he reminded his hearers, "is not a duty, it is only a necessity"— but it was also designed for the unknown future. This conception of the Constitution was the background against which he projected every inquiry into the scope of a specific power or specific limitation. That the Constitution is a framework of great governmental powers to be exercised for great public ends was for him not a pale intellectual concept. It dominated his process of constitutional adjudication. His opinions, composed in harmony with his dominating attitude toward the Constitution, recognized an organism within which the dynamic life of a free society can unfold and flourish. From his constitutional opinions there emerges the conception of a nation adequate to its national and international tasks, whose federated states, though subordinate to central authority for national purposes, have ample power for their divers local needs. He was mindful of the Union which he helped to preserve at Ball's Bluff, Antietam, and Fredericksburg. He was equally alert to assure scope for the states in matters peculiarly theirs because not within the reach of Congress.

The nation was nearly deprived of one of its great men because President Theodore Roosevelt resented that Holmes, in his estimate of John Marshall, should have subordinated the intellectual originality of the Chief Justice to his political significance. It was to be expected, therefore, that on the Supreme Court he would be left unimpressed by what are called great cases. What he cared about was transforming thought. "My keenest interest is excited, not by what are called great questions and great cases, but by little decisions which the common run of selectors would pass by because they did not deal with the Constitution or a telephone company, yet which have in them the germ of some wider theory, and therefore of some profound interstitial change in the very tissue of the law" (Collected Legal Papers, p. 269). Judged by conventional standards, therefore, his opinions not infrequently appeared to dispose rather cavalierly of controversies that were complicated in their facts and far-reaching in their immediate consequences. "This brief summary of the pleadings," he wrote of a litigation in which the record filled a five-foot shelf, "is enough to show the gravity and importance of the case. It concerns the expenditure of great sums and the welfare of millions of men. But cost and importance, while they add to the solemnity of our duty, do not increase the difficulty of decision except as they induce argument upon matters that with less mighty interests no one would venture to dispute" (Sanitary District v. United States, 266 U.S. 405, 425). With his vast learning he combined extraordinary rapidity of decision. His opinions were felicitous distillates of these faculties. His genius—put to service by rigorous self-discipline and deep learning—was to go for the essentials and express them with stinging brevity. He was impatient with laboring the obvious as a form of looseness, for looseness and stuffiness equally bored him. He genially suggested that judges need not be heavy to be weighty. ". . . our reports were dull because we had the notion that judicial dignity required solemn fluffy speech, as, when I grew up, everybody wore black frock coats and black cravats . . ." (*Letters*, II, 132).

In his opinions the thinker and the artist are superbly fused. In deciding cases, his aim was "to try to strike the jugular." His opinions appear effortless—birds of brilliant plumage pulled from the magician's sleeves. But his correspondence gives glimpses of the great effort that lay behind the seemingly easy achievement. "Of course in letters one simply lets oneself go without thinking of form but in my legal writing I do try to make it decent and I have come fully to agree with Flaubert. He speaks of writing French, but to write any language is enormously hard. To avoid vulgar errors and pitfalls ahead is a job. To arrange the thoughts so that one springs naturally from that which precedes it and to express them with a singing variety is the devil and all." And again: "The eternal effort of art, even the art of writing legal decisions, is to omit all but the essentials. The 'point of contact' is the formula, the place where the boy got his finger pinched; the rest of the machinery doesn't matter."

Whenever he disagreed with the majority of his brethren he was reluctant to express his dissenting views and did not often do so. In Massachusetts the number of his dissents was less than one per cent. of all his opinions. On the Supreme Court of the United States the expression of dissenting views on constitutional issues has, from the beginning, been deemed almost obligatory. In Washington, therefore, they came from Justice Holmes's pen more frequently and sometimes were written with "cold Puritan passion." He gave a public hint of the forces that clashed in the Supreme Court in the decorous form of a mere lawsuit when he said "we are very quiet there, but it is the quiet of a storm centre . . ." (*Collected Legal Papers*, p. 292). In a letter to Pollock he gave more than a hint of the inevitable conflicts within the Court: "Today I am stirred about a case that I can't mention yet to which I have sent round a dissent that was prepared to be ready as soon as the opinion was circulated. I feel sure that the majority will very highly disapprove of my saying what I think, but as yet it seems to me my duty. No doubt I shall hear about it on Saturday at our conference and perhaps be persuaded to shut up, but I don't expect it" (*Letters*, II, 29). Some of his weightiest utterances are dissents, but they are dissents that have shaped history. (See *Adair* v. *United States*, 208 U.S. 161, 190; *Hammer* v. *Dagenhart*, 247 U.S. 251, 277; *Abrams* v. *United States*, 250 U.S. 616, 624; *Evans* v. *Gore*, 253 U.S. 245, 264; *Adkins* v. *Children's Hospital*, 261 U.S. 525, 567; *Tyson & Bro.* v. *Banton*, 273 U.S. 418, 445; *United States* v. *Schwimmer*, 279 U.S. 644, 653; *Baldwin* v. *Missouri*, 281 U.S. 586, 595.) Disproportionate significance has been attached to his dissents, however; they are merely a part of a much larger, organic whole.

After his retirement he played briefly with the suggestion that he put his ultimate thoughts on law between the covers of a small book, but all his life he had been driven by the lash of some duty undone and at last he revelled in the joy of having no unfinished business. Moreover, he felt strongly that he had had his say in the way in which he most cared to express his reflections—scattered in his more than two thousand opinions and in his lean but weighty collection of occasional writings. "I am being happily idle," he wrote to Pollock, "and persuading myself that 91 has outlived duty. I can imagine a book on the law, getting rid of all talk of duties and rights—beginning with the definition of law in the lawyer's sense as a statement of the circumstances in which the public force will be brought to bear upon a man through the Courts, and expounding rights as a hypostasis of a prophecy—in short, systematizing some of my old chestnuts. But I don't mean to do it. . . ." (*Letters*, II, 307). He was no believer in systems. These, he felt, were heavy elaborations of a few insights —*aperçus*, to use his recurring word. Systems die; insights remain, he reiterated. Therefore, a few of his own *aperçus* will give the best clues to his philosophy of law and to his judicial technique in the most important field of his labors.

". . . the provisions of the Constitution are not mathematical formulas having their essence in their form; they are organic living institutions transplanted from English soil. Their significance is vital not formal; it is to be gathered not simply by taking the words and a dictionary, but by considering their origin and the line of their growth" (*Gompers* v. *United States*, 233 U.S. 604, 610).

". . . when we are dealing with words that also are a constituent act, like the Constitution of the United States, we must realize that they have called into life a being the development of which could not have been foreseen completely by the most gifted of its begetters. It was enough for them to realize or to hope that they had created an organism; it has taken a century and has cost their successors much sweat and blood to prove that they created a nation. The case before us must be considered in the light of our whole experience and not merely in that of what was said a hundred years ago" (*Missouri* v. *Holland*, 252 U.S. 416, 433).

"Great constitutional provisions must be administered with caution. Some play must be allowed for the joints of the machine, and it must be remembered that legislatures are ultimate guardians of the liberties and welfare of the people in quite as great a degree as the courts" (*Missouri, Kansas & Texas Ry. Co.* v. *May*, 194 U.S. 267, 270).

"While the courts must exercise a judgment of their own, it by no means is true that every law is void which may seem to the judges who pass upon it excessive, unsuited to its ostensible end, or based upon conceptions of morality with which they disagree. Considerable latitude must be allowed for differences of view as well as for possible peculiar conditions which this court can know but imperfectly, if at all. Otherwise a constitution, instead of embodying only relatively fundamental rules of right, as generally understood by all English-speaking communities, would become the partisan of a particular set of ethical or economical opinions, which by no means are held *semper ubique et ab omnibus*" (*Otis* v. *Parker*, 187 U.S. 606, 608–09).

". . . I should not dream of asking where the line can be drawn, since the great body of the law consists in drawing such lines, yet when you realize that you are dealing with a matter of degree you must realize that reasonable men may differ widely as to the place where the line should fall" (*Schlesinger* v. *Wisconsin*, 270 U.S. 230, 241).

It is futile to try to account for genius; and the term is not inaptly used for one whom so qualified an appraiser as Mr. Justice Cardozo deemed probably the greatest legal intellect in the history of the English-speaking judiciary. Holmes simply heeded his own deepest impulses. He was born to probe beyond the surface of things, to cut beneath the skin of formulas, however respectable. In his formative

years he found most congenial the company of speculative minds like
William James and Charles S. Pierce and Chauncey Wright . . .
All his life his pastime was not courtroom gossip but "twisting the tail
of the cosmos" (Perry, *The Thought and Character of William
James*, I, 504–19). Although native bent was powerfully reinforced
by his Civil War experience, the deeper ferment of his time also
worked in him. He came to maturity when Darwin began to disturb
ancient beliefs. If Genesis had to be "reinterpreted" no texts of the
law, however authoritative, could claim sanctity. By whatever combination of native disposition and outside influences it came to pass,
however, the result was that Holmes early rejected legal principles
as absolutes. He looked beneath their decorous formulations and saw
them for what they usually are—sententious expressions of overlap-
ping or conflicting social policies. The vital judicial issue is apt, therefore, to be their accommodation. Decisions thus become essentially
a matter of drawing lines. Again and again he adverted to that necessity, which he once summed up as follows: "I do not think we need
trouble ourselves with the thought that my view depends upon differences of degree. The whole law does so as soon as it is civilized. . . .
Negligence is all degree—that of the defendant here degree of the
nicest sort; and between the variations according to distance that I
suppose to exist and the simple universality of the rules in the Twelve
Tables or the Leges Barbarorum, there lies the culture of two thousand years" (*LeRoy Fibre Co.* v. *Chicago, Milwaukee & St. Paul Ry.*,
232 U.S. 340, 354). Such a view of law of course implies the exercise
of choice. But judicial judgment precluded the notion of capricious
choice. It assumes judgment between defined claims, each of recognized validity and with a cultural pedigree of its own, but all of
which necessarily cannot be completely satisfied. This process of
adjustment is bound increasingly to fall to the legislature as interests
and activities in society become more and more interdependent. The
considerations which thus prompt legislation and the intricate, dubious
materials out of which laws are written bring into sharp focus the
duty of deference to legislative determinations demanded from the
revisory process called adjudicative. In a thousand instances Holmes
was loyal to that philosophy. Thereby he resolved into comprehending larger truths the conflicting claims of state and nation, of liberty
and authority, of individual and society.

"It is right and proper that in the reading room of the Harvard Law School the portrait of Holmes should face in equal honor the portrait of Marshall" (A. D. Hill, *Harvard Graduates' Magazine, supra*, p. 284). There fell to Marshall, as Holmes took occasion to say, "perhaps the greatest place that ever was filled by a judge" (*Collected Legal Papers*, p. 270). That Marshall seized it, the rôle of the Supreme Court in American history bears witness. Holmes's claim to preëminence has a different basis. He is unsurpassed in the depth of his penetration into the nature of the judicial process and in the originality of its exposition. His conception of the Constitution cannot be severed from his conception of a judge's function in applying it; and his views of the judge's function derive from his intellectual presuppositions, that is, from his loyal adherence in judicial practice to his philosophic scepticism. His approach to judicial problems was inseparable from his consciously wrought notions of his relations to the universe. These abstractions appear far removed from the particular cases that came before him. But the clarity with which a specific controversy is seen, in the context of the larger intellectual issues beneath the formal surface of litigation, and the disinterestedness with which such analysis guides decision and opinion, are the ultimate determinants of American public law.

After a major operation in the summer of 1922, Holmes showed signs of age—he was then in his eighty-second year; but his marvelous physique gradually reasserted itself, though he strictly conserved his energy for his work. Some of his most powerful opinions were written in his ninth decade. Until near the end of his tenure he usually wrote more than his share of opinions. He was nearly eighty-nine when the illness and death of Chief Justice Taft cast upon Holmes for a considerable period the heavy burden of presiding in Court and the still more difficult task of guiding its deliberations at conferences. He did both, in the language of Mr. Justice Brandeis, "as to the manner born."

The machinery was running down, however, and on Jan. 12, 1932, he sent his resignation, in his own beautiful script, to the President— "the time has come and I bow to the inevitable." He continued his serene life, in Washington and in the summers at Beverly Farms, reading and being read to, enjoying the simple and familiar things of nature that had always refreshed him and the devoted attention of friends, especially the young. He had become a very old man but his faculties were never impaired. He had grown almost wistful in his gentleness. The fire of his exciting personality was dying down and on the morning of Mar. 6, 1935, came the end.

With the sure response of the mass of men—given enough time— to goodness and gallantry of spirit, Holmes, the fundamentally solitary thinker, had become a pervasive and intimate national possession. His death elicited an outpouring of feeling throughout the country. But of all the moving things that were said he would probably have most liked the few words of his old friend and his closest colleague for fifteen years, Mr. Justice Brandeis, when the news was brought to him: "And so the great man is gone." On his ninety-fourth birthday—a raw March day with snow gently falling—he was buried with due military honors, in the Arlington National Cemetery, alongside his wife and near his companions, known and unknown, of the Army of the Potomac.

OWEN J. ROBERTS

Charles Evans Hughes: The Administrative Master

Roberts, an Associate Justice from 1930 to 1945, was bound to
Chief Justice Hughes not only by friendship but by the common bonds of center-conservatism during the 1935–1937 crisis
within the Court over New Deal measures. On Hughes's death
in 1948, Roberts addressed a joint meeting of the Association
of the Bar of the City of New York and the New York County
Lawyers Association. "If ever a life could stand on the bare
record, without more," Roberts began, "his can." Speaking
"much as a son or younger brother might feel," Roberts focused his remarks on Hughes as captain of the Court. "His
greatest quality," said Roberts, "was balance," and this was
clearly the quality Roberts considered of paramount importance
in the "ideal" Justice.

Roberts had been appointed to the Court by President Hoover
in 1930. He had been an assistant district attorney for Philadelphia County, attorney for the Pennsylvania Railroad and
other large corporations, and a special prosecutor for President
Coolidge during the Teapot Dome investigation in 1924. In
1945 Roberts retired from the Court and became dean of the
University of Pennsylvania Law School. He died in 1955.

SOURCE: *Memorial Addresses of the Hon. Owen J. Roberts
and the Hon. Augustus N. Hand, December 12, 1948.*

[Charles Evans Hughes] became the head of the Court at a critical time in the nation's history, and during the span of his
service, the Court was confronted with constitutional questions novel
in character and critical to the preservation of our system. The Court
needed, as never before, cool, sane, courageous, and sagacious leadership.

The Chief Justice met the challenge of the task confronting him
in a way characteristic of him. I am sure that it was his inveterate
habit not to undertake any work without a careful and rational analysis of what was involved. Once he had made that analysis and had
satisfied himself of the course he should pursue, he laid aside all
further questions as to the program and plunged into it according to
his own blueprint, with amazing vigor and enthusiasm. I have never
known a man who patterned his life so meticulously and with such
obvious intellectual balance. He calculated with nicety how much of
his time he must devote to each of the departments of the Court's
work. He laid out his day, his week, and his month accordingly, and
he rigorously lived up to the schedule he had set himself.

He arose and breakfasted early. Immediately afterwards he went
for a brisk and a long walk. He was back at his desk shortly after
eight o'clock and from then until eleven-thirty he handled administrative matters, dealt with his correspondence, interviewed those who
had to see him on the business of the Court, and devoted what time
was left to study. At eleven-thirty he left his home for the Court.
In a brief interval of ten or fifteen minutes, he dealt with administrative matters after arriving at the courthouse. He was always in the
robing room a few minutes before twelve o'clock and, in the eleven
years of his tenure, he led the Court to the bench exactly as the clock
struck twelve. For two hours he presided over the proceedings with
alertness. No advocate ever had any doubt that the Chief Justice was
following him with acuteness and understanding. With urbanity, but
with persistence, he held counsel to the critical points in his case and
contrived to confine the arguments to the pivotal issues.

At two o'clock, Court would adjourn to an adjoining room for
luncheon. At once the Chief Justice relaxed and became the center

of a delightful half hour of talk which ranged from the merest local happening to world events. The current business of the Court was completely forgotten in the sociability of the group. Back on the bench at two-thirty, he again led the Court in the hearing of arguments. At the adjournment hour, he stepped into his office in the courthouse, perhaps saw one or two persons who had appointments with him, dispatched with great celerity certain administrative matters, and by five o'clock or sooner was on his way home.

On arrival, he and Mrs. Hughes would go for a stroll, and would return home for an early dinner. The evening was devoted to study, general reading, and family relationships. The Chief Justice retired at ten o'clock. During weeks when the Court was in recess and opinions were being prepared, he usually spent his entire day in his chambers at his home, studying, writing, and examining the opinions circulated to him by the other members of the Court.

The conferences of the Court took place on Saturdays at noon. If the Saturday in question fell in an argument week, the agenda for the conference might contain a half dozen jurisdictional statements on appeal, twenty to thirty petitions for certiorari, a few miscellaneous motions, and ten or fifteen cases which had been argued that week.

In the Supreme Court, the Chief Justice opens the discussion of all questions. Chief Justice Hughes would dispose of administrative matters with the greatest promptness. He would then take up the jurisdictional statements and petitions for certiorari. In each of these he had a typewritten memorandum of considerable length, evidently prepared by his clerks, but he did not rely on this memorandum in stating the case. He had a number of small white sheets on which he had scribbled notes in lead pencil. He would glance at one of these and then launch into a statement of the case. He had a marvelous power of condensing the facts without omitting any that were important, and, on the basis of this statement, he would announce his views as to the action the Court should take. So complete were his summaries, that in many cases nothing needed to be added by any of his associates. So comprehensive was his knowledge of the petitions, briefs, and records, that if any questions were raised by one of the brethren, the Chief Justice would reach for the printed book, which was full of white markers, turn to the appropriate place, and either summarize or read the material which supported the statement he had made. I do not remember an instance when he was found to have erred in his original statement.

Then came consideration of the argued cases. Again the Chief Justice spoke from lead pencil notes at which he occasionally glanced. His presentation of the facts of a case was full and impartial. His summary of the legal questions arising out of the facts was equally complete, dealing with the opposing contentions so as to make them stand out clearly. When this had been done, he would usually look up with a quizzical smile and say, "Now I will state where I come out," and would then outline what he thought the decision of the Court should be. Again, in many cases his treatment was so complete that little, if anything, further could be added by any of the Justices. In close and difficult cases, where there were opposing views, the discussion would go around the table from the senior to the junior, each stating his views and the reasons for his concurrence or his difference with those outlined by the Chief. After the Chief Justice had finished his statement of the case and others took up the discussion, I have never known him to interrupt or get into an argument with the Justice who was speaking. He would wait until the discussion had closed and then briefly and succinctly call attention to the matters developed in the discussion as to which he agreed or disagreed, giving his reasons. These conference sessions lasted from twelve o'clock sometimes to six, sometimes until six-thirty in the evening, and sometimes the session had to be adjourned until Monday afternoon to finish the business on hand. It is not hard to understand that, at the close of such a conference, most of the Justices were weary. The sustained intellectual effort demanded was great. The way the Chief Justice came through these difficult conferences was always a matter of wonder and admiration to me. After the conference was concluded, he sent for a clerk and assigned the cases. A slip of paper bearing the numbers of the cases assigned to each Justice was sent to his home within an hour and a half after the close of the conference.

Saturday evenings were the times of recreation for the Chief Justice and Mrs. Hughes. Each Saturday evening they would entertain or would be entertained at dinner. In the entire week, this was the only recreation the Chief Justice permitted himself during the term of the Court. So nicely did he allot his time to the various matters demanding attention, that, if his schedule were interrupted during the week by some unusual event, something he had laid out for himself to do had to go undone, and time had to be provided in the following week to take up the loss.

Again in the exercise of reasoned appraisal of himself and his work, which was the Chief Justice's inveterate habit, he evidently decided that he ought not only carry all the administrative work of the Court but do at least as much, and usually a little more than any of his brethren, in writing opinions. The record will show that year after year his product was as large, if not larger than that of any of his associates. He was very generous and considerate in the assigning of opinions to the members of the Court. He realized that in certain important cases he must speak for the Court, but he did not confine himself to those cases, but took a full share of the ordinary run of cases which came before the tribunal. Several of his associates suggested to him at various times that he ought to save himself for the important cases and ought to assign more of the relatively unimportant cases to his colleagues, but he would not tolerate the suggestion.

During his incumbency, the Court kept fully abreast of all its work. At each adjournment for the summer recess, all cases presented had been disposed of, except those as to which there was a division in the Court which required re-argument, or some other unavoidable reason for postponing the case until autumn. This accomplishment was due, not to any pressure which the Chief Justice exerted upon his brethren, but to his willingness to carry more than his fair share of the work of the Court and his obvious pride in the Court's accomplishment. His example was the greatest spur to his colleagues to do thorough work and to do it with reasonable promptness. The best reward any of the Justices could have for such a performance was the obvious satisfaction of the Chief at its accomplishment.

Chief Justice Hughes was a stickler for the proprieties. He had a deep sense of the dignity and importance of the Court over which he presided, and he instilled into every one of his brethren the same dignified attitude towards the work of the Court and the same sense of its importance. I am sure that it was part of a well thought out program that the Chief Justice, after the argument of the case and prior to the conference, did not discuss the merits of that case or the probable disposition of it with any of his brethren. He absorbed the arguments and the briefs of counsel. He read the records with greater care than any of us, and in his closet he wrestled with the problems presented and focused his superb abilities on their solution. What his conclusion was, none of us knew until he announced it at conference. He neither leaned on anyone else for advice nor did he proffer advice or assistance to any of us, but left us each to form his own conclusions to be laid on the table at conference in free and open discussion. A nice sense of propriety undoubtedly brought about this practice. Many of the associates between argument and conference would discuss the questions involved in the case and would exchange views with their brethren. Certainly there was nothing wrong with this practice, but it seems to me the Chief Justice held a far better position with his Court by not indulging in any such practice, but by beating out his conclusions himself, for announcement to the whole body of the Court in open conference. I am sure that this calculated course greatly strengthened his position and authority with his brethren.

The Chief Justice preserved and respected the proprieties in all his dealings with his brethren. There was some impalpable quality about him which would not permit disregard by them of the dignity and high-mindedness which ought to prevail in the tribunal. This high personal quality pervaded all the deliberations of the Court. Strong views were often expressed around the conference table, but never in eleven years did I see the Chief Justice lose his temper. Never did I hear him pass a personal remark. Never did I know him to raise his voice. Never did I witness his interrupting a Justice or getting into a controversy with him, and practically never did any one of his associates overstep the bounds of courtesy and propriety in opposing the views advanced by the Chief. The result was a feeling of personal cordiality and comradeship that I think was unique in a Court so seriously divided in its views on great matters of constitutional policy and law. Men whose views were as sharply opposed as those of Van Devanter and Brandeis, or those of Sutherland and Cardozo, were at one in their admiration and affectionate regard for their presiding officer.

FELIX FRANKFURTER
Chief Justices I Have Known

This was an "informal talk" given by the Justice ("just as it lies in my mind," he commented) at the University of Virginia Law School to law students and their ladies, on May 12, 1953. It was tape-recorded and then published in what might be called "transcript form" rather than "article form." Frankfurter began by noting that he had known six of the thirteen men who had served as Chief Justice of the United States—Melville Fuller, Edward D. White, William H. Taft, Charles E. Hughes, Harlan F. Stone, and Fred Vinson. He would talk about five, saying nothing, "of course, of the Chief Justice whom I've known longest in service, the present occupant of the seat," Fred Vinson. In its effervescence, its roaming yet pointed reflections, and its sense of the Supreme Court as an entity-in-history, this speech might be called "Vintage Frankfurter."

SOURCE: 39 *Virginia Law Review* 883 (1953).

I should say the three greatest Chief Justices we've had were John Marshall, Roger Taney, and Charles E. Hughes. It is an interesting thing that the first two of these between them, and in immediate succession, served for almost one half of the 164 years the show has been going. I mention the duration of their service—Marshall's and Taney's; Marshall from 1801 to 1834, thirty-three years, and Taney from '34 to '64—because the length of time during which a Chief Justice presides over the Court has, of course, a great deal to do with his place in history. Time is one of the most important factors in the realization of a man's potentialities.

Coming to the Chief Justices whom I've seen, whom I've seen in action, about whom professionally I may be allowed to have some judgment, let me come down to 1888 when Grover Cleveland appointed a man who was not known generally to the country at all. I suppose Melville Weston Fuller was a man about whom there was nothing in what newspapermen call the morgues of the leading newspapers in the country. He had no record to speak of, except a professional one. His appointment is an illustration, a striking illustration, of the contingencies of life. And I think he—and I shall speak of others—illustrates the importance of not having a fixed, specific ambition in life. The chance of realizing a specific ambition, the laws of chance, are so much against you, that, if I may say so, I do not think any of you should harbor an ambition to become Chief Justice of the United States. The likelihood that you will realize it—I don't know what the mathematicians, if there be any in this audience, would say—is worth nothing, and the likelihood that you will have an embittered life is very considerable. . . .

When Chief Justice Waite died, if a poll had been taken among lawyers and judges to determine the choice of a successor, I don't suppose a single vote would have been cast for Melville W. Fuller, certainly outside Chicago. Indeed, he was not Grover Cleveland's first choice. It was widely believed that a man named Edward J. Phelps of Vermont would become Chief Justice. He was a leader of the bar. He was an eminent man. He'd been Minister to Great Britain. But 1888 was a time when the so-called Irish vote mattered more than it has mattered in more recent years. Edward J. Phelps, as has been true of other ministers and ambassadors to Great Britain, made some speeches in England in which he said some nice things, believe it or not, about the British people. Patrick Collins, a Democratic leader, the then mayor of Boston, felt that that wouldn't do. A man who says nice things about the British can't possibly make a good Chief Justice of the United States. And since Patrick Collins was a powerful influence in the Democratic party, he advised President Cleveland that if he sent Phelps's name to the Senate, the chances of confirmation might not be very bright. Phelps's name was not sent to the Senate.

Melville Fuller was a Vermonter by birth, educated in Bowdoin, and the Harvard Law School. As a young man, after a little political activity in Augusta, Maine, he tried his luck in the beckoning West. He went to Chicago, where he was very active as a Democrat. In that way it chanced that Grover Cleveland came to know him, and knowing him, to respect him. After some maneuvering, Cleveland named Fuller, to the great surprise of the press of the country, and even of the profession. Fuller was confirmed, but with a very large vote in opposition. One of the opponents of confirmation was Senator Hoar of Massachusetts, then on the powerful Judiciary Committee, who afterwards did the handsome thing by saying how wrong he had been, just as in our day Senator Norris, who had opposed the confirmation of Harlan F. Stone, later publicly expressed his regret.

The point about Fuller was, or rather is, that he was a lawyer, and a lawyer only. I need hardly tell this audience that to me being a lawyer, with the full implications of responsibility and opportunity that the word carries, in a society like ours, in a government of laws under a written Constitution, is a calling second to none. Melville Fuller had held no public office of any kind, unless you call being a member of a constitutional convention public office. He was a practising lawyer. He was fifty-five years old when he was appointed to the Supreme Court, and he had not only had no judicial experience, he had had, as I have said, no official experience of any kind. I think Fuller was the only man, with the exception of his immediate predecessor, who came to the chief justiceship so wholly without a record in official public life.

When you deal with a number as small as that of the Chief Justices of the United States, any inference from one or more cases is statistically not of much validity. I merely point out parenthetically the fact that five Chief Justices came to the office without having had prior judicial experience. I don't want you to draw any inference from that fact which you cannot rationally defend. There's much to be said, and I haven't time to say it now, on the general question of the relevance of prior judicial experience as a qualification for membership on the Supreme Court. Perhaps I can sum up, parenthetically again, my own position by saying that prior judicial experience is neither a qualification nor a disqualification. I think that when the President of the United States comes to select someone to fill a vacancy on the

Supreme Court, no single factor should be the starting point in his
deliberation. He shouldn't say, "I want a man who has had experience
as a judge," or, "I want a man who hasn't had experience as a judge."
It is a fact that if you blot out the names of those who came to the
Supreme Court without any prior judicial experience, you blot out,
in my judgment, barring only two, the greatest names on the roster
of Supreme Court judges.

At all events, Fuller came to the court as a man who had had wide
experience at the bar, and, what is important, wide experience at the
bar of the Supreme Court and with the kind of business that came
before the Supreme Court in his day. He was a dapper little man.
I remember vividly—I still remember—seeing him for the first time.
I was a student at the Harvard Law School and he was president of
the Harvard Alumni Association. He was introducing the speaker
of the day, none other than William H. Taft, who had just returned
from the Philippines to become Secretary of War. Fuller had silvery
locks, more silvery and more—what shall I say—striking, because he
was a little man, than the locks of the former Senator from Texas,
Tom Connally. He was an extremely cultivated man, which is important. He read the classics. He was a student of history. He had
felicity of speech.

Fuller came to a Court which wondered what this little man was
going to do. There were titans, giants on the bench. They were powerful men, both in experience and in force of conviction, and powerful
in physique, as it happened. For myself, I think all Justices of the
Supreme Court should be strong, big, powerful-looking men! Certainly those whom he met there, who welcomed him courteously but
not hopefully, were as I've described them. Believe it or not, there's
ambition even in the breasts of men who sit on the Supreme Court
of the United States. There's a good deal to be said for the proposal
of Mr. Justice Roberts that no man should ever be appointed to the
Chief Justiceship from the Court.

Fuller met on that Court at least four or five men of great stature.
The senior among them was Samuel F. Miller, who had been appointed
by Lincoln, and whose career, incidentally, is an exciting story of
American life, because Miller started out as a physician, practised
medicine for ten-odd years, twelve-odd years, until he became a
lawyer and in very quick order a Justice of the Supreme Court. He

had great native ability, and he was a strong man. Fuller, if they had had the expression in those days, might have been called an egghead. He was a blue-blooded intellectual. The contrast was great. Then there was Harlan, a Kentuckian, six feet-three, a tobacco-chewing Kentuckian. You didn't have to come from Kentucky to chew tobacco in those days. They did it in Massachusetts. But Harlan was all Kentuckian. There was a smallish man whom I regard as one of the keenest, profoundest intellects that ever sat on that bench, Joseph Bradley of Jersey. And then there was Matthews of Ohio, and a six feet five or six inch giant from Massachusetts, Horace Gray. Those were the big men, the powerful men, the self-assured men, over whom Melville Fuller came to preside.

They looked upon him, as I've indicated, with doubt, suspicion, but he soon conquered them. He conquered them and they soon felt that the man who presided over them justly presided over them. He had gentle firmness. He had great courtesy. He had charm. He had lubricating humor. Justice Holmes was fond of telling a story. In his early days, he said, "I'm afraid my temper was a little short." And there could hardly be two men more different than Mr. Justice Holmes, who wielded a rapier, and Mr. Justice Harlan, who wielded a battle-axe. A rapier and a battle-axe locked in combat are likely to beget difficulties for innocent bystanders. Justice Harlan, who was oratorical while Justice Holmes was pithy, said something that seemed not ultimate wisdom to Holmes. Justice Holmes said he then did something that isn't done in the conference room of the Supreme Court. Each man speaks in order and there are no interruptions, no cut-ins —or cuts-in, whichever the plural is—because if you had that you would soon have a Donnybrook Fair instead of an orderly proceeding. But Holmes said, "I did lose my temper at something that Harlan said and sharply remarked, 'That won't wash. That won't wash.' " Tempers flared and something might have happened. But when Holmes said, "That won't wash," the silvery-haired, gentle, small, Chief Justice said, "Well, I'm scrubbing away. I'm scrubbing away."

Whether you're in a conference room of the Supreme Court, or en banc in a court of appeals, or at faculty meetings presided over by the irenic Dean Ribble, or in a law club, the same kind of thing happens. Men get short of temper and humor is a great solvent. Fuller had that. He presided with great courtesy. He presided with authority,

quiet authority, an authority unlike Hughes's, of whom I shall speak
shortly. He presided with great gentle firmness. You couldn't but
catch his own mood of courtesy. Counselors too sometimes lose their
tempers, or, in the heat of argument, say things, and there was a
subduing effect about Fuller. Soon these men, who looked at him
out of the corner of their eyes, felt that they were in the presence
of a Chief whom they could greatly respect. I have the authority of
Mr. Justice Holmes, who sat under four chief justices in Massachusetts before he came down to Washington, and under three in
Washington, that there never was a better presiding officer, or rather,
and more important in some ways, a better moderator inside the
council chamber, than this quiet gentleman from Illinois.

Somehow or other the felicity of his pen, more of his tongue, but
also his pen—if you will read a speech he made on the occasion of
the centennial of the founding of this country, reported in 132 United
States Reports—that charm which he had in occasional writings did
not manifest itself, or he did not exert it, in his opinions. You cannot
tell the quality or the importance of a man on the Supreme Court
solely from his opinions. Mr. Justice Van Devanter, in passing, is a
striking illustration of that. And so Fuller's opinions will give you
nothing of his charming qualities. He's rather diffuse. He quotes too
many cases. And generally he's not an opinion writer whom you read
for literary enjoyment, though you can profitably read his non-judicial
things for that purpose.

Fuller was invited to leave the Supreme Court, not to become governor of New York, but because Grover Cleveland was very anxious
to have him as his Secretary of State. An important document in the
history of the judiciary, and I think in the history of the law, is Fuller's
letter to President Cleveland stating why a man shouldn't leave the
chief justiceship, and, I should add, an associate justiceship, for any
political office. He was, as I said, fifty-five years old when he came
to the Court. He was Chief Justice for twenty-two years. The difference in functions between the Chief Justice and the other members
of the Court is, as Holmes said, mainly on the administrative side,
and there never was a better administrator on the Court than Fuller.

I ought to add one thing that seems to me not without interest and
not without pleasure to record. I said Fuller was appointed in 1888.
That was, let me remind you, a Presidential Election year. Like every

party out of power, the Republicans expected to be returned, as indeed they were. If mere partisanship had ruled, it would not have been difficult to await the result of the election and give the selection of a Chief Justice to the incoming Administration. Instead, the Senate confirmed the Democratic choice of President Cleveland. This broad-minded action reflects honor on all the Senators whose votes confirmed Fuller. Especial mention, however, should be made of Senator Shelby M. Cullom of Illinois, who knew Fuller and his qualifications as lawyer and man, and, transcending party considerations, pressed his confirmation. Now, that's a very gratifying thing to one, who, like myself, is out of party politics and party attachments—that politicians didn't play for position in relation to such a high office.

I must move on. Fuller died in 1910, and the appointment of his successor is a most interesting episode in American history, because Fuller died shortly after President Taft had named Governor Hughes of New York as an Associate Justice. As a matter of fact, Hughes had not even taken his place, when, in the summer, shortly after he was named, Fuller died. In offering Governor Hughes the place on the Supreme Court, President Taft—a great admirer, not unnaturally, of Hughes, who made the decisive campaign speech for Taft in 1908 at Youngstown, Ohio—Taft, with that charming exuberance, that charming forthrightness of his, indicated that Fuller can't live forever, and that, of course, he, Hughes, would be the natural choice of Taft for the chief justiceship. He indicated, as much as words can indicate, that he would name Hughes to be Chief Justice. Then, having doubt-less re-read the letter after he signed it, he scribbled under it a post-script, being fully aware of his delightful and generous indiscretion, "Of course, I do not make this as a firm promise," or words to that effect. I'm not quoting accurately. Governor Hughes, in accepting the position, told the President that of course he was as free as a bird as far as the chief justiceship was concerned.

Well, a vacancy in the chief justiceship did occur six weeks after this exchange of letters, and everybody expected Hughes to be made Chief Justice. Hughes took his seat, and it must have been extremely embarrassing for the baby member of the Court to be the heir apparent to the vacant chief justiceship. Some of the older fellows must have had thoughts. In fact, they had more than thoughts. They didn't like the idea. You know, the notion of a freshman runs all through life—

younger brother, younger sister, freshman at college, freshman on the Supreme Court.

By that time—1910—the Court had completely changed. Of the men whom Fuller found when he went there in 1888 only one survived, and that was Harlan. There were very strong men on the Court in 1910. It would be a pathetic Court indeed if there weren't always at least some strong men on it. By 1910 there were some new strong men. When Hughes joined the Court he found there in addition to Mr. Justice Harlan that nice bird-like creature with a beard, Mr. Justice McKenna of California. Holmes by that time was on and had been on for eight years. There was Mr. Justice White. There was a very strong man named Van Devanter. There was Mr. Justice Day, there was Mr. Justice Lamar.

They didn't like the idea of having this untried New York governor, New York politician, become Chief Justice. They drew up a round robin to present to Taft, who had appointed some of them. They saw President Taft, I believe, and indicated that they didn't like to have their junior member made Chief Justice. Mr. Justice Holmes, with his characteristic high honor, refused to join this kind of protest. He was perfectly ready to have Hughes become Chief Justice.

Taft appointed a member of the Court, a powerful member of the Court, Edward D. White of Louisiana. President Taft was glad to appoint—we are so much removed from 1910 in some ways—Taft found it appealing to appoint White as Chief Justice because White had been a Confederate. It wasn't until the 'eighties that a Confederate southerner had again been put on the Supreme Court. That was Lucius Quintus Cincinnatus Lamar of Mississippi. But to make a Confederate, an ex-Confederate—are Confederates ever "ex"?—Chief Justice was something that could contribute much, even then, so Taft thought, and I believe rightly, to the cohesion of our national life.

We shall never know what happened, but within twenty-four hours there was a change in the mind of Taft, and it was then that White became Chief Justice. There is the most absurd, and most absurdly contradictory, testimony of people who think they do know what happened. Within a half hour after Taft had summoned Hughes probably to tell him he was going to be Chief Justice, he cancelled the request that Hughes come. During that time something happened.

Anyhow, White was made Chief Justice. At the Saturday conference following the sending of White's name to the Senate, Hughes,
the junior member of the Court, made what I am told was one of
the most gracious speeches of welcome to the new Chief Justice,
Edward D. White.

Now let me tell you about him. He looked the way a Justice of
the Supreme Court should look, as I indicated a little while ago. He
was tall and powerful. I think a jowl also helps a Justice of the Supreme Court. He had an impressive jowl. He came from Louisiana,
as I've said. He was a drummer boy in the Confederacy, which had
upon him a very important influence, not only in life, but as a judge
—a very profound influence. It is a very interesting thing, but Edward
D. White, the Confederate drummer boy, was much more national-
istic, if that phrase carries the meaning I should like it to carry, was
far more prone to find State action forbidden as an interference with
federal power than was Holmes, the Union soldier, who went to his
death with three bullets in his body. White was so impressed with
the danger of divisiveness, with the danger of separatism, with the
intensification of local interest to the disregard of the common national
interest, that again and again and again he found that local action had
exceeded the bounds of local authority, because it might weaken and
endanger the bonds of national union. One of the most interesting
things is the division between him and Holmes in specific instances,
where White was, if one may use colloquial, inaccurate terms, for
centralization and Holmes was for "States' rights."

White "read" law. He didn't have the advantage that you and I
have had, of systematic training in the law in a university law school.
He was educated by the Jesuits—another very important part of his
life, because for him logic and logical analysis played a very important,
sometimes an excessive role. Very early he was put on the Supreme
Court of Louisiana, but he was there only two years because he was
then legislated out of office, or rather the court to which he belonged
was. So that he had only two years of relatively unimportant judicial
experience. During those two years he never had a case of the kind
which most frequently came to the Supreme Court after he became
a member of it. After his brief State judicial career, White practised
law and in 1891 was sent to the Senate of the United States on the
great issue of whether there should or shouldn't be a state lottery.

That's a profound question, isn't it? Anyhow, it took him to the Senate of the United States, where he began to play an important part. He was an effective speaker, much respected, a man of cultivation.

And then comes another one of those incidents which lead me to caution the young in this room not to fix their ambition on becoming Chief Justice or even an Associate Justice of the Supreme Court of the United States. Mr. Justice Blatchford of New York died and there were reasons why the natural thing was to pick a New Yorker for his place. This was in the second administration of Cleveland, after he had come back following Harrison's intervening Presidency. But the New York politicians had got into an awful row with Cleveland, and the Democratic Party in New York was split wide open. The leader of the anti-Cleveland forces, David B. Hill, was in the Senate of the United States. Mr. Cleveland, who was himself a lawyer of very considerable parts and knew the bar, first sent in the name of William B. Hornblower, a leading member of the New York bar. Senator Hill, acting in the historic tradition of—what is the phrase? I appeal to you on historic grounds; "personally obnoxious" or politically obnoxious—whatever the phrase is, said, "I oppose this nomination." If a Senator from the nominee's State is opposed to him and speaks the traditional words, the nomination fails. This works on the theory of "you scratch my back today and I'll scratch yours tomorrow." They all go in for that kind of thing. That's certainly a harmless way of putting it, isn't it?—"that kind of thing." So Mr. Hornblower's name fell by the wayside.

President Cleveland then sent in a second name, Wheeler H. Peckham of New York, another one of the really top-notch lawyers of his day. There was nothing against him except that he was a Cleveland man, but that was enough for David B. Hill, so he again arose, swirled the toga about him, and said that he was very sorry but that "Mr. Peckham, an otherwise estimable man, is personally obnoxious." And so Mr. Peckham's name was withdrawn. Cleveland was put to it, and he did what Presidents have done before and since. He drew on that powerful force, the club feeling of the Senate. And he said, "I'll fix you. I'll name a Senator to the Supreme Court." And they never reject Senators for anything, almost. So he named Senator White of Louisiana and Senator White was confirmed within fifteen minutes.

That's how White came on the Supreme Court in 1894. He sat for sixteen years as an Associate, a very significant member of the Court, until he was made Chief Justice at the age of sixty-five. He'd been a judge for sixteen years, but it's important to remember again that when he was made a judge he had only this rather unimportant, not very relevant, not quite two years on the Louisiana Supreme Court. He remained Chief Justice from 1910 to 1920.

An important thing in the work of a Chief Justice which distinguishes him from other members of the Court is that he is the presiding officer, and has guidance of the business of the Court in charge. It isn't what he says in his opinions that is more important than what his brethren say, but what he advises on the mechanics of doing the job —should we give a lawyer extra time, should we hear this case now or later, should we grant a rehearing if the Court is divided; things that pertain to the way that the business should be done, things that cannot properly be managed without knowledge of the nature of the business, or, since you deal with eight other human beings, without knowledge of the ways of the other eight Justices. It is thus very important, that number one, the Chief Justice should have had a good deal of familiarity with the business of the Court before he gets there, and, number two, that he start off on the right foot in his relations with his colleagues, whom he finds there. Of course, influence, influence in the sense of respect and deference, can be acquired in the course of time, but it makes a lot of difference if the start is a good one. White, when he came to be Chief Justice in 1910, dealt with men with whom he'd been a judge for periods varying in length from sixteen to a few years. But, as sometimes happens, there soon was a wholesale change in the Court. While a number of the Associates remained—McKenna, and Holmes, and Day—a new lot came on in the other places. A very able lot they were too.

I ought to say something about the differences in the nature of the business that has come to the Court in different periods. When Fuller assumed office in 1888, the Court dealt a great deal with problems arising from the vast industrialization which the Civil War had set into motion. It was also during Fuller's time that the war with Spain and the acquisition of territory led to new controversies. These events were reflected in the business of the Court because the Court is a good mirror, an excellent mirror, of which historians for some strange reason have little availed themselves, of the struggles of dominant forces outside the Court. Sooner or later the conflicts in the economic and social world result in litigation before the Court. De Tocqueville in 1832, when he wrote his great book, had the discernment to see what later writers have so often not seen that by the very nature of our Constitution practically every political question eventually, with us, turns into a judicial question. The question may become somewhat mutilated in the process, but come before the Court it will.

One sometimes reads stuff about the Supreme Court and wonders whether anyone ever studies history any longer. One would suppose that dissenting opinions were a recent discovery. In fact, I am sometimes told that they are an invention brought down by a Harvard professor. Well, the men on Fuller's Court divided drastically, and fiercely, and severely on the issues of their time. In the Insular cases, they wrote no fewer than 200 pages of opinions, which were illuminatingly summarized by that great philosopher, Mr. Dooley, when he said that so far as he could make out, "the Supreme Court decided that the Constitution follows the flag on Mondays, Wednesdays, and Fridays."

Beginning about in the 'seventies, the states, not yet the Federal Government, but the states began to regulate business. And there came before the Court a series of questions as to the power of the states, in view of the Civil War Amendments. With the Interstate Commerce Act of 1887, we enter upon an era where the Federal Government intervenes. It's the era we're still in, in which I suppose the statistically predominant issues concern the relations between government and business, broadly speaking. During Fuller's period, on the whole, the outlook of the Court was very—what shall I say?—inhospitable towards control of business. Restrictions upon the free activities of men came into Court, on the whole, under a serious handicap.

By the time White came to be Chief Justice the Federal Government had gone in for regulation more and more. Hughes was on the Court, with great experience, as governor of New York, in regulating business. During White's tenure, Brandeis came on the Court, without any previous judicial experience, but with, I suppose, unparalleled experience in the domain of practical economics, with an understanding of the relations of business to society. Yet, though White came to the chief justiceship with full knowledge of the Court's business and with a strong hold on his colleagues, if anybody thought that merely because of that there'd be unanimity of opinion, there'd be a want of differences, of course he was bound to be mistaken. And indeed, during White's tenure, the divisions became more and not fewer. But he was master of his job. There was something very impressive about him, both in appearance and otherwise. He was an impressive-looking person. He was also a great personality. He was a master of speech, though a master of too abundant speech. I should suppose, on the whole, his opinions are models of how not to write a legal opinion. He made three words grow, usually, where there was appropriate room only for one.

The Court became more and more divided in opinion during his period, not because of him, but because the issues became more contentious, the occasions for making broad decisions, broad rulings were fewer and matters became more and more, as Holmes early pointed out and for fifty years continued to point out, matters of degree.

White was Chief Justice only for ten years, and when he died an astonishing thing happened, unique in the history of this country and not likely to recur, at least as far as one can look ahead:—an ex-President of the United States became the Chief Justice of the United States. That was, of course, William H. Taft.

Now, his case, may contradict what I said about not fixing your ambition on a particular job, because William H. Taft, from the time he came to manhood, wanted to become a member of the Supreme Court. His great ambition in life was to be a Justice of the Supreme Court, and he finally not only attained it, but he attained it with, as it were, a dividend. He became Chief Justice of the United States. Yet, if I were you, I wouldn't draw too heavily on Taft for encouragement, let alone derive assurance from his case, that if you only want to be Chief Justice of the Supreme Court of the United States strongly enough, you'll get there. Let me tell you why.

Taft was a brilliant student, as we all know, at Yale. I think he would have continued to be even if he had gone to the Harvard Law School, as his son did after him. He went out to Cincinnati and had a quick career, which vindicated the promise of his youth. At 32 he was Solicitor General, having been on a lower court in Ohio before that. When the present system of Courts of Appeal, then called Circuit Courts of Appeals, was established in 1891, he became a circuit judge, and he was a very good judge, a notable judge, for nine years,

from 1891 to 1900, when McKinley sent him to the Philippines
as the civil governor general. While he was out there, vacancies occurred on the Supreme Court of the United States, and his then bosom
friend, Theodore Roosevelt, who knew of his ambition, twice offered
him a place on the Supreme court—twice. To the very great honor
of his name it is to be recorded that Taft twice refused that which his
personal ambition was most eager to have, because he thought he owed
it to the Philippine people whom he was then governing not to leave
—what's the phrase?—the plow in the furrow. So twice he put behind
him the realization of his personal ambition, because duty commanded
him otherwise.

Then he became Secretary of War, and then President of the
United States. His heart must have twinged more than once as he
had opportunity to put four men on the Supreme Court and fill places
that he himself so coveted. In 1913 Taft ceased to be President and
was promoted to be a professor of law. Well, if any man ever put
behind him the thought that he would ever be on the Court, it was
William H. Taft, when he went up to New Haven to profess law.
If you want to be foolish, if you want your life subject to the hazards
of such fortuities as those which determined the fate of William H.
Taft, then you can follow his example. Who would have thought that
the course of events would be such that in 1921 Warren Gamaliel
Harding would be President of the United States and would ask William H. Taft to be Chief Justice?

Taft became Chief Justice at the age of sixty-three, having been, as
I've indicated, a notable judge, but having been out of the business
of judging and out of touch with the Supreme Court, except for having filled four of its nine places, for twenty years. He was a very
rusty lawyer indeed when he came to preside over the Court. He
himself said, and he was very happy to say, with that generosity of
his which politicians would do well to, but do not often, imitate, that
whatever he did as Chief Justice was made possible by his great reliance on him whom he called his "lord chancellor," Mr. Justice Van
Devanter. Mr. Justice Van Devanter is a man who plays an important
role in the history of the Court, though you can't find it adequately
reflected in the opinions written by him, because he wrote so few.
But Van Devanter was a man of great experience. He'd been chief
justice of Wyoming. He was then made a circuit judge, a United

States circuit judge, and became a member of the Supreme Court in 1910. He had a very clear, lucid mind, the mind, should I say, of a great architect. He was a beautiful draftsman and an inventor of legal techniques who did much to bring about the reforms which, of course, were effectively accomplished by Taft as Chief Justice.

Taft's great claim, I think, in history will be as a law reformer. In the characteristic way of this country, various federal judges throughout the country were entirely autonomous; little independent sovereigns. Every judge had his own little principality. He was the boss within his district, and his own district was his only concern. A judge was a judge where he was, and although he may have had very little business, he couldn't be used in regions where the docket was congested. This, as you know was changed, and the change has been, of course, highly beneficial. An even more important reform for which Taft was effectively responsible was the legislation authorizing the Supreme Court to be master in its own household, which means that the business which comes to the Supreme Court is the business which the Supreme Court allows to come to it. No case can come up without getting prior permission, as it were, prior leave. So that cases which never should take the time, the energy, the thought of the ultimate tribunal in the land are allowed to rest, if they come from the federal courts, after those courts have had two goes at them, after, that is, Judge Dobie's or Judge Prettyman's court has reviewed the work of the district court, or, if the cases come from the state courts, after they have received the hierarchial adjudication provided by the state. So that no longer is it true, as it was before this legislation, that a case would come to the Supreme Court automatically after it had gone through, let us say, four other courts, as though having an endless litigation were one of the God-given rights of the American citizen.

So Chief Justice Taft, as I've said, has a place in history in my judgment next to Oliver Ellsworth, who originally devised the judicial system. Chief Justice Taft adapted it to the needs of a country that had grown from three million to a hundred and forty, a hundred and fifty, whatever it was.

Taft was, of course, very genial. He didn't have to learn to be genial. It's better to learn to be genial than not to be genial at all, but Taft was just instinctively genial, with great warmth, forth-putting, a great deal of comradery about him. When he came to the chief jus-

ticeship in 1921, the papers had been full, as the papers are from time
to time nowadays, of talk about the great divisions on the Court. Law-
men are constantly troubled, even lawyers when they lose a case, about
divisions on the Court. Why anyone in his senses should expect nine
men, presumably there because of their special capabilities, all to have
the same thoughts and views—one would suppose that nine men are
put there because you want variety of thoughts—why anyone should
expect that harmony and identity of views which do not exist even
among physicists, let alone among professors of sociology or history,
why they should expect nine people to know how to apply in unison
and in concord such delightfully vague phrases or concepts as "due
process of law," phrases, as a great judge once said, of "calculated
ambiguity," I do not understand, but anyhow it doesn't work out that
way, never has, and, if I may be a prophet, never will. To be sure,
there is no difference of opinion concerning the proposition that
twelve is twelve, and it is clear, therefore, that a jury must have
twelve members under the federal system. That's simple, that's easy.
But when it comes to things like when does a state encroach upon the
right of Congress to regulate commerce, or what kind of limitations
may you put upon people who want to speak at Hyde Park, or in
Union Square, or on the Lawn of the University of Virginia, well,
that's a different story.

So when Taft became Chief Justice there had been this succession
of great divisions on the Court—serious divisions on very serious
matters. And every once in a while there were five-to-four decisions.
Just as the newspapers don't print, "Mr. and Mrs. Jones have been
happily married for fifteen years this day. This is the fifteenth anniversary of the happy marriage of Mr. and Mrs. Jones," but they would
print somewhere in the paper that Mr. and Mrs. Jones are getting a
divorce, so the newspapers don't publicize the case in which the Court
is unanimous. I can assure you that there are a great many such—
most of them in fact. The newspapers do have headlines: "The Supreme Court divides on minimum wages. The Supreme Court divides
on child labor. The Supreme Court divides on this and that."

The appointment of Taft gave rise to the hope that all this would
end. "He's such a charming man, don't you know?" The only note I
did bring with me, because I like to read it, I like to recall it myself,
is of a newspaper editorial printed when Mr. Taft was appointed

Chief Justice in June, 1921. The present New York *Herald Tribune*, the then New York *Tribune*, commented, as did every paper in the country, on what a delightful man William H. Taft is, how charming, how everybody liked him, and now no more five-to-four opinions. I thought the *Tribune* put it best: "Mr. Taft has such tact and good humor, and has so unconquerable a spirit of fair play, that he is greatly beloved of his fellow citizens. These gifts and this character may not be the first ones sought for in a chief justice, but even the most eminent judges are none the worse for having them. With Justice Taft as a moderator"—now listen to this—"it is probable that not a few asperities that mar the harmony of the celestial chamber, the consulting room, not a few of those asperities will be softened and that not quite so often in the future will the court divide five and four."

I really think that's very funny. The assumption of this serious editorial writer that Taft, C.J., would just smile and then Holmes would say, "Aye, aye, sir," or Justice Van Devanter would say, "For ten years I've been disagreeing with Holmes, but now that you've smiled at both of us, why we just love each other." I've never done it, but my impression is strong that a count would show more five-to-four decisions during Taft's time than during White's time; or certainly just as many. Life was pleasant, very pleasant, with Taft as Chief Justice, but judicial conflicts existed because the problems before the Court evoked them. As for asperities during the period between '21 and '30, when Taft quit—well, I think, the conference was just as lively a place. I wasn't there, but the sparks even carried outside of the conference room to singe the pages of the United States Reports.

Well, of course Taft knew the men on the Court well, and he found there two whom he had appointed. That didn't prevent those two from disagreeing with him, I can assure you. One of the strongest, one of the most memorable of dissenting opinions against Taft was written by a man whom he had appointed. What judge would be worth his salt if it made any difference to him that the President who appointed him, whether he was on or off the Court disagreed with him? What judge worth his salt would have his convictions influenced by whether the Chief Justice is a charming man and a delightful raconteur, or not? That isn't the nature of the problems to be faced. That isn't the nature of the function. That isn't the nature of the enterprise.

In 1930 Taft became ill and retired. He always had the love and affection of his colleagues. He and Brandeis, when Taft was President, crossed swords very heavily—very fiercely indeed; Brandeis was counsel in the famous Pinchot-Ballinger attack on the administration. But they became fast friends on the Court. One of the things that people, laymen, even lawyers, do not always understand is indicated by the question you hear so often: "Does a man become any different when he puts on a gown?" I say, "If he's any good, he does."

Taft was followed, of course, by Hughes. Now the last thing that Hughes ever expected to be after he left the Court in 1916 to run for the Presidency—I have ventured to say in print that I believe this was the one act of his life which he regretted—then became Secretary of State, then became a member of the World Court, and finally returned to the bar to, I suppose, as vast a practice as that of any man at the bar in our time, or at any time in the history of this country—the last thing Hughes expected to become was Chief Justice. He was, of course, to Hoover's great surprise, subject to severe attack when his name was sent in. He finally was confirmed, though it was a nip and tuck business. He took his seat at the center of the Court, with a mastery, I suspect, unparalleled in the history of the Court, a mastery that derived from his experience, as diversified, as intense, as extensive, as any man ever brought to a seat on the Court, combined with a very powerful and acute mind that could mobilize these vast resources in the conduct of the business of the Court. There must be in this room lawyers who came before the Court when Chief Justice Hughes presided. To see him preside was like witnessing Toscanini lead an orchestra.

Aside from the power to assign the writing of opinions, which is his by custom, and of which I shall speak, a Chief Justice has no authority that any other member of the Court hasn't. That really is an institution in which every man is his own sovereign. The Chief Justice is *primus inter pares*. He presides. Somebody has to preside at a sitting of nine people, and he presides in Court and at conference. But Chief Justice Hughes radiated authority, not through any other quality than the intrinsic moral power which was his. He was master of the business. He could disembowel a brief and a record. He had an extraordinary memory and vast experience in the conduct of litigation, and of course he had been on the Court six years, from '10 to '16. And, he had intimate and warm relations with some of the men he found on the Court. He was a great admirer of that greatest mentality of all, that greatest intellect, in my judgment, who ever sat on the Court —I say intellect—Mr. Justice Holmes. He was an old friend at the bar of Mr. Justice Brandeis. He'd been one year in the Cabinet with Stone. So he not only felt at home in the courtroom, he felt at home with his colleagues.

I've often used a word which for me best expresses the atmosphere that Hughes generated; it was taut. Everything was taut. He infected and affected counsel that way. Everybody was better because of Toscanini Hughes, the leader of the orchestra. That was true of Cardozo, when he was chief judge of the New York Court of Appeals. One is told that the same men were somehow or other better when he was chief judge than they were the next day, after he had ceased to be chief judge. That's a common experience in life. One man is able to bring things out of you that are there, if they're evoked, if they're sufficiently stimulated, sufficiently directed. Chief Justice Hughes had that very great quality.

Chief Justice Stone is, of course, the antithesis, in the fate that was allotted to him, to Marshall and Taney and Fuller. If you're only Chief Justice for five years, as Stone was, even though you come to the chief justiceship after having been an Associate, the opportunities to realize on the moral opportunities that place gives you are necessarily very limited. Time plays a very important part. Stone came to the Court in '41. He'd been an Associate Justice since '25, been on the Court sixteen years. Before that he had been Attorney General, been a professor of law and dean of a law school, and an extensive practitioner in New York. He was familiar with the business of the Court. He was a very different personality from Hughes. Hughes was dynamic and efficient. That's a bad word to apply to Hughes, because it implies regimentation. It implies something disagreeable, at least to me. I don't like to have a man who is too efficient. He's likely to be not human enough. That wasn't true of Hughes. He simply was effective—not efficient, but effective. Stone was much more easy-going. The conference was more leisurely. The atmosphere was less taut, both in the courtroom and the conference room. It has been said that there wasn't free and easy talk in Hughes's day in the conference room. Nothing could be further from the truth. There was less wasteful talk. There was less repetitious talk. There was less foolish talk. You just didn't like to talk unless you were dead sure of your ground, because that gimlet mind of his was there ahead of you.

Stone was an "easy boss," as it were. Boss is the worse word to use with reference to the Chief Justice of the United States, because that's precisely what he isn't. Anybody who tried it wouldn't try it long. There is one function, however, that the Chief Justice has by virtue of being Chief Justice, other than being the administrator, presiding in open court and presiding at the conference and being the first man to lay open the problems before us—the cases that have been argued and the cases in which petitions have been filed. That other function is, I believe, the most important of all that pertains to the office of Chief Justice. I know not how it is in the Supreme Court of Appeals of Virginia. The method of designating the member of the court who writes the opinion for the court varies in the various state courts. In New York, for instance, it goes by rotation. That's a practice very common in this country. Even when it goes that way, even when it's so chancy a thing as it is in New York, a great man can make a dent on the accidental system by which cases come to him. They used to say, until they knew better, "Why is it that Chief Judge Cardozo, or Judge Cardozo, always gets the interesting cases?" The answer was that no matter what case he got, he made it interesting; and he didn't "get" it—it came to him in automatic order. I believe it is a fact, though it is so strange a fact that I shan't identify the state, but I'm assured on dependable authority that in the Supreme Court of at least one of our states, and not the least populous of states, they shake dice to determine who should write an opinion. Well, having it go in order lacks, for my taste, at least that aleatory aspect that dice have.

From Marshall's time in the Supreme Court the Chief Justice has designated the member of the Court who writes the opinion of the Court. As most of you know, we hear argument five days a week and on Saturday there's a conference. After everybody has had his say, beginning with the Chief Justice and following in order of seniority—everybody has his say and can say whatever he wants to say—there is a formal vote. In order that the junior shouldn't be influenced, everybody having already expressed his view, the formal voting begins with the junior. How careful we are not to coerce anybody! After conference, in cases in which the Chief Justice is with the majority, as he is in most instances, he designates the member of the Court who is to write the opinion. If he is in the minority, then the next senior Justice does the assigning. So that in most of the cases the Chief Justice decides who is to speak for the Court. Of course, as for dissents and concurrences—that's for each member to choose for himself.

You can see the important function that rests with the Chief Justice in determining who should be the spokesman of the Court in expressing the decision reached, because the manner in which a case is stated, the grounds on which a decision is rested—one ground rather than another, or one ground rather than two grounds—how much is said and how it is said, what kind of phrasing will give least trouble in the future in a system of law in which as far as possible you are to decide the concrete issue and not embarrass the future too much— all these things matter a great deal. The deployment of his judicial force by the Chief Justice is his single most influential function. Some do that with ease. Some do it with great anguish. Some do it with great wisdom. Some have done it with less than great wisdom.

No Chief Justice, I believe, equaled Chief Justice Hughes in the skill and the wisdom and the disinterestedness with which he made his assignments. Some cases are more interesting than others, and it is the prerogative of the Chief Justice not only to be kindly and fair and generous in the distribution of cases, but also to appear to be so. The task calls for qualities of tact, of understanding, and for skill in the effective utilization of the particular qualities that are available. Should one man become a specialist in a subject? Or is it important not to place too much reliance on one man because he's a great authority in the field? Should you pick the man who will write in the narrowest possible way? Or should you take the chance of putting a few seeds in the earth for future flowering? Those are all very difficult, very delicate, very responsible questions. . . .

I hope I've indicated enough, however, to disclose that in view of the functions of the Supreme Court, what you want in a Justice is not a specialist in this or that field, not necessarily a man who has had prior experience on the bench, not necessarily a man who has been broadened by high office, as was the case with Hughes, rather than broadened by the depth and range of his reading and his thinking, as in the case of Mr. Justice Holmes who never had any practical experience to speak of, in the narrow sense of the term.

What is essential for the discharge of functions that are almost too much, I think, for any nine mortal men, but have to be discharged by nine fallible creatures, what is essential is that you get men who bring to their task, first and foremost, humility and an understanding of the range of the problems and of their own inadequacy in dealing with them; disinterestedness, allegiance to nothing except the search, amid tangled words, amid limited insights, loyalty and allegiance to nothing except the effort to find their path through precedent, through policy, through history, through their own gifts of insight to the best judgment that poor fallible creatures can arrive at in that most difficult of all tasks, the adjudication between man and man, between man and state, through reason called law.

ROBERT H. JACKSON

Mr. Justice Brandeis: "Microscope and Telescope"

Robert Jackson was not one of Louis Brandeis's former law clerks nor a member of his inner circle of associates. Nor did Jackson serve with Brandeis on the Court, since Brandeis retired in 1939 and Jackson was appointed in 1941. But as an Assistant Attorney General, Solicitor General, and Attorney General during the first two Roosevelt Administrations, Jackson argued cases steadily before Mr. Justice Brandeis. Jackson's writings and speeches also drew heavily on Brandeis's opinions and his judicial philosophy. When he delivered this address, at the Brandeis Memorial Colony Dinner on June 23, 1943, Jackson had been on the Court for two years and had had the opportunity of testing his "outsider's" estimate of Brandeis's judicial role against the view of judicial qualities and performance which comes from inside the white Temple.

SOURCE: 9 *Vital Speeches* 664 (1943).

I believe it was Emerson who said that institutions are but the lengthened shadows of individuals. It is my purpose to speak of Mr. Justice Brandeis, the man under whose lengthened shadow we gather tonight.

The great work of his life, to which all else was prelude, was as a Justice of the United States Supreme Court. The character of such work is, to laymen, obscure and elusive. It does not lie on the surface, nor does it thrust itself upon lay attention. Even for lawyers, unless they follow the work of the Court closely, it is difficult to appraise. A Justice officially expresses himself in the technical language of the law, and he is as remote from the lay world as if he wrote in a dead language. When he speaks for the Court, his opinion is depersonalized by the necessity of adapting it to the several minds for which he speaks. While legislators may act as they want to act, judges often act as statutes tell them to act and render judgments that are the law's judgments rather than their personal ones. Oftentimes, too, the judge is legally bound to base his conclusions on facts as they are decided by someone else. As a result he appears to approve a good deal that in truth he has no say about.

Then, too, in many fields of law where there is no controlling legislation, judges must usually submit to the guidance of precedents. Justice Brandeis never carried regard for precedent to a worship of them. But he did accept, as all judges should, certain traditional restraints on personal judgment. Laymen often fail to see why this should be. The law is, after all, a rule for men to live by. They must have some way to find out how they should behave in order to avoid liabilities and punishments and troubles with the law. When there is no known rule except the personal will of the judge one happens to come before, one can never know how to conduct himself. Bentham said that judges, when they assume to make the law, do it "just as a man makes laws for his dog. When your dog does anything you want to break him of, you wait till he does it, and then beat him for it." I think we must agree that there is uncomforting truth in this criticism of judicial law-making, and that it is to be avoided so far as possible consistently with the view that law is a living and progressing body of learning.

The device by which judicial action is made at all predictable is the precedent. It is the doctrine that a court will give a word or phrase in a contract or statute the same meaning tomorrow that it did yesterday, that it will resort to the same principles to fashion future judgments that it employed in past ones. Of course, even at its best the endless variation in the facts of cases makes any prediction from precedent an imperfect one. But in its absence, or before judges with no regard for the true function of the precedent, there is no law but that day's opinion of the judge who perhaps accidentally gets the case. Brandeis, it seems to me, came near the golden mean in his attitude toward the precedents. He examined them patiently and followed them in the absence of grave reasons for a departure. If he departed, as he never feared to do, he paid his profession the respect of a searching, candid, and unequivocal opinion giving his reasons.

I often hear it said of Brandeis as if it characterized his life's work, "He was a great dissenter." Let me warn you against this popular but badly mistaken standard of appraisal. Dissenting opinions, of course, have a way of better pleasing those who read as well as those who write them. They are apt to be more individual and colorful. Opinions which must meet the ideas of many minds may in comparison seem dull and undistinguished. In the past few years a dozen, or perhaps a score, of really important decisions of the Supreme Court have been overruled. In consequence, minority opinions won belated vindication. The drama of a high court reversing itself has news value, and some have come to regard dissent as something worthy in itself.

Brandeis had no such delusion. It is not the number of his dissents, but the quality of his dissenting opinions, that is outstanding. The fact is that of the dissents that have been written in the history of the Court only a trifling proportion have later become law. The same is true of the dissenting opinions of individual Justices. In judicial thinking as elsewhere two good heads will average better results than one, and time more often vindicates majority opinions than minority ones.

The great work of Brandeis was done, not in opposing the Court, but in leading it. He was its spokesman in many difficult and complicated problems which covered the wide range of issues that come before it. It was for the Court that he wrote the greater number of his five hundred and twenty-eight opinions. They interpret the great life-giving clauses of the Constitution, pioneer in administrative law, deal with the law of public utilities, patents, monopolies and restraint of trade, labor relations and civil rights. In these he patiently gathered up the facts of record, examined the arguments of counsel, reconciled the views of his associates, and set forth the conclusion of the Court in clear, illuminating and unadorned language.

It was this constructive type of work on the Court for which his career at the bar peculiarly fitted him. His work as a lawyer was constructive, practical and bold. He pioneered in fields lawyers seldom entered and more rarely were distinguished in, and always he was building—building—building. I shall not dwell on these early activities. In them Woodrow Wilson with singular vision detected the making of a constructive jurist. He named lawyer Brandeis to the Supreme Court, fostered the nomination through a stormy confirmation, and gave to his country Mr. Justice Brandeis.

The period of his service began June 5, 1916, and ended by retirement February 13, 1939. In that almost quarter century unprecedented things came to pass. The United States went through the ordeal of one world war and stood on the precipice overlooking another. Between the two we harvested crops planted by a century of industrial revolution—speculation, extravagance, and inflation, with its aftercrop of depression, deflation and disaster. Paul Freund, one of the closest friends of the Justice, has recorded that when Brandeis was asked in the dark days of 1933 whether he believed the worst was over, he answered almost cheerfully that "the worst had happened before 1929."

This period of rapidly fluctuating price levels and economic chaos, of social unrest and upheaval, of political transition and experimentation, brought to his Court an unprecedented grist of difficult problems. Some of them the Court did not meet too well. On important occasions he was a vigorous and sometimes solitary dissenter. In earlier days he was sometimes joined by Mr. Justice Holmes, and later by Mr. Justice Cardozo, Mr. Justice Stone and Chief Justice Hughes. The message to Congress in which President Roosevelt proposed to reorganize the Court brought on some of the most critical moments of its long and not always tranquil history. Brandeis had protested some, though not all, of the decisions that had aggrieved the President and many others. In general the attack in the Court fight was against decisions that he had opposed in the Court. But while he was always ready to struggle within the Court, he would have no hands laid upon the institution from the outside. It mattered not that the outside hands would in the main uphold his views and would rebuke those with whom he had long and often disagreed. Brandeis valued its independence of decision even more than rightness of decision. He joined with Chief Justice Hughes in a letter to Senator Wheeler which did more than any one thing to turn the tide of the Court struggle.

I mention this because it revealed the man. I suppose perhaps eighty-five per cent of those who followed and revered him were in the camp of the President. I think ninety-five per cent of those who disliked or scorned him were in the opposition. But Brandeis did not determine his principles by counting heads. He simply thought his friends were wrong and his foes for once were right, and that was an end of the matter for him. He believed with all the intensity of his being that the country needed the institution he served, and that a court of courage, character and independence could exist only in an atmosphere of freedom from political pressures. But he believed the Justices maintain it by self-restraint and open-mindedness, by unbiased, patient and accurate application of the law, and by freedom from political ambition or partisanship.

The handiwork of his opinions measured up to this standard. He mastered completely the facts of his case, respecting facts for the stubborn things that they are. He set them forth with fidelity to the record and with unbiased emphasis. He analyzed them in the light of research, not only in the law, but in economics, science and history. As Mr. Freund, who served as his law clerk, tells us, when he had finally completed the many revisions of an opinion he said, "The opinion is now convincing, but what can we do to make it more instructive?" And instructive his opinions are. When one comes upon an opinion by Brandeis, it is like finding bedrock upon which it is safe to build.

He was not an ornamental writer. Clarity and simplicity were his aims, and so well did he achieve them that style never steals attention from the substance. He did not have the apt and cutting phrase that Holmes wielded so devastatingly. But while Holmes illuminated a subject like a flash of lightning, Brandeis illuminated it as does the noonday sun—steadily, evenly, completely. Chief Justice Hughes summed up his workmanship by describing him as "the master of both microscope and telescope. Nothing of importance, however minute, escapes his microscopic examination of every problem, and, through his powerful telescopic lens, his mental vision embraces distant scenes ranging far beyond the familiar worlds of conventional thinking."

Justice Brandeis greatly influenced many young men. He found time in some way to cultivate their acquaintance. His modest home on Sunday afternoon often gathered those who wanted to see him or to whom he had extended an invitation. He would draw them into conversation, fortify their courage if he found it failing. He saw life as it was lived by aspiring young men. He gave no encouragement to those who came to whine over their bruises. He sought no easy way to lift even men he liked into positions they had not earned. He did not tell every lad he could do great things, but he made them all feel they could be useful things, and he urged them to do well whatever task they had in hand. He urged them after enlarging their experiences and broadening their viewpoints to go home, to fill places in their own communities.

Brandeis has been called a reformer, and he had the passion for betterment that lies at the root of reform. But he never went off on any plan for making men into angels. His aim was only to make better men, and content if only a little better. Crusader, some called him, and he had the zeal, the consecration and the courage of one. But he stuck to practical jobs and left windmill-tilting to those whose emotions outrun their judgment. Friend of the poor and champion of the disadvantaged he was, but always he planned ways for them to help themselves and never sought to relieve them of work or responsibility, which he thought to be great educators. He was in no sense a collectivist or believer in centralized control of life or of industry.

Brandeis was labelled as a "liberal," and labels are tyrannical things. Because Brandeis had been a liberal in politics, many expected him as a judge to sustain all that was done in the name of liberalism. Those reckoned without knowledge of his high concept of his judicial office. He feared and distrusted large, unconfined and irresponsible power, whether in private or public hands. He would never accept it as wholesome merely because found at the time being put to good use by good hands. He knew that the powers which evil men misuse are often acquired because lodged in the hands of men on the argument that they were good men.

In the "Hot Oil" case and the N.R.A. case he joined in striking down as unconstitutional acts of Congress sponsored by the Administration and identified with its program of economic recovery. Although few were more sympathetic with debtors in the depression, he concurred in holding unconstitutional state legislation which deprived the creditor of all effective remedy, and wrote the opinion holding the Frazier-Lemke Act for the relief of farm debtors unconstitutional. In the Tennessee Valley Authority litigation, while he agreed that the

Act was constitutional, he would have refused to decide the point because he thought it not properly presented. Later he would have refused judgment sustaining the old age benefit provisions of the Social Security Act as constitutional, because he thought the procedure was not appropriate, but being overruled, he joined in holding the Act constitutional. In all of these matters he refused to yield his ideas of what was constitutional or as to appropriate procedures because of his political sympathies with the causes involved.

What was the general philosophy of this man? It is safer to seek it from his own words. Many admirers have tried to make Brandeis over in their own image. What he stood for is perhaps better and more shortly stated in his famous letter to Robert Bruere than anyone could do for him. Hence, I quote at length what I think could wisely be the basic creed of the modern liberal:

"Refuse to accept as inevitable any evil in business (e.g., irregularity of employment). Refuse to tolerate any immoral practice (e.g., espionage). But do not believe that you can find a universal remedy for evil conditions or immoral practices in effecting a fundamental change in society (as by State Socialism). And do not pin too much faith in legislation. Remedial institutions are apt to fall under the control of the enemy and to become instruments of oppression.

Seek for betterment within the broad lines of existing institutions. Do so by attacking evil in situ; and proceed from the individual to the general. Remember that progress is necessarily slow; that remedies are necessarily tentative; that because of varying conditions there must be much and constant inquiry into facts . . . and much experimentation; and that always and everywhere the intellectual, moral and spiritual development of those concerned will remain an essential—and the main factor—in real betterment.

This development of the individual is, thus, both a necessary means and the end sought. For our objective is the making of men and women who shall be free, self-respecting members of a democracy —and who shall be worthy of respect. Improvement in material conditions of the worker and ease are the incidents of better conditions—valuable mainly as they may ever increase opportunities for development.

The great developer is responsibility. Hence no remedy can be hopeful which does not devolve upon the workers' participation in responsibility for the conduct of business; and their aim should be the eventual assumption of full responsibility—as in cooperative enterprises. This participation in and eventual control of industry is likewise an essential of obtaining justice in distributing the fruits of industry.

But democracy in any sphere is a serious undertaking. It substitutes self-restraint for external restraint. It is more difficult to maintain than to achieve. It demands continuous sacrifice by the individual and more exigent obedience to the moral law than any other form of government. Success in any democratic undertaking must proceed from the individual. It is possible only where the process of perfecting the individual is pursued. His development is attained mainly in the processes of common living. Hence the industrial struggle is essentially an affair of the church and its imperative task."

Such was the philosophy, such the tough fibre of his mind, such the qualities which make his work pre-eminent among the many powerful men of his time.

FELIX FRANKFURTER

Justice Roberts and the "Switch in Time"

Given the divisions within the Supreme Court during the 1940's and 1950's, the following address by Justice Frankfurter has at least something of the nature of a sword stroke in the battle for historical judgment. What was at stake was the estimate of two men, Hughes and Roberts, and the truth about the famous accommodation by the Supreme Court in 1937 which upheld the National Labor Relations Act and other key New Deal measures and helped to bury the President's Court reform bill. To have known "what really happened" while many historians and political scientists were weaving elaborate myths about the Court's switch in 1937 must have been a heavy burden. Justice Frankfurter laid a bit of this load down with an address in 1955 printed here, certainly one of the most fascinating and revealing "disclosures" in out-of-Court commentary.

SOURCE: "Mr. Justice Roberts," 104 *University of Pennsylvania Law Review* 311 (1955).

The dictum that history cannot be written without documents is less than a half-truth if it implies that it can be written from them. Especially is this so in making an assessment of individual contributions to the collective results of the work of an institution like the Supreme Court, whose

241

labors, by the very nature of its functions, are done behind closed
doors and, on the whole, without leaving to history the documentation leading up to what is ultimately recorded in the United States
Reports. To be sure, the opinions of the different Justices tell things
about them—about some, more; about some, less. As is true of all
literary compositions, to a critic saturated in them, qualities of the
writer emerge from the writing. However, even in the case of an
opinion by a Justice with the most distinctive style, what is said and
what is left unsaid present to students of the Court a fascinating challenge of untangling individual influences in a collective judgment.

To discover the man behind the opinion and to estimate the influence he may have exerted in the Court's labors, in the case of Mr.
Justice Roberts, is an essentially hopeless task. Before I came on the
Court I had been a close student of its opinions. But not until I became
a colleague, and even then only after some time, did I come to realize
how little the opinions of Roberts, J., revealed the man and therefore
the qualities that he brought to the work of the Court. In his case
it can fairly be said the style—his judicial style—was not the man.

The esprit of Roberts's private communications leave little doubt
that when he came to writing his opinions he restrained the lively and
imaginative phases of his temperament. I speak without knowledge,
but he had evidently reflected much on the feel and flavor of a judicial opinion as an appropriate expression of the judicial judgment.
The fires of his strong feelings were banked by powerful self-discipline,
and only on the rarest occasion does a spark flare up from the printed
page. The sober and declaratory character of his opinions was, I believe, a form consciously chosen to carry out the judicial function as
he saw it. We are told that Judge Augustus N. Hand, in disposing of
a case that excited much popular agitation, set himself to writing an
opinion in which nothing was "quotable." The reasons behind this attitude doubtless guided Justice Roberts in fashioning his judicial style.
Moreover, his was, on the whole, a hidden rather than an obvious nature—hidden, that is, from the public view. His loyalties were deep,
as was his devotion to his convictions. Both were phases of an uncom-
promising honesty. They constituted the most guarded qualities of
his personality and he would not vulgarize them by public manifestation.

In not revealing, indeed in suppressing, the richer and deeper qualities of his mind and character, the Roberts opinions reflect his own underestimation of his work. Partly, he was a very modest man, partly his judicial self-depreciation expressed his sense of awe to be a member of the bench charged with functions, in the language of Chief Justice Hughes, "of the gravest consequence to our people and to the future of our institutions." Above all, the standards for his self-appraisal were, characteristically, judges of the greatest distinction in the Court's history. On leaving the bench, he wrote: "I have no illusions about my judicial career. But one can only do what one can. Who am I to revile the good God that he did not make me a Marshall, a Taney, a Bradley, a Holmes, a Brandeis or a Cardozo."

Roberts was unjust to himself. He contributed more during his fifteen years on the Court than he himself could appraise. His extensive, diversified experience at the bar and his informed common sense brought wisdom to the disposition of the considerable body of litigation, outside the passions of popular controversy, that still comes before the Court. Again, his qualities of character—humility engendered by consciousness of limitations, respect for the views of others whereby one's own instinctive reactions are examined anew, subordination of solo performances to institutional interests, courtesy in personal relations that derives from respect for the conscientious labor of others and is not merely a show of formal manners—are indispensable qualities for the work of any court, but pre-eminently for that of the Supreme Court. Probably no Justice in the Court's history attached more significance to these qualities than Mr. Justice Brandeis. It tells more than pages of argumentation that Brandeis held Roberts in especial esteem as a member of the Court.

It is one of the most ludicrous illustrations of the power of lazy repetition of uncritical talk that a judge with the character of Roberts should have attributed to him a change of judicial views out of deference to political considerations. One is more saddened than shocked that a high-minded and thoughtful United States Senator should assume it to be an established fact that it was by reason of "the famous switch of Mr. Justice Roberts" that legislation was constitutionally sustained after President Roosevelt's proposal for reconstructing the Court and because of it. The charge specifically relates to the fact that while Roberts was of the majority in *Morehead* v. *New York ex rel. Tipaldo*, 298 U.S. 587, decided June 1, 1936, in reaffirming *Adkins*

v. *Children's Hospital*, 261 U.S. 525, and thereby invalidating the New York Minimum Wage Law, he was again with the majority in *West Coast Hotel Co.* v. *Parrish*, 300 U.S. 379, decided on March 29, 1937, overruling the *Adkins* case and sustaining minimum wage legislation. Intellectual responsibility should, one would suppose, save a thoughtful man from the familiar trap of *post hoc ergo propter hoc*. Even those whose business it is to study the work of the Supreme Court have lent themselves to a charge which is refuted on the face of the Court records. It is refuted, that is, if consideration is given not only to opinions but to appropriate deductions drawn from data pertaining to the time when petitions for certiorari are granted, when cases are argued, when dispositions are, in normal course, made at Conference, and when decisions are withheld because of absences and divisions on the Court.

It is time that this false charge against Roberts be dissipated by a recording of the indisputable facts. Disclosure of Court happenings not made public by the Court itself, in its opinions and orders, presents a ticklish problem. The secrecy that envelops the Court's work is not due to love of secrecy or want of responsible regard for the claims of a democratic society to know how it is governed. That the Supreme Court should not be amenable to the forces of publicity to which the Executive and the Congress are subjected is essential to the effective functioning of the Court. But the passage of time may enervate the reasons for this restriction, particularly if disclosure rests not on tittle-tattle or self-serving declarations. The more so is justification for thus lifting the veil of secrecy valid if thereby the conduct of a Justice whose intellectual morality has been impugned is vindicated.

The truth about the so-called "switch" of Roberts in connection with the *Minimum Wage* cases is that when the *Tipaldo* case was before the Court in the spring of 1936, he was prepared to overrule the *Adkins* decision. Since a majority could not be had for overruling it, he silently agreed with the Court in finding the New York statute under attack in the *Tipaldo* case not distinguishable from the statute which had been declared unconstitutional in the *Adkins* case. That such was his position an alert reader could find in the interstices of the United States Reports. It took not a little persuasion—so indifferent was Roberts to misrepresentation—to induce him to set forth what can be extracted from the Reports.[1] Here it is:

"A petition for certiorari was filed in *Morehead* v. *Tipaldo*, 298 U.S. 587, on March 16, 1936. When the petition came to be acted upon, the Chief Justice spoke in favor of a grant, but several others spoke against it on the ground that the case was ruled by *Adkins* vs. *Children's Hospital*, 261 U.S. 525. Justices Brandeis, Cardozo and Stone were in favor of a grant. They, with the Chief Justice, made up four votes for a grant.

"When my turn came to speak I said I saw no reason to grant the writ unless the Court were prepared to re-examine and overrule the *Adkins* case. To this remark there was no response around the table, and the case was marked granted.

"Both in the petition for certiorari, in the brief on the merits, and in oral argument, counsel for the State of New York took the position that it was unnecessary to overrule the *Adkins* case in order to sustain the position of the State of New York. It was urged that further data and experience and additional facts distinguished the case at bar from the *Adkins* case. The argument seemed to me to be disingenuous and born of timidity. I could find nothing in the record to substantiate the alleged distinction. At conference I so stated, and stated further that I was for taking the State of New York at its word. The State had not asked that the *Adkins* case be overruled but that it be distinguished. I said I was unwilling to put a decision on any such ground. The vote was five to four for affirmance and the case was assigned to Justice Butler.

"I stated to him that I would concur in any opinion which was based on the fact that the State had not asked us to re-examine or overrule *Adkins* and that, as we found no material difference in the facts of the two cases, we should therefore follow the *Adkins* case. The case was originally so written by Justice Butler, but after a dissent had been circulated he added matter to his opinion, seeking to sustain the *Adkins* case in principle. My proper course would have been to concur specially on the narrow ground I had taken. I did not do so. But at conference in the Court I said that I did not propose to review and re-examine the *Adkins* case until a case should come to the Court requiring that this should be done.

"August 17, 1936, an appeal was filed in *West Coast Hotels* [*sic*] *Company* vs. *Parrish*, 300 U.S. 379. The Court as usual met to consider applications in the week of Monday, October 5, 1936, and concluded its work by Saturday, October 10. During the conferences the jurisdictional statement in the *Parrish* case was considered and the question arose whether the appeal should be dismissed [Evidently he meant, should be reversed summarily, since the Washington Supreme Court had sustained the statute.] on the authority of *Adkins* and *Morehead*. Four of those who had voted in the majority in the *Morehead* case voted to dismiss the appeal in the *Parrish* case. I stated that I would vote for the notation of probable jurisdiction. I am not sure that I gave my reason, but it was that in the appeal in the *Parrish* case the authority of *Adkins* was definitely assailed and the Court was asked to reconsider and overrule it. Thus, for the first time, I was confronted with the necessity of facing the soundness of the *Adkins* case. Those who were in the majority in the *Morehead* case expressed some surprise at my vote, and I heard one of the brethren ask another, 'What is the matter with Roberts?'

"Justice Stone was taken ill about October 14. The case was argued December 16 and 17, 1936, in the absence of Justice Stone, who at that time was lying in a comatose condition at his home. It came on for consideration at the conference on December 19. I voted for an affirmance. There were three other such votes, those of the Chief Justice, Justice Brandeis, and Justice Cardozo. The other four voted for a reversal.

"If a decision had then been announced, the case would have been affirmed by a divided Court. It was thought that this would be an unfortunate outcome, as everyone on the Court knew Justice Stone's views. The case was, therefore, laid over for further consideration when Justice Stone should be able to participate. Justice Stone was convalescent during January and returned to the sessions of the Court on February 1, 1937. I believe that the *Parrish* case was taken up at the conference on February 6, 1937, and Justice Stone then voted for affirmance. This made it possible to assign the case for an opinion, which was done. The decision affirming the lower court was announced March 29, 1937.

"These facts make it evident that no action taken by the President in the interim had any causal relation to my action in the *Parrish* case."

More needs to be said for Roberts than he cared to say for himself. As a matter of history it is regrettable that Robert's unconcern for his own record led him to abstain from stating his position. The occasions are not infrequent when the disfavor of separate opinions, on the part of the bar and to the extent that it prevails within the Court, should not be heeded. Such a situation was certainly presented when special circumstances made Roberts agree with a result but basically disagree with the opinion which announced it.

The crucial factor in the whole episode was the absence of Mr. Justice Stone from the bench, on account of illness, from October 14, 1936, to February 1, 1937, 299 U.S. III.

In *Chamberlain* v. *Andrews* and its allied cases, decided November 23, 1936, the judgments of the New York Court of Appeals sustaining the New York Unemployment Insurance law were "affirmed by an equally divided Court." 299 U.S. 515. The constitutional outlook represented by these cases would reflect the attitude of a Justice towards the issues involved in the *Adkins* case. It can hardly be doubted that Van Devanter, McReynolds, Sutherland and Butler, JJ. were the four Justices for reversal in *Chamberlain* v. *Andrews, supra*. There can be equally no doubt that Hughes, C.J., and Brandeis and Cardozo, JJ. were for affirmance. Since Stone, J. was absent, it must have been Roberts who joined Hughes, Brandeis and Cardozo. The appellants petitioned for a rehearing before the full bench, but since the position of Stone, as disclosed by his views in the *Tipaldo* case, would not have changed the result, *i.e.*, affirmance, the judgments were allowed to stand and the petition for rehearing was denied. Moreover, in preceding Terms, Roberts had abundantly established that he did not have the narrow, restrictive attitude in the application of the broad, undefined provisions of the Constitution which led to decisions that provoked the acute controversies in 1936 and 1937.

Indeed, years before the 1936 election, in the 1933 Term he was the author of the opinion in *Nebbia* v. *New York*, 291 U.S. 502, which evoked substantially the same opposing constitutional philosophy from Van Devanter, McReynolds, Sutherland and Butler, JJ., as their dissent expressed in *West Coast Hotel Co.* v. *Parrish, supra*. The result in the *Nebbia* case was significant enough. But for candor and courage, the opinion in which Roberts justified it was surely one of the most important contributions in years in what is perhaps the most far-reaching field of constitutional adjudication. It was an effective blow for liberation from empty tags and meretricious assumptions. In effect, Roberts wrote the epitaph on the misconception, which had gained respect from repetition, that legislative price-fixing as such was at least presumptively unconstitutional. In his opinion in *Parrish*, the Chief Justice naturally relied heavily on Roberts's opinion in *Nebbia*, for the reasoning of *Nebbia* had undermined the foundations of *Adkins*.

Few speculations are more treacherous than diagnosis of motives or genetic explanations of the position taken by Justices in Supreme Court decisions. Seldom can attribution have been wider of the mark than to find in Roberts's views in this or that case a reflection of economic predilection. He was, to be sure, as all men are, a child of his antecedents. But his antecedents united with his temperament to make him a forthright, democratic, perhaps even somewhat innocently trusting, generous, humane creature. Long before it became popular to regard every so-called civil liberties question as constitutionally self-answering, Roberts gave powerful utterance to his sensitiveness for those procedural safeguards which are protective of human rights in a civilized society, even when invoked by the least appealing of characters. See his opinions in *Sorrells* v. *United States*, 287 U.S. 435, 453, and *Snyder* v. *Massachusetts*, 291 U.S. 97, 123.

Owen J. Roberts contributed his good and honest share to that coral-reef fabric which is law. He was content to let history ascertain, if it would, what his share was. But only one who had the good fortune to work for years beside him, day by day, is enabled to say that no man ever served on the Supreme Court with more scrupulous regard for its moral demands than Mr. Justice Roberts.

FOOTNOTE

[1] Mr. Justice Roberts gave me this memorandum on November 9, 1945, after he had resigned from the bench. He left the occasion for using it to my discretion. For reasons indicated in the text, the present seems to me an appropriate time for making it public.

THREE

THE CONTEMPORARY SUPREME COURT

☆☆☆ Roles for the New Constitutionalism

EARL WARREN

A Sketch of the Supreme Court

Earl Warren, the present Chief Justice of the Court, had a successful career as a prosecutor, administrator and political leader before coming to the Court in 1953 as President Eisenhower's first appointee. Warren had been District Attorney of Alameda County (Oakland), California; Attorney General of California from 1938–1942; and Governor for three successive terms, 1942–1953. In the 1948 presidential election, he was Thomas Dewey's running mate on the Republican ticket. Most of Chief Justice Warren's speeches have been on state occasions and ceremonial functions at which he represents the Federal Judiciary. On one such occasion, his speeches to the American Law Institute each year, describing the past Term of the Supreme Court and the state of the federal judicial system in general, he has made interesting reportive comments about changes in the Court's rules and the state of the Court's docket. In this speech describing the basic place of the Supreme Court in the American constitutional framework, Chief Justice Warren addressed the judges of the Supreme Court of Civil and Criminal

Judicature, at Karlsruhe, Germany, on August 25th, during a trip the
Chief Justice made to Europe in 1959.

SOURCE: "Address," Karlsruhe, Germany, August 25, 1959.

The more I explore other systems of free government
o   o   o   the more I am convinced that there is no perfect
system; that forms of successful government are not copied, but grow
according to the spirit of the people who live under them, and that that
spirit springs inevitably from the history, traditions and experience of
the people themselves. There are today, as we all know, constitutions
drafted in the most eloquent and inspirational language that are not
worth the paper they are written on, because there is no spirit to make
the words meaningful. When I reflect on this subject, invariably there
comes to my mind the lines of the English poet, Alexander Pope, who
in his *Essay on Man* said:

> "For forms of government let fools contest;
> Whate'er is best administered is best."

We realize in America that while we revere our Constitution it was
not Godgiven to us alone. Few procedures, and no principles on
which it is premised, sprang full grown from the minds of our Founding Fathers, as did Minerva from the brain of Jupiter. It was an adaptation to our particular situation of universal principles that had developed throughout civilization. The drafters of our Constitution sat
for four hot summer months in an effort to reconcile economic differences, geographic problems, social customs and governmental concepts. They brought out a charter of government that was unlike
anything that had theretofore been devised; yet it contained principles
of representation and freedom that had evolved through the centuries.

You have asked me to speak to you on the position of our Supreme
Court in the American system.

I believe I should start by saying that it is unlike the highest court
of any other nation. The differences are not to be found necessarily
in ideologies, nor in juridical approach, nor even in results achieved.
They are to be found in the governmental structure, in the separation

of powers, in the division of functions between the national government and the states, and in the relations of our citizens to both governments. All of these relationships are different from those in other nations that pursue, as we do, the ideal of liberty under law. They developed out of our own experiences.

It must be remembered that when our Constitution was adopted we had not enjoyed a long existence as a Nation. Before 1776, when our Declaration of Independence was proclaimed, there was no cohesion between all the colonies and very little active cooperation between any of them. They were thirteen little English-owned colonies, scattered for a thousand miles along the Atlantic Coast, ruled by the Royal Governors from across the ocean who were arrogant, and in many instances oppressive. Some of the colonies were large by their standards while others were very small. Some were fairly affluent, others poor. Some were strictly agricultural, others commercial. Some claimed vast, uninhabited territory to the west, while others were definitely circumscribed as to size. They had fought together for freedom without any pattern of government. Each colony considered itself sovereign.

In 1781, the Articles of Confederation brought them together as an extremely loose Federation, but it soon became evident that the Federation could not command respect, either at home or abroad. There was grave danger of the entire structure falling and of the colonies becoming permanently isolated through the machinations of foreign governments. There was a general recognition that the situation should be strengthened, but in what manner and to what extent was a matter of sharp disagreement. Some wanted a strong national government, others only sufficient strength in the Federation to carry on as a Nation leaving the States in a sovereign capacity. Suspicion was rampant and animosities were common.

It was in this kind of atmosphere that the Constitutional Convention met in Philadelphia on May 17, 1787. It labored throughout the summer in secrecy, resolving differences, compromising and generalizing to avoid disruption. On September 16th, they emerged from their hall with a document of only 5000 words establishing the Government of the United States. It is said that as the delegates filed out a woman in the crowd, anxiously awaiting the results of the Convention, said to the venerable Benjamin Franklin, "Doctor Franklin, what kind of a government have you given us?" His answer was, "A Republic, Madame, if you can keep it."

One hundred and seventy-two years later, we are still working to keep it, adjusting differences, reconciling conflicting theories, and giving proper weight to divergent principles. In this phase of our Government, our Courts, of course, play a dominant part.

I shall not enter into a discussion of our Constitution other than to say that it provides for a federal government of delegated powers, reserving to the States and to the people all undelegated powers. As was not uncommon in the Constitutional Convention, when the situation became tense and threatened dissolution, the matter at hand was resolved in the most general of terms. And so it was with the Federal Judiciary. There were those who wanted no hierarchy of federal courts, who believed that the State courts would be sufficient for all purposes and there were those who were convinced that federal courts were essential to the preservation of the Constitution. The issue was resolved in this simple language:

"The judicial Power of the United States, shall be vested in one supreme Court, and in such inferior Courts as the Congress may from time to time ordain and establish. The Judges, both of the supreme and inferior Courts, shall hold their Offices during good Behaviour, and shall, at stated Times, receive for their Services, a Compensation, which shall not be diminished during their Continuance in Office."

It then provides:

"The judicial Power shall extend to all Cases, in Law and Equity, arising under this Constitution, the Laws of the United States, and Treaties made, or which shall be made, under their Authority;" etc.

Thereafter it enumerates the limited kind of cases in which the Supreme Court has original jurisdiction, and concludes:

"In all the other Cases before mentioned, the supreme Court shall have appellate Jurisdiction, both as to Law and Fact, with such Exceptions, and under such Regulations as the Congress shall make."

Thus it will be seen that the Constitution directly provided for only one court—the Supreme Court—and it with only limited original jurisdiction, i.e.; "to all Cases affecting Ambassadors, other public Ministers and Consuls," and those in which a state shall be Party. In this manner, the Constitutional Convention left it to the future and to the Congress to determine whether there would even be a federal system of lower Courts or whether all justiciable matters would be decided by the State courts, which were left in existence, subject only to such review as might later be prescribed, in the Supreme Court of the United States.

But Congress did not long delay. In its first session after ratification of the Constitution, it passed the Judiciary Act of 1789 in which it established a complete set of Federal Courts, fixed their original and appellate jurisdictions including the appellate jurisdiction of the Supreme Court. The debate in Congress concerning this act was almost as prolonged as that for the adoption of the Constitution itself. It has been acclaimed as one of the most outstanding pieces of legislation in our history. It, of course, developed some weaknesses as the country grew, but these have been rectified and it is still the basis of our federal court structure. It established a District Court in each State as the federal trial court. That court has jurisdiction over all cases in which the United States Government is a party. This now represents about one-third of all cases filed. It also has jurisdiction over civil cases between private parties which involve:

(1) federal questions covering all cases in law and equity arising under the Constitutional laws and treaties of the United States;

(2) diversity of citizenship; and

(3) admiralty.

As now developed, our appellate structure presently consists of eleven courts of appeals, which with some exceptions have appellate jurisdiction over all final judgments of the District Courts. In most of such appeals it becomes the court of last resort, because it is only through its supervisory power to insure that a fair proceeding has been had by the parties or where an important federal right has been allegedly infringed or where there has been a conflict between the circuits that the Supreme Court will review their judgments.

The Supreme Court consists of nine Justices—the Chief Justice of the United States and eight Associate Justices. The Court sits at

Washington, D.C., and has but one court term each year, commencing on the first Monday of October and continuing until all cases ready for decision have been heard and decided. The adjournment date in recent years has been approximately July 1st. During its last term the Court disposed of 1,761 cases which came from the following sources:

United States Courts of Appeals...................... 896
United States District Courts........................ 39
Special Federal Courts............................... 34
State Courts... 792

The state cases come to the Supreme Court only from a final judgment of the highest available court in the state, and then only when a federal claim has been raised and decided by that court. It might be of some interest to you to know that in all the State courts 1,250,000 civil cases and 312,000 criminal cases were filed last year in the courts of general jurisdiction. As I stated a moment ago, only seven hundred and ninety-two of this number reached the Supreme Court of the United States, and of this number only seventeen were reversed.

It may interest you to know how the Supreme Court, sitting always as a body, can dispose of 1,761 cases in nine months. It has not always been so. In 1925 the Court was very much behind in its work, but in that year the Congress provided for review through a statutory writ of certiorari which gave to the Supreme Court the right in all cases except direct appeals to deny the issuance of the writ summarily where the decision below is obviously correct, or where the question was not properly raised below, or where it is not of public importance or where for any reason the question is not ripe for decision.

Many appeals and petitions for writs of certiorari border on the frivolous and it would be a complete waste of time to hear them. Many of them raise a point that is not of general importance. In still others the petitioner might not have raised the federal question in the court below so as to enable it to pass upon the question, and lastly the court below might have rested its decision on an adequate state ground that obviates the necessity of reaching the federal question.

In all such cases the Supreme Court on the written petition for certiorari and the written response which are available to all the Justices, deny the petition without hearing argument, and without writing an opinion. The denial of the writ leaves the decision of the lower court in effect, but it has no other legal significance. It is not an affirmance of the judgment and does not mean that the Supreme Court necessarily agrees with it.

This is the fate of all but approximately one hundred and fifty cases each term. These are argued and usually result in a full legal opinion on the merits of the litigation. Perhaps half of these cases will be reversed, so at most not more than fifty cases of either federal or state courts suffer reversal in a year. Most of these are reversed because of ultra vires actions of public officials, misinterpretation of Federal laws or denial of due process, thus reducing the number of statutes, federal and state, which are declared unconstitutional to a minimum. In fact there have been fewer than eighty federal laws declared to be unconstitutional in the history of the nation. The right of judicial review is not mentioned in our Constitution, but it was a recognized principle in State judicial systems when John Marshall in the famous case of Marbury vs. Madison held that to decide between the Constitution and a law, when they conflict, is the very essence of judicial duty. Since that time it has become deeply imbedded in American law, but it still stirs up more emotion than any other judicial act. . . .

We are eternally grateful to those who drafted our Constitution, and whom we affectionally call the Founding Fathers. They gave us the charter of our freedom, the anchor of which is an independent judiciary as one of the three coordinate branches of our government. To those of us who sit on the courts of our nation, they left a daily challenge to protect and preserve that freedom in trust for those who are to follow us.

We are endeavoring to measure up to that challenge. . . .

WILLIAM J. BRENNAN, JR.

Fundamentals of Judicial Review

Judicial review of legislation by the Supreme Court in its basic elements is as old as *Marbury* v. *Madison* in 1803 and its unofficial precursors even earlier. Yet the way in which the Supreme Court conceives its power and scope of review has varied greatly from era to era. Today the Court operates in a climate of legal realism and sociological jurisprudence, with vast regulatory functions undertaken by government, and at a time of sharp tensions involving the status of minority groups and the liberty of radical dissenters from the American consensus. Justice Brennan sketched the role of judicial review in this contemporary context in an address to the Student Legal Forum at the University of Virginia Law School on February 17, 1959. Brennan, a Democrat appointed to the Court by President Eisenhower in 1956, is a Harvard Law School graduate who practiced trial and labor law in Newark, New Jersey. In 1949 a Republican governor appointed him to the New Jersey Superior Court and another Republican appointment placed him on the state Supreme Court in 1952. Within the Supreme Court of the United States, Brennan has become part of a liberal "bloc of four," including Justices Hugo Black and William O. Douglas and Chief Justice Earl Warren.

SOURCE: Manuscript copy of "Remarks," from Justice William J. Brennan, Jr., dated "1959."

I'm going to talk about the duty of the Court to declare in proper cases the unconstitutionality of federal and state laws or other governmental actions. This function goes by the name of judicial review. This seems to me to be an imprecise label since one might suppose that all of the Court's work comes under such a heading. However, it's the commonly used label for my subject and I'll use it tonight. The highest courts of the States, in passing on state action, also have this duty, of course, not only in applying the State Constitutions but also the Federal Constitution. Indeed, this role of the state courts, in its relation to State Constitutions, had become established before the Framers of the Federal Constitution provided for a National Supreme Court.

Let us first get the function in proper perspective in terms of the Court's work. The simple truth is that among the cases the Court decides each year the number which require any consideration at all of asserted challenges to the constitutional validity of federal or state laws or actions is very small, and the number of actual constitutional decisions still smaller. The major grist of the Court deals, as it invariably has dealt, with the construction of statutes enacted by the Congress. In cases coming to the Court there are few which do not involve a federal statute, obliquely if not directly. The Court, of course, does not construe state statutes. That is the function of the particular State's courts and the Court applies constitutional principles in light of the interpretation given a State's statute by its courts.

But the determinations of what Congress has meant by what it has said in a federal statute is the task of the federal courts. The job of finding that meaning is very often not an easy one, for the words used generally lend themselves to different meanings in the settings in which the statutes are applied. Even by resort to extrinsic aids to meaning—committee reports and congressional debates—the issue will frequently remain in doubt. Did Congress mean that an accused who wounded two federal officers with a single shot from a shotgun should be held to have violated once, or twice, the criminal statute constituting an assault upon a federal officer a crime? When Congress made it an antitrust violation for one corporation to acquire the stock of another corporation in certain circumstances, did the violation arise only upon the acquisition of the stock of a competing corporation or also when the acquisition is by a supplier corporation of the stock of a customer corporation? But difficult as the determination of meaning may be, a decision as to that meaning must be made by the Court, and always is. When Congress disagrees, the law is amended and the congressional meaning is clarified. This happens all the time as, of course, it should. I dare say the extent that Congress uses and has always used the amending process to revise judicial interpretations of its enactments is not fully appreciated. This has been a healthy interplay between the courts and the Congress in the areas of law-making which are the exclusive province of the Legislative Branch.

There is another area where there are constitutional overtones but where the amending process also operates. This is the area in which both Congress and the States have legislated on the same subject matter. A decision may be required whether the federal law has occupied the field in such manner that the Supremacy Clause of the Constitution requires a decision that the federal law foreclosed state action. When the Court's holding is that the federal law displaced state law on the same subject, if the Court misconceived the congressional purpose, the amending process can correct the error.

Let me now return to judicial review. How did that become a duty of the Supreme Court? The Constitution makes no reference to such a duty. Yet, certainly since Chief Justice Marshall's holding in *Marbury* v. *Madison* that, "It is emphatically the province and duty of the Judicial Department to say what the law is," the Court and the Country have accepted this role of the Court as a permanent and indispensable feature of our constitutional system. Did Marshall invent the concept? Professor Dietze, in his interesting article in last December's issue of the Virginia Law Review, says that "Judicial review seems to be vital for the protection of the individual's liberty in a democratic society" and naturally grew up in an American society imbued with "A desire to make the individual free from governmental oppression," to guarantee the individual's "Liberty under the law, his liberty from the law maker." Perhaps it comes to the same thing but judicial review was at all events an inevitable concomitant of the unique structure of our very special form of democratic government. We all know the history of the unending struggle between governments and people over where the power of rulers ends and where the freedom of the individual begins. The Founders of this Nation had this problem very much in mind when they wrote our Constitution and Bill of Rights. Their answer was to build in a way which would avoid concentration of the powers of government. They created a federalism by diffusing governmental power between two sets of sovereignties, national and state, prescribing limited powers for the National Government, and imposing restrictions applicable to both sovereignties and designed to prevent oppression of the individual.

None of the Founders, however, was so optimistic as to think that these paper delineations of power would be a sure and certain guarantee against all attempted abuse of governmental power. They were practical as well as wise men and we impugn their craftsmanship if we assume that they were unaware of the inevitability of conflicts among the departments within the National Government, between the National Government and the States, and between the individual and both Governments. Of course they knew that difficult problems of what belonged to which sovereignty, and how far either might interfere with the liberty of the citizen, would arise. There isn't a foot of ground in this vast Country, excepting only federal enclaves and the District of Columbia, and in some aspects, navigable waters, which does not experience the interplay of political authority in which two Governments are simultaneously operating, the State Government and the Federal Government. Such are the limitations of the human mind, of human imagination, that no genius of constitution-making could have delineated the precise boundaries of the powers assigned the several repositories of governmental power. Nor in the nature of things could the Framers have fashioned guide lines for the resolution of the myriad collisions between power exercised by any of these repositories, and the guarantees of individual liberty erected to restrain governmental oppression whatever its source.

It is obvious that somebody had to be provided to referee these conflicts and the evidence points to the Framers' choice of the Supreme Court to perform the duty. The Articles of Confederation had failed for lack of a federal judiciary to make final decisions on questions arising between the States, and between the States and National Government. Hamilton said: "A circumstance which crowns the defects of the Confederation . . . [is] the want of a judiciary power.

Laws are a dead letter without courts to expound and define their true meaning and operation. . . . To avoid the confusion which would unavoidably result from the contradictory decisions of a number of independent judicatories, all nations have found it necessary to establish one court paramount to the rest, possessing a general superintendence and authorized to settle and declare in the last resort a uniform rule of justice."

Also the 50-odd delegates to the Constitutional Convention well knew that state judges were holding state laws void. Actually two widely publicized instances of the exercise of this power by a state court occurred during the Convention. Moreover statements of delegates during the proceedings express this understanding. For example, Luther Martin of Maryland opposed the proposal to associate the federal judges with the President in a power to veto laws of Congress, because he said: "As to constitutionality of laws, that point will come before the judges in their proper official character. In this character, they have a negative on the laws. Join them with the Executive in the revision and they will have a double negative." So he reported to the Maryland Legislature: "Whether, therefore, any laws or regulations of the Congress, any acts of its President or other officers, are contrary to, or not warranted by the Constitution, rests only with the judges . . . to determine, by whose determination every State must be bound."

Hamilton, in The Federalist, speaking of Acts of Congress, wrote that the federal courts were intended to be "An intermediary body between the people and the legislature in order, among other things, to keep the latter within the limits assigned to their authority." And declared that the restraints imposed by the Constitution on Congress "Can be preserved in practice no other way than through the medium of courts of justice whose duty it must be to declare all Acts contrary to the manifest tenor of the Constitution void. Without this all the reservations of particular rights and privileges would amount to nothing."

Finally Madison, in 1831, was to say "a supremacy of the Constitution and Laws of the Union, without a supremacy in the exposition and execution of them, would be as much a mockery as a scabbard put into the hand of a soldier without a sword in it. I have never been able to see, that without such a view of the subject the Constitution itself would be the supreme law of the land; or that the uniformity of the federal authority throughout the parties to it could be preserved; or that without this uniformity anarchy and disunion would be prevented."

But I need not labor the obvious. You learned all this in grade school. From our beginning it has been the Supreme Court's duty to resolve issues between the Nation and the States, between the States themselves, and between individuals and governmental power, federal or state.

The function is performed without distinct guide lines in the Constitution. Some of the boundaries between national and state power are marked by only general language. Congress has power to "regulate commerce with foreign nations and among the several States." What is commerce? Is the power of Congress exclusive, or do the States have residual powers, at least until the Congress has acted? Congress has power "to provide for the punishment of counterfeiting the securities and current coin of the United States." May a State also make the passage of counterfeit coin within its borders an offense against the States' laws? And what about the prohibition that a State shall pass no "law impairing the obligation of contracts." What is a contract for this purpose? Does it include a grant or charter? What sort of action constitutes an impairment? And the guarantees of the individual in the Bill of Rights, if marked by language perhaps as precise as could have been used, are yet in language not wholly precise at that. The First Amendment says that "Congress shall make no law . . . abridging the freedom of speech or of the press." Congress enacted a law against use of the mails to distribute obscene matter. Obscenity is a form of speech. Does the First Amendment require the nullification of that law or is the language of the Amendment less prohibitive than its words imply? A federal officer is assaulted in the performance of his duty in a particular State. Although the assault is a crime against both sovereigns, is the Double Jeopardy Clause of the Fifth Amendment violated by successive state and federal prosecutions?

However, we know that the choice of general language was deliberate on the part of the Framers. They were wise men, as I have said, and were formulating a Constitution designed for the undefined and illimitable future. They wrote in broad outline so that the future would not be foreclosed, so that the past would not too much govern the future.

So it is that the economic and social conflicts of our history result in litigation which comes ultimately to the Court for final resolution. Over a century and a quarter ago De Tocqueville perceived what seemingly has escaped many later writers, namely, that by the very nature of our Constitution practically every political question in time comes to the Court in the guise of a judicial question. Still our history has been that many a controversy that elsewhere is settled by the conquest of arms, is, eventually anyhow, settled by force of reason.

The change in the distribution of governmental power effected by the Amendments which followed the end of our internal conflict in 1865 have had a profound bearing on the Court's duty to exercise this function. Limitations upon state powers then imposed had not theretofore existed. In consequence every enactment of every State, every action by the Governor of a State, any governmental act of any of the 49 States may be challenged at the Bar of the Court on the ground that such action, such legislation, is a deprivation of liberty without due process of law or denies the equal protection of the laws. What is "due," what is "equal," present questions among the most difficult and the most challenging to come before the Court. The constitutions of other federal governments do not include these standards for testing the constitutionality of the laws of the constituent States. These prohibitions are not to be found for example in the Constitutions of India, Canada or Australia. In the case of India their omission was the result of an express recommendation against their inclusion.

The complexity and range of constitutional issues before the Court changes to reflect the times. The Court's work is actually a mirror of the battles of forces going on outside the Court. You will remember that Mr. Justice Holmes sat for 20 years on the Massachusetts court before coming to the Supreme Court. That was in 1902. Shortly afterwards he alluded in a letter to his friend Sir Frederick Pollock to the contrast between his new work and his old. He said:

"Yes—here I am—and more absorbed, interested and impressed than ever I dreamed I might be. The work of the past is a finished book—locked up far away, and a new and solemn volume opens.

The variety and novelty to me of the questions, the remote spaces from which they come, the amount of work they require, all help the effect. I have written on the constitutionality of part of the Constitution of California, on the power of the Railroad Commissioner of Arkansas, on the question whether a law of Wisconsin impairs the obligation of the plaintiff's contract. I have to consider a question between a grant of the United States in aid of a military road and an Indian reservation on the Pacific Coast. I have heard conflicting mining claims in Arizona and whether a granite quarry is 'minerals' within an exception in railway grant, and fifty other things as remote from each other as these."

I find I share that experience since coming to the Court almost three years ago after eight years on New Jersey courts. But today's problems are more often raised by governmental action, state or federal, alleged to impair individual liberties than by governmental regulation of business, or by conflicts between state and federal regulations of business. When I wrote last year on the constitutionality of a provision of the Constitution of California, for example, the citizen was resting his claim of unconstitutionality upon an alleged violation of rights of freedom of speech secured to him by the First Amendment as applied to the States through the Fourteenth.

Now, what of the road by which a constitutional question gets to the Court? Is the way made easy or difficult? Does the Court keep the door open and the welcome mat out? To the disappointment of many, . . . parties desiring a constitutional decision from the Court are often denied one. The Court long ago developed principles under which constitutional decisions are made only when they are unavoidable. Since the Court is master in its own household, and its business is only what it allows to come to it, the Court first of all must agree to hear the case which raises the constitutional question. As you know, unless four members of the Court vote to grant certiorari, or, if it is an appeal, to note the appeal, the parties have no opportunity orally to argue and brief the question and the Court no occasion to prepare an opinion deciding it. We actually take something less than 7 or 8 percent of the cases we are asked to hear each year. Many which urge a constitutional question are not heard for a variety of reasons. Some may be cases in which the petitioner or appellant had no standing to raise the constitutional question. Some may be cases in which there was a failure to exhaust available administrative remedies. Some may be cases in which there was a failure properly to raise the constitutional question in the lower courts. Others may be state cases which have been decided on adequate state grounds supporting the result independently of the constitutional grounds. However substantial the constitutional question, the Court does not take and decide cases falling into any of those classes. And even among those taken and argued, decision of the constitutional question is not made if a nonconstitutional ground of decision is possible. This is particularly true where a federal statute is involved and the decision can turn on construction, even a strained construction, which avoids decision of the constitutional question. Or it may develop after argument of a state case, that there in fact exists an adequate state ground to support the state court's decision, although at the time of consideration of the petition for certiorari or appeal this was not apparent, or was debatable.

I thus conclude this obviously sketchy discussion of a duty, because of which, as my Brother Frankfurter said at this law school six years ago, "there ultimately rests [on this Court] the maintenance of the equilibrium between central authority and the constituent States, between the authority of government, whether state or national, and the liberties of the individual." Since it is a function of maintaining that equilibrium, perforce the Court rarely proceeds with the duty except in the midst of tensions. But the responsibility has always been faced when it should be faced and will, I know, continue to be. As one observer recently remarked "the Supreme Court does not sit to count votes. It is not its function to carry out the will of the majority. It is a fundamental basis of our governmental system that there are many things which a majority cannot do, and that there are many things on which the people of a State must yield to the greater national interest, as expressed in the Constitution. The Court interprets and applies the Constitution."

FELIX FRANKFURTER

The Process of Judging in Constitutional Cases

When Justice Frankfurter delivered this paper at the annual meeting of the American Philosophical Society, in Philadelphia, on April 22, 1954, he had been on the Supreme Court for fifteen years and had served with four Chief Justices and fifteen Associate Justices. Frankfurter—a close student and prolific writer about the Court's history, traditions, work, and values as a professor of law at Harvard before his appointment in 1938 —had as one of his major themes as a Justice that the making of wise constitutional law is too subtle a process to be imprisoned in new labels and formulas. Here, Frankfurter offers a statement about the creative role of the Justice and the relation of his judicial decisions to his economic and social values.

SOURCE: 98 *Proceedings of the American Philosophical Society* 233 (1954).

Those who know tell me that the most illuminating light on painting has been furnished by painters, and that the deepest revelations on the writing of poetry have come from poets. It is not so with the business of judging. The power of searching analysis of what it is that they are doing seems rarely to be possessed by judges, either because they are lacking in the art of critical exposition or because they are inhibited from practicing it. The fact is that pitifully little of significance has been contributed by judges regarding the nature of their endeavor, and, I might add, that which is written by those who are not judges is too often a confident caricature rather than a seer's vision of the judicial process of the Supreme Court.

We have, of course, one brave and felicitous attempt—Mr. Justice Cardozo's little classic. I have read and reread, and reread very recently, that charming book and yield to no one in my esteem for it. And yet you must not account it as immodesty or fractiousness if I say that the book would give me very little help in deciding any of the difficult cases that come before the Court. Why should a book about the judicial process by one of the great judges of our time shed relatively little light on the actual adjudicatory process of the Supreme Court? For the simple reason that *The Nature of the Judicial Process* derived from Cardozo's reflections while in Albany, before he came to Washington. The judicial business out of which Cardozo's experience came when he wrote the book was the business of the New York Court of Appeals, and that is very different business from the most important aspects of the litigation on which the Supreme Court must pass.

Let me indulge in one of the rare opportunities for the valid use of statistics in connection with the work of the Supreme Court. The reports of the New York decisions for the year during which Judge Cardozo delivered the lectures which comprise his book show that only about one out of a hundred cases before the New York Court of Appeals raised questions comparable to those that gave him most trouble in Washington. The year that he left Albany for Washington, 1932, only two opinions out of a hundred in the New York Reports raise the kind of questions that are the greatest concern for the Supreme Court. Cardozo wrote something like five hundred opinions on the New York Court of Appeals. In them he was concerned with matters that would not have been foreign, say, to Lord Mansfield or Lord Ellenborough, and would have been quite familiar to Cardozo's contemporaries on the English Supreme Court of Judicature.

After Cardozo came to Washington, he wrote 128 opinions for the Court during the tragically short period that fate allowed him there. He wrote twenty-one dissents. Of these 149 opinions only ten dealt with matters comparable to those which came before him while on the New York Court of Appeals. No one was more keenly aware than he of the differences between the two streams of litigation; no one more keenly alive than he to the resulting differences in the nature of the judicial process in which the two courts were engaged. Let me quickly add that such were the genius and the learning and, perhaps most important of all, the priestlike disinterestedness of his mind, that, even during his few brief years as a Justice, Cardozo became an outstanding contributor to the history of Supreme Court adjudication. What is relevant to our immediate purpose is realization of the important fact that the problems dealt with in Cardozo's illuminating little book, and in two other little books which played on the same theme, derive from an experience in the raw materials of the adjudicatory process very different from those that are the most anxious concern of the Supreme Court of the United States.

It is time for me to be explicit. I am advised by an arithmetically minded scholar that the Constitution of the United States is composed of some 6,000 words. Not every provision of that document that becomes controversial can come before the Supreme Court for adjudication. The questions that are not meet for judicial determination have elicited their own body of literature. A hint of the nature of such questions is given by their fair characterization as an exercise of judicial self-limitation. This area constitutes one very important and very troublesome aspect of the Court's functioning—its duty not to decide.

Putting to one side instances of this judicial self-restraint, De Tocqueville showed his characteristic discernment when he wrote: "Scarcely any political question arises in the United States that is not resolved sooner or later into a judicial question." (1 *Democracy in America* [Bradley ed., 1948], p. 280.) Those provisions of the Constitution that do raise justiciable issues vary in their incidence from time to time. The construction of all of them, however, is related to the circumambient condition of our Constitution—that our nation is a federalism. The most exacting problems that in recent years have come before the Court have invoked two provisions expressed in a few undefined words—the clause giving Congress power to regulate commerce among the States and the Due Process Clauses of the Fifth and Fourteenth Amendments.

A federalism presupposes the distribution of governmental powers between national and local authority. Between these two authorities there is shared the power entirely possessed by a unitary state. In addition to the provisions of our Constitution making this distribution of authority between the two governments, there is also in the United States Constitution a withdrawal of power from both governments, or, at least, the exercise of governmental power is subject to limitations protective of the rights of the individual. Of the two types of constitutional provision calling for construction from case to case, the limitation in the interest of the individual presents the most delicate and most pervasive of all issues to come before the Court, for these cases involve no less a task than the accommodation by a court of the interest of an individual over against the interest of society.

Human society keeps changing. Needs emerge, first vaguely felt and unexpressed, imperceptibly gathering strength, steadily becoming more and more exigent, generating a force which, if left unheeded and denied response so as to satisfy the impulse behind it at least in part, may burst forth with an intensity that exacts more than reasonable satisfaction. Law as the response to these needs is not merely a system of logical deduction, though considerations of logic are far from irrelevant. Law presupposes sociological wisdom as well as logical unfolding. The nature of the interplay of the two has been admirably conveyed, if I may say so, by Professor Alfred North Whitehead:

"It is the first step in sociological wisdom, to recognize that the major advances in civilization are processes which all but wreck the societies in which they occur:—like unto an arrow in the hand of a child. The art of free society consists first in the maintenance of the symbolic code; and secondly in fearlessness of revision, to secure that the code serves those purposes which satisfy an enlightened reason. Those societies which cannot combine reverence to their symbols with freedom of revision, must ultimately decay either from anarchy, or from the slow atrophy of a life stifled by useless shadows." (Whitehead, *Symbolism* [1927], p. 88.)

The Due Process Clauses of our Constitution are the vehicles for giving response by law to this felt need by allowing accommodations or modifications in the rules and standards that govern the conduct of men. Obviously, therefore, due process as a concept is neither fixed nor finished.

The judgment of history on the inherently living and therefore changing applicability of due process was thus pronounced by Mr. Justice Sutherland, one of the most traditionally minded of judges:

"Regulations, the wisdom, necessity and validity of which, as applied to existing conditions, are so apparent that they are now uniformly sustained, a century ago, or even half a century ago, probably would have been rejected as arbitrary and oppressive." (*Village of Euclid* v. *Ambler Realty Co.*, 272 U.S. 365, 387.)

A more expansive attempt at indicating the viable function of the guarantee of due process was made in a recent opinion:

"The requirement of 'due process' is not a fair-weather or timid assurance. It must be respected in periods of calm and in times of trouble; it protects aliens as well as citizens. But 'due process,' unlike some legal rules, is not a technical conception with a fixed content unrelated to time, place and circumstances. Expressing as it does in its ultimate analysis respect enforced by law for that feeling of just treatment which has been evolved through centuries of Anglo-American constitutional history and civilization, 'due process' cannot be imprisoned within the treacherous limits of any formula. Representing a profound attitude of fairness between man and man, and more particularly between the individual and government, 'due process' is compounded of history, reason, the past course of decisions, and stout confidence in the strength of the democratic faith which we profess. Due process is not a mechanical instrument. It is not a yardstick. It is a process. It is a delicate process of adjustment inescapably involving the exercise of judgment by those whom the Constitution entrusted with the unfolding of the process." (*Joint Anti-Fascist Refugee Committee* v. *McGrath*, 341 U.S. 123, 162–163, concurring opinion.)

This conception of due process meets resistance from what has been called our pigeonholing minds, which seek to rest uninquiringly on formulas—phrases which, as Holmes pointed out long ago, "by their very felicity delay further analysis," and often do so for a long time. This is, of course, a form of intellectual indulgence, sometimes called the law of imitation. "[T]raditions which no longer meet their original end" must be subjected to the critique of history whereby we are enabled "to make up our minds dispassionately whether the survival which we are enforcing answers any new purpose when it has ceased to answer the old." (Holmes, *Collected Legal Papers* [1920], p. 225.)

But a merely private judgment that the time has come for a shift of opinion regarding law does not justify such a shift. Departure from an old view, particularly one that has held unquestioned sway, "must be duly mindful of the necessary demands of continuity in a civilized society. A reversal of a long current of decisions can be justified only if rooted in the Constitution itself as an historic document designed for a developing nation." (*Graves* v. *N. Y. ex rel. O'Keefe,* 306 U.S. 466, 487–488, concurring opinion.) It makes an important difference, of course, if the validity of an old doctrine on which decisions were based was always in controversy and so did not embed deeply and widely in men's feelings justifiable reliance on the doctrine as part of the accepted outlook of society. What is most important, however, is that the Constitution of the United States, except in what might be called the skeleton or framework of our society—the anatomical as against the physiological aspects,—"was designed for a developing nation." As to those features of our Constitution which raise the most frequent perplexities for decision by the Court, they were drawn in many particulars with purposeful vagueness so as to leave room for the unfolding but undisclosed future.

At this point one wishes there were time to document these generalizations with concrete instances which would help to define the problem and illustrate generalities from which the Court starts and differences of opinion which naturally enough arise in their application. Such documentation would expose divergencies by which common starting points lead to different destinations because of differences in emphasis and valuation in the process of reasoning. They would also shed some light on the interplay between language and thought. Differences in style eventually may embody differences of content, just as a sonnet may sometimes focus thought more trenchantly than a diffuse essay.

The other major source of puzzling problems is the Commerce Clause. With us the Commerce Clause is perhaps the most fruitful and important means for asserting national authority against the particularism of state policy. The role of the Court in striking the balance between the respective spheres of federal and state power was thus adumbrated by the Court:

> "The interpenetrations of modern society have not wiped out state lines. It is not for us to make inroads upon our federal system either by indifference to its maintenance or excessive regard for the unifying forces of modern technology. Scholastic reasoning may prove that no activity is isolated within the boundaries of a single State, but that cannot justify absorption of legislative power by the United States over every activity. On the other hand, the old admonition never becomes stale that this Court is concerned with the bounds of legal power and not with the bounds of wisdom in its exercise by Congress. When the conduct of an enterprise affects commerce among the States is a matter of practical judgment, not to be determined by abstract notions. The exercise of this practical judgment the Constitution entrusts primarily and very largely to the Congress, subject to the latter's control by the electorate. Great power was thus given to the Congress: the power of legislation and thereby the power of passing judgment upon the needs of a complex society. Strictly confined though far-reaching power was given to this Court: that of determining whether the Congress has exceeded limits allowable in reason for the judgment which it has exercised. To hold that Congress could not deem the activities here in question to affect what men of practical affairs would call commerce, and to deem them related to such commerce merely by gossamer threads and not by solid ties, would be to disrespect the judgment that is open to men who have the constitutional power and responsibility to legislate for the Nation."
> (*Polish National Alliance* v. *Labor Board,* 322 U.S. 643, 650–651.)

The problems which the Commerce Clause raises as a result of the diffusion of power between a national government and its constituent parts are shared in variant forms by Canada, Australia, and India. While the distribution of powers between each national government and its parts varies, leading at times to different legal results, the problems faced by the United States Supreme Court under the Commerce Clause are not different in kind, as are the problems of judicial review under the Due Process Clause, from those which come before the Supreme Court of Canada and the High Court of Australia.

Judicial judgment in these two classes of the most difficult cases must take deep account, if I may paraphrase Maitland, of the day before yesterday in order that yesterday may not paralyze today, and it must take account of what it decrees for today in order that today may not paralyze tomorrow.

A judge whose preoccupation is with such matters should be compounded of the faculties that are demanded of the historian and the philosopher and the prophet. The last demand upon him—to make some forecast of the consequences of his action—is perhaps the heaviest. To pierce the curtain of the future, to give shape and visage to mysteries still in the womb of time, is the gift of imagination. It requires poetic sensibilities with which judges are rarely endowed and which their education does not normally develop. These judges, you will infer, must have something of the creative artist in them; they must have antennae registering feeling and judgment beyond logical, let alone quantitative, proof.

The decisions in the cases that really give trouble rest on judgment, and judgment derives from the totality of a man's nature and experience. Such judgment will be exercised by two types of men, broadly speaking, but of course with varying emphasis—those who express their private views or revelations, deeming them, if not *vox dei*, at least *vox populi*; or those who feel strongly that they have no authority to promulgate law by their merely personal view and whose whole training and proved performance substantially insure that their conclusions reflect understanding of, and due regard for, law as the expression of the views and feelings that may fairly be deemed representative of the community as a continuing society.

Judges are men, not disembodied spirits. Of course a judge is not free from preferences or, if you will, biases. But he may deprive a bias of its meretricious authority by stripping it of the uncritical assumption that it is founded on compelling reason or the coercive power of a syllogism. He will be alert to detect that though a conclusion has a logical form it in fact represents a choice of competing considerations of policy, one of which for the time has won the day.

An acute historian recently concluded that those "who have any share of political power . . . usually obtain it because they are exceptionally able to emancipate their purposes from the control of their unformulated wishes and impressions." (Richard Pares, "Human Nature in Politics—III," *The Listener*, Dec. 17, 1953, p. 1037.) For judges, it is not merely a desirable capacity "to emancipate their purposes" from their private desires; it is their duty. It is a cynical belief in too many quarters, though I believe this cult of cynicism is receding, that it is at best a self-delusion for judges to profess to pursue disinterestedness. It is asked with sophomoric brightness, does a man cease to be himself when he becomes a Justice? Does he change his character by putting on a gown? No, he does not change his character. He brings his whole experience, his training, his outlook, his social, intellectual, and moral environment with him when he takes a seat on the supreme bench. But a judge worth his salt is in the grip of his function. The intellectual habits of self-discipline which govern his mind are as much a part of him as the influence of the interest he may have represented at the bar, often much more so. For example, Mr. Justice Bradley was a "corporation lawyer" par excellence when he went on the Court. But his decisions on matters affecting corporate control in the years following the Civil War were strikingly free of bias in favor of corporate power.

To assume that a lawyer who becomes a judge takes on the bench merely his views on social or economic questions leaves out of account his rooted notions regarding the scope and limits of a judge's authority. The outlook of a lawyer fit to be a Justice regarding the role of a judge cuts across all his personal preferences for this or that social arrangement. The conviction behind what John Adams wrote in the provision of the Massachusetts Declaration of Rights regarding the place of the judiciary in our governmental scheme, and the considerations which led the framers of the Constitution to give federal judges life tenure and other safeguards for their independence, have, I believe, dominated the outlook and therefore the action of the generality of men who have sat on the Supreme Court. Let me recall the Massachusetts Declaration:

"It is essential to the preservation of the rights of every individual, his life, liberty, property, and character, that there be an impartial interpretation of the laws, and administration of justice. It is the right of every citizen to be tried by judges as free, impartial, and independent as the lot of humanity will admit. . . ." (Article XXIX.)

Need it be stated that true humility and its offspring, disinterestedness, are more indispensable for the work of the Supreme Court than for a judge's function on any other bench? These qualities alone will not assure another indispensable requisite. This is the capacity for self-searching. What Jacques Maritain said in another connection applies peculiarly to members of the Supreme Court. A Justice of that Court cannot adequately discharge his function "without passing through the door of the knowing, obscure as it may be, of his own subjective." (Maritain, *Creative Intuition in Art and Poetry* [1953], p. 114.)

This is not to say that the application of this view of the judge's function—that he is there not to impose his private views upon society, that he is not to enforce personalized justice—assures unanimity of judgments. Inevitably there are bound to be fair differences of opinion. And it would be pretense to deny that in the self-righteous exercise of this role obscurantist and even unjustifiable decisions are sometimes rendered. Why should anyone be surprised at this? The very nature of the task makes some differences of view well-nigh inevitable. The answers that the Supreme Court is required to give are based on questions and on data that preclude automatic or even undoubting answers. If the materials on which judicial judgments must be based could be fed into a machine so as to produce ineluctable answers, if such were the nature of the problems that come before the Supreme Court and such were the answers expected, we would have IBM machines doing the work instead of judges.

"How amazing it is that, in the midst of controversies on every conceivable subject, one should expect unanimity of opinion upon difficult legal questions! In the highest ranges of thought, in theology, philosophy and science, we find differences of view on the part of the most distinguished experts,—theologians, philosophers and scientists. The history of scholarship is a record of disagreements. And when we deal with questions relating to principles of law and their application, we do not suddenly rise into a stratosphere of icy certainty." (Address by Mr. Chief Justice Hughes, 13 *American Law Institute Proceedings* [1936], pp. 61, 64.)

The core of the difficulty is that there is hardly a question of any real difficulty before the Court that does not entail more than one so-called principle. Anybody can decide a question if only a single principle is in controversy. Partisans and advocates often cast a question in that form, but the form is deceptive. In a famous passage Mr. Justice Holmes has exposed this misconception:

"All rights tend to declare themselves absolute to their logical extreme. Yet all in fact are limited by the neighborhood of principles of policy which are other than those on which the particular right is founded, and which become strong enough to hold their own when a certain point is reached. . . . The boundary at which the conflicting interests balance cannot be determined by any general formula in advance, but points in the line, or helping to establish it, are fixed by decisions that this or that concrete case falls on the nearer or farther side." (*Hudson County Water Co. v. McCarter*, 209 U.S. 349, 355.)

This contest between conflicting principles is not limited to law. In a recent discussion of two books on the conflict between the claims of literary individualism and dogma, I came across this profound observation: "But when, in any field of human observation, two truths appear in conflict it is wiser to assume that neither is exclusive, and that their contradiction, though it may be hard to bear, is part of the mystery of things." ("Literature and Dogma," *Times Literary Supplement* [London], Jan. 22, 1954, p. 51.) But judges cannot leave such contradiction between two conflicting "truths" as "part of the mystery of things." They have to adjudicate. If the conflict cannot be resolved, the task of the Court is to arrive at an accommodation of the contending claims. This is the core of the difficulties and misunderstandings about the judicial process. This, for any conscientious judge, is the agony of his duty.

WILLIAM O. DOUGLAS

Judicial Review and the Protection of Liberty

William O. Douglas—law professor at Columbia and Yale, member and chairman of the Securities and Exchange Commission under President Franklin Roosevelt, and an outspoken, outdoor, "outsider" liberal—reached the Supreme Court in 1939, at a highly robust forty-two years of age. His energy has been bursting the seams of his judicial robes ever since. This is illustrated by the selection here, part of a chapter from a book of law lectures delivered by Justice Douglas in India, comparing the American and Indian judicial systems. *We, the Judges: Studies in American and Indian Constitutional Law from Marshall to Mukherjea* (New York: Doubleday & Co., 1956). Traveling from Asian steppes to Middle Eastern capitals and to Latin-American law schools, Justice Douglas has discussed with these foreign audiences what is and what he wishes could be in American constitutional law, particularly the law of civil liberties. Here, he assesses the present balance between legislative authority and judicial veto, and warns against a trend toward weakening judicial power to protect the individual from legislative and administrative oppression.

SOURCE: *We, The Judges* (New York: Doubleday & Co., 1956), 433.

In 1929, Lord Sankey, then the Lord Chancellor of England, spoke of the majestic function performed by the judiciary:

"Amid the cross-currents and shifting sands of public life the Law is like a great rock upon which a man may set his feet and be safe, while the inevitable inequalities of private life are not so dangerous in a country where every citizen knows that in the Law Courts, at any rate, he can get justice." [1]

In the same mood, the Committee on Ministers' Powers Report (1932) p. 114, noted:

"We are . . . unanimously of opinion that no considerations of administrative convenience, or executive efficiency, should be allowed to weaken the control of the Courts, and that no obstacle should be placed by Parliament in the way of the subject's unimpeded access to them."

These views need renewed emphasis today in America. For there has been a trend to weaken judicial authority and to aggrandize legislative authority. The trend has been growing in this century. But it reflects an appetite which is not new to legislatures. We experienced such tendencies before.

In 1781, Thomas Jefferson was greatly worried by the power of the legislative branch of government. He sounded an alarm and deplored the trend of events:

"All the powers of government, legislative, executive, and judiciary, result to the legislative body. The concentrating these in the same hands is precisely the definition of despotic government. It will be no alleviation that these powers will be exercised by a plurality of hands, and not by a single one. One hundred and seventy-three despots would surely be as oppressive as one. Let those who doubt it turn their eyes on the republic of Venice. As little will it avail us that they are chosen by ourselves. An *elective despotism* was not the government we fought for, but one which should not only be founded on free principles, but in which the powers of government should be so divided and balanced among several bodies of magistracy, as that no one could transcend their legal limits, without being effectually checked and restrained by the others. For this reason that convention which passed the ordinance of government, laid its foundation on this basis, that the legislative, executive, and judiciary departments should be separate and distinct, so that no person should exercise the powers of more than one of them at the same time. But no barrier was provided between these several powers. The judiciary and executive members were left dependent on the legislative, for their subsistence in office, and some of them for their continuance in it. If, therefore, the legislature assumes executive and judiciary powers, no opposition is likely to be made; nor, if made, can it be effectual; because in that case they may put their proceedings into the form of an act of assembly, which will render them obligatory on the other branches. They have, accordingly, in many instances, decided rights which should have been left to judiciary controversy; and the direction of the executive, during the whole time of their session, is becoming habitual and familiar. And this is done with no ill intention. The views of the present members are perfectly upright. When they are led out of their regular province, it is by art in others, and inadvertence in themselves. And this will probably be the case for some time to come. But it will not be a very long time. Mankind soon learn to make interested uses of every right and power which they possess, or may assume." *Notes on Virginia,* in Vol. II, *The Writings of Thomas Jefferson* (Memorial ed. 1903), pp. 162–164.

Jefferson knew of the excursions of the British Parliament into the judicial field. The legislature had punished men by legislative *fiat.* They called acts treason which were not treason when committed. The legislature, bent on political revenge or on vindication of party principle, convicted men on testimony that courts would not admit, violating established rules of evidence. Where the law provided one penalty, the legislature sometimes applied a heavier one. As Justice Chase said in *Calder* v. *Bull,* 3 Dall. 386, 389,

"The ground for the exercise of such *legislative* power was this, that the *safety* of the kingdom depended on the death, or other punishment, of the offender: as if traitors, when *discovered,* could be so formidable, or the government so insecure! With very few exceptions, the advocates of *such* laws were stimulated by ambition, or personal resentment, and vindictive malice. To prevent such, and similar, acts of violence and injustice, I believe, the Federal and State Legislatures, were prohibited from passing any bill of *attainder;* or any *ex post facto law.*"

The Virginia Declaration of Rights [2] of June 12, 1776, sounded the alarm against legislative encroachments on the liberties of the citizen. It asked for the separation of the legislative and executive powers from the judiciary. It also asked specific guarantees against the oppressive practices of both the legislative and the executive branches. Here are found the seeds of the American Bill of Rights. . . .

Roscoe Pound in *The Formative Era of American Law* (1938) has related how the American legislatures up to the middle of the last century thought of themselves as the dominant power of the nation:

"As late as the impeachment of Andrew Johnson it was confidently asserted that the executive was accountable to the legislative for the exercise of powers committed to the executive by the Constitution. All through the formative era legislative assemblies assumed that courts were accountable to them for the way in which they decided controversies. State legislatures summoned judges before them to be interrogated as to particular decisions exactly after the manner of the famous colloquy between James I and the judges of England. There was an idea of legislative omnicompetence. The earlier legislatures did not hesitate to enact statutes reversing judgments of the courts in particular cases. They sought to admit to probate wills rejected by the courts. They sought to dictate the details of administration of particular estates. By special laws they directed the details of local government for particular instances. They validated particular invalid marriages. They suspended the statute of limitations for a particular litigant in a particular case. They exempted a particular wrongdoer from liability for a particular wrong for which his neighbors would be held by the general law." *Id.*, 39–40.

In America, the pendulum swung away from the legislatures and toward the courts. It swung so far that by the turn of the century the judiciary assumed the dominant role. The reasons were varied, as Pound's analysis shows. *Id.*, 49 *et seq.*

The period of judicial supremacy was not to last long. By the mid-twentieth century the pendulum had swung again. This time legislative power overshadowed the other branches.

The judiciary lost some of its powers by forsaking the role of the super-legislature that it had assumed last century and in the first decades of the present century. But the principal reasons for the growth of legislative power at the expense of the other branches were: *first*, the massive appropriations made necessary by the world wars and by the great depression of the 1930's, and *second*, the vast growth of the federal bureaucracy. The power of government shifted from state to federal channels. Within the federal system, the power gravitated to the legislative branch. The hold which the legislature has over the purse strings makes its voice more and more felt. And, although the administrative agencies are parts of the executive branch, they are sensitive to congressional desires; they are subject to accounting at the hands of congressional committees; they are welded closely to congressional groups through a wide variety of lobbying agencies.

This growth in legislative power has had an important impact on both the executive and the judiciary.

Walter Lippmann in *The Public Philosophy* (1955) shows how the legislative branch more and more dominates the executive in the western world. The illustrations are numerous and needless to relate. In general, however, the legislative branch has more and more molded foreign policy, if not dictated it. More and more has the executive branch been under restraints of the legislative branch.

Lippmann has traced some of the ominous aspects of the tendency in the western world to subordinate executive power to legislative power. I mention it only in passing. For the main concern of these Lectures is with judicial power. It too has been eroded as legislative power has become more dominant.

The administrative agency is one example. The voice of the administrative agency has often been more powerful than that of the courts in disputes between competing interests. Judicial review of administrative action has of necessity been narrow and confined. Agency action has not carried finality as a matter of law; but it has been well-nigh conclusive in the run of cases. Agency action may involve liberty as well as property, the right to pursue a calling, as well as the right to indulge in certain business practices. Agency action speaks with decisiveness in the vital affairs of men. Courts are far removed from those contests and exert only a minor influence. This is not an erosion of judicial power in the sense of cutting down the courts' jurisdiction. It is, however, an erosion in the sense of a gradual displacement of judicial authority with administrative authority.

This growth of administrative authority has been a startling phenomenon. In 1818 a New Hampshire court held unconstitutional an act of the legislature awarding a new trial to a litigant in a probate case. *Merrill* v. *Sherburne*, 1 N.H. 199. The court noted that "a marked difference exists between the employments of judicial and legislative tribunals. The former decide upon the legality of claims and conduct; the latter make rules, upon which, in connexion with the constitution, those decisions should be founded." *Id.*, 204.

The judgment was sound by modern standards. But the concept of judicial power which the opinion reflects, and which was prevalent a century ago, has vastly changed. For today administrative agencies, as well as courts, "decide upon the legality of claims and conduct."

The administrative agency making the decision is closer to the political arena than the courts. Its members lack life tenure. Pressures that would be intolerable if applied to courts are constantly applied to the agencies. The "wrong" decision may result in an agency chairman answering to a congressional committee. Its procedures are sometimes intolerable by judicial standards.

This dilution in the power of courts is regretted by some because it deprives courts of power. That is not my primary concern. What gives me chief concern is the manner in which the liberty of the citizen suffers when he is subjected to unfair procedures.

One who for long views the administrative process from the vantage point of an appellate court is impressed with the variety of unfair practices and procedures that the administrative process nourishes. The records coming from the agencies show how rough-shod their approach often is. That procedure gives them flexibility, to be sure; but it often imperils the rights of the citizen and produces injustice.

A dramatic illustration, though by no means an isolated one, is *Bailey* v. *Richardson*, 182 F. 2d 46, which was affirmed by an equally divided Supreme Court, 341 U.S. 918. Miss Bailey was a government employee being screened by a Loyalty Board established in the Executive branch. The Board was empowered to disqualify a person for federal employment if "on all the evidence, reasonable grounds exist for belief that the person involved is disloyal to the Government of the United States."

Miss Bailey answered all the questions put to her by the Board and her answers were direct and specific. She asked for an administrative hearing, and one was granted her. At this hearing she testified and presented other witnesses who testified. No one appeared against her.

The Board rated her as ineligible for federal employment, finding that "reasonable grounds exist for belief" that she was "disloyal" to the United States. Miss Bailey appealed to the Review Board where she was given another hearing. No one other than she testified; and no affidavits other than hers were offered. The Review Board upheld the lower Board and requested the agency where she worked to remove her from the rolls.

Miss Bailey thereupon brought an action for declaratory judgment and an order directing her reinstatement.

It appeared that Miss Bailey was charged with being a Communist and with being active in a Communist "front organization." The Review Board stated that the case against her was based on reports, some of which came from "informants certified to us by the Federal Bureau of Investigation as experienced and entirely reliable."

Her counsel asked that their names be disclosed. The request was refused.

Her counsel asked if these informants had been active in a certain union. The chairman of the Review Board replied, "I haven't the slightest knowledge as to who they were or how active they have been in anything."

Her counsel asked if those statements were under oath. The chairman answered, "I don't think so."

The truth is that the Loyalty Board discharged Miss Bailey on evidence it could not even appraise.[3] The critical evidence of the unknown witness might have been the word of a person who, to use the words of Alan Barth in *The Loyalty of Free Men* (1951), p. 109, was "a paragon of veracity, a knave, or the village idiot." His identity, his reputation, his prejudices, his animus toward Miss Bailey, his trustworthiness were unknown to the administrative agency, to the accused employee, and to the reviewing court. The accused employee had no opportunity to show that the witness was venal, that he bore an old grudge, that he had an ax to grind in having her discharged.

Without knowing who the accuser was the employee had no way of defending. Her only defense was her own word and the character testimony of her friends. As dissenting Justices stated at the time:

"Dorothy Bailey was not, to be sure, faced with a criminal charge and hence not technically entitled under the Sixth Amendment to be confronted with the witnesses against her. But she was on trial for her reputation, her job, her professional standing. A disloyalty trial is the most crucial event in the life of a public servant. If condemned, he is branded for life as a person unworthy of trust or confidence. To make that condemnation without meticulous regard for the decencies of a fair trial is abhorrent to fundamental justice." See *Anti-Fascist Committee* v. *McGrath*, 341 U.S. 123, 180.

The courts permitted the growth of procedural rules and practices that were unfair to the citizen. Faceless informers grew in stature. Secret reports were used to condemn people—not to death but to the ranks of the jobless. The courts were not mindful of the advice of Justice Brandeis given years before.

"Experience should teach us to be most on our guard to protect liberty when the Government's purposes are beneficent. . . . The greatest dangers to liberty lurk in insidious encroachment by men of zeal, well-meaning but without understanding." *Olmstead* v. *United States*, 277 U.S. 438, 479.

The United States had an important problem to solve in ferreting out subversive agents, worming their way into government to ascertain secrets or to influence policy. The problem was to sort them out in a way that was fair to the innocent and guilty alike. Essentially unfair procedures cannot produce fair hearings. Yet the judicial branch did not insist upon the appropriate procedure.

The administrative agency moved more and more to the forefront as a censor of peoples' lives and activities. Lists of so-called "subversive" agencies were published by the government in proceedings that seemed to some judges to violate due process of law. *Anti-Fascist Committee* v. *McGrath*, 341 U.S. 123. And these lists had widespread impact across the nation. Teachers who were members of listed groups could not hold their jobs. *Adler* v. *Board of Education*, 342 U.S. 485. They had wide repercussions in the business community, driving customers from the doors of these organizations and sending them into bankruptcy or eclipse.

The probings by government agencies seemed endless. Not only were employees of state and federal governments discharged under procedures that were unfair by conventional legal standards. Men were discharged from their professions, not by reason of unfitness, but because of their unpopular political beliefs. *Barsky* v. *Board of Regents*, 347 U.S. 442.

The catalogue of these transgressions is unimportant. The important fact is that the judicial branch was lax in its insistence upon fair procedures. As a consequence, those who could command effective control over organs of publicity and propaganda brought great pressure to bear upon employers, school boards, government agencies, churches, and all other types of organizations to discharge those who were deemed "subversive."

Great impetus was given this drive by congressional committees investigating various aspects of American life. The excesses of these committees are notorious, all as recorded in Barth, *Government by Investigation*, and Taylor, *Grand Inquest*. Men were charged with all sorts of high crimes and misdemeanors by accusers who spoke under the protection of congressional immunity. They were pilloried before committees and given what a layman would consider a trial for their so-called offenses.

Often their offenses pertained to what they thought, not to what they had done. Men would be examined as to their political beliefs.

This growth of power in the administrative agency and in the congressional committee enabled those groups to use their authority as a powerful leverage over people and institutions. There seemed to be no restraint on their activities. Few restraints were self-imposed. Few statutes provided procedural safeguards. The courts were reluctant to interfere.

That chapter in American history shows the need for procedural rules that will insure fair hearings before both administrative agencies and congressional committees. Courts cannot fashion these rules; their drafting is for the legislative and executive branches. A fair hearing, however, demands minimum requirements.

The minimum requirements for fair hearings include the right to counsel. The average citizen is helpless before an agency or committee without the aid of an experienced hand.

A fair hearing also requires that anyone giving evidence against the citizen face the accused and submit to cross-examination. As stated by the dissenters in *United States* v. *Nugent,* 346 U.S. 1, 13–14:

"The use of statements by informers who need not confront the person under investigation or accusation has such an infamous history that it should be rooted out from our procedure. A hearing at which these faceless people are allowed to present their whispered rumors and yet escape the test and torture of cross-examination is not a hearing in the Anglo-American sense. We should be done with the practice—whether the life of a man is at stake, or his reputation, or any matter touching upon his status or his rights. If FBI reports are disclosed in administrative or judicial proceedings, it may be that valuable underground sources will dry up. But that is not the choice. If the aim is to protect the underground of informers, the FBI report need not be used. If it is used, then fairness requires that the names of the accusers be disclosed. Without the identity of the informer the person investigated or accused stands helpless. The prejudices, the credibility, the passions, the perjury of the informer are never known. If they were exposed, the whole charge might wither under the cross-examination."

The realm of the conscience should be placed beyond the reach of government. Political beliefs, like religious convictions, are one's own business. One should not be subject to an accounting for anything but his conduct.[4]

Man's struggle for freedom in the western world has largely been an effort to be free from the inquisition. The inquisition sought out the heretics—those who had deviated from the "true" faith. Man finally realized that there was too much diversity in life to regiment men under a single political creed, a single religion, a single school of philosophy. Yet once an agency or committee can probe one's secret thoughts or basic philosophy of life, the citizen can become the victim of an ugly public mood. Once that happens, the inquisition has returned under a new form.

The aim of procedural reforms should be to give an accused at least the same degree of protection and the same quality of safeguards when his reputation and his right to work are being litigated, as when his property is jeopardized. Whenever government reaches into the lives of citizens to deprive them of rights or to restrict their liberty, the steps it takes should be strictly measured by due process of law. . . .

The judiciary cannot, of course, make a lawsuit out of every congressional inquiry nor saddle administrative agencies with all the paraphernalia of court trials. Moreover, abiding reforms come not only from procedural reforms but also from the force of public opinion and an attitude of tolerance and fairness that permeates every agency and committee in the land. The judiciary plays an important role in educating the people as well as in deciding cases. It can and should, in the critical crises that affect the reputations and fortunes of men, be alert to create, if necessary, new safeguards for the liberty of the citizen. The judiciary sits in a quiet and dignified place, one that is far removed from the tumult and passions of crowds. It sits to make sure in cases coming before it that not even the humblest or the most unpopular citizen is the victim of any intolerance that sweeps the country.

The judiciary has no army or police force to execute its mandates or compel obedience to its decrees. It has no control over the purse strings of government. Those two historic sources of power rest in other hands. The strength of the judiciary is in the command it has over the hearts and minds of men. That respect and prestige are the product of innumerable judgments and decrees, a mosaic built from the multitude of cases decided. Respect and prestige do not grow suddenly; they are the products of time and experience. But they flourish when judges are independent and courageous. The court that raises its hand against the mob may be temporarily unpopular; but it soon wins the confidence of the nation. The court that fails to stand before the mob is not worthy of the great tradition.

The judiciary is in a high sense the guardian of the conscience of the people as well as of the law of the land. It is much further removed from the political arena than the administrative agencies or the legislative. It sits aloof and detached from the community, not subject to the political stresses and storms of the other branches. It is made up of men who have tenure and other protections against the political forces of the day. Its decisions are more apt to reflect tradition and first principles than political expediency.

Judicial review gives time for the sober second thought. It interrupts the administrative process, to be sure, and makes it more time-consuming. But there are few decisions that must move pell-mell into action. The cooling period is good for most hotly-contested issues. And where basic fundamental rights of the citizen are at stake, the contemplative pause, necessitated by judicial review, may be critical. The confidence of the citizen in modern government is increased by more, rather than less, judicial review of the administrative process. It assures that basic unfairness will be corrected. And the administrator who knows he must ultimately account to a judicial body for his actions will tend to be a more responsible public official.

FOOTNOTES

[1] Quoted in Hewart, *The New Despotism* (1929), p. 151.

[2] Appendix I, Lecture 8.

[3] The problem of the *Bailey* case came before the Court once more in *Peters* v. *Hobby*, 349 U.S. 331. Dr. Peters had been cleared of disloyalty charges by an administrative agency, but a Review Board had reexamined his case on its own motion and concluded that grounds for discharge existed. This conclusion was based on information supplied by "faceless informers" unknown to either Dr. Peters or the Review Board, information which Dr. Peters had no chance to refute by the time-tested method of cross-examination. Dr. Peters contended that this procedure violated the requirements of Due Process. A majority of the Court declined to reach the constitutional problems involved. The Court roundly denounced the Review Board, holding that the Board had no authority under the applicable Executive Order to conduct such review on its own motion.

[4] Those who support the legislative power to investigate the area of beliefs ground their position on *Dennis* v. *United States*, 341 U.S. 494, and related cases discussed in Lecture 9, which hold that Congress or a state legislature may restrict free expression where there is felt to be a "clear and present danger." Under that view, it is urged that Congress may investigate to determine whether a clear and present danger exists calling for legislative action. The reach of the investigative power and its impact on First Amendment rights was considered in *Barsky* v. *United States*, 167 F. 2d 241, and *United States* v. *Josephson*, 165 F. 2d 82, discussed in Lecture 4.

☆☆☆ The Techniques of Adjudication

TOM C. CLARK

How Cases Get into the Supreme Court

This "informal discussion," Justice Clark notes, deals with the appellate practice of the Supreme Court, based on "one decade" of his experience as a Justice. "After a couple of more decades," he told his audience, the University of Minnesota Law School Alumni, at Minneapolis, "I might be able to give you a real 'assist.' " Clark, a Texan and protégé of the late Representative and House Speaker Sam Rayburn, practiced law in Dallas County and then served as its Civil District Attorney. He entered the Department of Justice in 1937, and after serving in the antitrust, war frauds, and criminal divisions, became Attorney General in 1945. President Truman appointed him to the Court in 1949. A frequent speaker on the Court's work and practices in recent years, Justice Clark's discussion of the Court's handling of its appellate jurisdiction is particularly interesting in light of the debate over the press of cases and its impact upon the Court's quality of decisions.

SOURCE: "Some Thoughts on Supreme Court Practice," Address, April 13, 1959, manuscript copy from Mr. Justice Clark.

As you know the jurisdiction of the Court is set out in Article III of the Constitution. In addition to prescribing certain jurisdictional limits it authorizes the Congress to lay down further restrictions. Congress has exercised that authority by enacting laws from time to time, most of which have been codified in Chapter 81 of Title 28 of the United States Code. As thus defined by the Constitution and by Statute, Supreme Court jurisdiction is of two general types: original and appellate. The original jurisdiction is very narrow —limited generally to actions between states or a state and the federal government, or to cases affecting ambassadors of foreign nations—and is thus seldom exercised. In very few Terms does the Court dispose of more than two or three such cases; sometimes an entire Term will expire without the Court's having disposed of a single original case.

The Court's appellate jurisdiction is of three general types: by appeal, by writ of certiorari, and by certified questions. A case comes up by certified question when a United States Court of Appeals or the Court of Claims is of the opinion that a legal issue involved in a case before it should be decided by the Supreme Court. It frames the issue in the form of a question and asks the Court for instructions thereon. This type of jurisdiction also is seldom drawn into play. Thus the vast number of cases handled by the Court are those cases coming to it by appeal or by a petition for a writ of certiorari. The number of such cases ranges between 1600 and 1850 each Term.

Jurisdiction by appeal is said to be an "obligatory" jurisdiction. By that, it is meant that when a case properly comes before the Court, the appealing party is entitled as a matter of right to have the Court exercise its jurisdiction and decide the case one way or another. As a consequence, this type of jurisdiction is more narrowly drawn than is the certiorari jurisdiction which we will discuss presently. In general, a party has a right to appeal (1) from any federal court decision declaring an Act of Congress unconstitutional (if the United States is a party); (2) from an order granting or denying an injunction in any case required to be heard by any three-judge federal District Court; (3) in any case where a federal Court of Appeals has declared a state statute to be invalid under the Constitution or laws of the

United States; or (4) from a final judgment of a state court declaring a federal statute unconstitutional or upholding a state statute against a claim of invalidity under the laws or Constitution of the United States. Approximately 9% of the cases which come before the Court are presented by appeal.

The Court's certiorari jurisdiction is very broad—extending generally to all cases in the federal courts, and all cases in state courts where the controlling issue is one arising under the United States Constitution or under federal laws or treaties.

The Court's jurisdiction over writs of certiorari is entirely discretionary. By that, I mean that the Court may decide to take the case or not, as it sees fit. Incidentally, a petition is granted on only four affirmative votes from among the nine Justices. By a careful exercise of this discretion, the Court can devote its limited time and energies to those cases involving the more important issues. As the late Chief Justice Vinson once said, in an address before the American Bar Association:

> "The Supreme Court is not, and never has been, primarily concerned with the correction of errors in lower court decisions. The debates in the Constitutional Convention make clear that the purpose of the establishment of one supreme national tribunal was, in the words of John Rutledge of South Carolina, 'to secure the national rights and uniformity of judgments.' The function of the Supreme Court is, therefore, to resolve conflicts of opinion on federal questions that have arisen among lower courts, to pass upon questions of wide import under the Constitution, laws and treaties of the United States, and to exercise supervisory power over lower federal courts. To remain effective, the Supreme Court must continue to decide only those questions whose resolution will have immediate importance far beyond the particular facts and parties involved." [Address of Sept. 7, 1949, Stern and Gressman, *Supreme Court Practice*, p. 107.]

You will find a further summary of the factors governing the Court's exercise of certiorari jurisdiction in Rule 19 of the Supreme Court Rules.

You are probably curious as to how all this works out in practice. Taking the last Term as an example [October Term 1957], the Court disposed of 1646 cases. These included one case under the Court's original jurisdiction; no certified questions; 139 appeals; and 1506 petitions for certiorari. Of the latter, 1326 (or 81%) were disposed of by a simple denial of certiorari, leaving 319 (19%) of the appellate cases which were disposed of "on the merits." About two-thirds of the latter (200 cases) came from federal courts; the balance (119) coming from the various states.

A little over half the cases "on the merits" are disposed of without the Court's hearing oral argument; that is, summarily. This fact has given rise to critical comment during recent years. Perhaps some of the criticism has merit, but a large part of it stems from a failure to fully appreciate the nature of the cases so decided. To say that all of them are decided "on the merits" is a trifle misleading. For instance, last Term 20% of the cases in this category were appeals which were dismissed because they simply failed to present a substantial federal question. Another 20% were dismissed because the federal question presented, although substantial, was squarely governed by our prior decisions. Still another 13% of these cases, arising mostly from federal courts, were affirmed for somewhat the same reasons. Thus, if we add these up, we find that over half (53%) of these so-called cases on the merits actually presented no real question at all, or else one which had already been decided. In either case it would be a waste of the time and money of the parties to present oral argument. This sort of thing is not new, but, on the contrary, has been done by the Court throughout its entire history. It has been more noticeable in recent years because of the great increase in the number of cases reaching the Court.

The rest of these cases which are disposed of summarily fall into a number of categories. In some (8%), the cases are so similar to other cases which *are* being argued that the Court holds them in abeyance until the latter are decided and then disposes of them accordingly. The reason for this is to avoid unnecessary duplication in argument. Another group of cases (13%) is where the decision below is so clearly out of line with applicable authority that argument is unnecessary in order to reverse. An example of this sort of case was handed down just the other day. A federal District Court had held that the Agricultural Adjustment Act of 1938, which grants the government the power to assign quotas for certain crops, was unconstitutional when applied to a farmer who grew wheat for consumption on his own farm. Certainly this is, or at least was, a substantial federal question. Nevertheless, the Supreme Court had, 16 years earlier, unanimously decided the question to the contrary in the leading case of *Wickard* v. *Fillburn*, 317 U.S. 111. An analogous category (5%) is represented by those cases where the United States was the prevailing party below and where the Solicitor General himself confesses error. There remains only some 20% of those decided summarily. Some of those had become moot; some were remanded for reconsideration in the light of other opinions handed down by the Court subsequent to the lower court action; and the balance presented other situations calling for special treatment.

Now for some details in each of these areas of our jurisdiction. We shall skip the original jurisdiction since you would seldom be involved in such litigation.

Appeals—Obligatory Jurisdiction

In this area the appellant files a jurisdictional statement showing the basis of the Court's jurisdiction. The procedure is the product of Mr. Justice Van Devanter and was introduced in 1928. The statement must show that the federal question involved is substantial or, if from a federal court, sufficiently substantial to require argument. The appellee may then file a motion to dismiss or affirm the judgment appealed from, which the appellant may meet by a brief in opposition. The Court acts upon these papers, either permitting the case to be argued at a later setting or summarily disposing of it. When a question of jurisdiction is close, the Court may postpone the issue of jurisdiction to the argument on the merits, hearing all questions at the same time. In summary dispositions the Court may dismiss the appeal for want of jurisdiction or the lack of a substantial federal question, or may affirm.

Since the appellant comes to the Court as a matter of right and a summary disposition involves the merits, the jurisdictional statement is more narrowly drawn than the petition for certiorari. On certiorari the case involves the exercise of wide discretion by the Court and a denial has none of the consequences of an adjudication. Hence the petitioner must present much stronger grounds to be successful in having his case heard.

THE CERTIORARI SYSTEM—DISCRETIONARY ACTION

The petition for certiorari springs from the Judiciary Act of 1925 and, likewise, is the product of Mr. Justice Van Devanter. The general principles governing its exercise may be found in Rule 19.

It is impossible for one to follow any definite course which will lead to the granting of his petition. There is one thing, however, of which you can be sure. It is a "long shot," to use racing parlance. The average proportion of certiorari petitions granted during the past few Terms has been less than 13%. You should tell your client of this, so that when the denial comes along there will be less fuss about the fee. Invariably the client loses some of the vigor in the threat, "I'll take him *all the way* to the Supreme Court" when he hears about the 13% and the *costs* and the *fee*. I will, however, try to give you some of the ground rules, learned in a decade of considering some 20,000 such petitions.

First. On state cases you must show that a substantial federal question was necessarily decided by the highest state court in which a decision could be had, and, in addition, that the state's judgment cannot be supported on some independent state ground. The adequacy of the state ground is a question for the Supreme Court.

Second. Every petition for certiorari in a federal case must show that the question posed is of general importance—not a "sporting case." As I have said, the writ is "not in the mere interest of the litigants." This is true even though the case was decided wrongly below. However, if rightly decided this fact alone would not bar the petition from being granted.

Third. The rule requires that "special and important reasons" be shown to exist requiring a grant. The most compelling special and important reason is the existence of a conflict between the Circuits on the point involved; or, a conflict between the Court of Claims and a Circuit. This is true because one of the functions of the writ is to resolve such conflicts. However, this reasoning would not extend to District Court conflicts. Sometimes contrary decisions between different panels of the same Court of Appeals occur. But the conflict rule does not ordinarily reach them; those are domestic squabbles and must generally be resolved at home.

Naturally the conflict must be on the law and not reconcilable on the basis of factual differences. Sometimes even true conflicts are not taken if the impact is narrow, as in a case where the statute involved has been amended, or if it appears that subsequent cases in the Circuit have resolved it. However, conflicts still remain the safest vehicle for a grant.

Fourth. In non-conflict cases the test is not so easily stated. In general, however, the petitioner should emphasize the effect of the decision upon the administration of the law rather than the impact upon the litigants themselves. The existence of a substantial constitutional question, the construction of an important and far-reaching federal statute, a serious question of public law, or a decision in conflict with a controlling Supreme Court opinion should turn the trick. Remember, four votes of the Justices are sufficient for a grant. Questions of a "just result" or "better theory" are not for the Court at this stage of the proceeding. A lawyer should assess the chances of certiorari's being granted on entirely objective lines, not on the wishes of his client.

In connection with certiorari work let me dissipate a few rumors by quoting a few words from Chief Justice Hughes. He pointed out that some lawyers thought there was some "mystery about [the certiorari] work" of the Court, which the Chief insisted "should be dispelled." He found that some think that petitions "are distributed among the Justices ratably. Others think the Justice assigned to a Circuit deals with applications from the Circuit." My old bench partner and beloved friend, Mr. Justice Jackson, some 20 years later, put it this way: ". . . [A] suspicion has grown at the bar that the law clerks constitute a kind of junior court which decides the fate of certiorari petitions. This idea of the law clerks' influence," said the Justice, "gave rise to a lawyer's waggish statement that the Senate no longer need bother about confirmation of Justices but ought to confirm the appointment of law clerks." Needless to say, not one of these rumors has truth. Each Justice passes upon every application, of whatever kind, filed with the Court.

There is one additional form of petition that I must mention for

I would like you to interest yourselves in them. They are the *in forma pauperis* applications. They plague the Court, running some 800 to 1000 a year, mostly in criminal cases. The petition is usually *pro se,* a lawyer rarely participating. This lack of counsel at the petitioning stage is most unfortunate and stands as a blot on our profession. If criminal indigents were afforded legal aid through advice at this stage of the proceeding I am sure the applications would decrease appreciably. Moreover, the danger of meritorious cases not being adequately presented would be less. If you would examine our cases you would find that some of the most important pronouncements of the Court arise from indigent cases. These, of course, after certiorari is granted, are handled by attorneys assigned by the Court. They receive no fee. However, from our admission funds the Clerk pays the printing cost and the travel expense of assigned counsel. It is interesting to note—and I am proud to say—that some of the most distinguished lawyers in America have handled these cases on an assigned basis. It would be of immeasurable help to the Court if, through the good offices of the bar, legal assistance could be given to indigent prisoners, both state and federal, especially at the principal prisons. . . .

WILLIAM J. BRENNAN, JR.

Working at Justice

How the Court handles cases once they are accepted for decision—that is, what the procedures and traditions are behind the doors of the Conference Room and in the individual suites of the Justices—has always been a staple of judicial speechmaking. Partly to dispel myths about the Court's practices and partly to give listeners an inside feeling (without violating proprieties), the Justices today have developed a rather uniform word portrait of how a case is decided from application for certiorari until announcement of opinion in open court. This example of the standard text is by Justice Brennan, and was part of a talk delivered at the Florida Bar Convention in Miami Beach, Florida, on May 7, 1960.

SOURCE: "State Court Decisions and the Supreme Court," Address, Florida Bar Convention, Miami Beach, Florida, May 7, 1960, manuscript copy from Mr. Justice Brennan.

Our detailed procedure is really very simple.
Each application is usually in the form of a short petition, attached to which are any opinions of the State Courts in the case. The adversary may file a response—also, in practice, usually short. Both the petition and response should identify the Federal questions allegedly involved, argue their substantiality, whether they were properly raised in the State Courts, whether they were decided by the State

Court contrary to controlling Federal precedents, and whether in any event the State Court decision may rest on an independent State ground. Each Justice receives copies of the petition and response and also of such part of the record as the parties may submit. Each Justice then without any consultation at this stage with his brethren, reaches his own tentative conclusion whether the application should be granted or denied. The first consultation with his brethren about the case comes at the Court conference at which the case is listed for discussion on the agenda. We sit in conference each Friday during the Term with some exceptions not important here. Conferences begin at 11 in the morning and usually continue until the neighborhood of 6 except for a half hour recess for lunch. Only the Justices are present at conference. There are no law clerks, no stenographers, no secretaries, no pages—just the nine of us. The junior Justice acts as guardian of the door, receiving and delivering any messages that come in or go from the conference. The conferences for obvious reasons are carried on in absolute secrecy. But the secrecy is as to our deliberations. There is no secrecy as to how we operate at the conference.

The conference room is a beautifully oak paneled chamber with one side lined with books from floor to ceiling. Over the mantle of the exquisite marble fireplace at one end hangs the only adornment in the chamber—a portrait of Chief Justice John Marshall. In the middle of the room stands a rectangular table, not too large but large enough for the nine of us comfortably to gather around it. The Chief Justice sits at the south end and Mr. Justice Black, the senior Associate Justice at the north end. Along the side to the left of the Chief Justice sits Justices Stewart, Whittaker, Harlan and Frankfurter in that order. On the right side sit Justice Clark, myself and Justice Douglas in that order.

We are summoned to conference by a buzzer which rings in our several chambers five minutes before the hour. Upon entering the conference room each of us shakes hands with his colleagues. That tradition originated when Chief Justice Fuller presided many decades ago. It is a symbol that harmony of aims if not of views is the Court's guiding principle.

Each of us has his copy of the agenda of the day's cases before him. The agenda lists the cases applying for review. Each of us before coming to the conference has noted on his copy his tentative view of the proper disposition of each case. Most applications are petitions for certiorari but there are also always a few appeals. To keep the discussion of the list within manageable proportions all of us before the conference will have indicated to the Chief Justice which of the listed applications we think so lacking in merit as not to be worthy of discussion. Where we have unanimously agreed the cases are passed over in discussion.

The Chief Justice begins the discussion of each case. He then yields to the senior Associate Justice and discussion proceeds down the line seniority-wise until each Justice has spoken. Voting goes the other way following discussion. The junior Justice votes first and voting then proceeds up the line to the Chief Justice who votes last. Each of us has a docket containing a sheet for each case with appropriate places for recording the votes. When any case receives four votes, either to grant certiorari or to note or postpone an appeal, that case is then transferred to the oral argument list.

I mentioned earlier that of the 792 State cases in which review was sought last Term only 58 were granted review. You will inquire what is the status of the 734 which failed to get four votes. The answer is that the judgments of the State Courts remain undisturbed. Now I said "undisturbed"—I did not say "affirmed." A denial of certiorari is not an affirmance of the State Court judgment as some erroneously think. It means only that the petition for review did not get four votes and it means absolutely nothing more. The denial does not mean that the Court agrees with the result reached by the State Court or with the State Court's decision of the Federal question. Very often I have voted to deny an application when I thought that the State Court's result was very wrong. The six or more Justices voting to refuse review may and indeed, often do, differ upon the grounds of their common action. Some may conclude that the Federal question raised was not substantial, others that it had not been properly raised in the State Courts, others that in any event the State Court decisions rested on an independent State ground. Or some may have concluded that a case otherwise qualifying for review nevertheless raised an issue not appropriate at the time for review. Thus I emphasize a denial in nowise implies agreement with the State Court's decision of the Federal question even if that decision turned on that question. The Court may well take the very next case raising the same question and reach a different result on the merits.

Now what of the State Court decisions we do agree to review? How do we process them? First, I should say that while there are different standards determining acceptance of Federal Court decisions for review, the decisional process I'll describe applies without regard to whether the case reviewed comes from a State or Federal Court. There are rare occasions when the question is so clearly controlled by an earlier decision of our Court that a reversal of the lower court judgment is inevitable. In these rare instances we may summarily reverse without oral argument. The case must very clearly justify summary disposition, however, because our ordinary practice is not to reverse a State decision without oral argument. Indeed, oral argument of cases taken for review, whether from the State or Federal Courts is the usual practice. We rarely accept submissions of cases on briefs. Oral argument ordinarily occurs about four months after the application for review is granted. Each party at argument is usually allowed one hour, but in recent years we have limited oral argument to a half hour in cases thought to involve issues not requiring longer argument. Counsel submit their briefs and record in sufficient time for the distribution of one set to each Justice two or three weeks before the oral argument. Most of the members of the present Court follow the practice of reading the briefs before the argument. Some of us, and I am one, often have a bench memorandum prepared before the argument. This memorandum digests the facts and the arguments of both sides, highlighting the matters about which I may want to question counsel at the argument. Often I have an independent research made in advance of argument and incorporate the results in the bench memorandum.

We follow a schedule of two weeks of argument from Monday through Thursday, followed by two weeks of recess for opinion writing and the study of appeals and certiorari petitions. The argued cases are listed on the Friday conference agenda of the Friday following argument. Conference discussion of argued cases follows the same procedure I have described for the discussion of certiorari petitions. Of course, it is a much more extended discussion. Not infrequently discussion of particular cases may be spread over two or more conferences. Not until the discussion is completed and a vote is taken is the opinion assigned. The assignment is not made at the conference but formally in writing some few days after the conference. The Chief Justice assigns the opinions in those cases in which he has voted with the majority. The senior Associate Justice voting with the majority assigns the opinions in the other cases. The dissenters agree among themselves who shall write the dissenting opinion. Of course, each Justice is free to write his own opinion, concurring or dissenting.

The writing of an opinion is not easy work. It always takes weeks and sometimes months. The most painstaking research and care go into the task. Our law clerks are of invaluable assistance in getting the job done. We are also fortunate in having the splendid library in our own building which contains a most comprehensive collection of materials. We're even more fortunate in having an especially competent library staff upon whom we often call to assist us and our law clerks in doing the research work. The briefs of counsel are always helpful but each of us is better satisfied when he not only checks but also supplements those materials with independent research.

When the author of an opinion feels he has an unanswerable document he sends it to the print shop, which we maintain in our building. The printed draft may be revised several times before his proposed opinion is circulated among his brethren. Copies are sent to each member of the Court, those in the dissent as well as those in the majority. Now often comes the time when the author discovers that his work has only begun. He receives a return, ordinarily in writing, from each Justice who voted with him and usually also from the Justices who voted the other way. He learns who will write the dissent if one is to be written. But his particular concern is whether those who voted with him are still of his view and what they have to say about his proposed opinion. Often some who voted with him at conference will advise that they reserve final judgment pending the circulation of the dissent. It is a common experience that dissents change votes, even enough votes to become the majority. I have converted more than one proposed majority opinion into a dissent before the final decision was announced. I have also, however, had the more satisfying experience of rewriting a dissent as a majority opinion for the Court. Before everyone has finally made up his mind a constant interchange among us by memoranda, by telephone, at the lunch table, continues while we hammer out the final form of the opinion. I had one case during the past Term in which I circulated 10 printed drafts before one was approved as the Court opinion.

This brief sketch of our procedure was true for each of the 99 opinions for the Court we filed last Term, an average of 11 each. There were also 56 dissenting opinions filed, 28 concurring opinions and 11 separate opinions, a total of 194 opinions for the Term.

The point is that each Justice, unless he disqualifies himself in a particular case, passes on every piece of business coming to the Court. The Court does not function by means of committees or panels. Each Justice passes on each petition, each item, no matter how drawn, in long-hand, by typewriter, or on a press. Our Constitution vests the judicial power in only one Supreme Court. This does not permit Supreme Court action by committees, panels, or sections. The method that the several Justices use in meeting an enormous caseload varies. There is one uniform rule: Judging is not delegated. Each Justice studies each case in sufficient detail to resolve the question for himself. So that in a very real sense, each decision is an individual decision of every Justice. . . .

FELIX FRANKFURTER

Reflections on Reading Statutes

Many of the Justices have spoken about statutory construction
—Jackson, Douglas, and Frankfurter each delivered a speech on
the subject in recent years—and no topic surpasses this one for
unfolding the basic conceptions of a man about the Court's
role. Between the poles of manipulative "finding" of legislative
intent and a blindly passive literalness in using the words of a
statute as a master stencil lies a gray land of choice and balance.
The Justice has his roadmarks, as Justice Frankfurter notes here,
but they are hints on a treasure hunt rather than the firm sign-
posts of our concrete highways. This address was delivered as
the Benjamin N. Cardozo Lecture before the Association of
the Bar of the City of New York in March of 1947.

SOURCE: 2 *Record of the Association of the Bar of the City
of New York* 213–237 (1947).

A single volume of 320 octavo pages contains all the
laws passed by Congress during its first five years,
when measures were devised for getting the new government under way; 26 acts were passed in the 1789 session,
66 in 1790, 94 in 1791, 38 in 1792, 63 in 1793. For the single
session of the 70th Congress, to take a pre-depression period,
there are 993 enactments in a monstrous volume of 1014
pages—quarto not octavo—with a comparable range of
subject matter. . . . Inevitably the work of the Supreme

Court reflects the great shift in the center of gravity of law-making. Broadly speaking, the number of cases disposed of by opinions has not changed from term to term. But even as late as 1875 more than 40 per cent of the controversies before the Court were common-law litigation, fifty years later only 5 per cent, while today cases not resting on statutes are reduced almost to zero. It is therefore accurate to say that courts have ceased to be the primary makers of law in the sense in which they "legislated" the common law. It is certainly true of the Supreme Court, that almost every case has a statute at its heart or close to it.

This does not mean that every case before the Court involves questions of statutory construction. If only literary perversity or jaundiced partisanship can sponsor a particular rendering of a statute there is no problem. When we talk of statutory construction we have in mind cases in which there is a fair contest between two readings, neither of which comes without respectable title deeds. A problem in statutory construction can seriously bother courts only when there is a contest between probabilities of meaning.

DIFFICULTIES OF CONSTRUCTION

Though it has its own preoccupations and its own mysteries and above all its own jargon, judicial construction ought not to be torn from its wider, non-legal context. Anything that is written may present a problem of meaning, and that is the essence of the business of judges in construing legislation. The problem derives from the very nature of words. They are symbols of meaning. But unlike mathematical symbols, the phrasing of a document, especially a complicated enactment, seldom attains more than approximate precision. If individual words are inexact symbols, with shifting variables, their configuration can hardly achieve invariant meaning or assure definiteness. Apart from the ambiguity inherent in its symbols, a statute suffers from dubieties. It is not an equation or a formula representing a clearly marked process, nor is it an expression of individual thought to which is imparted the definiteness a single authorship can give. A statute is an instrument of government partaking of its practical purposes but also of its infirmities and limitations, of its awkward and groping efforts. . . .

The difficulties are inherent not only in the nature of words, of composition, and of legislation generally. They are often intensified by the subject matter of an enactment. The imagination which can draw an income tax statute to cover the myriad transactions of a society like ours, capable of producing the necessary revenue without producing a flood of litigation, has not yet revealed itself. . . . Moreover, government sometimes solves problems by shelving them temporarily. The legislative process reflects that attitude. Statutes as well as constitutional provisions at times embody purposeful ambiguity or are expressed with a generality for future unfolding. "The prohibition contained in the Fifth Amendment refers to infamous crimes— a term obviously inviting interpretation in harmony with conditions and opinions prevailing from time to time." [1] And Mr. Justice Cardozo once remarked, "a great principle of constitutional law is not susceptible of comprehensive statement in an adjective." [2]

The intrinsic difficulties of language and the emergence after enactment of situations not anticipated by the most gifted legislative imagination, reveal doubts and ambiguities in statutes that compel judicial construction. The process of construction, therefore, is not an exercise in logic or dialectic. The aids of formal reasoning are not irrelevant; they may simply be inadequate. The purpose of construction being the ascertainment of meaning, every consideration brought to bear for the solution of that problem must be devoted to that end alone. To speak of it as a practical problem is not to indulge a fashion in words. It must be that, not something else. Not, for instance, an opportunity for a judge to use words as "empty vessels into which he can pour anything he will"—his caprices, fixed notions, even statesmanlike beliefs in a particular policy. Nor, on the other hand, is the process a ritual to be observed by unimaginative adherence to wellworn professional phrases. To be sure, it is inescapably a problem in the keeping of the legal profession and subject to all the limitations of our adversary system of adjudication. When the judge, selected by society to give meaning to what the legislature has done, examines the statute, he does so not in a laboratory or in a classroom. Damage has been done or exactions made, interests are divided, passions have been aroused, sides have been taken. But the judge, if he is worth his salt, must be above the battle. We must assume in him not only personal impartiality but intellectual disinterestedness. In matters of statutory construction also it makes a great deal of difference whether you start with an answer or with a problem.

THE JUDGE'S TASK

Everyone has his own way of phrasing the task confronting judges when the meaning of a statute is in controversy. Judge Learned Hand speaks of the art of interpretation as "the proliferation of purpose." Who am I not to be satisfied with Learned Hand's felicities? And yet that phrase might mislead judges intellectually less disciplined than Judge Hand. It might justify interpretations by judicial libertines, not merely judicial libertarians. My own rephrasing of what we are driving at is probably no more helpful, and is much longer, than Judge Hand's epigram. I should say that the troublesome phase of construction is the determination of the extent to which extraneous documentation and external circumstances may be allowed to infiltrate the text on the theory that they were part of it, written in ink discernible to the judicial eye.

Chief Justice White was happily endowed with the gift of finding the answer to problems by merely stating them. Often have I envied him this faculty but never more than in recent years. No matter how one states the problem of statutory construction, for me, at least, it does not carry its own answer. Though my business throughout most of my professional life has been with statutes, I come to you empty-handed. I bring no answers. I suspect the answers to the problems of an art are in its exercise. Not that one does not inherit, if one is capable of receiving it, the wisdom of the wise. But I confess unashamedly that I do not get much nourishment from books on statutory construction, and I say this after freshly re-examining them all, scores of them.

When one wants to understand, or at least get the feeling of, great painting, one does not go to books on the art of painting. One goes to the great masters. . . .

And so I have examined the opinions of Holmes, Brandeis and

Cardozo and sought to derive from their treatment of legislation what conclusions I could fairly draw, freed as much as I could be from impressions I had formed in the course of the years.

Holmes came to the Supreme Court before the great flood of recent legislation, while the other two, especially Cardozo, appeared at its full tide. The shift in the nature of the Court's business led to changes in its jurisdiction, resulting in a concentration of cases involving the legislative process. Proportionately to their length of service and the number of opinions, Brandeis and Cardozo had many more statutes to construe. And the statutes presented for their interpretation became increasingly complex, bringing in their train a quantitatively new role for administrative regulations. Nevertheless, the earliest opinions of Holmes on statutory construction, insofar as he reveals himself, cannot be distinguished from Cardozo's last opinion, though the latter's process is more explicit.

A judge of marked individuality stamps his individuality on what he writes, no matter what the subject. What is however striking about the opinions of the three Justices in this field is the essential similarity of their attitude and of their appraisal of the relevant. Their opinions do not disclose a private attitude for or against extension of governmental authority by legislation, or towards the policy of particular legislation, which consciously or imperceptibly affected their judicial function in construing laws. It would thus be a shallow judgment that found in Mr. Justice Holmes' dissent in the *Northern Securities* case (193 U.S. 197, 400) an expression of his disapproval of the policy behind the Sherman Law. His habit of mind—to be as accurate as one can be—had a natural tendency to confine what seemed to him familiar language in a statute to its familiar scope. But the proof of the pudding is that his private feelings did not lead him to invoke the rule of indefiniteness to invalidate legislation of which he strongly disapproved (Compare *Nash* v. *United States*, 229 U.S. 373, and *International Harvester Co.* v. *Kentucky*, 234 U.S. 216), or to confine language in a constitution within the restrictions which he gave to the same language in a statute. (Compare *Towne* v. *Eisner*, 245 U.S. 418, and *Eisner* v. *Macomber*, 252 U.S. 189.)

The reservations I have just made indicate that such differences as emerge in the opinions of the three Justices on statutory construction, are differences that characterize all of their opinions, whether they are concerned with interpretation or constitutionality, with admiralty or patent law. They are differences of style. In the case of each, the style is the man.

If it be suggested that Mr. Justice Holmes is often swift, if not cavalier, in his treatment of statutes, there are those who level the same criticism against his opinions generally. It is merited in the sense that he wrote, as he said, for those learned in the art. I need hardly add that for him "learned" was not a formal term comprehending the whole legal fraternity. When dealing with problems of statutory construction also he illumined whole areas of doubt and darkness with insights enduringly expressed, however briefly. To say "We agree to all the generalities about not supplying criminal laws with what they omit, but there is no canon against using commonsense in construing laws as saying what they obviously mean," *Roschen* v. *Ward*, 279 U.S. 337, 339, is worth more than most of the dreary writing on how to construe penal legislation. Again when he said that "the meaning of a sentence is to be felt rather than to be proved," *United States* v. *Johnson*, 221 U.S. 488, 496, he expressed the wholesome truth that the final rendering of the meaning of a statute is an act of judgment. He would shudder at the thought that by such a statement he was giving comfort to the school of visceral jurisprudence. Judgment is not drawn out of the void but is based on the correlation of imponderables all of which need not, because they cannot, be made explicit. He was expressing the humility of the intellectual that he was, whose standards of exactitude distrusted pretensions of certainty, believing that legal controversies that are not frivolous almost always involve matters of degree, and often degree of the nicest sort. Statutory construction implied the exercise of choice, but precluded the notion of capricious choice as much as choice based on private notions of policy. One gets the impression that in interpreting statutes Mr. Justice Holmes reached meaning easily, as was true of most of his results, with emphasis on the language in the totality of the enactment and the felt reasonableness of the chosen construction. He had a lively awareness that a statute was expressive of purpose and policy, but in his reading of it he tended to hug the shores of the statute itself, without much re-enforcement from without.

Mr. Justice Brandeis, on the other hand, in dealing with these problems as with others, would elucidate the judgment he was exercising by proof or detailed argument. In such instances, especially when in dissent, his opinions would draw on the whole arsenal of aids to construction. More often than either Holmes or Cardozo, Brandeis would invoke the additional weight of some "rule" of construction. But he never lost sight of the limited scope and function of such "rules." Occasionally, however, perhaps because of the nature of a particular statute, the minor importance of its incidence, the pressure of judicial business or even the temperament of his law clerk, whom he always treated as a co-worker, Brandeis disposed of a statute even more dogmatically, with less explicit elucidation, than did Holmes.

For Cardozo, statutory construction was an acquired taste. He prefered common law subtleties, having great skill in bending them to modern uses. But he came to realize that problems of statutory construction had their own exciting subtleties and gave ample employment to philosophic and literary talents. Cardozo's elucidation of how meaning is drawn out of a statute gives proof of the wisdom and balance which, combined with his learning, made him a great judge. While the austere style of Brandeis seldom mitigated the dry aspect of so many problems of statutory construction, Cardozo managed to endow even these with the warmth and softness of his writing. The differences in the tone and color of their style as well as in the moral intensity of Brandeis and Cardozo made itself felt when they wrote full-dress opinions on problems of statutory construction. Brandeis almost compels by demonstration; Cardozo woos by persuasion.

Scope of the Judicial Function

From the hundreds of cases in which our three Justices construed statutes one thing clearly emerges. The area of free judicial movement is considerable. These three remembered that laws are not abstract propositions. They are expressions of policy arising out of specific situations and addressed to the attainment of particular ends. The difficulty is that the legislative ideas which laws embody are both explicit and immanent. And so the bottom problem is: What is below the surface of the words and yet fairly a part of them? Words in statutes are not unlike words in a foreign language in that they too have "associations, echoes, and overtones." [3] Judges must retain the associations, hear the echoes, and capture the overtones. In one of his very last opinions, dealing with legislation taxing the husband on the basis of the combined income of husband and wife, Holmes wrote: "The statutes are the outcome of a thousand years of history. . . . They form a system with echoes of different moments, none of which is entitled to prevail over the other." [4]

What exactions such a duty of construction places upon judges, and with what freedom it entrusts them! John Chipman Gray was fond of quoting from a sermon by Bishop Hoadley that "Whoever hath an *absolute authority* to *interpret* any written or spoken laws, it is he who is truly the law-giver to all intents and purposes, and not the person who first wrote or spoke them." Gray, *Nature and Sources of the Law* (2nd ed. 1921), 102, 125, 172. By admitting that there is some substance to the good Bishop's statement, one does not subscribe to the notion that they are law-givers in any but a very qualified sense.

Even within their area of choice the courts are not at large. They are confined by the nature and scope of the judicial function in its particular exercise in the field of interpretation. They are under the constraints imposed by the judicial function in our democratic society. As a matter of verbal recognition certainly, no one will gainsay that the function in construing a statute is to ascertain the meaning of words used by the legislature. To go beyond it is to usurp a power which our democracy has lodged in its elected legislature. The great judges have constantly admonished their brethren of the need for discipline in observing the limitations. A judge must not rewrite a statute, neither to enlarge nor to contract it. Whatever temptations the statesmanship of policymaking might wisely suggest, construction must eschew interpolation and evisceration. He must not read in by way of creation. He must not read out except to avoid patent nonsense or internal contradiction. "If there is no meaning in it," said Alice's King, "that saves a world of trouble, you know, as we needn't try to find any." Legislative words presumably have meaning and so we must try to find it.

This duty of restraint, this humility of function as merely the translator of another's command, is a constant theme of our Justices. It is on the lips of all judges, but seldom, I venture to believe, has the restraint which it expresses, or the duty which it enjoins, been observed with so consistent a realization that its observance depends on self-conscious discipline. Cardozo put it this way: "We do not pause to consider whether a statute differently conceived and framed would yield results more consonant with fairness and reason. We take this statute as we find it." [5] It was expressed more fully by Mr. Justice Brandeis when the temptation to give what might be called a more liberal interpretation could not have been wanting: "The particularization and detail with which the scope of each provision, the amount of the tax thereby imposed, and the incidence of the tax, were specified, preclude an extension of any provision by implication to any other subject. . . . What the Government asks is not a construction of a statute, but, in effect, an enlargement of it by the court, so that what was omitted, presumably by inadvertence, may be included within its scope." [6] An omission, at the time of enactment, whether careless or calculated, cannot be judicially supplied however much later wisdom may recommend the inclusion.

The vital difference between initiating policy, often involving a decided break with the past, and merely carrying out a formulated policy, indicates the relatively narrow limits within which choice is fairly open to courts and the extent to which interpreting law is inescapably making law. To say that, because of this restricted field of interpretive declaration, courts make law just as do legislatures is to deny essential features in the history of our democracy. It denies that legislation and adjudication have had different lines of growth, serve vitally different purposes, function under different conditions, and bear different responsibilities. The judicial process of dealing with words is not at all Alice in Wonderland's way of dealing with them. Even in matters legal some words and phrases, though very few, approach mathematical symbols and mean substantially the same to all who have occasion to use them. Other law terms like "police power" are not symbols at all but labels for the results of the whole process of adjudication. In between lies a gamut of words with different denotations as well as connotations. There are varying shades of compulsion for judges behind different words, differences that are due to the words themselves, their setting in a text, their setting in history. In short, judges are not unfettered glossators. They are under a special duty not to overemphasize the episodic aspects of life and not to undervalue its organic processes—its continuities and relationships. For judges at least it is important to remember that continuity with the past is not only a necessity but even a duty.

There are not wanting those who deem naive the notion that judges

are expected to refrain from legislating in construing statutes. They
may point to cases where even our three Justices apparently supplied
an omission or engrafted a limitation. Such an accusation cannot be
rebutted or judged in the abstract. In some ways, as Holmes once
remarked, every statute is unique. Whether a judge does violence to
language in its total context is not always free from doubt. Statutes
come out of the past and aim at the future. They may carry implicit
residues or mere hints of purpose. Perhaps the most delicate aspect
of statutory construction is not to find more residues than are implicit
nor purposes beyond the bound of hints. Even for a judge most sensitive to the traditional limitation of his function, this is a matter for
judgment not always easy of answer. But a line does exist between
omission and what Holmes called "misprision or abbreviation that does
not conceal the purpose." [7] Judges may differ as to the point at which
the line should be drawn, but the only sure safeguard against crossing
the line between adjudication and legislation is an alert recognition
of the necessity not to cross it and instinctive, as well as trained, reluctance to do so.

In the realms where judges directly formulate law because the
chosen lawmakers have not acted, judges have the duty of adaptation
and adjustment of old principles to new conditions. But where policy
is expressed by the primary law-making agency in a democracy, that
is by the legislature, judges must respect such expressions by adding
to or subtracting from the explicit terms which the lawmakers used
no more than is called for by the shorthand nature of language. Admonitions, like that of Justice Brandeis in the *Iselin* case, that courts
should leave even desirable enlargement to Congress will not by itself
furnish the meaning appropriate for the next statute under scrutiny.
But as is true of other important principles, the intensity with which
it is believed may be decisive of the outcome.

THE PROCESS OF CONSTRUCTION

Let me descend to some particulars.

The text.—Though we may not end with the words in construing
a disputed statute, one certainly begins there. You have a right to think
that a hoary platitude, but it is a platitude too often not observed at

the bar. In any event, it may not take you to the end of the road. The Court no doubt must listen to the voice of Congress. But often Congress cannot be heard clearly because its speech is muffled. Even when it has spoken, it is as true of Congress as of others that what is said is what the listener hears. Like others, judges too listen with what psychologists used to call the apperception mass, which I take it means in plain English that one listens with what is already in one's head. One more caution is relevant when one is admonished to listen attentively to what a statute says. One must also listen attentively to what it does not say.

We must, no doubt, accord the words the sense in which Congress used them. That is only another way of stating the central problem of decoding the symbols. It will help to determine for whom they were meant. Statutes are not archaeological documents to be studied in a library. They are written to guide the actions of men. As Mr. Justice Holmes remarked upon some Indian legislation "The word was addressed to the Indian mind," *Fleming* v. *McCurtain*, 215 U.S. 56, 60. If a statute is written for ordinary folk, it would be arbitrary not to assume that Congress intended its words to be read with the minds of ordinary men. If they are addressed to specialists, they must be read by judges with the minds of the specialists.

And so we assume that Congress uses common words in their popular meaning, as used in the common speech of men. The cases speak of the "meaning of common understanding," "the normal and spontaneous meaning of language," "the common and appropriate use," "the natural straightforward and literal sense," and similar variants. In *McBoyle* v. *United States*, 283 U.S. 25, 26, Mr. Justice Holmes had to decide whether an aeroplane is a "motor vehicle" within the meaning of the Motor Vehicle Theft Act. He thus disposed of it: "No doubt etymologically it is possible to use the word to signify a conveyance working on land, water or air, and sometimes legislation extends the use in that direction. . . . But in everyday speech 'vehicles' calls up a picture of a thing moving on land."

Sometimes Congress supplies its own dictionary. It did so in 1871, in a statute defining a limited number of words for use as to all future enactments. It may do so, as in recent legislation, by a section within a statute containing definitions for that statute. Or, there may be indications from the statute that words in it are employed in a distinctive sense. "If Congress has been accustomed to use a certain phrase with a more limited meaning than might be attributed to it by common practice, it would be arbitrary to refuse to consider that fact when we come to interpret a statute. But, as we have said, the usage of Congress simply shows that it has spoken with careful precision, that its words mark the exact spot at which it stops." [8] Or, words may acquire scope and function from the history of events which they summarize or from the purpose which they serve.

"However colloquial and uncertain the words had been in the beginning, they had won for themselves finally an acceptance and a definiteness that made them fit to play a part in the legislative process. They came into the statute . . . freighted with the meaning imparted to them by the mischief to be remedied and by contemporaneous discussion. . . . In such conditions history is a teacher that is not to be ignored." [9]

Words of art bring their art with them. They bear the meaning of their habitat whether it be a phrase of technical significance in the scientific or business world, or whether it be loaded with the recondite connotations of feudalism. Holmes made short shrift of a contention by remarking that statutes used "familiar legal expressions in their familiar legal sense." [10] The peculiar idiom of business or of administrative practise often modifies the meaning that ordinary speech assigns to language. And if a word is obviously transplanted from another legal source, whether the common law or other legislation, it brings the old soil with it.

The context.—Legislation is a form of literary composition. But construction is not an abstract process equally valid for every composition, not even for every composition whose meaning must be judicially ascertained. The nature of the composition demands awareness of certain pre-suppositions. For instance, the words in a constitution may carry different meanings from the same words in a statute precisely because "it is a constitution we are expounding." The reach of this consideration was indicated by Mr. Justice Holmes in language that remains fresh no matter how often repeated:

". . . when we are dealing with words that also are a constituent act, like the Constitution of the United States, we must realize that they have called into life a being the development of which could not have been foreseen completely by the most gifted of its begetters. It was enough for them to realize or to hope that they had created an organism; it has taken a century and has cost their successors much sweat and blood to prove that they created a nation. The case before us must be considered in the light of our whole experience and not merely in that of what was said a hundred years ago." [11]

And so, the significance of an enactment, its antecedents as well as its later history, its relation to other enactments, all may be relevant to the construction of words for one purpose and in one setting but not for another. Some words are confined to their history; some are starting points for history. Words are intellectual and moral currency. They come from the legislative mint with some intrinsic meaning. Sometimes it remains unchanged. Like currency, words sometimes appreciate or depreciate in value.

Frequently the sense of a word cannot be got except by fashioning a mosaic of significance out of the innuendoes of disjointed bits of statute. Cardozo phrased this familiar phenomenon by stating that "the meaning of a statute is to be looked for, not in any single section, but in all the parts together and in their relation to the end in view." [12] And to quote Cardozo once more on this phase of our problem: "There is need to keep in view also the structure of the statute, and the relation, physical and logical, between its several parts." [13]

The generating consideration is that legislation is more than composition. It is an active instrument of government which, for purposes of interpretation, means that laws have ends to be achieved. It is in this connection that Holmes said "Words are flexible." [14] Again it was Holmes, the last judge to give quarter to loose thinking or vague yearning, who said that "the general purpose is a more important aid to the meaning than any rule which grammar or formal logic may lay down." [15] And it was Holmes who chided courts for being "apt to err by sticking too closely to the words of a law where those words import a policy that goes beyond them." [16] Note, however, that he found the policy in "those words"!

"Proliferation of Purpose"

You may have observed that I have not yet used the word "intention." All these years I have avoided speaking of the "legislative intent" and I shall continue to be on my guard against using it. The objection to "intention" was indicated in a letter by Mr. Justice Holmes which the recipient kindly put at my disposal:

> "Only a day or two ago—when counsel talked of the intention of a legislature, I was indiscreet enough to say I don't care what their intention was. I only want to know what the words mean. Of course the phrase often is used to express a conviction not exactly thought out—that you construe a particular clause or expression by considering the whole instrument and any dominant purposes that it may express. In fact intention is a residuary clause intended to gather up whatever other aids there may be to interpretation beside the particular words and the dictionary."

If that is what the term means, it is better to use a less beclouding characterization. Legislation has an aim; it seeks to obviate some mischief, to supply an inadequacy, to effect a change of policy, to formulate a plan of government. That aim, that policy is not drawn, like nitrogen, out of the air; it is evinced in the language of the statute, as read in the light of other external manifestations of purpose. That is what the judge must seek and effectuate, and he ought not be led off the trail by tests that have overtones of subjective design. We are not concerned with anything subjective. We do not delve into the mind of legislators or their draftsmen, or committee members. Against what he believed to be such an attempt Cardozo once protested:

> "The judgment of the court, if I interpret the reasoning aright, does not rest upon a ruling that Congress would have gone beyond its power if the purpose that it professed was the purpose truly cherished. The judgment of the court rests upon the ruling that another purpose, not professed, may be read beneath the surface, and by the purpose so imputed the statute is destroyed. Thus the process of psychoanalysis has spread to unaccustomed fields. There is a wise and ancient doctrine that a court will not inquire into the motives of a legislative body. . . ." [17]

The difficulty in many instances where a problem of meaning arises is that the enactment was not directed towards the troubling question. The problem might then be stated, as once it was by Mr. Justice Cardozo, "which choice is it the more likely that Congress would have made?" [18] While in its context the significance and limitations of this question are clear, thus to frame the question too often tempts inquiry into the subjective and might seem to warrant the court in giving answers based on an unmanifested legislative state of mind. But the purpose which a court must effectuate is not that which Congress should have enacted, or would have. It is that which it did enact, however inaptly, because it may fairly be said to be imbedded in the statute, even if a specific manifestation was not thought of, as is often the very reason for casting a statute in very general terms.

Often the purpose or policy that controls is not directly revealed in the particular enactment. Statutes cannot be read intelligently if the eye is closed to considerations evidenced in affiliated statutes, or in the known temper of legislative opinion. Thus, for example, it is not lightly to be presumed that Congress sought to infringe on "very sacred rights." [19] This improbability will be a factor in determining whether language, though it should be so read if standing alone, was used to effect such a drastic change.

More frequently still it becomes important to remember, as in recent regulatory statutes, that the judicial task in marking out the extent to which Congress has exercised its constitutional power over commerce, is not that of devising an abstract formula. The task is one of accommodation as between assertions of new federal authority and historic functions of the individual States. Federal legislation of this character cannot therefore be construed without regard to the implications of our dual system of government. In such cases, for example, it is not to be assumed as a matter of course that when Congress adopts a new scheme for federal industrial regulation, it deals with all situations falling within the general mischief which gave rise to the legislation. The underlying assumptions of our dual form of government, and the consequent presuppositions of legislative draftsmanship which are expressive of our history and habits, cut across what might otherwise be the implied range of legislation. The history of congressional legislation regulating not only interstate commerce as such but also activities intertwined with it, justify the generalization that,

when the federal government takes over such local radiations in the
vast network of our national economic enterprise and thereby radically
readjusts the balance of State and national authority, those charged
with the duty of legislating are reasonably explicit and do not entrust its attainment to that retrospective expansion of meaning which
properly deserves the stigma of judicial legislation.

SEARCH FOR PURPOSE

How then does the purpose which a statute expresses reveal itself,
particularly when the path of purpose is not straight and narrow? The
English courts say: look at the statute and look at nothing else. . . .
[As Lord Haldane said in a 1922 decision,] "In *Millar* v. *Taylor* the
principle of construction was laid down in words, which have never,
so far as I know, been seriously challenged, by Willes J. as long ago as
in 1769: 'The sense and meaning of an Act of Parliament must be
collected from what it says when passed into a law; and not from the
history of changes it underwent in the house where it took its rise.
That history is not known to the other house or to the sovereign.' "
These current English rules of construction are simple. They are
too simple. If the purpose of construction is the ascertainment of meaning, nothing that is logically relevant should be excluded. The rigidity
of English courts in interpreting language merely by reading it disregards the fact that enactments are, as it were, organisms which exist
in their environment. One wonders whether English judges are confined psychologically as they purport to be legally. The judges deem
themselves limited to reading the words of a statute. But can they really
escape placing the words in the context of their minds, which after all
are not automata applying legal logic but repositories of all sorts of
assumptions and impressions? Such a modest if not mechanical view
of the task of construction disregards legal history. In earlier centuries
the judges recognized that the exercise of their judicial function to understand and apply legislative policy is not to be hindered by artificial
canons and limitations. . . .
At the beginning, the Supreme Court reflected the early English
attitude. With characteristic hardheadedness Chief Justice Marshall
struck at the core of the matter with the observation "Where the

mind labours to discover the design of the legislature, it seizes everything from which aid can be derived." [20] This commonsensical way
of dealing with statutes fell into disuse, and more or less catchpenny
canons of construction did service instead. To no small degree the
vogue of a more wooden treatment of legislation arose, I suspect, because the need for keeping vividly in mind the occasions for drawing
on all aids in the process of distilling meaning from legislation was comparatively limited. As the area of regulation steadily widened, the impact of the legislative process upon the judicial brought into being, and
compelled consideration of, all that convincingly illumines an enactment, instead of merely that which is called, with delusive simplicity,
"the end result." Legislatures themselves provided illumination by general definitions, special definitions, explicit recitals of policy, and
even directions of attitudes appropriate for judicial construction. Legislative reports were increasingly drawn upon, statements by those in
charge of legislation, reports of investigating committees, recommendations of agencies entrusted with the enforcement of laws, etc. etc. When
Mr. Justice Holmes came to the Court, the United States Reports
were practically barren of references to legislative materials. These
swarm in current volumes. And let me say in passing that the importance that such materials play in Supreme Court litigation carry
far-reaching implications for bench and bar.

The change I have summarized was gradual. Hesitations were felt
and doubts were expressed even after the Court broke out of the
mere language of a law. We find Mr. Justice Holmes saying, "It is a
delicate business to base speculations about the purposes or construction of a statute upon the vicissitudes of its passage." [21] And as late as
1925 he referred to earlier bills relating to a statute under review, with
the reservation "If it be legitimate to look at them." [22]

Such hesitations and restraints are in limbo. Courts examine the
forms rejected in favor of the words chosen. They look at later statutes
"considered to throw a cross light" upon an earlier enactment.[23] The
consistent construction by an administrative agency charged with ef-
fectuating the policy of an enactment carries very considerable weight.
While assertion of authority does not demonstrate its existence, long-
continued, uncontested assertion is at least evidence that the legislature
conveyed the authority. Similarly, while authority conferred does not

atrophy by disuse, failure over an extended period to exercise it is some proof that it was not given. And since "a page of history is worth a volume of logic," [24] courts have looked into the background of statutes, the mischief to be checked and the good that was designed, looking sometimes far afield and taking notice also as judges of what is generally known by men.

Unhappily, there is no table of logarithms for statutory construction. No item of evidence has a fixed or even average weight. One or another may be decisive in one set of circumstances, while of little value elsewhere. A painstaking, detailed report by a Senate Committee bearing directly on the immediate question may settle the matter. A loose statement even by a chairman of a committee, made impromptu in the heat of debate, less informing in cold type than when heard on the floor, will hardly be accorded the weight of an encyclical.

Spurious use of legislative history must not swallow the legislation so as to give point to the quip that only when legislative history is doubtful do you go to the statute. While courts are no longer confined to the language, they are still confined by it. Violence must not be done to the words chosen by the legislature. Unless indeed no doubt can be left that the legislature has in fact used a private code, so that what appears to be violence to language is merely respect to special usage. In the end, language and external aids, each accorded the authority deserved in the circumstances, must be weighed in the balance of judicial judgment. Only if its premises are emptied of their human variables, can the process of statutory construction have the precision of a syllogism. We cannot avoid what Mr. Justice Cardozo deemed inherent in the problem of construction, making "a choice between uncertainties. We must be content to choose the lesser." [25] But to the discerning and disinterested eye, the scales will hardly escape appearing to tip slightly on the side of a more probable meaning.

"Canons of Construction"

Nor can canons of construction save us from the anguish of judgment. Such canons give an air of abstract intellectual compulsion to what is in fact a delicate judgment, concluding a complicated process of balancing subtle and elusive elements. All our three Justices have at one time or another leaned on the crutch of a canon. But they have done so only rarely, and with a recognition that these rules of construction are not in any true sense rules of law. So far as valid, they are what Mr. Justice Holmes called them, axioms of experience.[26] In many instances, these canons originated as observations in specific cases from which they were abstracted, taken out of the context of actuality, and, as it were, codified in treatises. . . .

Insofar as canons of construction are generalizations of experience, they all have worth. In the abstract, they rarely arouse controversy. Difficulties emerge when canons compete in soliciting judgment, because they conflict rather than converge. For the demands of judgment underlying the art of interpretation, there is no vade-mecum.

But even generalized restatements from time to time may not be wholly wasteful. Out of them may come a sharper rephrasing of the conscious factors of interpretation; new instances may make them more vivid but also disclose more clearly their limitations. Thereby we may avoid rigidities which, while they afford more precise formulas, do so at the price of cramping the life of law. To strip the task of judicial reading of statutes of rules that partake of the mysteries of a craft serves to reveal the true elements of our problem. It defines more accurately the nature of the intellectual responsibility of a judge and thereby subjects him to more relevant criteria of criticism. Rigorous analysis also sharpens the respective duties of legislature and courts in relation to the making of laws and to their enforcement.

Fair Construction and Fit Legislation

The quality of legislative organization and procedure is inevitably reflected in the quality of legislative draftsmanship. Representative Monroney told the House last July that "95 percent of all the legislation that becomes law passes the Congress in the shape that it came from our committees. Therefore if our committee work is sloppy, if it is bad, if it is inadequate, our legislation in 95 percent of the cases will be bad and inadequate as well." And Representative Lane added that "In the second session of the 78th Congress 953 bills and and resolutions were passed, of which only 86 were subject to any real discussion." [27] But what courts do with legislation may in turn deeply affect what Congress will do in the future. Emerson says somewhere that mankind is as lazy as it dares to be. Loose judicial reading makes for loose legislative writing. It encourages the practise illustrated in a recent cartoon in which a senator tells his colleagues "I admit this new bill is too complicated to understand. We'll just have to pass it to find out what it means." A modern Pascal might be tempted at times to say of legislation what Pascal said of students of theology when he charged them with "a looseness of thought and language that would pass nowhere else in making what are professedly very fine distinctions." And it is conceivable that he might go on and speak, as did Pascal, of the "insincerity with which terms are carefully chosen to cover opposite meanings." [28]

But there are more fundamental objections to loose judicial reading. In a democracy the legislative impulse and its expression should come from those popularly chosen to legislate and equipped to devise policy, as courts are not. The pressure on legislatures to discharge their responsibility with care, understanding and imagination should be stiffened, not relaxed. Above all, they must not be encouraged in irresponsible or undisciplined use of language. In the keeping of legislatures perhaps more than in that of any other group is the well-being of their fellow-men. Their responsibility is discharged ultimately by words. They are under a special duty therefore to observe that "Exactness in the use of words is the basis of all serious thinking. You will get nowhere without it. Words are clumsy tools, and it is very easy to cut one's fingers with them, and they need the closest attention in handling; but they are the only tools we have, and imagination itself cannot work without them. You must master the use of them, or you will wander forever guessing at the mercy of mere impulse and unrecognized assumptions and arbitrary associations, carried away with every wind of doctrine." [29]

Perfection of draftsmanship is as unattainable as demonstrable correctness of judicial reading of legislation. Fit legislation and fair adjudication are attainable. The ultimate reliance of society for the proper fulfillment of both these august functions is to entrust them only to those who are equal to their demands.

Footnotes

[1] Mr. Justice Brandeis in *United States* v. *Moreland*, 258 U.S. 433, 451.

[2] *Carter* v. *Carter Coal Co.*, 298 U.S. 238, 327.

[3] See Sir Ernest Barker's Introduction to his translation of Aristotle's *Politics*, p. lxiii.

[4] *Hoeper* v. *Tax Commission*, 284 U.S. 206, 219.

[5] *Anderson* v. *Wilson*, 289 U.S. 20, 27.

[6] *Iselin* v. *United States*, 270 U.S. 245, 250–51.

[7] *St. Louis-San Francisco Ry.* v. *Middlekamp*, 256 U.S. 226, 232.

[8] *Boston Sand Co.* v. *United States*, 278 U.S. 41, 48.

[9] Cardozo, *Duparquet Co.* v. *Evans*, 297 U.S. 216, 220–21.

[10] *Henry* v. *United States*, 251 U.S. 393, 395.

[11] *Missouri* v. *Holland*, 252 U.S. 416, 433.

[12] *Panama Refining Co.* v. *Ryan*, 293 U.S. 388, 433, 439.

[13] *Duparquet Co.* v. *Evans*, 297 U.S. 216, 218.

[14] *International Stevedoring Co.* v. *Haverty*, 272 U.S. 50, 58.

[15] *United States* v. *Whitridge*, 197 U.S. 135, 143.

[16] *Olmstead* v. *United States*, 277 U.S. 438, 469.

[17] *United States* v. *Constantine*, 296 U.S. 287 at 298–99.

[18] *Burnet* v. *Guggenheim*, 288 U.S. 280, 285.

[19] *Milwaukee Publishing Co.* v. *Burleson*, 255 U.S. 407, 438.

[20] *United States* v. *Fisher*, 2 Cranch 358, 386.

[21] *Pine Hill Co.* v. *United States*, 259 U.S. 191, 196.

[22] *Davis* v. *Pringle*, 268 U.S. 315, 318.

[23] See *United States* v. *Aluminum Co. of America*, 148 F. 2d. 416, 429.

[24] *N.Y. Trust Co.* v. *Eisner*, 256 U.S. 345, 349.

[25] *Burnet* v. *Guggenheim*, 288 U.S. 280, 288.

[26] See *Boston Sand Co.* v. *United States*, 278 U.S. 41, 48.

[27] See 92 Congressional Record, pp. 10040 and 10054, July 25, 1946.

[28] See Pater, *Miscellaneous Studies*, Essay on Pascal, pp. 48, 51.

[29] See J. W. Allen's Essay on Jeremy Bentham, in *The Social and Political Ideas of the Revolutionary Era* (ed. by Hearnshaw), pp. 181, 199.

WILLIAM O. DOUGLAS
The Decline of Stare Decisis

Justice Robert Jackson, who had experienced the iron bonds of precedent in arguing New Deal cases before the "old" Court in the 1930's, when Jackson was an Assistant Attorney General and Solicitor General, delivered an address in 1944 on "Decisional Law and *Stare Decisis*." He noted that "our times have witnessed considerable relaxation in the authority of the precedent." Discussing the reasons for this and the policy behind the principle of "let the decision stand," Jackson observed: "I cannot believe that any person who at all values the judicial process or distinguishes its method and philosophy from those of the political and legislative process would abandon or substantially impair the rule of *stare decisis*. Unless the assumption is substantially true that cases will be disposed of by application of known principles and previously disclosed courses of reasoning, our common-law process would become the most intolerable kind of *ex post facto* judicial law-making. Moderation in change is all that makes judicial participation in the evolution of law tolerable. . . . To overrule an important precedent is serious business. It calls for sober appraisal of the disadvantages of innovation as well as those of the questioned case, a weighing of practical effects of one against the other" (30 *A.B.A.J.* 334 [1944]).

In the selection which follows, Justice William O. Douglas takes a view of *stare decisis* which has a different emphasis from that of the quotation from Justice Jackson, though not openly antagonistic to Jackson's thought. The address was given as a

Benjamin N. Cardozo Lecture before the Association of the Bar of the City of New York, in April of 1949.

SOURCE: 4 *Record of the Association of the Bar of the City of New' York* 152–179 (1949).

We live in an age of doubt and confusion. Rules that once seemed fixed and certain today seem beclouded. Principles of law have been challenged and judges asked to refashion them. Many raised their voices in protest. Some were special pleaders with a stake in existing law. Others had a sincere belief that the foremost function of law in these days of stress and strain is to remain steady and stable so as to promote security. Thus judges have been admonished to hold steadfast to ancient precedents lest the courts themselves add fresh doubt, confusion, and concern over the strength of our institutions.

This search for a static security—in the law or elsewhere—is misguided. The fact is that security can only be achieved through constant change, through the wise discarding of old ideas that have outlived their usefulness, and through the adapting of others to current facts. There is only an illusion of safety in a Maginot Line. Social forces like armies can sweep around a fixed position and make it untenable. A position that can be shifted to meet such forces and at least partly absorb them alone gives hope of security.

I speak here of long-term swings in the law. I do not suggest that *stare decisis* is so fragile a thing as to bow before every wind. The law is not properly susceptible to whim or caprice. It must have the sturdy qualities required of every framework that is designed for substantial structures. Moreover, it must have uniformity when applied to the daily affairs of men.

Uniformity and continuity in law are necessary to many activities. If they are not present, the integrity of contracts, wills, conveyances and securities is impaired.[1] And there will be no equal justice under law if a negligence rule is applied in the morning but not in the afternoon. *Stare decisis* provides some moorings so that men may trade and arrange their affairs with confidence. *Stare decisis* serves to take the capricious element out of law and to give stability to a society. It is a strong tie which the future has to the past.

It is easy, however, to overemphasize *stare decisis* as a principle in the lives of men. Even for the experts law is only a prediction of what judges will do under a given set of facts—a prediction that makes rules of law and decisions not logical deductions but functions of human behavior.[2] There are usually plenty of precedents to go around; and with the accumulation of decisions, it is no great problem for the lawyer to find legal authority for most propositions. The difficulty is to estimate what effect a slightly different shade of facts will have and to predict the speed of the current in a changing stream of the law. The predictions and prophecies that lawyers make are indeed appraisals of a host of imponderables. The decisions of yesterday or of the last century are only the starting points.

As for laymen, their conception of the rules of law that govern their conduct is so nebulous that in one sense, as Gray said, the law in its application to their normal affairs is to a very considerable extent *ex post facto*.[3]

The place of *stare decisis* in constitutional law is even more tenuous. A judge looking at a constitutional decision may have compulsions to revere past history and accept what was once written. But he remembers above all else that it is the Constitution which he swore to support and defend, not the gloss which his predecessors may have put on it. So he comes to formulate his own views, rejecting some earlier ones as false and embracing others. He cannot do otherwise unless he lets men long dead and unaware of the problems of the age in which he lives do his thinking for him.

This re-examination of precedent in constitutional law is a personal matter for each judge who comes along. When only one new judge is appointed during a short period, the unsettling effect in constitutional law may not be great. But when a majority of a Court is suddenly reconstituted, there is likely to be substantial unsettlement. There will be unsettlement until the new judges have taken their positions on constitutional doctrine. During that time—which may extend a decade or more—constitutional law will be in flux. That is the necessary consequence of our system and to my mind a healthy one. The alternative is to let the Constitution freeze in the pattern which one generation gave it. But the Constitution was designed for the vicissitudes of time. It must never become a code which carries the overtones of one period that may be hostile to another.

So far as constitutional law is concerned *stare decisis* must give way before the dynamic component of history. Once it does, the cycle starts again. Today's new and startling decision quickly becomes a coveted anchorage for new vested interests. The former proponents of change acquire an acute conservatism in their new *status quo*. It will then take an oncoming group from a new generation to catch the broader vision which may require an undoing of the work of our present and their past.

Much of what courts do is little understood by laymen. Very few portions of the press undertake to show the social, economic, or political significance of the work of the judiciary or to educate the public on long-term trends. Lawyers often do not see the broader view which is exposed by the narrow and intensely personal efforts of a client to vindicate a position or gain an advantage. Yet the work of a court may send a whole economy in one direction or help shape the manifest destiny of an era. Two illustrations from different periods of our history will indicate what I mean.

For at least a decade or more it was commonly assumed that the Fourteenth Amendment was adopted to protect negroes in their newly won rights. Other interests had sought to creep under its wing. Thus corporations claimed they were persons within the meaning of the equal protection clause. Woods (then circuit judge) thought the language of the Amendment and its history too clear to admit of doubt on the point. In 1870 he rejected the contention in *Insurance Co.* v. *New Orleans*, 1 Woods 85. Sixteen years passed. Woods was now a member of the Court of which Waite was Chief Justice. A railroad company pressed its claim that California's tax assessment against it violated the Equal Protection Clause of the Fourteenth Amendment. Before the point was even argued, Waite announced from the bench that the Court did not care to hear argument on the question whether the clause applied to corporations. "We are all of opinion that it does," he said.[4] Thus without argument or opinion on the point the *Santa Clara* case became one of the most momentous of all our decisions. It was not long before the same constitutional doctrine was extended to the Due Process Clause.[5] Again the decision was cryptic and oracular, without exposition or explanation.

These decisions, whether right or wrong, sound or unsound, may have changed the course of our industrial history. Corporations were now armed with constitutional prerogatives. And so armed, they proceeded to the development and exploitation of a continent in a manner never equalled before or since. Some think these decisions helped give corporations what Parrington has called "the freedom of buccaneers." [6] They doubtless did release some of the dynamic quality of the drive that built industrial America in a brilliant (albeit ruthless) way.

These unexplained (and certainly not obvious) decisions are now so implicit in the financial and industrial undertaking of the nation that a recent challenge of them had a resounding effect.[7] Such is the hold of *stare decisis* on the profession.

A half century passed and the Court made another decision whose impact on industrial America was almost as profound.

In 1918 the Court in the *Dagenhart* case (*Hammer* v. *Dagenhart*, 247 U.S. 251) had decided that Congress had no power to regulate the production of goods for commerce where the goods themselves were harmless. It thus struck down a child labor law. A process of erosion soon set in. Distinctions and qualifications were made in a long line of decisions. Finally in 1941 in a case involving the constitutionality of the Fair Labor Standards Act (*United States* v. *Darby*, 312 U.S. 100) a unanimous Court overruled the earlier five-to-four decision. Stone's exposition of the Commerce Clause in the *Darby* case was undoubtedly more faithful to Marshall's conception of it [8] than that espoused by a bare majority of the Court in the *Dagenhart* case. However that may be, the *Darby* case gave sanction to a new centralized force in American industrial and social life.

Some have thought that but for the philosophy which it represents and the power of the Federal Government which it sanctions, the nation would not have been able to marshall all the strength and to develop all the ingenuity and resourcefulness necessary to deal with the increasingly national problems of the age.

The decision of the Court in the *Santa Clara* case protected the forces of free enterprise that were building America. We can never know how much the spectre of socialism and the fear of assaults on capitalism contributed to the decision. But the end result is plain: the Court itself became part of the dynamic component of history. It did not live aloof from the turbulence of the times. It was part of the life of the community, absorbed from it the dominant attitudes and feelings of the day, and moved with the impetus of the era.

The Court in the *Darby* case was likewise extremely sensitive to the critical problems of another day. The whole of the democratic world had long been reexamining the conditions that had produced the misery of depressions. It is a soul-searching decision when one is asked to deny the existence of the power of government to correct a social evil. The unanimity of the Court in the *Darby* case indicated how high experience had piled since *Dagenhart* was decided.

Neither the Court in the *Santa Clara* case nor the Court in the *Darby* case was insensitive to the implications of the decisions. Precedents are made or unmade not on logic and history alone. The choices left by the generality of a constitution relate to policy. That is why laymen and lawyers alike must look widely and diversely for understanding. The problem of the judge is to keep personal predilections from dictating the choice and to be as faithful as possible to the architectural scheme. We can get from those who preceded a sense of the continuity of a society. We can draw from their learning a feel for the durability of a doctrine and a sense of the origins of principles. But we have experience that they never knew. Our vision may be shorter or longer. But it is ours. It is better that we make our own history than be governed by the dead. We too must be dynamic components of history if our institutions are to be vital, directive forces in the life of our age.

One can respect the policy decision both in the *Santa Clara* case and in the *Darby* case. But whatever the view on the merits all will agree, I think, that the recent Court was more faithful to the democratic tradition. It wrote in words that all could understand why it did what it did. That is vital to the integrity of the judicial process.

The periods in which the *Santa Clara* and the *Darby* cases were decided were both turbulent. It is of interest to look at them comparatively for insight into the problem of stability of judicial precedents. The latter period closes in some respects a cycle started by the first.

One measure of stability is the extent to which precedents are overruled.

During the thirty-year period between 1860 and 1890, the Court on eighteen occasions overruled (expressly or in effect) controlling precedents. In 10 of these the Court was unanimous. In 13 of the overruled cases the Court had been unanimous. Eight of these cases involved constitutional issues. Ten involved questions of state law and common law and interpretations of statutes.

The most important of the constitutional decisions were the *Legal Tender Cases* (11 Wall. 682, 12 Wall. 457) that overruled the *Hepburn* case (*Hepburn* v. *Griswold*, 8 Wall. 603) decided the previous year. The *Hepburn* case, decided by a 4-3 vote in 1870, held that a creditor need not take United States notes as payment under contracts made prior to the Act of Congress declaring the notes legal tender. The next year the minority of three became a majority of five through the appointment of Strong and Bradley by President Grant.

Feeling of the day ran high. Strange comrades were aligned on both sides of the debate. There was bitter argument by the public. Charges of court-packing reverberated through the country. Many who opposed the first decision likewise opposed the second. The debate shook the country. But the judges then as now spoke their minds. These were men of strong convictions; and they gave the government the flexible control over currency which they thought the Constitution intended.

Hughes once said of this decision, "From the standpoint of the effect on public opinion, there can be no doubt that the reopening of the case was a serious mistake and the overruling in such a short time, and by one vote, of the previous decision shook popular respect for the Court." [9] My own view is different. In some cases it is of course more important that a rule be announced and a dispute put at rest than that a decision be made one way or the other. But when it comes to a constitutional question, especially the authority of government to act, the decision where possible should reflect views of the full court.

The reversal of the Court in the *Legal Tender Cases* had a healthy effect. Management of currency was left in the legislative field, where the school of which Cardozo was a conspicuous member thinks most social and economic problems should remain. It was left so that the people could experiment even unwisely. That is a part of the adventure in democratic government—a view expressed by Bradley in the *Legal Tender Cases*, 12 Wall. p. 562, when he stated, "Questions of political expediency belong to the legislative halls, not to the judicial forum."

In the decade preceding 1860, the Court had held that the admiralty jurisdiction depended on the navigable character of the water, not upon the ebb and flow of the tide thus overruling a leading case from the preceding generation.[10] In the 1868 Term the Court made the foundation of admiralty even firmer by holding, contrary to a ten-year-old decision that admiralty jurisdiction extended to commerce on navigable waters though the transportation was wholly within a state; and further that the action *in rem* was limited to the admiralty court.[11]

In the early part of the period from 1860–1890, the Court gave broad leeway to state regulations of interstate commerce.[12] It sustained a Wisconsin rate even on interstate commerce since Congress had not acted.[13] It held valid a tax on a railroad's gross receipts from inter-state commerce.[14] It allowed a State to impose a nondiscriminatory li-cense tax on an interstate business.[15] The first two of these decisions were by a divided Court; the third was unanimous.

But in only a few years important and rather basic shifts on these matters were made. The silence of Congress—the fact that it had not regulated a particular matter—was given increasing weight as evidence of an intent to leave interstate commerce free from regulation. The Court undertook a stricter application of constitutional principles designed to keep the arteries of commerce open and to free the inter-state aspects of business from state control whether by taxes or regu-lation.[16]

State regulation of discriminatory interstate rates of carriers was annulled in the October Term, 1886.[17] In the same Term a unanimous Court held unconstitutional an unapportioned tax on the gross receipts of interstate commerce.[18] The following Term a unanimous Court overturned its previous unanimous decision and held that a license tax on an interstate business was unconstitutional.[19] Shortly thereafter it struck down a state law regulating the sale of liquor in the original package by the importer and with it a forty-three-year-old prece-dent.[20] Even the evils of alcohol were considered less weighty than the evils of a constrained interstate commerce. Field's view that (apart from strictly local aspects of commerce) the silence of Congress was the "equivalent to its declaration that commerce in the matter shall be free" [21] was in the ascendancy.

In this period the Court also rejected a fifty-nine-year-old precedent and held that Congress had no power to commit for contempt incurred by refusal to obey and respect an order in a Congressional investigation.[22] In the 1824 Term Marshall had ruled that the question whether a suit is against a State within the prohibition of the Eleventh Amendment is determined by reference to the parties of record. After a checkered career that doctrine was finally excised from the law.[23]

These were the eight cases overruling precedents on constitutional law.

The other ten involved more mundane subjects. . . .

A number of decisions in the latter group involved overruling the Court's prior construction of Acts of Congress. These precedents were overruled against objections, at times vigorous, that the correction of the error, if any, should be left to Congress.

In the period from 1937–March 28, 1949, the Court in 30 cases overruled earlier decisions. In 21 of these the reversals were on constitutional grounds. In the great majority of the 30 cases the cases overruled had been decided within the previous 20 years.

These cases are too fresh in memory to require much space for discussion. The largest group—8 in number—related to the taxing power of state and federal governments. Tax rates had become more burdensome than ever before in our history; and tax exemptions were being closely scrutinized as the government's need for revenue grew.

The new approach was largely fashioned by Hughes. He held for the Court that a nondiscriminatory federal income tax upon the lessee of a State was not open to the objection that it was a tax on an instrumentality of the State (*Helvering* v. *Producers Corp.*, 303 U.S. 376). Two decisions, one from that decade and one from the preceding decade, fell.[24] The new doctrine was applied to sustain an Oklahoma estate tax on Indian property [25] previously held exempt under the federal instrumentality doctrine.[26] And finally in *Oklahoma Tax Commission* v. *Texas Co.*, decided March 7, 1949, the rest of the cases by which tax immunities had been acquired in Indian property under the instrumentality theory were overruled.[27]

Other private tax exemptions, riding on the concept of sovereign immunity from taxation, were reexamined and eliminated. Salaries of federal employees were placed within the reach of the state-taxing power, and the salaries of state employees within the reach of the national power.[28] A state tax on a private contractor was upheld, even though its burden would eventually be passed on to the federal government.[29] This tendency closely to scrutinize tax privileges led to the taxation of the salaries of federal judges appointed after the taxing statute.[30]

A ten-year-old precedent [31] was overruled and a State was allowed to levy an inheritance tax on shares of a corporation incorporated under its law, although the deceased had been domiciled elsewhere.[32] In another tax case [33] the Court repudiated a newly spun theory of the privileges and immunity clause [34] which promised to throttle state power over business affairs.

In other ways too, the Court enlarged the regulatory power of the States in the field of economic affairs—by a less restrictive reading of the equal-protection clause; [35] by a more pervasive view of state regulation of local aspects of interstate industries; [36] by tolerance of price-fixing by the States.[37]

A judicially created restraint on the power of Congress over commerce was also removed in the *Darby* case.[38] And contrary to long-standing rulings on the character of insurance,[39] that business was held covered by the Sherman Act.[40] During this period the Court also strengthened the federal eminent domain power [41] by eliminating private property interests which had been judicially created in the bed of a navigable stream.[42]

In the field of civil liberties the Court decided and then rather promptly reversed two decisions: it held that a State could not require school children to perform a flag salute in opposition to their religious beliefs [43] and it struck down a license tax imposed on the dissemination of religious literature by a religious group.[44] It also reversed a nine-year-old precedent [45] and held that where a primary election was an integral part of the elective process for nominating candidates for Congress, a State could not exclude a person from the right to vote in it on account of race or color.[46]

In the divorce field the Court reconstrued the Full Faith and Credit Clause so as to give the state of the domicile of one spouse more power over dissolution of the marriage relation.[47]

In *Erie R. Co.* v. *Tompkins*, 304 U.S. 64, the Court rid the federal system of a precedent almost a century old,[48] and with the latter went others that became "obsolete." [49] The Court saw its earlier holding as inviting discrimination by nonresidents of one State against residents of another in diversity cases. It therefore took a step towards uniformity by making local law as construed by state agencies controlling in federal courts in that type of case. And finally in *Lincoln Union* v. *Northwestern Co.*, 335 U.S. 525, decided January 3, 1949, it sustained the constitutionality of state laws outlawing the closed shop. In doing so it repudiated some precedents [50] by which the constitutional standard of Due Process had absorbed economic theories of the judiciary. It returned closer to the earlier constitutional pronouncements that the States have the power "to legislate against what are found to be injurious practices in their internal commercial and business affairs, so long as their laws do not run afoul of some specific federal constitutional prohibition, or of some valid federal law." *Id.*, at p. 536.

Those were the cases reflecting rights-about-face in constitutional law during this recent period. There were others which have been important in the affairs of the nation. A ruling that a utility's depreciation had to be taken at present value rather than cost was rejected.[51] The rule that he who sells an unpatented part of a combination for use in the assembled machine may be guilty of contributory infringement was rejected where a combination patent was being used to protect an unpatented part from competition.[52] It was held that in admiralty the warranty of seaworthiness extended to the appliances and the place of work and that the owner was not relieved of liability because an employee negligently chose defective equipment where sound equipment was available.[53]

In five cases the Court overruled decisions involving interpretations of Acts of Congress and thus cleared the stream of law of derelicts of its own creation, not waiting for Congress to act. It held that private operators of vessels under certain contracts with the government could be sued for torts, the claimants not being restricted to suits against the United States under the Suits in Admiralty Act.[54] It gave a restrictive interpretation to a statute declaratory of the power of federal courts to punish for contempt [55] and thus returned to earlier views of the law. It changed its prior construction of the statute governing naturalization so as to do away with the requirement of an oath to bear arms as a condition of citizenship.[56] It overruled two four-year-old precedents construing the provision of the Revenue Act of 1926 that deals with transfers "intended to take effect in possession or enjoyment" at or after the grantor's death.[57] And just the other day it overruled a nineteen-year-old decision in the same field.[58]

In these cases, as in the ones from the 1860–1890 period already noticed, the Court rejected numerous pleas to let Congress correct mistakes that the Court had created. It was also reluctant to find in the silence of Congress approval of the statutory interpretations which it had adopted.

It is, I think, a healthy practice (too infrequently followed) for a court to re-examine its own doctrine. Legislative correction of judicial errors is often difficult to effect. Moreover, responsible government should entail the undoing of wrongs committed by the department in question. That course is faithful to democratic traditions. Respect for any tribunal is increased if it stands ready (save where injustice to intervening rights would occur) [59] not only to correct the errors of others but also to confess its own. This was the philosophy expressed by a judge of the New York Court of Appeals almost a century ago when he proclaimed it "the duty of every judge and every court to examine its own decisions, . . . without fear, and to revise them without reluctance." [60] That is to heed Shakespeare's warning in *The Merchant of Venice*,

> " 'Twill be recorded for a precedent;
> And many an error, by the same example
> Will rush into the state."

I said that one measure of instability in the law is represented by the overruling of precedents. But the overruling itself is at times not the true measure of the change. Commonly the change extended over a long period; the erosion of a precedent was gradual. The overruling did not effect an abrupt change in the law; it rather recognized a *fait accompli*.

In other words the distinguishing of precedents is often a gradual and reluctant way of overruling cases. In modern times the House of Lords has rarely overruled a precedent. But as Radin has shown it has carried the technique of distinguishing precedents "to a very high pitch of ingenuity." [61] And for us the process of distinguishing may indeed do service for overruling or have the same effect, as Brandeis observed in *Burnet* v. *Coronado Oil & Gas Co.*, 285 U.S. 393, 408.

Hammer v. *Dagenhart*, 247 U.S. 251, had a checkered career. Its principle sometimes seemed to be on the wane and then to be restored. It was, for example, held not to forbid federal punishment of the transportation of stolen motor vehicles (*Brooks* v. *United States*, 267 U.S. 432) or of goods made by convict labor (*Kentucky Whip & Collar Co.* v. *Illinois Central R. Co.*, 299 U.S. 334). Yet federal control of the wages, hours and working conditions of miners engaged in producing coal was invalidated (*Carter* v. *Carter Coal Co.*, 298 U.S. 238). But that was the last burst of vitality of the doctrine. *Labor Board* v. *Jones & Laughlin*, 301 U.S. 1, decided in 1937, upheld the Wagner Act as applied to a company producing goods for commerce, and foreshadowed the demise of the *Dagenhart* case. Thus it had been at least substantially impaired before *United States* v. *Darby*, 312 U.S. 100, laid it finally to rest. . . .

Thus the actual overruling of cases is no true measure of the rate of change in the law. The overruling may come at the end of a cycle of change and not mark its commencement. It is this gradual process of erosion of constitutional doctrine that has the true unsettling effect. It is this which often breeds wasteful uncertainty. As the first landmark falls, the outsider may have few clues as to the importance of the shift. The overruling may and often does presage a sweeping change in constitutional doctrine. Years of litigation may be needed to rid the law of mischievous decisions which should have fallen with the first of the series to be overruled.

That is why it is my belief that it would be wise judicial administration when a landmark decision falls to overrule expressly all the cases in the same genus as the one which is repudiated, even though they are not before the Court. There is candor in that course. *Stare decisis* then is not used to breed the uncertainty which it is supposed to dispel.

The development of exceptions or qualifications to constitutional doctrine can have a profound unsettling effect. An excellent example comes from the period 1860–1890.

The power of the states to fix utility rates was a new issue for the

Court at that time. The issue was conceived from the conflict between business interests and midwestern farmers, who were rapidly being impoverished by low prices, high interest, and high freight rates. They organized the Grange movement, which succeeded in exerting pressure in midwestern legislatures and obtaining legislation which provided limitations on rates.

It was in this setting that the issue was brought to the Supreme Court in a case involving the power of Illinois to fix the maximum rates for storage of grain in warehouses (*Munn* v. *Illinois*, 94 U.S. 113). A year passed between argument and the rendering of decision in the case. Two important conclusions were reached in this first important case on the subject of rate-making. (1) The power of a State to regulate industries "affected with a public interest" was upheld and the character of business falling in that category was broadly defined. (2) Recourse for correction of the rates was directed to the legislature and not to the courts. Field, in a vigorous dissent, joined in by Strong, viewed the conclusions of the Court as "subversive of the rights of private property" which the judiciary were duty-bound by the Constitution to defend. This dissent backed by the vigor of Field was to have telling effect in succeeding years.

There soon began a process of qualification which narrowed the category of businesses whose prices could be fixed by a State. The most striking restrictions on legislative power to fix prices were reached in the '20's by a closely divided Court. (*Tyson & Bro.* v. *Banton*, 273 U.S. 418, *Ribnik* v. *McBride*, 277 U.S. 350.) Those decisions marked the floodtide of exceptions and qualifications to the principle of *Munn* v. *Illinois*.

Beginning last century, Field's dissent as to the power of the courts to review utility rates had a powerful influence. There was at first some yielding to Field's view. Then came a change in personnel of the Court. Field's views became the law.[62] In 1890, the Court ruled that the question of reasonableness of rates was not entirely a legislative matter but was ultimately a judicial questioning arising under the Due Process Clause.[63] Then in 1898, came *Smyth* v. *Ames*, 169 U.S. 466, whose spirit many a judge wished were unblessed. It set constitutional standards for rate-making which haunted utility regulation.

Field's philosophy was that the "present assault upon capital is but the beginning" and only the "stepping-stone to others, larger and more sweeping, till our political contests will become a war of the poor against the rich; a war constantly growing in intensity and bitterness." [64] That philosophy merged with political power to give direction to the age. The spectre of confiscation rode high. Security was thought to be dependent upon keeping capital unfettered.

Today there is greater realization that survival lies in the development of a cooperative society where the security of capital rests on the broad base of the prosperity of the multitude. Today the accepted view is that property need not be made tyrant in order to give men freedom and incentive to acquire it, own it, and manage it and to unleash the great productive power of free enterprise.

Much of the unsettling influence of the Court since 1937 has been in removing from constitutional doctrine excrescences produced early in the century. The tendency has been to return to older views of constitutional interpretation, and to sanction governmental power over social and economic affairs which the Court beginning in the '80's and particularly in the preceding ten to thirty years had denied. Only if this is understood can the work of the period be put into clear historical perspective.

As respects price-fixing the process of restoration of the principle of *Munn* v. *Illinois* started almost at once after the flood of exceptions and qualifications had been reached. The ebb was clear and distinct.[65] The tide had started running back to *Munn* v. *Illinois* at least by 1934 when *Nebbia* v. *New York*, 291 U.S. 502, upheld the power of New York to fix the retail price of milk. *Olsen* v. *Nebraska*, 313 U.S. 236, decided April 28, 1941, merely marked the low tide. We returned in less than 70 years substantially to our starting point. *Munn* v. *Illinois* regained its lost vitality so far as price-fixing was concerned. Field's fear that "the prices of everything, from a calico gown to a city mansion, may be the subject of legislative direction" (94 U.S. p. 152) came true.

But that was only one phase of a basic shift in constitutional doctrine which took place during the recent period. Waite in *Munn* v. *Illinois* expressed in homely and unsophisticated terms the importance of judicial self-denial in review of social legislation. It was the view so ably espoused in later years by Holmes, Brandeis, Cardozo, and Stone. In *Munn* v. *Illinois*, 94 U.S. p. 134, Waite said, "For protection against abuses by legislatures the people must resort to the polls, not to the courts."

That principle was largely abandoned in the intervening years. The courts became the place to get relief from the pinch of legislation deemed to be improvident and unwise or hostile to the dominant interests of the day. But in the period from 1937–1949 Waite's view has been in process of restoration. The wisdom of legislation is to be tested by political processes, not by litigation. There are numerous instances during the recent period where that view has been applied. The recent closed-shop decision (*Lincoln Union* v. *Northwestern Co.*, 335 U.S. 525) is perhaps the best example. In the whole field of social legislation we have in a sense closed the cycle by returning to the philosophy of *Munn* v. *Illinois* and by wiping out the large group of intervening decisions which were hostile to legislative power and jealous of judicial power.[66]

The weakening of Field's influence on judicial review of utility rates has not been as complete. The force of the precedents forged in his era (and later strengthened by *Smyth* v. *Ames*, 169 U.S. 466) has been considerably dissipated, though they have not been overruled. Recent cases,[67] however, adopted a more pragmatic basis for rate-making, though the full-blown rule of legislative power in rate-making which *Munn* v. *Illinois* sponsored was not restored.

There are other factors of change and unsettlement in the law which defy statistical treatment. A rule of law correcting a social evil may be announced. But if it is not applied in the life of the community, there is no change. In spite of a new and unsettling pronouncement the course of the law may go on its way, undisturbed. On the other hand, if the Court as a matter of judicial administration pursues the matter and applies the principle with care and vigor in case after case, the effect of the change may be profound. We can only tell whether the Court is working in that direction by examining the cases which it takes and the manner of its disposition of them.

On what manner of cases does the Court spend its time? How is the discretionary certiorari jurisdiction employed? To what problems is the Court giving emphasis?

A few examples from the current period will illustrate how this matter of emphasis has caused substantial changes in law administration and in statutory interpretation.

There has been increasing scrutiny of charges that confessions in

criminal cases were coerced and a growing hostility to traces of
third-degree methods of the police in criminal prosecutions.[68] There
has been an increasing attention to the constitutional requirement of
counsel in criminal cases.[69] One product of that scrutiny has been
fundamental changes in the practice in some States, notably Missouri
and Illinois.[70] There has been increasing attention to Federal Employer
Liability Act cases that an indifferent or unfriendly attitude had per-
meated with a philosophy hostile to that reflected in the legislation.[71]

The study of changes in judicial precedents gives, of course, a distorted view. It is like the study of pathological cases in social or medi-
cal sciences. The norm is robust and enduring. The case that gets
into the books often has an unsettling effect. Yet we are apt to forget
that "the fact that a case is in the reports at all is in itself uncertain." [72]
The great body of law is unperturbed by events that may rock a nation.

When the changing stream of public law is studied there are three
considerations to keep in mind.

First. We have had only one major dispute that struck at the vitals
of our federalism. That was the Civil War. Our controversies and quar-
rels even at the level of constitutional law have been of a lesser kind.
They have been disputes calling for adjustment within the framework
of our Charter not for repudiation of it. As one of my Brethren recently stated,[73] they have not involved reconsideration of our basic
constitutional tenets which have been accepted since the days of Marshall. They have entailed argument over the application of established
doctrine. The problem has been to free the system for growth un-
hampered by the crippling restraints which men of cramped and narrow vision placed on it. In considering the charges leveled against
those of any period who are responsible for giving new or broader interpretations to the Constitution or discarding precedents it is well to
remember these words of Thayer,[74]

"And so it happens, as one looks back over our history and the field
of political discussions in the past, that he seems to see the whole
region strewn with the wrecks of the Constitution—of what people
have been imagining and putting forward as the Constitution. That
it was unconstitutional to buy Louisiana and Florida; that it was

unconstitutional to add new states to the Union from territory not belonging originally to it; that it was unconstitutional to govern the territories at all; that it was unconstitutional to charter a bank, to issue paper money, to make it a legal tender, to enact a protective tariff,—that these and a hundred other things were a violation of the Constitution has been solemnly and passionately asserted by statesmen and lawyers. Nothing that is now going forward can exceed the vehemence of denunciation, and the pathetic and conscientious resistance of those who lifted up their voices against many of these supposed violations of the Constitution. The trouble has been, then as now, that men imputed to our fundamental law their own too narrow construction of it, their own theory of its purposes and its spirit, and sought thus, when the question was one of mere power, to restrict its great liberty."

Second. It is sometimes thought to be astute political management of a shift in position to proclaim that no change is under way. That is designed as a sedative to instill confidence and allay doubts. It has been a tool of judges as well as other officials. Precedents, though distinguished and qualified out of existence, apparently have been kept alive. The theory is that the outward appearance of stability is what is important.

The idea that any body of law, particularly public law, should appear to stay put and not be in flux is an interesting phenomenon that Frank has explored in *Law and the Modern Mind*. He points out how it is—in law and in other fields too—that men continue to chant of the immutability of a rule in order to "cover up the transformation, to deny the reality of change, to conceal the truth of adaptation behind a verbal disguise of fixity and universality." [75] But the more blunt, open, and direct course is truer to democratic traditions. It reflects the candor of Cardozo. The principle of full disclosure has as much place in government as it does in the market place. A judiciary that discloses what it is doing and why it does it will breed understanding. And confidence based on understanding is more enduring than confidence based on awe.

Third. From age to age the problem of constitutional adjudication is the same. It is to keep the power of government unrestrained by the social or economic theories that one set of judges may entertain.

It is to keep one age unfettered by the fears or limited vision of another. There is in that connection one tenet of faith which has crystal-
lized more and more as a result of our long experience as a nation. It
is this: If the social and economic problems of state and nation can be
kept under political management of the people, there is likely to be
long-run stability. It is when a judiciary with life tenure seeks to write
its social and economic creed into the Charter that instability is created.
For then the nation lacks the adaptability to master the sudden storms
of an era. It must be remembered that the process of constitutional
amendment is a long and slow one.

That philosophy is reflected in what Thomas Jefferson wrote about
the Constitution.[76]

"Some men look at constitutions with sanctimonious reverence, and
deem them like the ark of the covenant, too sacred to be touched.
They ascribe to the men of the preceding age a wisdom more than
human, and suppose what they did to be beyond amendment. I
knew that age well; I belonged to it, and labored with it. It deserved
well of its country. It was very like the present, but without the
experience of the present; and forty years of experience in government is worth a century of book-reading; and this they would say
themselves, were they to rise from the dead."

Jefferson's words are *a fortiori* germane to the fashioning of constitutional law and to the lesser lawmaking in which the judiciary
necessarily indulges.

Footnotes

[1] See *United States* v. *Title Ins. Co.,* 265 U.S. 472, 486–487.
[2] Holmes, The Path of the Law, 10 Harv. L. Rev. 457, 459–461; Cohen,
Transcendental Nonsense and The Functional Approach, 35 Col. L. Rev. 809,
842 *et seq.;* Moore, Rational Basis of Legal Institutions, 23 Col. L. Rev. 609;
Frank, Law and the Modern Mind, pp. 100–159.
[3] Gray, The Nature and Sources of Law, § 225.
[4] *Santa Clara Co.* v. *Southern Pac. R. Co.,* 118 U.S. 394, 396.
[5] *Minneapolis R. Co.* v. *Beckwith,* 129 U.S. 26, 28, decided in 1889.
[6] Main Currents in American Thought.
[7] Black dissenting in *Connecticut General Co.* v. *Johnson,* 303 U.S. 77, 85.
[8] *Gibbons* v. *Ogden,* 9 Wheat. 1, 196.

9 Hughes, The Supreme Court of the United States, p. 52.

10 *The Thomas Jefferson*, 10 Wheat. 428 overruling *The Genesee Chief*, 12 How. 443.

11 *The Belfast*, 7 Wall. 624, overruling *Allen v. Newbury*, 21 How. 244.

12 These decisions, like *Munn* v. *Illinois*, 94 U.S. 135, itself, reflected the tolerance for local regulations expressed in *Cooley* v. *Board of Wardens*, 12 How. 299, 319.

13 *Peik* v. *Chicago & N. Ry. Co.*, 94 U.S. 164.

14 *State Tax on Railway Gross Receipts*, 15 Wall. 284.

15 *Osborne* v. *Mobile*, 16 Wall. 479.

16 For longer and more fundamental cyclical swings under the Commerce Clause see Rutledge, A Declaration of Legal Faith; Ribble, State and National Power over Commerce.

17 *Wabash, St. L. & P. Ry. Co.* v. *Illinois*, 118 U.S. 557.

18 *Philadelphia Steamship Co.* v. *Pennsylvania*, 122 U.S. 326.

19 *Leloup* v. *Port of Mobile*, 127 U.S. 640.

20 *Leisy* v. *Hardin*, 135 U.S. 100, overruling *Pierce* v. *New Hampshire*, 5 How. 504.

21 *Bowman* v. *Chicago & N. Ry. Co.*, 125 U.S. 465, 508.

22 *Kilbourn* v. *Thompson*, 103 U.S. 168, overruling *Anderson* v. *Dunn*, 6 Wheat. 204.

23 *In re Ayres*, 123 U.S. 443, overruling in part *Osborn* v. *U.S. Bank*, 9 Wheat. 738.

24 *Gillespie* v. *Oklahoma*, 257 U.S. 501; *Burnet* v. *Coronado Oil & Gas Co.*, 285 U.S. 393.

25 *Oklahoma Tax Comm'n* v. *United States*, 319 U.S. 598.

26 *Childers* v. *Beaver*, 270 U.S. 555.

27 *Howard* v. *Gipsy Oil Co.*, 247 U.S. 503; *Large Oil Co.* v. *Howard*, 248 U.S. 549; *Oklahoma* v. *Barnsdall Refineries*, 296 U.S. 521; *Choctaw & Gulf R. Co.* v. *Harrison*, 235 U.S. 292; *Indian Oil Co.* v. *Oklahoma*, 240 U.S. 522.

28 *Graves* v. *New York ex rel O'Keefe*, 306 U.S. 466, overruling *Collector* v. *Day*, 11 Wall. 113 and *New York ex rel. Rogers* v. *Graves*, 299 U.S. 401.

29 *Alabama* v. *King & Boozer*, 314 U.S. 1, overruling *Panhandle Oil Co.* v. *Knox*, 277 U.S. 218 and *Graves* v. *Texas Co.*, 298 U.S. 393.

30 *O'Malley* v. *Woodrough*, 307 U.S. 277, overruling *Miles* v. *Graham*, 268 U.S. 501.

31 *First National Bank* v. *Maine*, 284 U.S. 312.

32 *State Tax Commission* v. *Aldrich*, 316 U.S. 174.

33 *Madden* v. *Kentucky*, 309 U.S. 83.

34 *Colgate* v. *Harvey*, 296 U.S. 404.

35 *Tigner* v. *Texas*, 310 U.S. 141, overruling *Connolly* v. *Union Sewer Pipe Co.*, 184 U.S. 540.

36 *California* v. *Thompson*, 313 U.S. 109, overruling *Di Santo* v. *Pennsylvania*, 273 U.S. 34.

37 *Olsen* v. *Nebraska*, 313 U.S. 236, overruling *Ribnik* v. *McBride*, 277 U.S. 350.

38 *United States* v. *Darby*, 312 U.S. 100, reversing *Hammer* v. *Dagenhart*, 247 U.S. 251.

39 *Paul* v. *Virginia*, 8 Wall. 168.

[40] *United States* v. *Underwriters Ass'n.*, 322 U.S. 533.

[41] *United States* v. *Chicago, M. St. P. & P. R. Co.*, 312 U.S. 592.

[42] *United States* v. *Lynah*, 188 U.S. 445.

[43] *Board of Education* v. *Barnette*, 319 U.S. 624, overruling *Minersville School Dist.* v. *Gobitis*, 310 U.S. 586.

[44] *Jones* v. *Opelika*, 319 U.S. 103, overruling *Jones* v. *Opelika*, 316 U.S. 584.

[45] *Grovey* v. *Townsend*, 295 U.S. 45.

[46] *Smith* v. *Allwright*, 321 U.S. 649.

[47] *Williams* v. *North Carolina*, 317 U.S. 287, overruling *Haddock* v. *Haddock*, 201 U.S. 562, and *Sherrer* v. *Sherrer*, 334 U.S. 343, overruling in part, *Andrews* v. *Andrews*, 188 U.S. 14.

[48] *Swift* v. *Tyson*, 16 Pet. 1.

[49] Cf. *Angel* v. *Bullington*, 330 U.S. 183, 194, with *Lupton's Sons Co.* v. *Automobile Club*, 225 U.S. 489.

[50] *Adair* v. *United States*, 208 U.S. 161, and *Coppage* v. *Kansas*, 236 U.S. 1.

[51] *Federal Power Commission* v. *Hope Gase Co.*, 320 U.S. 591, overruling that part of *United Railways* v. *West*, 280 U.S. 234.

[52] *Mercoid Corp.* v. *Mid-Continent Co.*, 320 U.S. 661, overruling *Leeds & Catlin Co.* v. *Victor Talking Machine Co. (No. 2)*, 213 U.S. 325.

[53] *Mahnich* v. *Southern S. S. Co.*, 321 U.S. 96, overruling *Plamals* v. *Pinar Del Rio*, 277 U.S. 151.

[54] *Brady* v. *Roosevelt S. S. Co.*, 317 U.S. 575, overruling *Fleet Corp.* v. *Lustgarten*, 280 U.S. 320.

[55] *Nye* v. *United States*, 313 U.S. 33, overruling *Toledo Newspaper Co.* v. *United States*, 247 U.S. 402.

[56] *Girouard* v. *United States*, 328 U.S. 61, overruling *United States* v. *Schwimmer*, 279 U.S. 644, *United States* v. *Macintosh*, 283 U.S. 605, *United States* v. *Bland*, 283 U.S. 636.

[57] *Helvering* v. *Hallock*, 309 U.S. 106, overruling *Helvering* v. *St. Louis Trust Co.*, 296 U.S. 39, and *Becker* v. *St. Louis Trust Co.*, 296 U.S. 48.

[58] *Commissioner* v. *Church*, 335 U. S. 632, overruling *May* v. *Heiner*, 281 U.S. 238.

[59] On the prospective overruling of precedents to prevent such hardship see *Great Northern Ry. Co.* v. *Sunburst Co.*, 287 U.S. 358; *Aero Spark Plug Co.* v. *B. G. Corporation*, 130 F. 2d 290, 296–299.

[60] *Baker* v. *Lorillard*, 4 N.Y. 257, 261.

[61] The Trail of the Calf, 32 Corn. L.Q. 137, 143.

[62] See *Federal Power Commission* v. *Natural Gas Pipeline Co.*, 315 U.S. 575, 600.

[63] *Chicago, M. & St. P. R. Co.* v. *Minnesota*, 134 U.S. 418.

[64] See *Pollock* v. *Farmers Loan & Trust Co.*, 157 U.S. 429, 607.

[65] See *Tagg Bros.* v. *United States*, 280 U.S. 420; *O'Gorman & Young* v. *Hartford Fire Ins. Co.*, 282 U.S. 251.

[66] The durability of *Munn* v. *Illinois* on another point should be mentioned. Waite ruled that grain warehouses though instruments of interstate commerce could be regulated by the States until Congress acted (94 U.S. p. 135). Congress did act in 1916. By the United States Warehouse Act (39 Stat. 486) it made federal regulation subservient to state regulation. In 1931 it altered the scheme of the Act, making federal regulation exclusive of state regulation as respects

the matters covered by the federal act. See *Rice* v. *Santa Fe Elevator Corp.*, 331 U.S. 218.

[67] *Federal Power Commission* v. *Natural Gas Pipeline Co.*, 315 U.S. 575; *Federal Power Commission* v. *Hope Gas Co.*, 320 U.S. 591.

[68] See *Chambers* v. *Florida*, 309 U.S. 227; *Ashcraft* v. *Tennessee*, 322 U.S. 143; *Malinski* v. *New York*, 324 U.S. 401; *Haley* v. *Ohio*, 332 U.S. 596.

[69] See *Williams* v. *Kaiser*, 323 U.S. 471; *Hawk* v. *Olson*, 326 U.S. 271; *De Meerleer* v. *Michigan*, 329 U.S. 663.

[70] Rule 27A, 400 Ill. 22; Judicial Conference of Missouri, Executive Council, Special Report No. 3, February 8, 1945; Special Report No. 4, February 20, 1945. Special Report No. 9, November 8, 1945. See also 1 Journ. of Missouri Bar 73; 2 Journ. of Missouri Bar, 17, 28.

[71] See *Wilkerson* v. *McCarthy*, 336 U.S. 53, for a review of these cases since the 1943 Term.

[72] Radin, The Trail of the Calf, 32 Corn. L.Q. 137, 148.

[73] Reed, "Stare Decisis and Constitutional Law," 35 Penna. Bar Assoc. Quart. 131, 139-140. "No responsible official, jurist or statesman, has ever suggested that an effort should be made to ask reconsideration of the doctrine of dual sovereignty, the separation of powers or the supremacy of the Federal Constitution. It is the applications of the established doctrine that fill the courts and, indeed, the nation with controversy. Those applications are properly and continuously subject to critical reexamination. No threat of a challenge to established constitutional principles is on the horizon. The most likely controversies as to constitutional principle, in the immediate future, will be over the interrelation or interaction of one principle upon another."

[74] Legal Essays, p. 158.

[75] Law and The Modern Mind, p. 293. Cf. Fortas & Chisholm, The Psychiatry of Enduring Peace and Social Progress, 9 Journ. Biol. & Path. of Interpersonal Rel. 1, 3.

[76] Letter to Samuel Kercheval, July 12, 1816.

☆☆☆ The Frontiers of Constitutional Policy

WILLIAM J. BRENNAN, JR.
State Court and Supreme Court

During the 1950's, criticism of the Supreme Court's tendency to overturn the judgments of state courts reached a high point. A majority of the state supreme court chief justices issued a lengthy report in 1957, for example, challenging what was called the Court's interference with state criminal procedures, its willingness to find federal preemption of areas formerly under state jurisdiction, and its insensitivity to the needs of order where subversive activity was concerned. Those in Congress who shared these critical views—and there were many—sponsored bills to withdraw appellate jurisdiction from the Supreme Court over several areas of state action, such as admission to the bar, state teacher loyalty programs, and state segregation cases. The argument that Justices should have prior judicial experience to be appointed was also revived, and bills to set this as an absolute requirement were filed by congressional critics. The sole member of the Court who had had prior judicial experience as a state judge was Justice Brennan, whose service on the Superior and Supreme Courts of New Jersey made him a prototype of

348

the "right kind of man." Unhappily for the critics, Brennan was a member of the liberal bloc of four, and remarkably vocal about why a Supreme Court Justice cannot function exactly as a state court judge does. The selection printed here is one version of a speech discussing the two spheres of judicial activity which Justice Brennan delivered frequently in 1959 and 1960.

SOURCE: "Notes on the Supreme Court," Address at the Law Review Banquet, University of Pennsylvania Law School, March 10, 1960.

[A] comment recently made to me by one of my former law partners suggested what I think is a wholly appropriate subject. He said he thought some recent opinions of mine indicated I had changed some views I had expressed when a member of the New Jersey Supreme Court. But I suggested to my old friend that perhaps what to him seems to reflect a changed viewpoint may with greater accuracy be said to reflect a change of function. For unmistakably a high State court judge and a United States Supreme Court Justice must often look at the same case with different eyeglasses. Our States are not mere provinces of an all-powerful central government. As has been well said "they are political units with hard-core constitutional status, with plenary governmental responsibility for much that goes on within their borders." But they are nevertheless units of the nation and in our federal structure held to the commands of the national Constitution and the national laws. It should not be surprising that the State judge faced with a case presenting a conflict of State interests with the national Constitution and laws will sometimes react in a way which reflects zealousness to maintain the integrity of his State's sovereign powers. But occasionally he is stirred to resentment if the United States Supreme Court reaches a different judgment on the question whether the State action he approves must give way to the commands of the national Constitution and laws. When this happens he may have overlooked that when the States which formed the national Constitution agreed in that document to the supremacy of the national Constitution and national laws in proper cases, the very first Congress as one of its very first acts enacted the famous provision of the Judiciary Act of 1789 which explicitly provided for the performance by the Supreme Court of the function of finally passing on the question whether actions of the States violated the Federal Constitution or laws. Even if we assume that this function might have been reserved to the Congress, or have been assigned to some other tribunal, the hard fact is that since our beginnings as a nation it has been and yet remains a function required by law to be exercised by the Supreme Court. The word "usurpative" has a strange ring when applied to this function. As Professor Charles Black has said in his recent and very interesting little book *The People and the Court*—"the Court did not arrogate this function to itself; it was directed by Congress to assume it." He goes on to say that, "Nothing could be more obvious, [yet] nothing arouses greater occasional resentment, than the fact that the states must be subjected, as a last resort, to the requirements of the national Constitution and laws. Nothing could be more obvious, [yet] nothing raises this occasional resentment to higher pitches or fury, than the fact that, in the real world, this must mean that the actions of the states have to be submitted to control and possible invalidation by some national tribunal. Nothing could be more obvious, [yet] nothing could inspire resentment to shriller tones of invective, than the fact that, again in the real world, the national Constitution and laws to which the states must be subjected can be nothing else than the national Constitution and laws as interpreted by the national tribunal entrusted with this task of supervision, even though that interpretation may in some particular case not be the one arrived at, or even passionately held, by the dominant interest in the affected state."

However, the Supreme Court Justice can't look at a State case at all unless a claim is made that the action in issue violates a federal right. The high State court judge on the other hand must examine all the questions in the case, and this includes the federal questions. Professor Black suggests that when the State judge passes on the federal questions, he may be at a disadvantage for he "utters the best understanding *of the state* as to the meaning of commands placed upon the whole nation, by the whole nation, for the benefit of the whole nation. The finally authoritative utterance, in such a case, must be that of someone who represents the whole nation." The 1789 Act nominated the Supreme Court to be the national voice in this regard and "The Supreme Court reviewed its first state court case [and the state court cases it has since reviewed] * in obedience to a direct command laid on it in a statute passed by the First Congress and signed into law by President Washington."

Perhaps I can illustrate the different functions of the high State court and the Supreme Court judge in State cases by telling you of four cases decided while I was on the New Jersey Court which raised problems also presented in other cases since I came on the Supreme Court.

First, however, to put the situation in proper perspective, the review of State cases for test of State action against the commands of the national Constitution and laws is involved in only a small number of the total number of cases we decide each year.

I dare say questions as to constitutionality of laws and actions of the Congress or the Executive; as to the meaning and application of federal statutes; as to whether the actions of the numerous federal administrative agencies are within bounds; and the supervision of the administration of criminal justice in the federal courts; these take the larger part of our time. Such cases present problems of a nature not at all unfamiliar to the high State Court judge for most of them have their counterparts in the judicial grist which arises under State Constitutions and State Governments similar in form. The former State judge who comes to the Supreme Court finds that his State Court experience with the principles and techniques guiding judgment in cases of that kind can be very helpful.

But when the Supreme Court must examine State judicial action, the former State judge finds that the point from which he now looks at State action often requires him to affirm State Court action which he disapproved as a State judge, or disapprove State Court action which he found correct when a State Court judge. Let me proceed to my four illustrative cases.

The first of the cases involved the question whether State Courts could act to regulate peaceful organizational picketing where the National Labor Relations Board had declined jurisdiction on the ground that although the particular business was in commerce and subject to its jurisdiction the amount of its business did not warrant the Board's attention to its complaint against the picketing union. The business picketed was a retail store of a national jewelry chain. The New

* Insertion by Justice Brennan.

Jersey trial court enjoined the picketing on the ground that if the National Board would not act the State Courts should so that the employer would not be denied all remedy. When the case came to the New Jersey Supreme Court it was urged that the pre-emption doctrine as applied to these cases, a doctrine then in process of evolution in cases before the United States Supreme Court, excluded the operation of State law as to businesses in commerce despite the National Labor Relations Board's refusal to accept jurisdiction. But there was no decision of the United States Supreme Court so holding and indeed what statements there were touching the question in opinions might be read as recognizing State power in the circumstances. Although the injunction was reversed on other grounds, the opinion I wrote for the New Jersey Court adopted the view that if the National Board declined jurisdiction the States necessarily were free to apply their own law.

It was not long after I came to the Supreme Court when the precise question was presented in a case from the Supreme Court of Utah. Plainly enough my function was now different from what it was on the New Jersey Court. The Supreme Court, as the ultimate judicial authority for interpretation of the meaning and scope of federal legislation, was squarely faced with deciding whether the federal act left any latitude for State power merely because the National Board administering that act declined jurisdiction of a case concededly within its jurisdiction. Looking at the problem from that standpoint I found I had to conclude that the area over which Congress had exercised its legislative power was wide indeed and correspondingly that the area within which the States may continue to operate was very narrowly drawn. Against this background of the formulation by the Congress of a comprehensive code of conduct, which in addition to protecting the rights of employees to organize and engage in concerted activity outlawed certain aspects of labor union activity, it seemed apparent that the Congress intended that the States should be deprived of all regulatory power and made no exception for cases where the National Board declined to exercise its jurisdiction. In other words, the State oriented view of the State judge had no place in the exercise of the new function.

But I suppose the problems in the pre-emption area hardly present the difficulties and complexities of challenges to State action under the Fourteenth Amendment. I dare say the function of umpire of our federalism became particularly delicate when some 90 years ago in consequence of the adoption of that Amendment, every enactment of every State, every action by the Governor of a State, any governmental act of any of the 50 States including judicial actions might in a proper case be challenged at the bar of the Supreme Court on the ground that such action, such legislation, such State Court decision is a deprivation of liberty without due process of law or denies equal protection of the laws. What is "due," what is "equal," present the Court with some of the most difficult among the always difficult problems which it must resolve. Take this case which came to the New Jersey Court. An accused charged with murder made a confession after prolonged interrogation. Two months or more after he signed the confession counsel were assigned to defend him. The accused had not been given a copy of the confession and had no memory of its contents. His counsel applied to the Court for an order directing the prosecutor to supply a copy or at least to allow counsel to read the signed confession. The application was denied and the New Jersey Supreme Court affirmed with me and two others in dissent. The majority saw the problem as merely one of pretrial discovery in criminal cases and since State constitutional guarantees prevented evenhanded discovery concluded that a procedure not available to the State against the accused should not be available to the accused even if limited to discovery of his own confession. In dissent I expressed outrage that an accused with life at stake should not be allowed a copy of his own confession when in any negligence case an insurance company must provide the plaintiff before trial with a copy of the plaintiff's signed statement. But the question for the Federal Supreme Court was whether New Jersey's refusal to allow pretrial discovery of the accused's own confession denied due process, or, perhaps, whether its denial in a criminal case, while providing for pretrial discovery of like statements in civil cases, offended the guarantee of equal protection of the laws. The case did not get to the Supreme Court directly from the New Jersey Court but on review of the Court of Appeals for the Third Circuit affirming a District Court's denial of federal habeas corpus sought after the accused was convicted and sentenced to death, and that conviction and sentence had been affirmed by the New Jersey Court. Whether New Jersey's action offended the Fourteenth Amendment implicated principally the extent to which the guarantees of that Amendment circumscribed a State's power to fashion discovery procedures to be applied in criminal causes in its courts.

Since the Fourteenth Amendment as presently interpreted by the Court does not command the States to have any particular form of discovery practice in criminal cases or indeed any discovery practice at all, and there was no particular constitutional infirmity otherwise disclosed by the facts of the case, I had to agree that there was no error in the lower court's denial of habeas corpus. Quite clearly my expressed sense of outrage at the procedure while on the New Jersey Court was not an appropriate consideration. Innumerable State decisions are invulnerable to attack under the Fourteenth Amendment without regard to my personal views of their soundness. Obviously the Supreme Court may not intrude merely because the State Court result offends its members' sensibilities.

The next case is *State* v. *Hoag* which involved successive prosecutions for the same criminal act. Five patrons of a tavern were the victims of an armed robbery. New Jersey first indicted Hoag for the armed robbery of three of the patrons. On the trial of that indictment Hoag was acquitted. New Jersey then secured Hoag's indictment for the robbery of a fourth victim. Hoag unsuccessfully pleaded double jeopardy in violation of the New Jersey Constitution. At the trial the State's evidence was virtually the same as that at the former trial. Hoag was convicted. His appeal came to the New Jersey Supreme Court while I was a member of that Court. The conviction was sustained with myself and two colleagues in dissent. The majority held that the first prosecution for the robbery of A, B and C was for a different offense from the second prosecution for the robbery of D, even though the robberies were committed simultaneously. The view of the dissent which I joined was that the test of double jeopardy in light of the history and purpose of that guarantee was whether the accused was being harassed by successive trials, whether he was being required to marshall more than once the resources and energies necessary for his defense of what essentially was the same alleged criminal act. By that test it was clear to me that Hoag's defense of double jeopardy was good and should have defeated the second prosecution.

After I came on the Supreme Court, however, we had to deal with

Abbate v. *United States.* During a strike against the Southern Bell Telephone Company, the defendants conspired in Chicago to dynamite substations of the Telephone Company located in Mississippi. The substations carried coaxial cables which were essential parts of our federal military communications system. The State of Illinois indicted the defendants for conspiracy to injure or destroy the property of another in violation of an Illinois statute. The defendants pleaded guilty to that indictment and were sentenced to an Illinois prison. Thereafter the defendants were indicted in a federal court for conspiracy to commit an offense against the United States, namely to destroy a communication system operated and controlled by the United States. The defendants interposed the defense of double jeopardy. It was overruled and they were convicted. Plainly enough the defendants, like Hoag, were being subjected to successive prosecutions. The acts which were the basis of the federal prosecutions were the same acts which were the basis of the Illinois convictions. However, I wrote the opinion for the Court sustaining the federal prosecution. How did I differ *Hoag? Hoag* involved successive prosecutions by the same sovereignty, namely the State of New Jersey. *Abbate*, on the other hand, involved a federal prosecution following a State prosecution. *Abbate*, therefore, raised the question of the scope of the Fifth Amendment provision against subjecting an accused "for the same offense to be twice put in jeopardy of life or limb." But the Federal Government had not put *Abbate* and his codefendants to the harassment of successive trials. There were successive trials for the same acts, but the first was a State trial and the second was a federal trial. We held that the double jeopardy provision of the Fifth Amendment was a guarantee only as against successive federal prosecutions, that an act denounced as a crime by both national and state sovereignties is an offense against both and may be punished by each. This was more than a mere distinction of form. It was a distinction compelled, as I thought, by our concept of federalism. To the demands of federalism had to give way my views as a State judge in *Hoag* that nothing can be more repugnant than successive trials and punishments for the same criminal act.

Finally there is the particularly sensitive area of federal habeas corpus. This was involved in another case on which I sat in the New Jersey Court. In *State* v. *DeVita*, three young men committed a robbery murder on Newark's crowded main street on a busy Saturday afternoon. All three were convicted. Two of them received the death sentence and the third life imprisonment. We of the New Jersey Supreme Court unanimously affirmed the convictions and sentences. The United States Supreme Court refused review. Thereafter a motion was made in the trial court for a new trial on the ground that one of the jurors had been the victim of an armed robbery on the same street only a short time before the murder and had not disclosed this fact before being accepted as a juror. The motion was denied and we of the New Jersey Supreme Court unanimously affirmed. Again the United States Supreme Court denied review. An alleged federal constitutional infirmity in the conviction arising from the juror's conduct was asserted in the motion for a new trial but the New Jersey Supreme Court turned its affirmance primarily on State law and procedure. The opinion, however, did refer to the fact that a motion for a new trial had asserted a denial of due process of law. Thereafter federal habeas corpus was sought in the United States District Court.

Now the federal habeas corpus statute, you will remember, was adopted by Congress almost a century ago. It expanded the federal habeas corpus jurisdiction to embrace all persons allegedly restrained of their liberty in violation of the Federal Constitution, including persons detained under authority of State law. What constitutes a denial by a State of Federal constitutional rights in the prosecution and conviction of an accused under State laws necessarily must ultimately be determined by the United States Supreme Court which has the responsibility for constitutional interpretation. The ways in which State criminal prosecutions offend due process and equal protection of the laws have been developing over the years in Supreme Court decisions of concrete cases. While the obligation rests upon State courts, equally with the federal courts, to guard, enforce and protect every right granted or secured by the Federal Constitution, the Congress in the Federal Habeas Corpus Act has provided a federal remedy for adjudication of such constitutional claims. The rub has been that State judges have expressed irritation that this statute allows the intervention of the lower federal courts in the habeas corpus process. I think it is fair to say that State judicial tempers often rise to the boiling point when they contemplate the possibility that lower federal courts may set aside State criminal convictions which have been sustained by the State's highest court and particularly when the State Court decision has been denied review by the United States Supreme Court. I remember that on the New Jersey Court I shared the indignation of other members of that court that the *DeVita* case, to which we had given such close attention and review of which had twice been denied by the United States Supreme Court, might result in the setting aside by a single federal district judge of the convictions which we had sustained. It seemed to me too at that time that the respect due the highest court of a sovereign State required that if our judgments in these cases were to be federally reviewed they should be reviewed only by the federal tribunal charged with responsibility to speak the final word. I, therefore, was a supporter, with other New Jersey colleagues, of the proposal then before the Congress which would have had the effect of requiring that substantially all applications for writs of federal habeas corpus on behalf of State prisoners be made directly to the Supreme Court of the United States. But I now have an entirely different view. First of all I more fully appreciate the essential necessity for the federal habeas corpus statute if alleged federal constitutional infirmities in State convictions are to be heard and adjudicated. Many of these cases depend on factfinding which is not made at the original trial. For example, the facts bearing on a claim that the conviction was obtained through the knowing use by the State of perjured evidence won't be found in the trial record. Direct review by the United States Supreme Court of the original trial record will, therefore, not present such a federal constitutional claim. Where is the necessary record to be made? We would hope that it could be made in some State post conviction procedure. It is unfortunate, but true, however, that too many State post conviction procedures are not adequate. Indeed many which in form are adequate to deal with such questions require presentation by a skilled lawyer. But the States, by and large, do not require representation by a lawyer and, of course, our Court has said that except in capital cases the Fourteenth Amendment does not require that the States make provision for representation by counsel. The prisoner must struggle along as best he can through the maze of techniques which often confront him under State procedures. Until the States provide procedures adequate to permit a hearing and adjudication of such federal constitutional claims, I see no alternative but the provision of a federal habeas corpus procedure for the determination of the claims. There is an encouraging trend in many States toward the adoption of adequate procedures. If such procedures were to be generally adopted the reason for State judicial irritation toward the federal habeas corpus procedure should largely disappear. Resort to that procedure should not be so often necessary and federal judicial review limited to such as would be allowed by the United States Supreme Court would more often be possible.

Now none should mistake the difference in character of the functions as a difference in the exacting nature of the tasks performed by the judges of both State and Federal Supreme Courts. Actually the composite work of the courts of the 50 States probably has greater significance in measuring how well America attains the ideal of equal justice for all. I suppose the State courts of all levels must annually hand down literally millions of decisions which determine vital issues of life, liberty and property of human beings of this nation. Even the yearly total of decisions handed down by the highest courts of the 50 States must run into the tens of thousands. We should remind ourselves that it is these State court decisions which finally determine the overwhelming total of all legal controversies in this nation. For, of course, our system of justice intrudes the Supreme Court between the State courts and litigants only in that most narrow class of litigation which deals with federal questions. How infinitesimally small is that class is evident when I tell you that last Term in only 792 State cases did losers knock on the Supreme Court's door seeking review of State court judgments against them. Nine out of 10 of even that scant number did not get in. We turned away 734 or 93%. We could find only 58 which justified our inquiry into the merits of what the State courts had done. And even federal habeas corpus practice annually brings less than 3 dozen State criminal cases to the point of hearing in the District Courts. You will remember Mr. Justice Cardozo's views on the relative significance of his State and Supreme Court service. He said, "Whether the new field of usefulness is greater I don't know. Perhaps the larger opportunity was where I have been."

And even in the handful of cases where both the State courts and the Supreme Court function, the correct analysis of their respective responsibilities for decision is not in terms of which has the greater and which the lesser burden. The responsibilities are of the same gravity. The difference lies merely in the fact that the Supreme Court has the final word on federal questions. Judges of both courts, like other human beings responsible for other human institutions are on the dubious waves of error tossed. But in performing their respective tasks in cases where both must function, there can be no reason for contest, not even for petty quarrel.

Doubtless you wonder whether I believe that prior State judicial service is good preparation for service on the Supreme Court. Of course, I believe that it is. However, I do not think that it can fairly be maintained that prior State judicial service is necessarily a preferred preparation. The point may not be what particular prior experience it would be well for all nine Justices to have. I have misgivings whether it would be desirable to have a Court of nine who had the same preparation. The underlying problem manifested by the question can perhaps best be answered that as an institution having unique responsibilities the Court is best served when it can draw its members from among all the diverse roles followed by the legal profession.

ROBERT H. JACKSON

The Supreme Court as a Political Institution

Robert Jackson, a successful lawyer and advocate in upstate
New York, joined the New Deal at its start, working in the
Treasury Department. He stayed on to become one of Franklin Roosevelt's most useful and powerful legal captains. Appointed to the Supreme Court in 1941, his early decisions seemed
to mark a shift from his outspoken pre-Court "anti-ideological"
and "pragmatic" philosophy to a strict judicial activism on behalf of civil liberties, as typified by his ringing majority opinion
in the flag-salute cases, *West Virginia Board of Education* v.
Barnette, 319 U.S. 624 (1943). By the late 1940's, however, he
began to enunciate a position in sharp opposition to the liberal
activism of Justices Black, Douglas, Murphy, and Rutledge,
urging instead a selective intervention by the Court which
would hold the "great balances" between minority rights and
the majority's power and responsibility to govern. In 1954
Jackson accepted an invitation to deliver the Godkin Lectures
at Harvard University. This was an opportunity to draw together the themes he had been voicing in a battery of speeches
about the Court's work and his own judicial philosophy. In
October of 1954, he died suddenly of a heart attack. The lectures were substantially completed and revised, and with some
final arrangement by the Justice's son and one of his law clerks,
they appeared in book form. This selection is Chapter III of the
book.

SOURCE: *The Supreme Court in the American System of Government* (Cambridge: Harvard University Press, 1955), 53–83.

Few accusations against the Supreme Court are made with more heat and answered with less candor than that it makes political decisions. Of course, the line between political science and legal science is not fixed and varies with one's definition of his terms. Any decision that declares the law under which a people must live or which affects the powers of their institutions is in a very real sense political. I have previously quoted Judge Cardozo, who contrasted the New York Court of Appeals and the United States Supreme Court in these terms: "It [the New York Court of Appeals] is a great common law court; its problems are lawyers' problems. But the Supreme Court is occupied chiefly with statutory construction—which no man can make interesting—and with politics." [1] Of course, he used "politics" in no sense of partisanship but in the sense of policy-making. His remarks point to some features of the federal judicial power which distinguish it from the functions of the usual law court.

As already noted, the Constitutional Convention deliberately withheld from the Supreme Court power that was political in form, such as a forthright power to veto or revise legislation, and in that spirit the Court has held itself without power to render advisory opinions for the guidance even of the President.

The Court has also observed a number of other self-limitations which are intended to keep it out of active participation in the political processes. It has refused to inquire whether a state government complies with the guarantee of a republican form of government [2] or has properly ratified a proposed constitutional amendment.[3] It has given finality to the certification by the other branches of government that a federal statute is as signed, as against a claim of variance with the language actually adopted.[4] The duration of a state of war,[5] the abrogation of treaties,[6] the recognition or nonrecognition of foreign governments,[7] and matters of foreign policy [8] generally, have been held to be political questions.

Even more controversial has been the effort to use the Supreme Court to control the districting of states for the elections of members of Congress,[9] to fix the terms on which a new political party may go on the state ballot,[10] and to abolish the "county unit" system used in some states.[11] Of course, it would be nice if there were some authority to make everybody do the things we ought to have done and leave undone the things we ought not to have done. But are the courts the appropriate catch-all into which every such problem should be tossed? One can answer "Yes" if some immediate political purpose overshadows concern for the judicial institution. But in most such cases interference by the Court would take it into matters in which it lacks special competence, let alone machinery of implementation.

The judicial power of the Supreme Court, however, does extend to all cases arising under the Constitution, to controversies to which the United States is a party, and to those between two or more states. Thus, the Court must face political questions in legal form, for surely a controversy between two separately organized political societies does present a political question, even if waged with the formalities of a lawsuit. And any decision which confirms, allocates, or shifts power as between different branches of the Federal Government or between it and a constituent state is equally political, no matter whether the decision be reached by a legislative or a judicial process. Our Constitution was the product and expression of a virile political philosophy held by those who wrote it. Controversies over its meaning often spring from political motives, for the object of politics always is to obtain power. Such controversies have to be solved either by consideration of the experiences and statements of the framers which indicate the original will, or by reference to some relevant subsequent events and currents of opinion deemed controlling. And all constitutional interpretations have political consequences.

We must not forget that, at bottom, the Civil War was fought over constitutional doctrine. It oversimplifies that tragedy to say that it was a war over slavery, an institution which many southern leaders had come to deplore and one which Mr. Lincoln did not propose to abolish in the states where it existed. The controversy was over the power of the Federal Government to control the spread of slavery into new territory, and over the voluntary or compulsory character of the federal compact. These, like most other questions which have deeply agitated our people, found their way to the Supreme Court in the guise of private controversies between litigating parties.

Only those heedless of legal history can deny that in construing the Constitution the Supreme Court from time to time makes new constitutional law or alters the law that has been. And it is idle to say that this is merely the ordinary process of interpretation, as in the law of negotiable instruments, for example. While a vast and respectable body of learning on the law of bills and notes existed in the Western World, the federal judiciary was not bound to apply it. The Supreme Court had even less jurisprudential guidance in solving its political or public law problems than in solving those of private law. The organic document itself was novel in phrase and philosophy, and there was no judicial experience and no very persuasive body of learning to aid in the interpretation of the instrument. True, the Privy Council in colonial times may have dealt with analogous controversies as to the *ultra vires* character of colonial acts, or as to the powers of colonial governments under Royal Charters. But in the original states the people appear to have been highly sensitive about the newly acquired position of each state as a sovereign power, won by the treaty which recognized their independence: as parties to the federal compact the states were not the equivalent of chartered colonial corporations. Small wonder, then, that Marshall's great constitutional decisions cite no precedents, that they are argued out of political philosophy, and that later courts again and again have overruled outmoded doctrines and turned to new ones as political or economic conditions changed.

The question that the present times put into the minds of thoughtful people is to what extent Supreme Court interpretations of the Constitution will or can preserve the free government of which the Court is a part. A cult of libertarian judicial activists now assails the Court almost as bitterly for renouncing power as the earlier "liberals" once did for assuming too much power. This cult appears to believe that the Court can find in a 4,000-word eighteenth-century document or its nineteenth-century Amendments, or can plausibly supply, some clear bulwark against all dangers and evils that today beset us internally. This assumes that the Court will be the dominant factor in shaping the constitutional practice of the future and can and will maintain, not only equality with the elective branches, but a large measure of supremacy and control over them. I may be biased against this attitude because it is so contrary to the doctrines of the critics of the Court, of whom I was one, at the time of the Roosevelt proposal to reorganize the judiciary. But it seems to me a doctrine wholly incompatible with faith in democracy, and in so far as it encourages a belief that the judges may be left to correct the result of public indifference to issues of liberty in choosing Presidents, Senators, and Representatives, it is a vicious teaching.

I shall pass over as not germane to my subject the question whether the Constitution itself is adequate for the security problems, the economic problems, and the political problems of our day. But I do not think that would be an academic question. We face the rivalry, which may break into the hostility, of concentrated governments that can decide quickly and secretly on their policies. Our power is so dispersed that nothing can be decided quickly or secretly. But I assume the permanence of our constitutional scheme, if for no other reason than our inability to agree on any other. The difficulties of amendment are such that many look to interpretation rather than amendment as a means of change.

But before we take the measure of the values the Court should and in some degree can protect, we must not overlook the things now practically beyond its control. Two of the greatest powers possessed by the political branches, which seem to me the disaster-potentials in our system, are utterly beyond judicial reach. These are the war power and the money, taxing, and spending power, which is the power of inflation. The improvident use of these powers can destroy the conditions for the existence of liberty, because either can set up great currents of strife within the population which might carry down constitutional forms and limitations before them.

The Constitution made what in its day was a logical division of the war power, delegating to Congress the power to declare war and to the President, as Commander in Chief, the power to conduct it. But the twentieth century ushered in an era of undeclared wars and thereby drained much of the substance out of the congressional power to declare war. It is apparent now that the President can so handle foreign affairs and the armed forces as to leave Congress no real choice but to declare war or as to involve us in warfare without any declaration. Korea stands as an example of the actual concentration of the war power in the President. That wars and rumors of wars are the great threats to political stability and to liberty needs no demonstration. Total war means total subjection of the individual to the state. We may resist "creeping socialism" or the coming of the omnipotent socialized state in peacetime. But manpower, labor, property, material, profit, rent, and even food are subject to the planned economy and galloping socialism of modern war. This form of military socialization is accepted as patriotic, and dissenters are coerced into obedience. But it sets a pattern which is not easily changed when peace is restored, and it is no accident that the doctrines of Marx were sterile until the era of total wars and then took their deepest root in countries most deeply affected by war.

The other disaster-potential is the power over our money system and the power to tax and spend for the public welfare. In the famous Agricultural Adjustment Act case the political branches lost a case and won a cause. Even in holding that Act invalid, the Supreme Court adopted the Federalist view of the spending power and declared, "It results that the power of Congress to authorize expenditure of public moneys for public purposes is not limited by the direct grants of legislative power found in the Constitution." [12] The Court earlier had held that a suit by a federal taxpayer to restrain expenditures of public money on the ground that the controlling statute is invalid cannot be maintained and that a state may not institute such an action to protect her citizens.[13]

Thus the two disaster-potential powers are insulated from all judicial control—the war power practically in the hands of the President, the spending power in the hands of Congress. Either improvidently used can bring catastrophe so extensive as to carry down with it all else that we value. War and inflation and their kin have released the evil forces which have destroyed liberty elsewhere. No protection against these catastrophic courses can be expected from the judiciary. The people must guard against these dangers at the polls.

The political function which the Supreme Court, more or less effectively, may be called upon to perform comes to this: In a society in which rapid changes tend to upset all equilibrium, the Court, without exceeding its own limited powers, must strive to maintain the great system of balances upon which our free government is based. Whether these balances and checks are essential to liberty elsewhere in the world is beside the point; they are indispensable to the society we know. Chief of these balances are: first, between the Executive and Congress; second, between the central government and the states; third, between state and state; fourth, between authority, be it state or national, and the liberty of the citizen, or between the rule of the majority and the rights of the individual.

I have said that in these matters the Court must respect the limitations on its own powers because judicial usurpation is to me no more justifiable and no more promising of permanent good to the country than any other kind. So I presuppose a Court that will not depart from the judicial process, will not go beyond resolving cases and controversies brought to it in conventional form, and will not consciously encroach upon the functions of its coordinate branches. Whether in case of a clearly unconstitutional usurpation of power by one of the other branches the Court would be justified in stepping out of its judicial role and itself exercising a usurped counterbalancing power, I do not stop to consider, because I think in such an event the judicial voice would be little heeded in the chaos.

EXECUTIVE V. LEGISLATIVE

It is hard to conceive a task more fundamentally political than to maintain amidst changing conditions the balance between the executive and legislative branches of our federal system. The Supreme Court often is required to arbitrate between the two because litigation in one form or another raises questions as to the legitimacy of the acts of one branch or the other under the doctrine of separation of powers. In such cases the Court has found no precedent from any other country or in the judicial interpretation of any similar written instrument, and it has had to devise its own doctrine from time to time.

The Court, both before and after the Roosevelt influence was felt in its appointments, has tended strongly to support the power of the President in matters involving foreign affairs.[14] On the other hand, where only internal affairs are involved, the Court has been more inclined to restrict executive power. It halted a presidential effort indirectly to control the policies of the administrative agencies by removal of a Federal Trade Commissioner.[15] In the cases striking down the NIRA, the Court refused to sanction the congressional practice of delegating power to the President to make codes for industry that would be the equivalent of new laws.[16] The Court has kept the Executive from usurping the adjudicative function through military trials of offenders by holding such trials illegal in *Ex parte Milligan*, 4 Wall. (71 U.S.) 2, after, however, they had been running riot for a number of years. In the more recent case of *United States ex rel. Quirin* v. *Cox*, 317 U.S. 1, the Court met in special session to review the legality of the conviction of the eight German saboteurs who had been tried by a military commission set up by President Roosevelt, although his proclamation and order of July 2, 1942, provided that they should not be privileged "to seek any remedy or maintain any proceeding directly or indirectly, or to have any such remedy or proceeding sought on their behalf, in the courts. . . ." [17] This part of the President's proclamation was quietly rejected and the saboteurs were given a full hearing, as a result of which, however, the trial was found to have been legal and the convictions were sustained.

In the more recent Steel Seizure case [18] the Court refused to sanction a presidential seizure of private property without congressional authorization, holding that the President has no such inherent power under the Constitution. But I felt constrained in that case to point out the inadequacies of judicial power to appraise or control the realistic balance of power between Congress and the President.[19] This is because of the gap that exists between the President's paper powers and his actual powers. The real potency of the Executive office does not show on the face of the Constitution. The relative influence of the President and of the Congress has fluctuated widely, depending on the personal and political strength of the particular President as compared with that of the congressional leadership. A Congress stampeded by a powerful leader like Thaddeus Stevens may cripple a President who is politically vulnerable, and a senatorial coalition may break the foreign policy of even an able and strong President like Wilson. On the other hand, a White House tenant who is a skillful manipulator of his extralegal influences may force an unwelcome program through Congress.

What are these sources of presidential strength? First, the Executive power is concentrated in a single head in whose choice the whole nation has a part, making him the focus of public hopes and expectations. No collection of local representatives can rival him in prestige. None can gain such ready and effective access to the modern means of communication with the masses or exert such influence on public opinion; this is one of his most effective leverages upon those in Congress who are supposed to balance his power. As the nation's activities have spread, the President wields the power of appointment and promotion over a vast multitude of our people. He is not merely the Chief Magistrate of the Republic; he is the titular and usually the actual head of the prevailing political party, whose loyalties and interest enable him to win as political leader what he could not command under the Constitution. Woodrow Wilson summed it all up in the observation that "if he rightly interpret the national thought and boldly insist upon it, he is irresistible. . . . His office is anything he has the sagacity and force to make it." [20]

Yet it depends not upon the President alone but upon his sagacity and force measured against that of the Congress as manifested in its leadership. If Congress forfeits the respect of the country, it will not be able to balance the power of the Executive. No matter what the Supreme Court opines, only Congress itself can keep its power from slipping through its fingers.

FEDERAL POWER V. STATE POWER

It is the maintenance of the constitutional equilibrium between the states and the Federal Government that has brought the most vexatious questions to the Supreme Court. That it was the duty of the Court, within its own constitutional functions, to preserve this balance has been asserted by the Court many times; that the Constitution is vague and ambiguous on this subject is shown by the history preceding our Civil War. It is undeniable that ever since that war ended we have been in a cycle of rapid centralization, and Court opinions have sanctioned a considerable concentration of power in the Federal Government with a corresponding diminution in the authority and prestige of state governments. Indeed, long ago an acute foreign observer declared the United States to be "a nation concealed under the form of a federation." [21] As respected an authority as Charles Evans Hughes declared nearly three decades ago that "far more important to the development of the country, than the decisions holding acts of Congress to be invalid, have been those in which the authority of Congress has been sustained and adequate national power to meet the necessities of a growing country has been found to exist within constitutional limitations." [22]

Here again the principal causes of this concentration have not been within judicial control. Improved methods of transportation and communication; the increasing importance of foreign affairs and of interstate commerce; the absorption of revenue sources by the nation with the consequent appeal by distressed localities directly to Washington for relief and work projects, bypassing the state entirely; the direct election of Senators; and various other factors—all have contributed to move the center of gravity from the state capital to that of the nation.

I think it is a mistake to lump all states' rights together as is done so frequently in political discussions.

There can be no doubt that in the original Constitution the states surrendered to the Federal Government the power to regulate interstate commerce, or commerce among the states. They did so in the light of a disastrous experience in which commerce and prosperity were reduced to the vanishing point by states discriminating against each other through devices of regulation, taxation and exclusion. It is more important today than it was then that we remain one commercial and economic unit and not a collection of parasitic states preying upon each other's commerce. I make no concealment of and offer no apology for my philosophy that the federal interstate commerce power should be strongly supported and that the impingement of the states upon that commerce which moves among them should be restricted to narrow limits.

It was early perceived that to allow the Federal Government to spend money for internal improvement would aggrandize its powers as against those of the states. It was not until the famous decision holding the Social Security Act constitutional that this controversy over the federal power to tax and spend for the general welfare was settled, and settled in favor of the existence of that power in the Federal Government.[23] I believe that this controversy was rightly settled, but there is no denying that the power is vast and, uncontrolled, leads to the invasion of sources of revenue and builds up the Federal Government by creating organizations to make the expenditures. But here we are dealing with powers granted to the Federal Government, if not entirely without ambiguity, at least in language which fairly admits of the construction given it and which fairly warned those who adopted the Constitution that such results might follow.

Considerations of a different nature arise from interferences with states' rights under the vague and ambiguous mandate of the Fourteenth Amendment. The legislative history of that Amendment is not enlightening, and the history of its ratification is not edifying. I shall not go into the controversy as to whether the Fourteenth Amendment, by a process of incorporation or impregnation, directs against the states prohibitions found in the earlier Amendments. Whether it does or not, I think the Fourteenth Amendment has been considerably abused.

For more than half a century the Supreme Court found in the Fourteenth Amendment authority for striking down various social experiments by the states. The history of judicial nullification of state social and economic legislation is too well known to justify repetition here. It came to its culmination when the Court wound up the October 1935 Term by declaring that there was no power in either state or nation to enact a minimum wage law,[24] a position repudiated within a few months by the conventions of both political parties and retracted by the Court itself with some haste. That retraction probably brought an end to the use of the Fourteenth Amendment to prevent experiments by the states with economic and social and labor legislation.

The states have probably been more venturesome and radical in their experimentation than the Congress. This is perhaps explainable by the fact that their experiments are more easily modified if unsuccessful. In the Granger movement and in the social legislation that followed it the states took the lead. On the other hand, they have enacted more extreme legislation for the control and restriction of labor unions when the tide ran the other way. In each instance the interest adversely affected has sought to obtain a holding that due process of law prevented the state from controlling its affairs and also prevented the nation from interfering, thus disabling either from exerting effective control. It is my basic view that whenever any organization or combination of individuals, whether in a corporation, a labor union or other body, obtains such economic or legal advantage that it can control or in effect govern the lives of other people, it is subject to the control of the Government, be it state or federal, for the Government can suffer no rivals in the field of coercion. Liberty requires that coercion be applied to the individual not by other individuals but by the Government after full inquiry into the justification.

Today, however, we have a different application of the Fourteenth Amendment. Today it is being used not to restrain state legislatures but to set aside the acts of state courts, particularly in criminal matters. This practice has proceeded to a point where the federal courts are in acute controversy with the state courts, and the assembled Chief Justices of the state courts have adopted severe resolutions condemning the federal intervention. I must say that I am rather in sympathy with the Chief Justices of the state courts on this subject. I believe we are unjustifiably invading the rights of the states by expanding the constitutional concept of due process to include the idea that the error of a trial court deprives it of "jurisdiction," [25] by including in the concept by interpretation all other constitutional provisions not literally incorporated in the Fourteenth Amendment, and, in the alternative, by incorporating into it all of our ideas of decency, even to the point of making a constitutional issue of rulings upon evidence.

The Court has been drawing into the federal system more and more control by federal agencies over local police agencies. I have no doubt that the latter are often guilty of serious invasions of individual rights. But there are more fundamental questions involved in the interpretation of the antiquated, cumbersome, and vague civil rights statutes which give the Department of Justice the right to prosecute state officials.[26] If the Department of Justice must prosecute local officials, the FBI must investigate them, and no local agency which is subject to federal investigation, inspection, and discipline is a free agency. I cannot say that our country could have no central police without becoming totalitarian, but I can say with great conviction that it cannot become totalitarian without a centralized national police. At his trial Hermann Goering, with great candor, related the steps by which the Nazi party obtained complete domination of Germany, and one of the first was the establishment of the supremacy of the national over the local police authorities. So it was in Russia, and so it has been in every totalitarian state. All that is necessary is to have a national police competent to investigate all manner of offenses, and then, in the parlance of the street, it will have enough on enough people, even if it does not elect to prosecute them, so that it will find no opposition to its policies. Even those who are supposed to supervise it are likely to fear it. I believe that the safeguard of our liberty lies in limiting any national policing or investigative organization, first of all to a small number of strictly federal offenses, and secondly to nonpolitical ones. The fact that we may have confidence in the administration of a federal investigative agency under its existing heads does not mean that it may not revert again to the days when the Department of Justice was headed by men to whom the investigatory power was a weapon to be used for their own purposes.

It is a difficult question and always will remain a debatable question where, in particular instances, federal due process should step into state court proceedings and set them aside. When the state courts render harsh or unconsidered judgments, they invite this power to be used. But I think in the long run the transgressions of liberty by the Federal Government, with its all-powerful organization, are much more to be feared than those of the several states, which have a greater capacity for self-correction.

State v. State

Another clearly political type of litigation is that of state against state. It was logical that in a federation the different units should have some arbiter to settle their differences. Congress was made a supervisor of their separate compacts or agreements. The Supreme Court was made the arbiter of their controversies. Here was the precedent for an international court, for the states waived their sovereignty sufficiently to submit to a compulsory jurisdiction over their controversies with each other. This seems a hopeful precedent for an alternative to war and chaos and reprisals. Under this head of jurisdiction the Court has settled boundary disputes,[27] apportioned the debts of a divided state between the two new divisions,[28] and determined many disputes over rivers and waters.[29]

To what source may the Court look for law to govern such controversies? The actual practice perhaps is well illustrated in Mr. Justice Cardozo's opinion in *New Jersey* v. *Delaware,* 291 U.S. 361. His search carried him through many ancient documents, which he interpreted according to the common law of property, and he compared the claims of the two states in the light of that body of learning. But this was inadequate for the solution of the case and resort was had to international law. He traced international law through the Court's own decisions and through all of the conventional authorities, American and foreign. He found international law inconclusive and no positive law applicable. He declared that "International law, or the law that governs between states, has at times, like the common law within states, a twilight existence during which it is hardly distinguishable from morality or justice, till at length the *imprimatur* of a court attests its jural quality." [30] He concluded that in these circumstances it was within the power of the judicial process to develop and apply a formula consonant with justice and with the political and social needs of the interstate or international legal system. Reduced to its simplest terms, what the Court seemed to be saying in that case was that it found no controlling law and was obliged to declare some, in the light of the experience and learning of the law in similar situations. The Court has no escape in many cases of this character from the undesirable alternatives of refusing to obey its duty to decide the case or of devising some rule of decision which has no precedent or positive law authority.

I know that it is now regarded as more or less provincial and reactionary to cite the Tenth Amendment, which reserves to the states and the people the powers not delegated to the Federal Government. That Amendment is rarely mentioned in judicial opinions, rarely cited in argument. But our forefathers made it a part of the Bill of Rights in order to retain in the localities certain powers and not to allow them to drift into centralized hands. Perhaps the Tenth Amendment is drifting into oblivion as constitutional provisions may sometimes do. . . .

MAJORITY V. INDIVIDUAL

Perhaps the most delicate, difficult and shifting of all balances which the Court is expected to maintain is that between liberty and authority.

It is not so easy as some people believe to determine what serves liberty best by way of restriction of authority. For example, the removal of the Japanese from the West Coast during the War, which seemed to me plainly unconstitutional as applied to citizens, was rationalized as a service to ultimate liberty.[31] And I suppose no one would be more likely than Abraham Lincoln to win recognition by common vote as the greatest servant of freedom; yet President Lincoln, at the outset of his administration, suspended the writ of habeas corpus and resorted to wholesale arrest without warrant, detention without trial, and imprisonment without judicial conviction. Private mail was opened, and Cabinet officers simply sent telegrams ordering persons to be arrested and held without communication or counsel. The power was given to generals of various of the northern states to suppress newspapers and suspend the writ. President Lincoln, in his famous letter to Erastus Corning and others, defended his conduct, saying all that ever could be said and what always will be said in favor of such policies in time of emergency.[32] Those policies were sharply but unavailingly condemned in May of 1861 by the aged Chief Justice Taney, and he has said all that can be said on the other side.[33] Had Mr. Lincoln scrupulously observed the Taney policy, I do not know whether we would have had any liberty, and had the Chief Justice adopted Mr. Lincoln's philosophy as the philosophy of the law, I again do not know whether we would have had any liberty.

Lord Acton has said that liberty is a term of two hundred definitions.[34] About all I am sure of is that it is something never established for the future, but something which each age must provide for itself. I think we are given the rough outlines of a free society by our Bill of Rights. Liberty is not the mere absence of restraint, it is not a spontaneous product of majority rule, it is not achieved merely by lifting underprivileged classes to power, nor is it the inevitable by-product of technological expansion. It is achieved only by a rule of law.

But we must bear in mind that in the protection of individual or minority rights, we are often impinging on the principle of majority rule. Judicial opinions rarely face this dilemma. Let us take, for example, a community engaged largely in steel work, many of whose inhabitants are employed on night shifts and get their rest by day. Acting through regularly chosen representatives, the municipality duly enacts a regulation that precludes doorbell ringing in the distribution of literature or goods. A religious faction insists upon ringing doorbells to summon the occupant to the door to receive religious tracts that attack his religion and seek to convert him to the faith of the caller. If the Court holds that the right of free speech includes the right to enter upon private property and summon the owner to the door, it necessarily holds that a majority of a community are without the right to protect their hours of rest against such religiously inspired aggression.

In case after case in which so-called civil rights are involved, the question simmers down to one of the extent to which majority rule will be set aside. This issue has been debated,[35] but it has by no means been settled, and views shift as the occasion for judicial intervention shifts from case to case. About all we need to note, unless we were to go into a lengthy discussion of the particular cases of application of the power, is that the power of the Court to protect individual or minority rights has on the other side of the coin the power to restrain the majority. Some profound political philosophers, among them Mr. Jefferson, doubted the advisability of such intervention. Mr. Jefferson asked where else we may "find the origin of *just* powers, if not in the majority of the society? Will it be in the minority? Or in an individual of that minority?"[36] Perhaps we should say that it is only to be found in the law, in rationally and dispassionately devised rules which limit the majority's control over the individual and the minority. But even with the best draftsmanship possible such rules cannot but leave many questions for interpretation.

Moreover, we must remember that the Supreme Court is not the only force that is operating upon the Constitution. Custom, even in most vital matters, may serve to alter it. I suppose the election of a President is the most decisive and important recurring event in our national life. Nothing concerned the forefathers more, and they set up an elaborate and original system to assure nonpartisan, deliberative choice from among all the citizens by electors selected for their leadership and judgment. This system has been suffocated by custom. The American public now sits at its television, entertained by the antics of two national conventions which limit their practicable choice of President to two men. Neither of these conventions nor the parties holding them has the slightest recognition in the Constitution, whose framers took every precaution to prevent the emergence of parties.

The Supreme Court, in the exercise of its power, has repeatedly come into collision with the strong executives of the nation. Jefferson, Jackson, Lincoln, and Franklin Roosevelt have been in open conflict with it. The clash has occurred where the Court was believed to be entering political realms through the passageway of private litigation. It would serve no purpose to review the merits of the conflict here, but in almost every instance it has occurred in such form as really to raise the question of minority and individual rights against majority rule: in each instance the President has been the representative of a powerful, popular majority. This is one of the great dilemmas of judicial power and one most avoided in discussion of the subject. So far as I can see, nothing has been accomplished in any of the controversies to settle or put at rest the questions which cause them. Judicial power to nullify a law duly passed by the representative process is a restriction upon the power of the majority to govern the country. Unrestricted majority rule leaves the individual in the minority unprotected. This is the dilemma and you have to take your choice. The Constitution-makers made their choice in favor of a limited majority rule.

In interpreting that limitation, of course, the Supreme Court from time to time makes and alters the law of the Constitution. It is idle to say that this is merely the ordinary process of private law interpretation. When the Court goes too far in interfering with the processes of the majority, it will again encounter a drive against its power or personnel. The power which has been exerted by the Court and which lies at the root of the controversies with the Executive has no more been renounced by the post-Roosevelt Court than it was by the pre-Roosevelt Court, though the lack of novel and progressive legislation has offered less occasion for its exercise. My philosophy has been and continues to be that such an institution, functioning by such methods, cannot and should not try to seize the initiative in shaping the policy of the law, either by constitutional interpretation or by statutory construction. While the line to be drawn between interpretation and legislation is difficult, and numerous dissents turn upon it, there is a limit beyond which the Court incurs the just charge of trying to supersede the law-making branches. Every Justice has been accused of legislating and every one has joined in that accusation of others. When the Court has gone too far, it has provoked reactions which have set back the cause it is designed to advance, and has sometimes called down upon itself severe rebuke.

If an organized society wants the kind of justice that an independent, professional judicial establishment is qualified to administer, our judiciary is certainly a most effective instrument for applying law and justice to individual cases and for cultivating public attitudes which rely upon law and seek justice. But I know of no modern instance in which any judiciary has saved a whole people from the great currents of intolerance, passion, usurpation, and tyranny which have threatened liberty and free institutions. The Dred Scott decision did not settle the question of the power to end slavery, and I very much doubt that had Mr. Justice McLean not dissented in that case it would have done any more to avoid war. No court can support a reactionary regime and no court can innovate or implement a new one. I doubt that any court, whatever its powers, could have saved Louis XVI or Marie Antoinette. None could have avoided the French Revolution, none could have stopped its excesses, and none could have prevented its culmination in the dictatorship of Napoleon. In Germany a courageous court refused to convict those whom the Nazi government sought to make the scapegoats for the Reichstag fire, clandestinely set by the Nazis themselves, and other courts decreed both the Nazi and the Communist parties to be illegal under German law. Those judgments fell on deaf ears and became dead letters because the political forces at the time were against them.

It is not idle speculation to inquire which comes first, either in time or importance, an independent and enlightened judiciary or a free and tolerant society. Must we first maintain a system of free political government to assure a free judiciary, or can we rely on an aggressive, activist judiciary to guarantee free government? While each undoubtedly is a support for the other, and the two are frequently found together, it is my belief that the attitude of a society and of its organized political forces, rather than its legal machinery, is the controlling force in the character of free institutions.

I am a fairly consistent reader of British newspapers. I have been repeatedly impressed with the speed and certainty with which the slightest invasion of British individual freedom or minority rights by officials of the government is picked up in Parliament, not merely by the opposition but by the party in power, and made the subject of persistent questioning, criticism, and sometimes rebuke. There is no waiting on the theory that the judges will take care of it. In this country, on the contrary, we rarely have a political issue made of any kind of invasion of civil liberty. On the contrary, district attorneys who have been rebuked by the courts are frequently promoted by the public. The attitude seems to be, leave it to the judges. Years after the event takes place, the judges make their pronouncement, often in the form of letting some admittedly guilty person go, and that ends the matter. In Great Britain, to observe civil liberties is good politics and to transgress the rights of the individual or the minority is bad politics. In the United States, I cannot say that this is so. Whether the political conscience is relieved because the responsibility here is made largely a legal one, I cannot say, but of this I am sure: any court which undertakes by its legal processes to enforce civil liberties needs the support of an enlightened and vigorous public opinion which will be intelligent and discriminating as to what cases really are civil liberties cases and what questions really are involved in those cases. I do not think the American public is enlightened on this subject.

Sometimes one is tempted to quote his former self, not only to pay his respects to the author but to demonstrate the consistency of his views, if not their correctness. On the 150th anniversary of the Supreme Court, speaking for the executive branch of the Government as Attorney General, I said to the Justices:

"However well the Court and its bar may discharge their tasks, the destiny of this Court is inseparably linked to the fate of our democratic system of representative government. Judicial functions, as we have evolved them, can be discharged only in that kind of society which is willing to submit its conflicts to adjudication and to subordinate power to reason. The future of the Court may depend more upon the competence of the executive and legislative branches of government to solve their problems adequately and in time than upon the merit which is its own." [37]

FOOTNOTES

[1] The statement was a personal one made to Mr. Justice Jackson and is recorded in Jackson, *Full Faith and Credit*, p. 2 (1945).

2 E.g., *Cochran* v. *Louisiana State Board*, 281 U.S. 370; *Mountain Timber Co.* v. *Washington*, 243 U.S. 219; *Pacific States Telephone & Telegraph Co.* v. *Oregon*, 223 U.S. 118.

3 E.g., *Coleman* v. *Miller*, 307 U.S. 433; *Leser* v. *Garnett*, 258 U.S. 130; *Luther* v. *Borden*, 7 How. (48 U.S.) 1.

4 E.g., *Field* v. *Clark*, 143 U.S. 649; *Harwood* v. *Wentworth*, 162 U.S. 547; *Flint* v. *Stone Tracy Co.*, 220 U.S. 107, 143.

5 E.g., *Ludecke* v. *Watkins*, 335 U.S. 160; *Commercial Trust Co.* v. *Miller*, 262 U.S. 51. Cf. *Woods* v. *Cloyd W. Miller Co.*, 333 U.S. 138, 146 (concurring opinion).

6 E.g., *Clark* v. *Allen*, 331 U.S. 503; *Terlinden* v. *Ames*, 184 U.S. 270; *Doe* v. *Braden*, 16 How. (57 U.S.) 635.

7 E.g., *United States* v. *Pink*, 315 U.S. 203; *Oetjen* v. *Central Leather Co.*, 246 U.S. 297; *Kennett* v. *Chambers*, 14 How. (55 U.S.) 38.

8 E.g., *Harisiades* v. *Shaughnessy*, 342 U.S. 580; *Chicago & Southern Air Lines, Inc.* v. *Waterman S.S. Corp.*, 333 U.S. 103; *In re Cooper*, 143 U.S. 472; *Foster* v. *Neilson*, 2 Pet. (27 U.S.) 253.

9 E.g., *Wood* v. *Broom*, 287 U.S. 1; *Colegrove* v. *Green*, 328 U.S. 549; *Anderson* v. *Jordan*, 343 U.S. 912.

10 E.g., *MacDougall* v. *Green*, 335 U.S. 281; *Illinois ex rel. Sankstone* v. *Jarecki*, 346 U.S. 861; *White* v. *Howard*, 347 U.S. 910.

11 E.g., *Cook* v. *Fortson*, *Turman* v. *Duckworth*, 329 U.S. 675; *South* v. *Peters*, 339 U.S. 276.

12 *United States* v. *Butler*, 297 U.S. 1, 66.

13 *Massachusetts* v. *Mellon*, 262 U.S. 447.

14 E.g., *United States* v. *Curtiss-Wright Export Corp.*, 299 U.S. 304; *Chicago & Southern Air Lines, Inc.* v. *Watermann S.S. Corp.*, 253 U.S. 103.

15 *Humphrey's Executor* v. *United States*, 295 U.S. 602.

16 *Panama Refining Co.* v. *Ryan*, 293 U.S. 388; *A.L.A. Schechter Poultry Corp.* v. *United States*, 295 U.S. 495.

17 Proclamation 2561, 7 Fed. Reg. 5101.

18 *Youngstown Sheet & Tube Co.* v. *Sawyer*, 343 U.S. 579.

19 *Id.*, at 634 (concurring opinion).

20 Wilson, *Constitutional Government in the United States*, 68, 69 (1911).

21 Dicey, *Law of the Constitution*, App. 604. (9th ed. 1939).

22 Hughes, *The Supreme Court of the United States*, 96 (1928).

23 *Helvering* v. *Davis*, 301 U.S. 619.

24 *Morehead* v. *New York ex rel. Tipaldo*, 298 U.S. 587.

25 *Johnson* v. *Zerbst*, 304 U.S. 458, 467–468; see also *Brown* v. *Allen*, 344 U.S. 443, 532 (concurring opinion). [Mr. Justice Jackson had written "Johnson" next to this note.]

26 See *Screws* v. *United States*, 325 U.S. 91.

27 E.g., *Maryland* v. *West Virginia*, 217 U.S. 1; *Indiana* v. *Kentucky*, 163 U.S. 520; *Missouri* v. *Iowa*, 7 How. (48 U.S.) 660.

28 *Virginia* v. *West Virginia*, 206 U.S. 290.

29 E.g., *New Jersey* v. *Delaware*, 291 U.S. 361; *Wisconsin* v. *Illinois*, 278 U.S. 367; *Kansas* v. *Colorado*, 206 U.S. 46.

30 291 U.S., at 383.

31 *Korematsu* v. *United States*, 323 U.S. 214.

[32] VIII *Complete Works of Abraham Lincoln* (ed. Nicolay and Hay), 298 (*c.* 1894).

[33] *Ex parte Merryman*, Reports of Cases at Law and Equity and in the Admiralty determined in the Circuit Court of the United States for the District of Maryland by Roger Brooke Taney, 246 (1871).

[34] Acton, *Essays on Freedom and Power*, 14 (1948).

[35] *West Virginia State Board of Education* v. *Barnette*, 319 U.S. 624.

[36] Letter to Major John Cartwright, June 5, 1824, VII *Writings of Thomas Jefferson* (ed. Washington), 356 (1861).

[37] 309 U.S. v, vii.

HUGO BLACK

The Bill of Rights

In 1960, after twenty-one years of general unavailability for
direct public discussion of the Court's work, Hugo Black delivered the first James Madison Lecture at New York University Law School. A group of politically sensitive cases involving the "Communist issue" in 1958–1959 had produced an
unusually sharp clash between the Black position (shared by
Warren, Douglas and Brennan) and the position of the Court
majority. While the focus of the Madison Lecture was the
historical and philosophical basis of "absolutes" in the Bill of
Rights, Black used the subject as a chance to attack the 1958–
1959 Court majority's "balancing" doctrine. The packed audience which watched Black deliver this speech saw him re-create
his earlier roles as soft-spoken but razor-sharp Southern prosecutor and Senate investigator. An Alabaman, Black had practiced law in Birmingham, served as a police court judge and
county solicitor, and had spent a decade in the United States
Senate as a Southern progressive. President Roosevelt appointed him in 1938 as his first nominee to the Court, no doubt
savoring the fact that senatorial courtesy would prevent serious
opposition to a man who had been a zealous investigator of
business chicanery, a stalwart New Dealer, a critic of Supreme
Court rulings favoring property rights, and a supporter of the
Roosevelt Court bill in 1937.

SOURCE: 35 *New York University Law Review* 865 (1960).

What is a bill of rights? In the popular sense it is any document setting forth the liberties of the people. I prefer to think of our Bill of Rights as including all provisions of the original Constitution and Amendments that protect individual liberty by barring government from acting in a particular area or from acting except under certain prescribed procedures. I have in mind such clauses in the body of the Constitution itself as those which safeguard the right of habeas corpus, forbid bills of attainder and ex post facto laws, guarantee trial by jury, and strictly define treason and limit the way it can be tried and punished. I would certainly add to this list the last constitutional prohibition in Article Six that "no religious Test shall ever be required as a Qualification to any Office or public Trust under the United States."

I shall speak to you about the Bill of Rights only as it bears on powers of the Federal Government. Originally, the first ten amendments were not intended to apply to the states but, as the Supreme Court held in 1833 in *Barron* v. *Baltimore*,[1] were adopted to quiet fears extensively entertained that the powers of the big new national government "might be exercised in a manner dangerous to liberty." I believe that by virtue of the Fourteenth Amendment, the first ten amendments are now applicable to the states, a view I stated in *Adamson* v. *California*.[2] I adhere to that view. In this talk, however, I want to discuss only the extent to which the Bill of Rights limits the Federal Government.

In applying the Bill of Rights to the Federal Government there is today a sharp difference of views as to how far its provisions should be held to limit the lawmaking power of Congress. How this difference is finally resolved will, in my judgment, have far-reaching consequences upon our liberties. I shall first summarize what those different views are.

Some people regard the prohibitions of the Constitution, even its most unequivocal commands, as mere admonitions which Congress need not always observe. This viewpoint finds many different verbal expressions. For example, it is sometimes said that Congress may abridge a constitutional right if there is a clear and present danger that the free exercise of the right will bring about a substantive evil that Congress has authority to prevent. Or it is said that a right may be abridged where its exercise would cause so much injury to the public that this injury would outweigh the injury to the individual who is deprived of the right. Again, it is sometimes said that the Bill of Rights' guarantees must "compete" for survival against general powers expressly granted to Congress and that the individual's right must, if outweighed by the public interest, be subordinated to the Government's competing interest in denying the right. All of these formulations, and more with which you are doubtless familiar, rest, at least in part, on the premise that there are no "absolute" prohibitions in the Constitution, and that all constitutional problems are questions of reasonableness, proximity, and degree. This view comes close to the English doctrine of legislative omnipotence, qualified only by the possibility of a judicial veto if the Supreme Court finds that a congressional choice between "competing" policies has no reasonable basis.

I cannot accept this approach to the Bill of Rights. It is my belief that there *are* "absolutes" in our Bill of Rights, and that they were put there on purpose by men who knew what words meant, and meant their prohibitions to be "absolutes." The whole history and background of the Constitution and Bill of Rights, as I understand it, belies the assumption or conclusion that our ultimate constitutional freedoms are no more than our English ancestors had when they came to this new land to get new freedoms. The historical and practical purposes of a Bill of Rights, the very use of a written constitution, indigenous to America, the language the Framers used, the kind of three-department government they took pains to set up, all point to the creation of a government which was denied all power to do some things under any and all circumstances, and all power to do other things except precisely in the manner prescribed. In this talk I will state some of the reasons why I hold this view. In doing so, however, I shall not attempt to discuss the wholly different and complex problem of the marginal scope of each individual amendment as applied to the particular facts of particular cases. For example, there is a question as to whether the First Amendment was intended to protect speech that courts find "obscene." I shall not stress this or similar differences of construction, nor shall I add anything to the views I expressed in the recent case of *Smith* v. *California*.[3] I am primarily discussing here whether liberties *admittedly* covered by the Bill of Rights can nevertheless be abridged on the ground that a superior public interest justifies the abridgment. I think the Bill of Rights made its safeguards superior.

Today most Americans seem to have forgotten the ancient evils which forced their ancestors to flee to this new country and to form a government stripped of old powers used to oppress them. But the Americans who supported the Revolution and the adoption of our Constitution knew firsthand the dangers of tyrannical governments. They were familiar with the long existing practice of English persecutions of people wholly because of their religious or political beliefs, They knew that many accused of such offenses had stood, helpless to defend themselves, before biased legislators and judges.

John Lilburne, a Puritan dissenter, is a conspicuous example.[4] He found out the hard way that a citizen of England could not get a court and jury trial under English law if Parliament wanted to try and punish him in some kind of summary and unfair method of its own. Time and time again, when his religious or political activities resulted in criminal charges against him, he had demanded jury trials under the "law of the land" but had been refused. Due to "trials" either by Parliament, its legislative committees, or courts subservient to the King or to Parliament, against all of which he vigorously protested as contrary to "due process" or "the law of the land," Lilburne had been whipped, put in the pillory, sent to prison, heavily fined and banished from England, all its islands and dominions, under penalty of death should he return. This last sentence was imposed by a simple Act of Parliament without any semblance of a trial. Upon his defiant return he was arrested and subjected to an unfair trial for his life. His chief defense was that the Parliamentary conviction was a nullity, as a denial of "due process of law," which he claimed was guaranteed under Magna Charta, the 1628 Petition of Right, and statutes passed to carry them out. He also challenged the power of Parliament to enact bills of attainder on the same grounds—due process of law. Lilburne repeatedly and vehemently contended that he was entitled to notice, an indictment, and court trial by jury under the known laws of England; that he had a right to be represented by counsel; that he had a right to have witnesses summoned in his behalf and be confronted by the witnesses against him; that he could not be compelled to testify against himself. When Lilburne finally secured a jury, it courageously acquitted him, after which the jury itself was severely punished by the court.

Prompted largely by the desire to save Englishmen from such legislative mockeries of fair trials, Lilburne and others strongly advocated adoption of an "Agreement of the People" which contained most of the provisions of our present Bill of Rights. That Agreement would have done away with Parliamentary omnipotence. Lilburne pointed out that the basic defect of Magna Charta and statutes complementing it was that they were not binding on Parliament since "that which is done by one Parliament, as a Parliament, may be undone by the next Parliament: but an Agreement of the People begun and ended amongst the People can never come justly within the Parliament's cognizance to destroy." [5] The proposed "Agreement of the People," Lilburne argued, could be changed only by the people and would bind Parliament as the supreme "law of the land." This same idea was picked up before the adoption of our Federal Constitution by Massachusetts and New Hampshire, which adopted their constitutions only after popular referendums. Our Federal Constitution is largely attributable to the same current of thinking.

Unfortunately, our own colonial history also provided ample reasons for people to be afraid to vest too much power in the national government. There had been bills of attainder here; women had been convicted and sentenced to death as "witches"; Quakers, Baptists and various Protestant sects had been persecuted from time to time. Roger Williams left Massachusetts to breathe the free air of new Rhode Island. Catholics were barred from holding office in many places. Test oaths were required in some of the colonies to bar any but Christians from holding office. In New England Quakers suffered death for their faith. Baptists were sent to jail in Virginia for preaching, which caused Madison, while a very young man, to deplore what he called that "diabolical hell-conceived principle of persecution." [6]

In the light of history, therefore, it is not surprising that when our Constitution was adopted without specific provisions to safeguard cherished individual rights from invasion by the legislative, as well as the executive and judicial departments of the National Government, a loud and irresistible clamor went up throughout the country. These protests were so strong that the Constitution was ratified by the very narrowest of votes in some of the states. It has been said, and I think correctly, that had there been no general agreement that a supplementary Bill of Rights would be adopted as soon as possible after Congress met, the Constitution would not have been ratified. It seems clear that this widespread demand for a Bill of Rights was due to a common fear of political and religious persecution should the national legislative power be left unrestrained as it was in England.

The form of government which was ordained and established in 1789 contains certain unique features which reflected the Framers' fear of arbitrary government and which clearly indicate an intention absolutely to limit what Congress could do. The first of these features is that our Constitution is written in a single document. Such constitutions are familiar today and it is not always remembered that our country was the first to have one. Certainly one purpose of a written constitution is to define and therefore more specifically limit government powers. An all-powerful government that can act as it pleases wants no such constitution—unless to fool the people. England had no written constitution and this once proved a source of tyranny, as our ancestors well knew. Jefferson said about this departure from the English type of government: "Our peculiar security is in the possession of a written Constitution. Let us not make it a blank paper by construction." [7]

A second unique feature of our Government is a Constitution supreme over the legislature. In England, statutes, Magna Charta and later declarations of rights had for centuries limited the power of the King, but they did not limit the power of Parliament. Although commonly referred to as a constitution, they were never the "supreme law of the land" in the way in which our Constitution is, much to the regret of statesmen like Pitt the elder. Parliament could change this English "Constitution"; Congress cannot change ours. Ours can only be changed by amendments ratified by three-fourths of the states. It was one of the great achievements of our Constitution that it ended legislative omnipotence here and placed all departments and agencies of government under one supreme law.

A third feature of our Government expressly designed to limit its powers was the division of authority into three coordinate branches none of which was to have supremacy over the others. This separation of powers with the checks and balances which each branch was given over the others was designed to prevent any branch, including the legislative, from infringing individual liberties safeguarded by the Constitution.

Finally, our Constitution was the first to provide a really independent judiciary. Moreover, as the Supreme Court held in *Marbury* v. *Madison*,[8] correctly I believe, this judiciary has the power to hold legislative enactments void that are repugnant to the Constitution and the Bill of Rights. In this country the judiciary was made independent because it has, I believe, the primary responsibility and duty of giving force and effect to constitutional liberties and limitations upon the executive and legislative branches. Judges in England were not always independent and they could not hold Parliamentary acts void. Consequently, English courts could not be counted on to protect the liberties of the people against invasion by the Parliament, as many unfortunate Englishmen found out, such as Sir Walter Raleigh, who was executed as the result of an unfair trial, and a lawyer named William Prynne, whose ears were first cut off by court order and who subsequently, by another court order, had his remaining ear stumps gouged out while he was on a pillory. Prynne's offenses were writing books and pamphlets.

All of the unique features of our Constitution show an underlying purpose to create a new kind of limited government. Central to all of the Framers of the Bill of Rights was the idea that since government, particularly the national government newly created, is a powerful institution, its officials—all of them—must be compelled to exercise their powers within strictly defined boundaries. As Madison told Congress, the Bill of Rights' limitations point "sometimes against the abuse of the Executive power, sometimes against the Legislative, and in some cases against the community itself; or, in other words, against the majority in favor of the minority." [9] Madison also explained that his proposed amendments were intended "to limit and qualify the powers of Government, by excepting out of the grant of power those cases in which the Government ought not to act, or to act only in a particular mode." [10] In the light of this purpose let us now turn to the language of the first ten amendments to consider whether their provisions were written as mere admonitions to Congress or as absolute commands, proceeding for convenience from the last to the first.

The last two Amendments, the Ninth and Tenth, are general in character, but both emphasize the limited nature of the Federal Government. Number Ten restricts federal power to what the Constitution delegates to the central government, reserving all other powers to the states or to the people. Number Nine attempts to make certain that enumeration of some rights must "not be construed to deny or disparage others retained by the people." The use of the words, "the people," in both these Amendments strongly emphasizes the desire of the Framers to protect individual liberty.

The Seventh Amendment states that "In Suits at common law, where the value in controversy shall exceed twenty dollars, the right of trial by jury shall be preserved. . . ." This language clearly requires that jury trials must be afforded in the type of cases the Amendment describes. The Amendment goes on in equally unequivocal words to command that "no fact tried by a jury, shall be otherwise reexamined in any Court of the United States, than according to the rules of the common law."

Amendments Five, Six, and Eight relate chiefly to the procedures that government must follow when bringing its powers to bear against any person with a view to depriving him of his life, liberty, or property.

The Eighth Amendment forbids "excessive bail," "excessive fines," or the infliction of "cruel or unusual punishments." This is one of the less precise provisions. The courts are required to determine the meaning of such general terms as "excessive" and "unusual." But surely that does not mean that admittedly "excessive bail," "excessive fines," or "cruel punishments" could be justified on the ground of a "competing" public interest in carrying out some generally granted power like that given Congress to regulate commerce.

Amendment Six provides that in a criminal prosecution an accused shall have a "speedy and public trial, by an impartial jury of the State and district wherein the crime shall have been committed, which district shall have been previously ascertained by law, and to be informed of the nature and cause of the accusation; to be confronted with the witnesses against him; to have compulsory process for obtaining witnesses in his favor, and have the Assistance of Counsel for his defence." All of these requirements are cast in terms both definite and absolute. Trial by jury was also guaranteed in the original Constitution. The additions here, doubtless prompted by English trials of Americans away from their homes, are that a trial must be "speedy and public," "by an impartial jury," and in a district which "shall have been previously ascertained by law." If there is any one thing that is certain it is that the Framers intended both in the original Constitution and in the Sixth Amendment that persons charged with crime by the Federal Government have a right to be tried by jury. Suppose juries began acquitting people Congress thought should be convicted. Could Congress then provide some other form of trial, say by an administrative agency, or the military, where convictions could be more readily and certainly obtained, if it thought the safety of the nation so required? How about secret trials? By *partial* juries? Can it be that these are not absolute prohibitions?

The Sixth Amendment requires notice of the cause of an accusation, confrontation by witnesses, compulsory process and assistance of counsel. The experience of centuries has demonstrated the value of these procedures to one on trial for crime. And this Amendment purports to guarantee them by clear language. But if there are no absolutes in the Bill of Rights, these guarantees too can be taken away by Congress on findings that a competing public interest requires that defendants be tried without notice, without witnesses, without confrontation, and without counsel.

The Fifth Amendment provides:

"No person shall be held to answer for a capital, or otherwise infamous crime, unless on a presentment or indictment of a Grand Jury, except in cases arising in the land or naval forces, or in the Militia, when in actual service in time of War or public danger; nor shall any person be subject for the same offence to be twice put in jeopardy of life or limb; nor shall be compelled in any criminal case to be a witness against himself, nor be deprived of life, liberty, or property, without due process of law; nor shall private property be taken for public use, without just compensation."

Most of these Fifth Amendment prohibitions are both definite and unequivocal. There has been much controversy about the meaning of "due process of law." Whatever its meaning, however, there can be no doubt that it must be granted. Moreover, few doubt that it has an historical meaning which denies Government the right to take away life, liberty, or property without trials properly conducted according to the Constitution and laws validly made in accordance with it. This, at least, was the meaning of "due process of law" when used in Magna Charta and other old English Statutes where it was referred to as "the law of the land."

The Fourth Amendment provides:

"The right of the people to be secure in their persons, houses, papers, and effects, against unreasonable searches and seizures, shall not be violated, and no Warrants shall issue, but upon probable cause, supported by Oath or affirmation, and particularly describing the place to be searched, and the persons or things to be seized."

The use of the word "unreasonable" in this Amendment means, of course, that not *all* searches and seizures are prohibited. Only those which are *unreasonable* are unlawful. There may be much difference of opinion about whether a particular search or seizure is unreasonable and therefore forbidden by this Amendment. But if it *is* unreasonable, it is absolutely prohibited.

Likewise, the provision which forbids warrants for arrest, search or seizure without "probable cause" is itself an absolute prohibition.

The Third Amendment provides that:

"No Soldier shall, in time of peace be quartered in any house, without the consent of the Owner, nor in time of war, but in a manner to be prescribed by law."

Americans had recently suffered from the quartering of British troops in their homes, and so this Amendment is written in language that apparently no one has ever thought could be violated on the basis of an overweighing public interest.

Amendment Two provides that:

"A well regulated Militia, being necessary to the security of a free State, the right of the people to keep and bear Arms, shall not be infringed."

Although the Supreme Court has held this Amendment to include only arms necessary to a well-regulated militia, as so construed, its prohibition is absolute. This brings us to the First Amendment. It reads:

"Congress shall make no law respecting an establishment of religion, or prohibiting the free exercise thereof; or abridging the freedom of speech, or of the press; or the right of the people peaceably to assemble, and to petition the Government for a redress of grievances."

The phrase "Congress shall make no law" is composed of plain words, easily understood. The Framers knew this. The language used by Madison in his proposal was different, but no less emphatic and unequivocal. That proposal is worth reading:

"The civil rights of none shall be abridged on account of religious belief or worship, nor shall any national religion be established, nor shall the full and equal rights of conscience be in any manner, or on any pretext, infringed.

"The people shall not be deprived or abridged of their right to speak, to write, or to publish their sentiments; and the freedom of the press, as one of the great bulwarks of liberty, shall be inviolable.

"The people shall not be restrained from peaceably assembling and consulting for their common good; nor from applying to the Legislature by petitions, or remonstrances, for redress of their grievances." [11]

Neither as offered nor as adopted is the language of this Amendment anything less than absolute. Madison was emphatic about this. He told the Congress that under it "The right of freedom of speech is secured; the liberty of the press is expressly declared to be *beyond the reach of this Government.* . . ." [12] (Emphasis added in all quotations.) Some years later Madison wrote that "it would seem scarcely possible to doubt that *no power whatever* over the press was supposed to be delegated by the Constitution, as it originally stood, and that the amendment was intended as a *positive and absolute reservation of it.*" [13] With reference to the positive nature of the First Amendment's command against infringement of religious liberty, Madison later said that "there is not a shadow of right in the general government to intermeddle with religion," [14] and that "this subject is, for the honor of America, perfectly free and unshackled. The *government has no jurisdiction over it.*" [15]

To my way of thinking, at least, the history and language of the

Constitution and the Bill of Rights, which I have discussed with you, make it plain that one of the primary purposes of the Constitution with its amendments was to withdraw from the Government all power to act in certain areas—whatever the scope of those areas may be. If I am right in this then there is, at least in those areas, no justification whatever for "balancing" a particular right against some expressly granted power of Congress. If the Constitution withdraws from Government all power over subject matter in an area, such as religion, speech, press, assembly, and petition, there is nothing over which authority may be exerted.

The Framers were well aware that the individual rights they sought to protect might be easily nullified if subordinated to the general powers granted to Congress. One of the reasons for adoption of the Bill of Rights was to prevent just that. Specifically the people feared that the "necessary and proper" clause could be used to project the generally granted Congressional powers into the protected areas of individual rights. One need only read the debates in the various states to find out that this is true. But if these debates leave any doubt, Mr. Madison's words to Congress should remove it. In speaking of the "necessary and proper" clause and its possible effect on freedom of religion he said, as reported in the *Annals of Congress:*

> "Whether the words are necessary or not, he did not mean to say, but they had been required by some of the State Conventions, who seemed to entertain an opinion that under the clause of the Constitution, which gave power to Congress to make all laws *necessary and proper* to carry into execution the Constitution, and the laws made under it, enabled them to make laws of such a nature as might infringe the rights of conscience, and establish a national religion; to prevent these effects he presumed the amendment was intended, and he thought it as well expressed as the nature of the language would admit." [16]

It seems obvious to me that Congress, in exercising its general powers, is expressly forbidden to use means prohibited by the Bill of Rights. Whatever else the phrase "necessary and proper" may mean, it must be that Congress may only adopt such means to carry out its powers as are "proper," that is, not specifically prohibited.

It has also been argued that since freedom of speech, press, and religion in England were narrow freedoms at best, and since there were many English laws infringing those freedoms, our First Amendment should not be thought to bar similar infringements by Congress. Again one needs only to look to the debates in Congress over the First Amendment to find that the First Amendment cannot be treated as a mere codification of English law. Mr. Madison made a clear explanation to Congress that it was the purpose of the First Amendment to grant greater protection than England afforded its citizens. He said:

"In the declaration of rights which that country has established, the truth is, they have gone no farther than to raise a barrier against the power of the Crown; the power of the Legislature is left altogether indefinite. Although I know whenever the great rights, the trial by jury, freedom of the press, or liberty of conscience, come in question in that body, the invasion of them is resisted by able advocates, yet their Magna Charta does not contain any one provision for the security of those rights, respecting which the people of America are most alarmed. The freedom of the press and rights of conscience, those choicest privileges of the people, are unguarded in the British Constitution.

"But although the case may be widely different, and it may not be thought necessary to provide limits for the legislative power in that country, yet a different opinion prevails in the United States." [17]

It was the desire to give the people of America greater protection against the powerful Federal Government than the English had had against their government that caused the Framers to put these freedoms of expression, again in the words of Madison, "beyond the reach of this Government."

When closely analyzed the idea that there can be no "absolute" constitutional guarantees in the Bill of Rights is frightening to contemplate even as to individual safeguards in the original Constitution. Take, for instance, the last clause in Article Six that "no religious Test shall ever be required" for a person to hold office in the United States. Suppose Congress should find that some religious sect was dangerous because of its foreign affiliations. Such was the belief on which English test oaths rested for a long time and some of the states had test oaths on that assumption at the time, and after, our Constitution was adopted in 1789. Could Congress, or the Supreme Court, or both, put this precious privilege to be free from test oaths on scales, find it outweighed by some other public interest, and therefore make United States officials and employees swear they did not and never had belonged to or associated with a particular religious group suspected of disloyalty? Can Congress, in the name of overbalancing necessity, suspend habeas corpus in peacetime? Are there circumstances under which Congress could, after nothing more than a legislative bill of attainder, take away a man's life, liberty, or property? Hostility of the Framers toward bills of attainder was so great that they took the unusual step of barring such legislative punishments by the States as well as the Federal Government. They wanted to remove any possibility of such proceedings anywhere in this country. This is not strange in view of the fact that they were much closer than we are to the great Act of Attainder by the Irish Parliament, in 1688, which condemned between two and three thousand men, women, and children to exile or death without anything that even resembled a trial.[18]

Perhaps I can show you the consequences of the balancing approach to the Bill of Rights liberties by a practical demonstration of how it might work. The last clause of the Fifth Amendment is: "nor shall private property be taken for public use, without just compensation." On its face this command looks absolute, but if one believes that it should be weighed against the powers granted to Congress, there might be some circumstances in which this right would have to give way, just as there are some circumstances in which it is said the right of freedom of religion, speech, press, assembly and petition can be balanced away. Let us see how the balancing concept would apply to the just compensation provision of the Bill of Rights in the following wholly imaginary judicial opinion of Judge X:

"This case presents an important question of constitutional law. The United States is engaged in a stupendous national defense undertaking which requires the acquisition of much valuable land throughout the country. The plaintiff here owns 500 acres of land. The location of the land gives it a peculiarly strategic value for carrying out the defense program. Due to the great national emergency that exists, Congress concluded that the United States could not afford at this time to pay compensation for the lands which it needed to acquire. For this reason an act was passed authorizing seizure without compensation of all the lands required for the defense establishment.

"In reaching a judgment on this case, I cannot shut my eyes to the fact that the United States is in a desperate condition at this time. Nor can I, under established canons of constitutional construction, invalidate a Congressional enactment if there are any rational grounds upon which Congress could have passed it. I think there are such grounds here. Highly important among the powers granted Congress by the Constitution are the powers to declare war, maintain a navy, and raise and support armies. This, of course, means the power to conduct war successfully. To make sure that Congress is not unduly restricted in the exercise of these constitutional powers, the Constitution also gives Congress power to make all laws 'necessary and proper to carry into execution the foregoing powers. . . .' This 'necessary and proper' clause applies to the powers to make war and support armies as it does to all the other granted powers.

"Plaintiff contends, however, that the Fifth Amendment's provision about compensation is so absolute a command that Congress is wholly without authority to violate it, however great this nation's emergency and peril may be. I must reject this contention. We must never forget that it is a constitution we are expounding. And a constitution, unlike ordinary statutes, must endure for ages; it must be adapted to changing conditions and the needs of changing communities. Without such capacity for change, our Constitution would soon be outmoded and become a dead letter. Therefore its words must never be read as rigid absolutes. The Bill of Rights' commands, no more than any others, can stay the hands of Congress from doing that which the general welfare imperatively demands. When two great constitutional provisions like these conflict—as here the power to make war conflicts with the requirements for just compensation—it becomes the duty of courts to weigh the constitutional right of an individual to compensation against the power of Congress to wage a successful war.

"While the question is not without doubt, I have no hesitation in finding the challenged Congressional act valid. Driven by the absolute necessity to protect the nation from foreign aggression, the national debt has risen to billions of dollars. The Government's credit is such that interest rates have soared. Under these circumstances, Congress was rationally entitled to find that if it paid for all the lands it needs it might bankrupt the nation and render it helpless in its hour of greatest need. Weighing as I must the loss the individual will suffer because he has to surrender his land to the nation without compensation against the great public interest in conducting war, I hold the act valid. A decree will be entered accordingly."

Of course, I would not decide this case this way nor do I think any other judge would so decide it today. My reason for refusing this approach would be that I think the Fifth Amendment's command is absolute and not to be overcome without constitutional amendment even in times of grave emergency. But I think this wholly fictitious opinion fairly illustrates the possibilities of the balancing approach, not only as to the just compensation clause, but as to other provisions of the Bill of Rights as well. The great danger of the judiciary balancing process is that in times of emergency and stress it gives Government the power to do what it thinks necessary to protect itself, regardless of the rights of individuals. If the need is great, the right of Government can always be said to outweigh the rights of the individual. If "balancing" is accepted as the test, it would be hard for any conscientious judge to hold otherwise in times of dire need. And laws adopted in times of dire need are often very hasty and oppressive laws, especially when, as often happens, they are carried over and accepted as normal. Furthermore, the balancing approach to basic individual liberties assumes to legislators and judges more power than either the Framers or I myself believe should be entrusted, without limitation, to any man or any group of men.

It seems to me that the "balancing" approach also disregards all of the unique features of our Constitution which I described earlier. In reality this approach returns us to the state of legislative supremacy which existed in England and which the Framers were so determined to change once and for all. On the one hand, it denies the judiciary its constitutional power to measure acts of Congress by the standards set down in the Bill of Rights. On the other hand, though apparently reducing judicial powers by saying that acts of Congress may be held unconstitutional only when they are found to have no rational legislative basis, this approach really gives the Court, along with Congress, a greater power, that of overriding the plain commands of the Bill of Rights on a finding of weighty public interest. In effect, it changes the direction of our form of government from a government of limited powers to a government in which Congress may do anything that Courts believe to be "reasonable."

Of course the decision to provide a constitutional safeguard for a particular right, such as the fair trial requirements of the Fifth and Sixth Amendments and the right of free speech protection of the First, involves a balancing of conflicting interests. Strict procedures may release guilty men; protecting speech and press may involve dangers to a particular government. I believe, however, that the Framers themselves did this balancing when they wrote the Constitution and the Bill of Rights. They appreciated the risks involved and they decided that certain rights should be guaranteed regardless of these risks. Courts have neither the right nor the power to review this original decision of the Framers and to attempt to make a different evaluation of the importance of the rights granted in the Constitution. Where conflicting values exist in the field of individual liberties protected by the Constitution, that document settles the conflict, and its policy should not be changed without constitutional amendments by the people in the manner provided by the people.

Misuse of government power, particularly in times of stress, has brought suffering to humanity in all ages about which we have authentic history. Some of the world's noblest and finest men have suffered ignominy and death for no crime—unless unorthodoxy is a crime. Even enlightened Athens had its victims such as Socrates. Because of the same kind of bigotry, Jesus, the great Dissenter, was put to death on a wooden cross. The flames of inquisitions all over the world have warned that men endowed with unlimited government power, even earnest men, consecrated to a cause, are dangerous.

For my own part, I believe that our Constitution, with its absolute guarantees of individual rights, is the best hope for the aspirations of freedom which men share everywhere. I cannot agree with those who think of the Bill of Rights as an 18th Century straitjacket, unsuited for this age. It is old but not all old things are bad. The evils it guards against are not only old, they are with us now, they exist today. Almost any morning you open your daily paper you can see where some person somewhere in the world is on trial or has just been convicted of supposed disloyalty to a new group controlling the government which has set out to purge its suspected enemies and all those who had dared to be against its successful march to power. Nearly always you see that these political heretics are being tried by military tribunals or some other summary and sure method for disposition of the accused. Now and then we even see the convicted victims as they march to their execution.

Experience all over the world has demonstrated, I fear, that the distance between stable, orderly government and one that has been taken over by force is not so great as we have assumed. Our own free system to live and progress has to have intelligent citizens, citizens who cannot only think and speak and write to influence people, but citizens who are free to do that without fear of governmental censorship or reprisal.

The provisions of the Bill of Rights that safeguard fair legal procedures came about largely to protect the weak and the oppressed from punishment by the strong and the powerful who wanted to stifle the voices of discontent raised in protest against oppression and injustice in public affairs. Nothing that I have read in the Congressional debates on the Bill of Rights indicates that there was any belief that the First Amendment contained any qualifications. The only arguments that tended to look in this direction at all were those that said "that all paper barriers against the power of the community are too weak to be worthy of attention." [19] Suggestions were also made in and out of Congress that a Bill of Rights would be a futile gesture since there would be no way to enforce the safeguards for freedom it provided. Mr. Madison answered this argument in these words:

> "If they [the Bill of Rights amendments] are incorporated into the Constitution, independent tribunals of justice will consider themselves in a peculiar manner the guardians of those rights; they will be an impenetrable bulwark against any assumption of power in the Legislative or Executive; they will be naturally led to resist every encroachment upon rights expressly stipulated for in the Constitution by the declaration of rights." [20]

I fail to see how courts can escape this sacred trust.

Since the earliest days philosophers have dreamed of a country where the mind and spirit of man would be free; where there would be no limits to inquiry; where men would be free to explore the unknown and to challenge the most deeply rooted beliefs and principles. Our First Amendment was a bold effort to adopt this principle—to establish a country with no legal restrictions of any kind upon the subjects people could investigate, discuss and deny. The Framers knew, better perhaps than we do today, the risks they were taking. They knew that free speech might be the friend of change and revolution. But they also knew that it is always the deadliest enemy of tyranny. With this knowledge they still believed that the ultimate happiness and security of a nation lies in its ability to explore, to change, to grow and ceaselessly to adapt itself to new knowledge born of inquiry free from any kind of governmental control over the mind and spirit of man. Loyalty comes from love of good government, not fear of a bad one.

The First Amendment is truly the heart of the Bill of Rights. The Framers balanced its freedoms of religion, speech, press, assembly and petition against the needs of a powerful central government, and decided that in those freedoms lies this nation's only true security. They were not afraid for men to be free. We should not be. We should be as confident as Jefferson was when he said in his First Inaugural Address:

> "If there be any among us who would wish to dissolve this Union or to change its republican form, let them stand undisturbed as monuments of the safety with which error of opinion may be tolerated where reason is left free to combat it." [21]

FOOTNOTES

[1] 32 U.S. (7 Pet.) 242, 249 (1833).
[2] 332 U.S. 46, 71–72 (1947) (dissenting opinion).
[3] 361 U.S. 147, 155 (1959) (concurring opinion).
[4] See The Trial of John Lilburn and John Wharton (Star Chamber 1637) in 3 How. St. Tr. 1315 (1816).
[5] Leveller Manifestoes of the Puritan Revolution 423 (Wolfe ed. 1944).
[6] 1 Rives, History of the Life and Times of James Madison 44 (1859).
[7] 4 Jefferson, Writings 506 (Washington ed. 1859).
[8] 5 U.S. (1 Cranch) 137 (1803).
[9] 1 Annals of Cong. 437 (1789).

10 Ibid.

11 1 Annals of Cong. 434 (1789).

12 1 Annals of Cong. 738 (1789).

13 6 Madison, Writings 391 (Hunt ed. 1906).

14 5 Madison, Writings 176 (Hunt ed. 1904).

15 Id. at 132.

16 1 Annals of Cong. 730 (1789). (Emphasis added.)

17 1 Annals of Cong. 436 (1789).

18 See Joint Anti-Fascist Refugee Comm. *v.* McGrath, 341 U.S. 123, 146–49 (1951) (appendix to concurring opinion of Black, J.).

19 1 Annals of Cong. 437 (1789).

20 1 Annals of Cong. 439 (1789).

21 8 Jefferson, Writings 2–3 (Washington ed. 1859).

HUGO BLACK

Further Thoughts on the "*Absolute*" Bill of Rights

Following delivery of the Madison Lecture just printed, an animated discussion arose among lawyers, political scientists, and journalists about Justice Black's definition of "absolutes." Several commentators pointed out that in his two decades on the Supreme Court, Justice Black had not always voted for such a total concept in specific circumstances. One of the leading examples of a more limited pre-1960 position, for instance, was Chaplinsky v. New Hampshire, 315 U.S. 568 (1942). A unanimous opinion for the Court had upheld the conviction of a religious-sect speaker under an ordinance forbidding the utterance of "offensive, derisive or annoying" words to another person in a public place. Black had joined the Court's opinion stating in unequivocal terms that:

[T]he right of free speech is not absolute at all times and under all circumstances. There are certain well-defined and narrowly limited classes of speech, the prevention and punishment of which have never been thought to raise any Constitutional problem. These include the lewd and obscene, the profane, the libelous, and the insulting or "fighting" words—those which by their very utterance inflict injury or tend to incite an immediate breach of the peace.

The author of those words for the unanimous Court was the civil-liberties stalwart, Justice Frank Murphy, and, along with Justice Black, the statement was approved by Justices William

O. Douglas and Wiley Rutledge of the libertarian activist group within the Court.

Perhaps it was to explain and further clarify his position, and to carry forward the public debate, that Justice Black consented in the spring of 1962 to take part in an unusual event, a public "interview" in depth about his views, conducted not by a journalist but by a professor of law, and before an audience with sophistication in Bill of Rights issues and judicial review. On Saturday evening, April 14, 1962, at a banquet in honor of his twenty-five years of service on the Supreme Court tendered him by the American Jewish Congress, Justice Black was "interviewed" by Professor Edmond Cahn of New York University Law School. Professor Cahn was, by his own description, in thoroughgoing agreement with the Black position; the interview was thus a wholly friendly one with critics unrepresented. The questions were not submitted to Justice Black in advance, and when the interview was later published in pamphlet form and in a law review, it was noted that the transcript "was not submitted to Justice Black for correction."

SOURCE: *Justice Black and the First Amendment—"Absolutes": A Public Interview*, 37 New York University Law Review 569 (1962).

CAHN: Let me start by explaining the purpose of this interview. Two years ago, when you delivered your James Madison Lecture [1] at New York University, you declared your basic attitude toward our Bill of Rights. This was the positive side of your constitutional philosophy. Tonight I propose we bring out the other side, that is, your answers to the people who disagree with and criticize your principles. The questions I will ask, most of them at least, will be based on the criticisms. As you know, I consider your answers so convincing that I want the public to have them.

Suppose we start with one of the key sentences in your James Madison Lecture where you said, "It is my belief that there *are* 'absolutes' in our Bill of Rights, and that they were put there on purpose by men who knew what words meant and meant their prohibitions to be 'absolutes.'" Will you please explain your reasons for this?

JUSTICE BLACK: My first reason is that I believe the words do mean what they say. I have no reason to challenge the intelligence, integrity or honesty of the men who wrote the First Amendment. Among those I call the great men of the world are Thomas Jefferson, James Madison, and various others who participated in formulating the ideas behind the First Amendment for this country and in writing it.

I learned a long time ago that there are affirmative and negative words. The beginning of the First Amendment [2] is that "Congress shall make no law." I understand that it is rather old-fashioned and shows a slight naïveté to say that "no law" means no law. It is one of the most amazing things about the ingeniousness of the times that strong arguments are made, which *almost* convince me, that it is very foolish of me to think "no law" means no law. But what it *says* is "Congress shall make no law respecting an establishment of religion," and so on.

I have to be honest about it. I confess not only that I think the Amendment means what it says but also that I may be slightly influenced by the fact that I do not think Congress *should* make any law with respect to these subjects. That has become a rather bad confession to make in these days, the confession that one is actually for something because he believes in it.

Then we move on, and it says "or prohibiting the free exercise thereof." I have not always exercised myself in regard to religion as much as I should, or perhaps as much as all of you have. Nevertheless, I want to be able to do it when I want to do it. I do not want anybody who is my servant, who is my agent, elected by me and others like me, to tell me that I can or cannot do it. Of course, some will remark that that is too simple on my part. To them, all this discussion of mine is too simple, because I come back to saying that these few plain words actually mean what they say, and I know of no college professor or law school professor, outside of my friend, Professor Cahn here, and a few others, who could not write one hundred pages to show that the Amendment does not mean what it says.

Then I move on to the words "abridging the freedom of speech or of the press." It *says* Congress shall make no law doing that. What it *means*—according to a current philosophy that I do not share—is that Congress shall be able to make just such a law unless we judges object too strongly. One of the statements of that philosophy is that if it shocks us too much, then they cannot do it. But when I get down to the really basic reason why I believe that "no law" means no law,

I presume it could come to this, that I took an obligation to support and defend the Constitution as I understand it. And being a rather backward country fellow, I understand it to mean what the words say. Gesticulations apart, I know of no way in the world to communicate ideas except by words. And if I were to talk at great length on the subject, I would still be saying—although I understand that some people say that I just say it and do not believe it—that I believe when our Founding Fathers, with their wisdom and patriotism, wrote this Amendment, they knew what they were talking about. They knew what history was behind them and they wanted to ordain in this country that Congress, elected by the people, should not tell the people what religion they should have or what they should believe or say or publish, and that is about it. It says "no law," and that is what I believe it means.

CAHN: Some of your colleagues would say that it is better to interpret the Bill of Rights so as to permit Congress to take what it considers reasonable steps to preserve the security of the nation even at some sacrifice of freedom of speech and association. Otherwise what will happen to the nation and the Bill of Rights as well? What is your view of this?

JUSTICE BLACK: I fully agree with them that the country should protect itself. It should protect itself in peace and in war. It should do whatever is necessary to preserve itself. But the question is: Preserve what? And how?

It is not very much trouble for a dictator to know how it is best to preserve his government. He wants to stay in power, and the best way to stay in power is to have plenty of force behind him. He cannot stay in power without force. He is afraid of too much talk; it is dangerous for him. And he should be afraid, because dictators do not have a way of contributing very greatly to the happiness, joy, contentment, and prosperity of the plain, everyday citizen. Their business is to protect themselves. Therefore, they need an army; they need to be able to stop people from talking; they need to have one religion, and that is the religion they promulgate. Frequently in the past it has been the worship of the dictator himself. To preserve a dictatorship, you must be able to stifle thought, imprison the human mind and intellect.

I want this Government to protect itself. If there is any man in the United States who owes a great deal to this Government, I am that man. Seventy years ago, when I was a boy, perhaps no one who knew me thought I would ever get beyond the confines of the small country county in which I was born. There was no reason for them to suspect that I would. But we had a free country and the way was open for me. The Government and the people of the United States have been good to me. Of course, I want this country to do what will preserve it. I want it to be preserved as the kind of Government it was intended to be. I would not desire to live at any place where my thoughts were under the suspicion of government and where my words could be censored by government, and where worship, whatever it was or wasn't, had to be determined by an officer of the government. That is not the kind of government I want preserved.

I agree with those who wrote our Constitution, that too much power in the hands of officials is a dangerous thing. What was government created for except to serve the people? Why was a Constitution written for the first time in this country except to limit the power of government and those who were selected to exercise it at the moment?

My answer to the statement that this Government should preserve itself is yes. The method I would adopt is different, however, from that of some other people. I think it can be preserved only by leaving people with the utmost freedom to think and to hope and to talk and to dream if they want to dream. I do not think this Government must look to force, stifling the minds and aspirations of the people. Yes, I believe in self-preservation, but I would preserve it as the Founders said, by leaving people free. I think here, as in another time, it cannot live half slave and half free.

CAHN: . . . In order to preserve the guaranteed freedom of the press, are you willing to allow sensational newspaper reports about a crime and about police investigation of the crime to go so far that they prejudice and inflame a whole state and thus deprive the accused of his right to a fair jury?

JUSTICE BLACK: The question assumes in the first place that a whole state can be inflamed so that a fair trial is not possible. On most of these assumptions that are made with reference to the dangers of the spread of information, I perhaps diverge at a point from many of those who disagree with my views. I have again a kind of old-fashioned trust in human beings. I learned it as a boy and have never wholly lost that faith.

I believe in trial by jury. Here again perhaps I am a literalist. I do not think that trial by jury is a perfect way of determining facts, of adjudicating guilt, or of adjudicating controversies. But I do not know of a better way. That is where I stand on that.

I do not think myself that anyone can say that there can be enough publicity completely to destroy the ideas of fairness in the minds of people, including the judges. One of the great things about trials by jury in criminal cases that have developed in this country—I refer to criminal cases because there is where most of the persecutions are found in connection with bringing charges against unpopular people or people in unpopular causes—we should not forget that if the jury happens to go wrong, the judge has a solemn duty in a criminal case not to let an unfair verdict stand. Also, in this country, an appellate court can hear the case.

I realize that we do not have cases now like the ones they had when William Penn was tried for preaching on the streets of London. The jury which was called in to send him off quickly to jail refused to do so, and suffered punishment from the judge because they would not convict a man for preaching on the streets. But that is a part of history, and it is but one of thousands of cases of the kind. Those people had publicity; that is why they would not convict William Penn. They knew, because the people had been talking, despite the fact that there was so much censorship then, that William Penn was being prosecuted largely because he was a dissenter from the orthodox views. So they stood up like men and would not convict. They lost their property, some of them their liberty. But they stood up like men.

I do not myself think that it is necessary to stifle the press in order to reach fair verdicts. Of course, we do not want juries to be influenced wrongfully. But with our system of education we should be in better condition than they were in those days in England, when they found that the jury was one of the greatest steps on their way to freedom. As a matter of fact, Madison placed trial by jury along with freedom of the press and freedom of conscience as the three most highly cherished liberties of the American people in his time.

I do not withdraw my loyalty to the First Amendment or say that the press should be censored on the theory that in order to preserve fair trials it is necessary to try the people of the press in summary contempt proceedings and send them to jail for what they have published. I want both fair trials and freedom of the press. I grant that you cannot get everything you want perfectly, and you never will. But you won't do any good in this country, which aspires to freedom, by saying just give the courts a little more power, just a little more power to suppress the people and the press, and things will be all right. You just take a little chunk off here and a little bit there. I would not take it off anywhere. I believe that they meant what they said about freedom of the press just as they meant what they said about establishment of religion, and I would answer this question as I have answered the other one.

CAHN: Do you make an exception in freedom of speech and press for the law of defamation? That is, are you willing to allow people to sue for damages when they are subjected to libel or slander?

JUSTICE BLACK: My view of the First Amendment, as originally ratified, is that it said Congress should pass none of these kinds of laws. As written at that time, the Amendment applied only to Congress. I have no doubt myself that the provision, as written and adopted, intended that there should be no libel or defamation law in the United States under the United States Government, just absolutely none so far as I am concerned.

That is, no federal law. At that time—I will have to state this in order to let you know what I think about libel and defamation—people were afraid of the new Federal Government. I hope that they have not wholly lost that fear up to this time because, while government is a wonderful and an essential thing in order to have any kind of liberty, order or peace, it has such power that people must always remember to check them here and balance them there and limit them here in order to see that you do not lose too much liberty in exchange for government. So I have no doubt about what the Amendment intended. As a matter of fact, shortly after the Constitution was written, a man named St. George Tucker, a great friend of Madison's, who served as one of the commissioners at the Annapolis Convention of 1786 which first attempted to fill the need for a national constitution, put out a revised edition of Blackstone. In it he explained what our Constitution meant with reference to freedom of speech and press. He said there was no doubt in his mind, as one of the earliest participants in the development of the Constitution, that it was intended that there should be no libel under the laws of the United States. Lawyers might profit from consulting Tucker's edition of Blackstone on that subject.

As far as public libel is concerned, or seditious libel, I have been very much disturbed sometimes to see that there is present an idea that because we have had the practice of suing individuals for libel, seditious libel still remains for the use of government in this country. Seditious libel, as it has been put into practice throughout the centuries, is nothing in the world except the prosecution of people who are on the wrong side politically; they have said something and their group has lost and they are prosecuted. Those of you who read the newspaper see that this is happening all over the world now, every week somewhere. Somebody gets out, somebody else gets in, they call a military court or a special commission, and they try him. When he gets through sometimes he is not living.

My belief is that the First Amendment was made applicable to the states by the Fourteenth. I do not hesitate, so far as my own view is concerned, as to what should be and what I hope will sometime be the constitutional doctrine that just as it was not intended to authorize damage suits for mere words as distinguished from conduct as far as the Federal Government is concerned, the same rule should apply to the states.

I realize that sometimes you have a libel suit that accomplishes some good. I practiced law twenty years. I was a pretty active trial lawyer. The biggest judgment I ever got for a libel was $300. I never took a case for political libel because I found out that Alabama juries, at least, do not believe in political libel suits and they just do not give verdicts. I knew of one verdict given against a big newspaper down there for $25,000, and the Supreme Court of Alabama reversed it. So even that one did not pan out very well.

I believe with Jefferson that it is time enough for government to step in to regulate people when they *do* something, not when they *say* something, and I do not believe myself that there is *any* halfway ground if you enforce the protections of the First Amendment.

CAHN: Would it be constitutional to prosecute someone who falsely shouted "fire" in a theater?

JUSTICE BLACK: I went to a theater last night with you. I have an idea if you and I had gotten up and marched around that theater, whether we said anything or not, we would have been arrested. Nobody has ever said that the First Amendment gives people a right to go anywhere in the world they want to go or say anything in the world they want to say. Buying the theater tickets did not buy the opportunity to make a speech there. We have a system of property in this country which is also protected by the Constitution. We have a system of property, which means that a man does not have a right to do anything he wants anywhere he wants to do it. For instance, I would feel a little badly if somebody were to try to come into my house and tell me that he had a constitutional right to come in there because he wanted to make a speech against the Supreme Court. I realize the freedom of people to make a speech against the Supreme Court, but I do not want him to make it in my house.

That is a wonderful aphorism about shouting "fire" in a crowded theater. But you do not have to shout "fire" to get arrested. If a person creates a disorder in a theater, they would get him there not because of *what* he hollered but because he *hollered*. They would get him not because of any views he had but because they thought he did not have any views that they wanted to hear there. That is the way I would answer: not because of what he shouted but because he shouted.

CAHN: Is there any kind of obscene material, whether defined as hard-core pornography or otherwise, the distribution and sale of which can be constitutionally restricted in any manner whatever, in your opinion?

JUSTICE BLACK: I will say it can in this country, because the courts have held that it can.

CAHN: Yes, but you won't get off so easily. I want to know what you think.

JUSTICE BLACK: My view is, without deviation, without exception, without any ifs, buts, or whereases, that freedom of speech means that you shall not do something to people either for the views they have or the views they express or the words they speak or write.

There is strong argument for the position taken by a man whom I admire very greatly, Dr. Meiklejohn, that the First Amendment really was intended to protect *political* speech, and I do think that was the basic purpose; that plus the fact that they wanted to protect *religious* speech. Those were the two main things they had in mind.

It is the law that there can be an arrest made for obscenity. It was the law in Rome that they could arrest people for obscenity after Augustus became Caesar. Tacitus says that then it became obscene to criticize the Emperor. It is not any trouble to establish a classification so that whatever it is that you do not want said is within that classification. So far as I am concerned, I do not believe there is any halfway ground for protecting freedom of speech and press. If you say it is half free, you can rest assured that it will not remain as much as half free. Madison explained that in his great Remonstrance when he said in effect, "If you make laws to force people to speak the words of Christianity, it won't be long until the same power will narrow the sole religion to the most powerful sect in it." I realize that there are dangers in freedom of speech, but I do not believe there are any halfway marks.

CAHN: Do you subscribe to the idea involved in the clear and present danger rule?

JUSTICE BLACK: I do not.

CAHN: By way of conclusion, Justice Black, would you kindly summarize what you consider the judge's role in cases arising under the First Amendment and the Bill of Rights?

JUSTICE BLACK: The Bill of Rights to me constitutes the difference between this country and many others. I will not attempt to say most others or nearly all others or all others. But I will say it constitutes the difference to me between a free country and a country that is not free.

My idea of the whole thing is this: There has been a lot of trouble in the world between people and government. The people were afraid of government; they had a right to be afraid. All over the world men had been destroyed—and when I say "government" I mean the individuals who actually happened to be in control of it at the moment, whether they were elected, whether they were appointed, whether they got there with the sword, however they got there—the people always had a lot of trouble because power is a heady thing, a dangerous thing. There have been very few individuals in the history of the world who could be trusted with complete, unadulterated, omnipotent power over their fellowmen.

Millions of people have died throughout the world because of the evils of their governments. Those days had not wholly passed when the Pilgrims came over to this country. Many of them had suffered personally. Some of them had their ears cut off. Many of them had been mutilated. Many of their ancestors had. Some of your ancestors came here to get away from persecution. Certainly, mine did.

There had been struggles throughout the ages to curb the dangerous power of governors. Rome had a sound government at one time. Those who study it carefully will find that, except for the slave class, they had, so far as most of the people were concerned, a good form of government. But it turned, and then they had Augustus and the other Caesars, and the Neros and Caligulas and Tiberiuses.

One of the interesting things about Tiberius is that in all the history I have read he is about the only man of great prominence who ever defended informers. He made the statement that the informers were the guardians of Rome. Recently I have heard that said here once or twice.

When our ancestors came over here and started this country, they had some more persecutions of their own. It was not limited to any one religion. A lot of my Baptist brethren got into trouble; a lot of the Methodist brethren got into trouble; a lot of the Episcopal Church got in trouble, the Congregational Church—each of them in turn. A lot of the Catholics got in trouble. Whichever sect was in control in a state for a time, they would say that the others could not hold office, which is an easy way of getting rid of your adversaries if you can put it over. Even for half a century after the Constitution was adopted, some of the states barred the members of certain faiths from holding office.

Throughout all of this—as the Jewish people know as well as any people on earth—persecutions were abroad everywhere in the world. A man never knew, when he got home, whether his family would be there, and the family at home never knew whether the head of the family would get back. There was nothing strange about that when Hitler did it. It was simply a repetition of the course of history when people get too much power.

I like what the Jewish people did when they took what amounted to a written constitution. Some of the states did it before the time of the Federal Constitution; they adopted written constitutions. Why? Because they wanted to mark boundaries beyond which government could not go, stripping people of their liberty to think, to talk, to write, to work, to be happy.

So we have a written Constitution. What good is it? What good is it if, as some judges say, all it means is: "Government, you can still do this unless it is so bad that it shocks the conscience of the judges." It does not say that to me. We have certain provisions in the Constitution which say, "Thou shalt not." They do not say, "You can do this unless it offends the sense of decency of the English-speaking world." They do not say that. They do not say, "You can go ahead and do this unless it is offensive to the universal sense of decency." If they did, they would say virtually nothing. There would be no definite, binding place, no specific prohibition, if that were all it said.

I believe with Locke in the system of checks and balances. I do not think that the Constitution leaves any one department of government free without there being a check on it somewhere. Of course, things are different in England; they do have unchecked powers, and they also have a very impressive history. But it was *not* the kind of history that suited the people that formed our Constitution. Madison said that explicitly when he offered the Bill of Rights to the Congress. Jefferson repeated it time and time again. Why was it not? Because it left Parliament with power to pass such laws as it saw fit to pass. It was not the kind of government they wanted. So we have a Bill of Rights. It is intended to see that a man cannot be jerked by the back of the neck by any government official; he cannot have his home invaded; he cannot be picked up legally and carried away because his views are not satisfactory to the majority, even if they are terrible views, however bad they may be. Our system of justice is based on the assumption that men can best work out their own opinions, and that they are not under the control of government. Of course, this is particularly true in the field of religion, because a man's religion is between himself and his Creator, not between himself and his government.

I am not going to say any more except this: I was asked a question about preserving this country. I confess I am a complete chauvinist. I think it is the greatest country in the world. I think it is the greatest because it has a Bill of Rights. I think it could be the worst if it did not have one. It does not take a nation long to degenerate. We saw, only a short time ago, a neighboring country where people were walking the streets in reasonable peace one day and within a month we saw them marched to the back of a wall to meet a firing squad without a trial.

I am a chauvinist because this country offers the greatest opportunities of any country in the world to people of every kind, of every type, of every race, of every origin, of every religion—without regard to wealth, without regard to poverty. It offers an opportunity to the child born today to be reared among his people by his people, to worship his God, whatever his God may be, or to refuse to worship anybody's God if that is his wish. It is a free country; it will remain free only, however, if we recognize that the boundaries of freedom are not so flexible; they are not made of mush. They say, "Thou shalt not," and I think that is what they mean.

Now, I have read that every sophisticated person knows that you cannot have any absolute "thou shalt nots." But you know when I drive my car against a red light, I do not expect them to turn me loose if I can prove that though I was going across that red light, it was not offensive to the so-called "universal sense of decency." I have an idea there are some absolutes. I do not think I am far in that respect from the Holy Scriptures.

The Jewish people have had a glorious history. It is wonderful to think about the contributions that were made to the world from a small, remote area in the East. I have to admit that most of my ideas stem basically from there.

It is largely because of these same contributions that I am here tonight as a member of what I consider the greatest Court in the world. It is great because it is independent. If it were not independent, it would not be great. If all nine of those men came out each Monday morning like a phonograph speaking one voice, you could rest assured it would not be independent. But it does not come that way. I want to assure you that the fact that it does not come that way does not mean that there is not a good, sound, wholesome respect on the part of every justice for every other justice.

I do hope that this occasion may cause you to think a little more and study a little more about the Constitution, which is the source of your liberty; no, not the source—I will take that back—but a protection of your liberty. Yesterday a man sent me a copy of a recent speech entitled "Is the First Amendment Obsolete?" The conclusion of the writer, who is a distinguished law school dean, was that the Amendment no longer fits the times and that it needs to be modified to get away from its rigidity. The author contends that the thing to do is to take the term "due process of law" and measure everything by that standard, "due process of law" meaning that unless a law is so bad that it shocks the conscience of the Court, it cannot be unconstitutional. I do not wish to have to pass on the laws of this country according to the degree of shock I receive! Some people get shocked more readily than others at certain things. I get shocked pretty quickly, I confess, when I see—and this I say with trepidation because it is considered bad to admit it—but I do get shocked now and then when I see some gross injustice has been done, although I am solemnly informed that we do not sit to administer justice, we sit to administer law in the abstract.

I am for the First Amendment from the first word to the last. I believe it means what it says, and it says to me, "Government shall keep its hands off religion. Government shall not attempt to control the ideas a man has. Government shall not attempt to establish a religion of any kind. Government shall not abridge freedom of the press or speech. It shall let anybody talk in this country." I have never been shaken in the faith that the American people are the kind of people and have the kind of loyalty to their government that we need not fear the talk of Communists or of anybody else. Let them talk! In the American way, we will answer them.

FOOTNOTES

[1] The lecture, entitled "The Bill of Rights," was delivered at the New York University School of Law on February 17, 1960. It is published in 35 N.Y.U.L. Rev. 865 (1960).

[2] The First Amendment reads as follows: "Congress shall make no law respecting an establishment of religion, or prohibiting the free exercise thereof; or abridging the freedom of speech, or of the press; or the right of the people peaceably to assemble, and to petition the Government for a redress of grievances."

WILLIAM J. BRENNAN, JR.

The Bill of Rights and the States

The issues of federalism—what powers belong to the States
and what to the Nation—have been matters of fighting words
and even of Civil War since the founding of the Republic. There
are still important cases presenting economic issues of federalism—such as who owns tideland rights, or whether the States
can tax corporations from out of state who do solicitation
business in the taxing jurisdiction, or how much control over
labor relations remains in the States after passage of the National
Labor Relations Act and the Taft-Hartley and Landrum-Griffin
Amendments. One of the main battlegrounds today for federalism questions is in the area of the Bill of Rights. Not only segregation practices of the States and cities from Dade County,
Florida, to New Rochelle, New York, are involved, but also
the full range of issues involving fair procedure, religious freedom, separation of church and state, freedom of speech and
press, and the other foundation blocks of the Constitution which
make up the first eight Amendments. Ever since the Fourteenth
Amendment in 1868 shifted the constitutional boundary between State and Nation, particularly in terms of what the Supreme Court *could* place under national protection, the relation
of the Bill of Rights to the States has been a shifting but constant
battleground within the Court. The speech on this topic which
Justice Brennan delivered here was given as the second James
Madison Lecture at the New York University Law School.

Source: 36 *New York University Law Review* 761 (1961).

I am deeply conscious of the honor of standing at this podium to deliver one of the lectures which, in James Madison's name, review the safeguards of liberty which he did so much to weave into our constitutional fabric. We owe a great debt to every Framer without exception. But we justly reserve for Madison alone the title of Father of the Constitution. It was he who drafted the Virginia plan which became the framework for the Constitution of the United States. It was he whose inspired leadership gave us the Bill of Rights.

These remarks will discuss the application of the Bill of Rights to the states. The seeds of that controversial subject were sown before the nation was formed. When the Declaration of Independence severed the tie that bound the colonies to the Throne of England, each colony fell back upon its own inherent sovereignty, and the people of each, with the exceptions at first of Connecticut and Rhode Island, formed for themselves a constitution, local, separate, and apart. Each state, formerly a colony, took fierce pride in its separate sovereignty. The states formed a Confederation, but so jealous was each of its sovereign prerogatives that too few powers essential to union were surrendered, and the enterprise foundered.

The constitutions of the original states anticipated the national Constitution in declaring the doctrine that there are human liberties which are inalienable. This doctrine has ever since been the center and core of the American idea of limited government. The government of each state was the creation of the people of the state; the source of power was the people of that state. The only end and aim of government was to secure the people in their natural and civil rights. However, union under the Articles of Confederation, and later under the Constitution, was not effected by the people as a mass, but by the several peoples of the several states. In other words, the nation was created by the states and the people of the states, and not by the people separate from the states. The states remained possessed of every power of sovereignty which the several peoples of the several states had not delegated to the United States. This feature was basic to both the Articles of Confederation and to the Constitution. A purpose of the Constitution was to improve upon the Articles of Confederation, and "to form a more perfect union" of states. The Framers' aim was to grant the national government only such powers of sovereignty as were necessary to attain ends better secured by a national government than by the states individually or in confederation. Powers of sovereignty as they affected only a state and the people of the state were reserved to the state. "The powers reserved to the several States," said Madison, "will extend to all the objects which, in the ordinary course of affairs, concern the lives, liberties and properties of the people, and the internal order, improvement and prosperity of the State." [1]

In contrast, the national government might exercise only the powers enumerated in the Constitution, together with the power to make all laws necessary and proper for carrying into execution the enumerated powers. Even these limitations were not enough for the peoples of some of the states. So widespread was the fear that the national government might encroach upon the sovereignty of the states, and the sovereign rights of the peoples of the several states that a number of states were reluctant to ratify the new Constitution without an express limitation on the authority of the national government to exercise certain powers. This was the genesis of the Bill of Rights.

It is natural then that the first ten amendments should have been conceived only as a bulwark to the states, and the peoples of the states, against encroachments of the national government upon the sovereignty which the people of each state reserved to themselves and to their state government. Protection against encroachment on individual rights by a state government was a matter for the state constitution. This division of sovereign powers between the states and the nation gave us, said John Quincy Adams, "the most complicated government on the face of the globe." [2] The proper preservation of that division constituted from the beginning, and constitutes still, an important value in every consideration of the application of the Federal Bill of Rights to the states. It is from this division that the concepts derive which we call "states' rights" or "the demands of our federalism." For "it may be not unreasonably said that the preservation of the States, and the maintenance of their governments, are as much within the design and care of the Constitution as the preservation of the Union and the maintenance of the National government." [3]

Yet there was support for the inclusion in the Constitution of restraints against encroachment by state governments upon rights of the peoples of the several states. Indeed, the Framers did include some restraints of this nature in the body of the Constitution itself. The prohibitions in article I, section 10, which forbid every state to pass any bill of attainder or ex post facto law or law impairing the obligation of contracts, are examples. Madison himself wanted more such restraints in the Constitution. He was by no means happy with the bills of rights which at that time were in the state constitutions. Said he: "[S]ome States have no bills of rights [four states had none], there are others provided with very defective ones, and there are others whose bills of rights are not only defective, but absolutely improper; instead of securing some in the full extent which republican principles would require, they limit them too much to agree with the common ideas of liberty." [4]

Madison proposed not ten, but, in the form the House sent them to the Senate, seventeen amendments. The House and Senate finally agreed on twelve to be submitted to the states. Only the last ten of the twelve were ratified to become the first ten amendments. Among the proposals which the Senate rejected was Number XIV of the seventeen submitted by the House. Number XIV—a number prophetic of things to come seventy-nine years later—read: "No State shall infringe the right of trial by Jury in criminal cases, nor the rights of conscience, nor the freedom of speech, or of the press." [5] Madison thought that these restrictions on state power were "of equal, if not greater importance than those already made" [6] in article I, section 10. There was, he said, "more danger of those powers being abused by the State Governments than by the Government of the United States." [7] Indeed, he "conceived this to be the most valuable amendment in the whole list. If there were any reason to restrain the Government of the United States from infringing upon these essential rights, it was equally necessary that they should be secured against the State Governments." [8] It is only conjecture that Number XIV was defeated in the Senate by the votes of states whose systems of established churches would have been outlawed under this proposal. Some states (Massachusetts until 1833) maintained established churches long after the First Amendment became effective.

Plainly enough, however, Madison had no thought that any of the first eight amendments which were adopted extended to the states. Yet as early as 1825, a textbook, the work of William Rawle, a Philadelphia lawyer who had served as United States Attorney, argued that except for the First and Seventh Amendments, the guarantees of the Bill of Rights

form parts of the declared rights of the people, of which neither the state powers nor those of the Union can ever deprive them. . . . A declaration of rights . . . equalizes all and binds all. It becomes part of the general compact. Each state is obliged while it remains a member of the Union, to preserve the republican form of government in all its purity and all its strength. The people of each state, by the amended constitution, pledge themselves to each other for the sacred preservation of certain detailed principles, without which the republican form of government would be impure and weak.[9]

Rawle's mistake was in conceiving that "We the people" in the Preamble meant that the Constitution was the creation of the American people compounded into one common mass; the Constitution was in fact the creation of states and of people within each of the states.

Eight years later, in 1833, the Supreme Court made this clear in *Barron* v. *Baltimore*,[10] the first case to present the question of the application of a provision of the Bill of Rights to a state. The City of Baltimore made street improvements which destroyed the commercial use of a wharf. The owner of the wharf sought damages from the city. The Maryland Court of Appeals held that he was not entitled to any. The wharf owner contended in the United States Supreme Court that the Maryland judgment violated the provision of the Fifth Amendment, "nor shall private property be taken for public use, without just compensation." That provision, the owner argued, "being in favor of the liberty of the citizen, ought to be so construed as to restrain the legislative power of a state, as well as that of the United States." [11] Marshall thought the argument was "not of much difficulty." The Bill of Rights, he said, did not operate against state, but only federal power. The Federal Constitution, Marshall went on,

was ordained and established by the people of the United States for themselves, for their own government, and not for the government of the individual states. Each state established a constitution for itself, and, in that constitution, provided such limitations and restrictions on the powers of its particular government, as its judg-

ment dictated. The people of the United States framed such a government for the United States as they supposed best adapted to
their situation and best calculated to promote their interests. The
powers they conferred on this government were to be exercised by
itself; and the limitations on power, if expressed in general terms,
are naturally, and, we think, necessarily, applicable to the government created by the instrument. They are limitations of power
granted in the instrument itself; not of distinct governments, framed
by different persons and for different purposes.[12]

The Court reaffirmed this proposition in a number of cases decided
over the next twenty-five years.[13]

Each of the states in time adopted a bill of rights. Many of these
followed the federal pattern. From all that appears, until the Civil
War, they bore out Madison's prophesy that "if once bills of rights
are established in all the States as well as the Federal Constitution, we
shall find that, although some of them are rather unimportant, yet,
upon the whole, they will have a salutary tendency." [14]

It was after the Civil War that the demand arose for national protection against alleged abuses of state power. It was charged that the
former Confederate states denied freedmen the protections for life,
liberty, and property accorded the white man under state constitutions and laws. The constitutionality of remedial legislation passed by
Congress was thought to be doubtful. This doubt led to the proposal
for a constitutional amendment to remove any question of congressional power. This amendment became the Fourteenth Amendment.

Deep passions and extreme partisanship marked the controversy
in and out of Congress over the adoption of the Fourteenth Amendment. It was the "Age of Hate in American politics." [15] The opponents'
most powerful argument, repeated and repeated in the debates in
Congress and up and down the land, was that the grant of powers
under the amendment would mean that the sovereign powers reserved
to the states, the keystone of the structure erected by the Framers,
would be transferred to the national government. Senator Browning
of Illinois said:

If the proposed amendments of the Constitution be adopted, new
and enormous power will be claimed and exercised by Congress, as
warranted by such amendments, and the whole structure of our

Government will perhaps gradually but yet surely be revolutionized. And so with the Judiciary. If the proposed amendments be adopted, they may and certainly will be used substantially to annihilate the State judiciaries. . . . Be assured, if this new provision be engrafted in the Constitution, it will, in time, change the entire texture and structure of our Government, and sweep away all the guarantees of safety devised and provided by our patriotic sires of the revolution. . . .[16]

This argument was not without force when directed to the first section of the amendment as originally proposed. That proposal read: "Congress shall have power to make all laws which shall be necessary and proper to secure to citizens of each State all privileges and immunities of citizens in the several States . . . and to all persons in the several States equal protection in the rights of life, liberty and property. . . ." [17] This certainly sounded like an affirmative grant of power to the Congress to supersede state laws. This version, however, never got beyond committee. There was quickly substituted the language now in the first section of the amendment, "No state shall make or enforce any law which shall abridge the privileges or immunities of citizens of the United States; nor shall any state deprive any person of life, liberty or property without due process of law; nor deny to any person within its jurisdiction the equal protection of the laws." That language, like the language of Article I, Section 10 of the Constitution, is language of limitation. On its face it appears simply to impose limits upon, and not to authorize Congress to displace, the states in the exercise of their traditional authority to legislate directly upon all their citizens in regard to life, liberty, and property. But Section 5 of the amendment does grant the Congress affirmative authority to enforce these prohibitions by appropriate legislation. The substituted provision in no wise stilled the cries that the amendment would effect a disruption of the historic distribution of sovereign powers and bring an end to the noble plan of the Framers. The opponents could not prevent the adoption of the amendment. But it cannot be said that they were completely vanquished. For events were to prove that the Supreme Court would interpret the amendment in a way which would go far to relieve their worry that its restraints effected the loss of separate and independent autonomy to the states.

The first case that came to the Court did not present the question of the application of a specific guarantee of the Federal Bill of Rights to the states. It is an interesting conjecture whether state power would have been vindicated had such been the case. The first decision, known as the *Slaughter-House Cases*,[18] came down in 1872. There was involved the constitutionality of a Louisiana statute which put certain New Orleans butchers out of business by conferring on a single corporation a monopoly of the business of slaughtering cattle. The affected butchers claimed that they were denied one of the "privileges or immunities of citizens of the United States" protected from abridgment by the states under the Amendment.

There is much evidence that those who coined the phrase the "privileges or immunities of citizens of the United States" were not certain what privileges and immunities were covered by these words. The Court held by a five-to-four vote that whatever privileges or immunities were included, the privilege of following the butcher calling in the State of Louisiana was not one of them. The privilege of following that calling was a privilege not of United States citizenship, but of state citizenship, and the prohibition of the calling by Louisiana was therefore inoffensive to the prohibition of the Fourteenth Amendment.

Nothing in the words themselves compelled that conclusion. Many still believe that the dissenting opinion in the *Slaughter-House Cases* expressed the sounder view. The Court was later to acknowledge that "Criticism of . . . [the *Slaughter-House Cases*] has never entirely ceased, nor has it ever received universal assent by members of this court. Undoubtedly, it gave much less effect to the Fourteenth Amendment than some of the public men active in framing it intended, and disappointed many others." [19] But the prevailing opinion frankly disclosed the basic concern of the Justices who subscribed to it. To embrace, among "the privileges or immunities of citizens of the United States," the privilege of a Louisiana citizen to follow the butcher's trade, would be, the Court declared,

> to transfer the security and protection of all the civil rights . . . to the Federal government[,] . . . to bring within the power of Congress the entire domain of civil rights heretofore belonging exclusively to the States [.] . . .

[The effect of] so great a departure from the structure and spirit of our institutions . . . is to fetter and degrade the State governments by subjecting them to the control of Congress, in the exercise of powers heretofore universally conceded to them of the most ordinary and fundamental character. . . .

We are convinced that no such results were intended by the Congress . . . nor by the legislatures . . . which ratified . . . [this amendment].[20]

But what of the privileges and immunities declared in the Federal Bill of Rights? Might not they be considered the logical referent of "privileges or immunities of citizens of the United States," since they are expressly declared in the United States Constitution itself? The Supreme Court was soon to reject that interpretation.

In case after case, beginning in 1875—each case presenting the question as to a different guarantee [21]—the Court held that the guarantees in the Federal Bill of Rights were not among "the privileges or immunities of citizens of the United States." The process was completed in a series of cases decided from 1887 to 1908 in which the Court time after time rejected efforts to persuade it that the federal list of rights in its entirety came within the protected privileges or immunities.[22]

I should complete here the story of the so-called "incorporation theory"—that is, the theory that the Fourteenth Amendment was intended to make all of the Federal Bill of Rights applicable to the states. This view had the strong support of the first Justice Harlan, of Mr. Justice Brewer, and of Mr. Justice Field as early as 1892.[23] It was espoused in 1947 by Mr. Justice Black in his famous dissent in *Adamson* v. *California*.[24] Mr. Justice Black believes that in the earlier cases the Court fell into error in failing sufficiently to consult the history of the Fourteenth Amendment. He reads that history as demonstrating that the Framers of the Fourteenth Amendment intended to enfold the Federal Bill of Rights within its commands.

My study of the historical events that culminated in the Fourteenth Amendment, and the expressions of those who sponsored and favored, as well as those who opposed its submission and passage, persuades me that one of the chief objects that the provisions of the Amendment's first section, separately, and as a whole, were intended to accomplish was to make the Bill of Rights, applicable to the states. With full knowledge of the import of the *Barron* decision, the framers and backers of the Fourteenth Amendment proclaimed its purpose to be to overturn the constitutional rule that case had announced.[25]

Three other Justices shared this view with Mr. Justice Black in 1947,[26] but it has yet to command the support of a majority of the Court.

However, the rejection of the incorporation theory, and the disregard of the privileges and immunities clause, have not closed every door in the Fourteenth Amendment against the application of the Federal Bill of Rights to the states. The Court has opened a door through the Fourteenth Amendment's due process clause. During the last half century the Court has opened that door to admit some of the federal list. Moreover, the Court has indicated that the door may be opened to still more. True, it is often insisted that the application to the states of a safeguard embodied in the first eight amendments is not made "because those rights are enumerated in the first eight Amendments, but because they are of such a nature that they are included in the conception of due process of law." [27] In other words, the insistence is that the due process clause is infused with "an independent potency" not resting upon the Bill of Rights.[28] With all respect, I think that Mr. Justice Cardozo's analysis is more accurate. In 1937, he described what the Court has done as a process by which the guarantees "have been taken over from the earlier articles of the federal bill of rights and brought within the Fourteenth Amendment by a *process of absorption.* . . . [T]he *process of absorption* has had its source in the belief that neither liberty nor justice would exist if . . . [those guarantees] were sacrificed." [29] The criteria by which judgments have been made in the past as to which specifics should be absorbed, and which not, are neither precise nor definitive. The Court early said: "Few phrases of the law are so elusive of exact apprehension as . . . [due process of law]. . . . This court has always declined to give a comprehensive definition of it, and has preferred that its full meaning should be gradually ascertained by the process of inclusion and exclusion in the course of the decisions of cases as they arise." [30]

The considerations of federalism of course loom large. A decision rejecting absorption of a particular guarantee will usually be made to rest on the inconsistency of its absorption with "the full power of the State to order its own affairs and govern its own people." [31] Where this consideration has been overborne, and the absorption of some specific has been decreed, the Court has said of that specific that it is "of the very essence of a scheme of ordered liberty," [32] or that it is included among "those fundamental principles of liberty and justice which lie at the base of all our civil and political institutions," [33] or that it is among those personal immunities "so rooted in the traditions and conscience of our people as to be ranked as fundamental." [34]

How many of the specifics of the Bill of Rights have been held to be absorbed by the Fourteenth Amendment? We start with the First Amendment.

By one or more of the tests all of the protections of the First Amendment have been held to extend to the exercise of state power. This development has taken place in a series of decisions handed down over the last thirty-five years. As recently as 1922, in *Prudential Insurance Co.* v. *Cheek*,[35] the Court had held that the Fourteenth Amendment did not make the protections of the First Amendment binding on the states. Since 1925, however, decisions have extended against state power the amendment's protections for religion, speech, press, assembly, and petition.[36] Of freedom of thought and speech, said Mr. Justice Cardozo, "one may say that it is the matrix, the indispensable condition, of nearly every other form of freedom." [37] Occasionally a member of the Court has suggested that the freedom of speech and of the press may be secured by the Fourteenth Amendment less broadly than it is secured by the First,[38] but this view has never persuaded even a substantial minority of the Court.

The first Amendment's protections for the cherished rights of mind and spirit thus stand guard against both state and federal governments. Voices are heard, however, which insist that these protections have not been as vigorously enforced against either federal or state power as they should be that the judiciary, as to First Amendment rights particularly, have not justified Madison's faith that "independent tribunals of justice will consider themselves in a peculiar manner the guardians of those rights." [39] Last year my colleague, Mr. Justice Black, opened these lectures with his distinguished paper on the subject whether the guarantees of the Bill of Rights, or at least most of them, are "absolutes" which strictly limit the exercise of congressional power, or are to be regarded merely as caution signals—"admonitions" —which Congress need not always observe.[40] Madison's unsuccessful effort to add a counterpart of the First Amendment to the Constitution, his Proposal XIV prohibiting the states from infringing the rights of conscience, and freedom of speech and press, strikingly evidences his concern for their fullest protection. For him, the suppression of individuality was the deadly enemy of the spirit, making a mockery of the dignity of man. Hence his warning that, because a representative government like ours expresses the majority will, "The prescriptions in favor of liberty ought to be levelled against that quarter where the greatest danger lies, namely, that which possesses the highest prerogative of power. But this is not found in either the Executive or Legislative departments of Government, but in the body of the people, operating by the majority against the minority." [41]

Besides the First Amendment guarantees, only three specifics of the federal list, as such, have so far been held to be absorbed by the due process clause. Due process applies to the states the Fifth Amendment's requirement that "just compensation" shall be paid for private property taken for public use.[42] Thus the Fourteenth Amendment imposes the requirement which Marshall held in *Barron* v. *Baltimore* that the Federal Constitution did not originally impose upon the states. Due process requires the states to appoint counsel for an accused charged with an offense punishable by death, in accordance with the Sixth Amendment's requirement that an accused shall have "the assistance of counsel for his defense." [43] Finally, due process applies to the states the Fourth Amendment's guarantees against unreasonable searches and seizures. After holding in 1914 that the Fourth Amendment was not directed against state officials,[44] the Court in 1949 held that "The security of one's privacy against arbitrary intrusion by the police . . . is . . . implicit in 'the concept of ordered liberty' and as such enforceable against the States through the Due Process Clause." [45]

But considerations of federalism have thus far overborne the arguments in favor of the extension, as such, of the rest of the list. It may surprise many of you that some of these should not be regarded as among "the fundamental principles of liberty and justice which lie at the base of all our civil and political institutions." [46] For example, the right to trial by jury, highly valued by most of us, has been said not to be fundamental. The Court has held that the Seventh Amendment's requirement of a common law jury in civil causes does not apply to the states.[47] Many states try civil causes before juries of less than twelve and have abolished the common law requirement of a unanimous verdict. Perhaps Madison would have agreed that a proper deference to states' rights justified this holding as to the Seventh Amendment. One doubts, however, that he would be as readily reconciled to the Court's dicta that the Sixth Amendment's guarantee to one accused of crime of the right to trial by a jury of his peers is not binding on the states. These dicta say not only that the Fourteenth Amendment does not absorb this guarantee, but indeed that the Constitution does not prevent a state from abolishing trial by jury in criminal causes altogether.[48] You will recall that Madison's rejected Proposal XIV embodied protections against state power not only for conscience, speech, and press, but also provided that "No State shall infringe the right of trial by Jury in criminal cases." The right of the accused to trial by jury was, said Madison, "as essential to secure the liberty of the people as any one of the pre-existent rights of nature." [49] The Court's extension to the states of the First Amendment's protections accords with Madison's judgment that indeed neither liberty nor justice would exist if these guarantees were sacrificed. It remains to be seen whether his judgment will also be confirmed if the Court is ever faced with a case in which a state has abolished trial by jury for serious criminal offenses.

The Court has held that the Sixth Amendment's guarantee of the right of an accused to have the assistance of court-appointed counsel for his defense is not, in non-capital cases, a fundamental principle absorbed by the Fourteenth Amendment.[50] It is only " 'where the gravity of the crime and other factors—such as the age and education of the defendant, the conduct of the court or the prosecuting officials, and the complicated nature of the offense charged and the possible defenses thereto—render criminal proceedings without counsel so apt to result in injustice as to be fundamentally unfair'. . . ." that the state has been held to have denied due process to a defendant tried for a noncapital offense.[51]

Only three weeks ago, I recorded my disagreement with this limitation of the extension of this specific of the Sixth Amendment to the states.[52] Rawle may have been in error in believing in 1825 that the Constitution without the Fourteenth Amendment imposed upon the states a duty to provide counsel in all state prosecutions. But none can deny Rawle's picture of the perilous position of the accused who must defend himself without a lawyer against the might of the state. "The most innocent man," Rawle said, "pressed by the awful solemnities of a public accusation and trial, may be incapable of supporting his own cause. He may be utterly unfit to cross-examine the witnesses against him, to point out the contradictions or defects of their testimony, and to counteract it by properly introducing and applying his own." [53] Without the help of a lawyer, all the other safeguards of a fair trial may be empty.

And it is not the due process clause that is alone involved here. The equal protection clause of the Fourteenth Amendment is also implicated. For a state cannot, consistently with the Federal Constitution, deny a citizen accused of crime the right to the assistance of counsel if he can afford to pay his own lawyer. The victims of the limitation upon the state's obligation to provide counsel are the indigent—they are the helpless, the weak, the outnumbered in our society.

> The result of our decisions is to refuse a State the power to force a person into a criminal trial without a lawyer if he wants one and can afford to hire one, but to deny the same protection to an accused who is too poor to retain counsel. This draws a line between rich and poor that is repugnant to due process. The need of counsel is the same, whatever the economic status of the accused. If due process requires that a rich man who wants a lawyer be allowed the opportunity to obtain one before he is tried, why should not due process give the same protection to the accused who is indigent? [54]

A state may violate the equal protection clause if it fails at its expense to provide a convicted indigent defendant with a transcript of the trial proceedings for purposes of appeal.[55] The denial of counsel to an indigent accused seems almost to be an a fortiori case of the violation of the guarantee of equal protection of the laws.

The test of "fundamental unfairness" as a criterion applied to state prosecutions is not unique to cases involving the denial of counsel. For example, the values underlying the Fifth Amendment's privilege against self-incrimination are sufficiently absorbed by the due process clause to invalidate a state conviction obtained with the aid of a confession, however true, which was secured from the accused by duress or coercion. The Court has said, "The abhorrence of society to the use of involuntary confessions does not turn alone on their inherent untrustworthiness. It also turns on the deep-rooted feeling that the police must obey the law while enforcing the law; that in the end life and liberty can be as much endangered from illegal methods used to convict those thought to be criminals as from the actual criminals themselves." [56]

One may well ask why some of the safeguards for the just administration of criminal laws should be absorbed not at all, or only partially, in due process, when the protections of the First Amendment are absorbed in full. The Court has certainly recognized the paramount importance of procedural safeguards in criminal prosecutions. The Court has forged standards for federal prosecutions which go even beyond the demands of the Federal Bill of Rights as presently construed.[57] True, these standards have been fashioned under the Court's inherent powers to supervise the administration of justice in the lower federal courts, while intervention in the administration of the criminal laws of the states implicates considerations of federalism. But federalism should not be raised to the plane of an absolute, nor the Bill of Rights be reduced to a precatory trust, and the Court within the last half-century has dealt increasingly with state administration of criminal justice in constitutional terms.[58]

The history of the Court's treatment of the application of the Fourth Amendment to the states is a good example. I have mentioned that in 1914 the Court held that the "Fourth Amendment is not directed to individual misconduct of . . . [state] officials. Its limitations reach the Federal Government and its agencies." [59] But, in 1949, the Court held that the due process clause had absorbed the Fourth Amendment's protections.[60] The 1914 decision had also held that evidence illegally seized by state officers might be received in a federal prosecution. Last Term, the Court reconsidered this holding, now that the Fourth Amendment's protections are held to apply to the states, and held that evidence seized in violation of that amendment, whether by federal or state officers, is not to be received in a federal prosecution.[61]

However, the 1949 decision left the states free to use in state courts evidence illegally obtained by state officers, if permitted under the state's rules of evidence. In other words, the exclusionary rule has not thus far been held to be a constitutional requirement woven into the Fourth Amendment's guarantees. Last Term's decision excluding the evidence in a federal prosecution was expressly grounded in the Court's inherent authority to supervise the administration of justice in federal courts and not on the Constitution.

Should the exclusionary rule be treated as a mere rule of evidence or does it take on constitutional mien in the context of the Fourth Amendment? There are members of the Court who insist that the rule must be treated as a constitutional requisite or the 1949 extension of the Fourth Amendment's protections to state power has been a meaningless exercise.[62] They point out that state officers have little incentive to obey the Fourth Amendment's commands if evidence seized in defiance of them may be used against the victims in state courts. Those who find it surprising that a state should be allowed to send a man to prison or to his death on evidence which state officials have obtained in disregard of the Constitution of the United States believe that inevitably the Court must reconsider its 1949 holding.*

Fifty-four of the ninety-two Justices who have sat on the Court have participated in decisions which have considered the application to the states of one or more of the federal list. For all of these Justices, decision has involved choice among competing values. Some have claimed for due process that its special character, to use words Cardozo employed in another context, is "its power of adaptation, its suppleness, its play." [63] Federalism makes its own contribution to the preservation of our freedoms. The specifics of the Bill of Rights so far absorbed in due process have enhanced, not diminished, that contribution. The absorption of more can only further increase respect for our federalism. As Mr. Justice Schaefer of Illinois said in his Holmes Lecture at Harvard two years ago:

> Considerations of federalism of course remain important. But in the world today they must be measured against the competing de-

* [In *Mapp* v. *Ohio*, 367 U.S. 643 (1961), the Supreme Court, by a 5–4 majority, overruled the 1949 *Wolf* ruling and held evidence obtained by state police through unconstitutional methods to be inadmissible in state trials. Justice Tom Clark wrote the majority opinion joined by Chief Justice Warren and Justices Black, Douglas and Brennan. In dissent were Justices Frankfurter, Harlan, Stewart and Whittaker. Note by the Editor.]

mands arising out of the relation of the United States to the rest of the world. The quality of a nation's civilization can be largely measured by the methods it uses in the enforcement of its criminal law. That measurement is not taken merely in retrospect by social historians of the future. It is taken from day to day by the peoples of the world, and to them the criminal procedure sanctioned by any of our states is the procedure sanctioned by the United States.[64]

The Court has other compelling reasons for the application to the states of more of the specifics of the Bill of Rights. The absence in our country of the turbulence witnessed in other lands cannot obscure the fact that crises at hand and in prospect are creating, and will create, more and more collisions between the citizen and his government. The need for vigilance to prevent government from whittling away the rights of the individual was never greater. Today, as rarely before, case after case comes to the Court which finds the individual battling to vindicate a claim under the Bill of Rights against the powers of government, federal and state.

The Bill of Rights is the primary source of expressed information as to what is meant by constitutional liberty. The safeguards enshrined in it are deeply etched in the foundations of America's freedoms. Among the important specifics of the Bill of Rights still not fully applied to the states are those which are pertinent to the standards which should govern the administration of criminal justice. Each is a protection with centuries of history behind it, often dearly bought with the blood and lives of people determined to prevent oppression by their rulers. Would Madison have thought that the right of a person not to be twice put in jeopardy of life or limb for the same offense; not to be compelled in any criminal case to be a witness against one's self; as an accused, to enjoy the right in criminal prosecutions to a speedy and public trial by an impartial jury of twelve, to be informed of the nature and cause of the accusation, to be confronted with the witnesses against him, to have compulsory process for obtaining witnesses in his favor, and to have the assistance of counsel for his defense, were rights unnecessary to "the very essence of a scheme of ordered liberty," or that any was not among "the fundamental principles of liberty and justice which lie at the base of all our civil and political institutions," or not among those personal immunities which are "so rooted in the traditions and conscience of our people as to be ranked as fundamental"? In any event, what due process under the Fourteenth Amendment meant to the wisdom of other days cannot be its measure to the vision of our time. The importance of keeping aglow the fires of freedom was never greater. Excessive emphasis upon states' rights must not make the process of absorption "a license to the judiciary to administer a watered-down, subjective version of the individual guarantees of the Bill of Rights when state cases come before" the Court.[65]

It is reason for deep satisfaction that many of the states effectively enforce the counterparts in state constitutions of the specifics of the Bill of Rights. Indeed, some have been applied by states to an extent beyond that required of the national government by the corresponding federal guarantee.[66] But too many state practices fall far short. Far too many cases come from the states to the Supreme Court presenting dismal pictures of official lawlessness, of illegal searches and seizures, illegal detentions attended by prolonged interrogation and coerced admissions of guilt, of the denial of counsel, and downright brutality.[67] Judicial self-restraint which defers too much to the sovereign powers of the states and reserves judicial intervention for only the most revolting cases will not serve to enhance Madison's priceless gift of "the great rights of mankind secured under this Constitution." [68] For these secure the only climate in which the law of freedom can exist.

FOOTNOTES

[1] The Federalist No. 45, at 290 (Lodge ed. 1891).
[2] Adams, The Jubilee of the Constitution 115 (1839).
[3] Texas v. White, 74 U.S. (7 Wall.) 700, 725 (1868).
[4] 1 Annals of Cong. 439 (1789).
[5] See Dumbauld, The Bill of Rights and What It Means Today 215 (1957).
[6] 1 Annals of Cong. 440 (1789).
[7] Ibid.
[8] Id. at 755.
[9] Rawle, A View of the Constitution of the United States of America 120–21 (1825).
[10] 32 U.S. (7 Pet.) 243 (1833).
[11] Id. at 246.
[12] Id. at 247.
[13] See, e.g., Lessee of Livingston v. Moore, 32 U.S. (7 Pet.) 469, 551–52 (1833); Permoli v. Municipality No. 1, 44 U.S. (3 How.) 589, 609 (1845) (dictum); Fox v. Ohio, 46 U.S. (5 How.) 410, 434–35 (1847); Smith v. Maryland,

59 U.S. (18 How.) 71, 76 (1855); Withers v. Buckley, 61 U.S. (20 How.) 84, 89–91 (1857).

14 1 Annals of Cong. 436 (1789).

15 Fairman, "Does the Fourteenth Amendment Incorporate the Bill of Rights? —The Original Understanding," 2 Stan. L. Rev. 5, 9 (1949).

16 Public Letter by Orville H. Browning, Oct 13, 1866, Cincinnati Commercial, Oct. 26, 1866, p. 2, col. 4, quoted in Fairman, supra note 15, at 78.

17 Fairman, supra note 15, at 21.

18 83 U.S. (16 Wall.) 36 (1872).

19 Twining v. New Jersey, 211 U.S. 78, 96 (1908).

20 83 U.S. (16 Wall.) at 77–78.

21 See Walker v. Sauvinet, 92 U.S. 90 (1875); United States v. Cruikshank, 92 U.S. 542, 552–56 (1875); Hurtado v. California, 110 U.S. 516 (1884); Presser v. Illinois, 116 U.S. 252, 263–68 (1886).

22 In re Kemmler, 136 U.S. 436, 448 (1890); McElvaine v. Brush, 142 U.S. 155, 158–59 (1891); O'Neil v. Vermont, 144 U.S. 323, 332 (1892) (dictum); Maxwell v. Dow, 176 U.S. 581, 597–98 (1900); Twining v. New Jersey, 211 U.S. 78, 96 (1908). See Spies v. Illinois, 123 U.S. 131 (1887). See generally Morrison, "Does the Fourteenth Amendment Incorporate the Bill of Rights?—The Judicial Interpretation," 2 Stan. L. Rev. 140 (1949).

23 O'Neil v. Vermont, supra note 22, at 363, 370 (dissenting opinions).

24 332 U.S. 46, 68 (1947). For contrasting views of the incorporation of the first eight amendments by the Fourteenth Amendment, compare Flack, The Adoption of the Fourteenth Amendment (1908), with Fairman, supra note 15.

25 332 U.S. at 71–72.

26 Mr. Justice Douglas joined in Mr. Justice Black's opinion. Mr. Justice Murphy stated that he and Mr. Justice Rutledge would go further: "I agree that the specific guarantees of the Bill of Rights should be carried over intact into the first section of the Fourteenth Amendment. But I am not prepared to say that the latter is entirely and necessarily limited by the Bill of Rights. Occasions may arise where a proceeding falls so far short of conforming to fundamental standards of procedure as to warrant constitutional condemnation in terms of a lack of due process despite the absence of a specific provision in the Bill of Rights." Id. at 124.

27 Twining v. New Jersey, 211 U.S. 78, 99 (1908).

28 Adamson v. California, 332 U.S. 46, 66 (1947) (concurring opinion).

29 Palko v. Connecticut, 302 U.S. 319, 326 (1937). (Emphasis added.)

30 Twining v. New Jersey, 211 U.S. 78, 99–100 (1908).

31 Id. at 106.

32 Palko v. Connecticut, 302 U.S. 319, 325 (1937).

33 Hurtado v. California, 110 U.S. 516, 535 (1884).

34 Snyder v. Massachusetts, 291 U.S. 97, 105 (1934).

35 259 U.S. 530, 543 (1922).

36 See West Virginia State Bd. of Educ. v. Barnette, 319 U.S. 624, 633 (1943); Bridges v. California, 314 U.S. 252, 277 (1941); Cantwell v. Connecticut, 310 U.S. 296, 303 (1940); De Jonge v. Oregon, 299 U.S. 353, 364 (1937); Near v. Minnesota ex rel. Olson, 283 U.S. 697, 707 (1931); Gitlow v. New York, 268 U.S. 652, 666 (1925). See generally Dumbauld, supra note 5, at 133–34.

37 Palko v. Connecticut, 302 U.S. 319, 327 (1937).

[38] See Smith v. California, 361 U.S. 147, 169 (1959) (separate opinion by Mr. Justice Harlan); Roth v. United States, 354 U.S. 476, 505–06 (1957) (separate opinion by Mr. Justice Harlan); Beauharnais v. Illinois, 343 U.S. 250, 288 (1952) (dissenting opinion by Mr. Justice Jackson).

[39] 1 Annals of Cong. 439 (1789).

[40] Black, The Bill of Rights, 35 N.Y.U.L. Rev. 865 (1960).

[41] 1 Annals of Cong. 437 (1789).

[42] Chicago, B. & Q.R.R. v. Chicago, 166 U.S. 226, 241 (1897).

[43] Powell v. Alabama, 287 U.S. 45, 68–69 (1932).

[44] Weeks v. United States, 232 U.S. 383, 398 (1914).

[45] Wolf v. Colorado, 338 U.S. 25, 27–28 (1949).

[46] Hebert v. Louisiana, 272 U.S. 312, 316 (1926).

[47] Walker v. Sauvinet, 92 U.S. 90 (1875).

[48] E.g., Palko v. Connecticut, 302 U.S. 319, 324 (1937).

[49] 1 Annals of Cong. 437 (1789).

[50] Betts v. Brady, 316 U.S. 455 (1942).

[51] McNeal v. Culver, 365 U.S. 109, 111 (1961), quoting Uveges v. Pennsylvania, 335 U.S. 437, 441 (1948).

[52] Id. at 117 (concurring opinion).

[53] Rawle, supra note 9, at 127–28.

[54] McNeal v. Culver, 365 U.S. 109, 118 (1961) (concurring opinion).

[55] Griffin v. Illinois, 351 U.S. 12 (1956).

[56] Spano v. New York, 360 U.S. 315, 320–31 (1959).

[57] See, e.g., Elkins v. United States, 364 U.S. 206 (1960); Mallory v. United States, 354 U.S. 449 (1957); McNabb v. United States, 318 U.S. 332 (1943).

[58] E.g., mob domination of a trial: Moore v. Dempsey, 261 U.S. 86 (1923); the right to counsel: Powell v. Alabama, 287 U.S. 45 (1932); the effect of perjured testimony: Mooney v. Holohan, 294 U.S. 103 (1935); Alcorta v. Texas, 335 U.S. 28 (1957) (per curiam); coerced confessions: Brown v. Mississippi, 297 U.S. 278 (1936); double jeopardy: Palko v. Connecticut, 302 U.S. 319 (1937); Hoag v. New Jersey, 356 U.S. 464 (1958); Ciucci v. Illinois, 356 U.S. 571 (1958) (per curiam).

[59] Weeks v. United States, 232 U.S. 383, 398 (1914).

[60] Wolf v. Colorado, 338 U.S. 25 (1949).

[61] Elkins v. United States, 364 U.S. 206 (1960).

[62] Wolf v. Colorado, 338 U.S. 25, 40, 41, 47 (1949) (dissenting opinions of Justices Douglas, Murphy and Rutledge).

[63] Cardozo, The Nature of the Judicial Process 84 (1921).

[64] Schaefer, Federalism and State Criminal Procedure, 70 Harv. L. Rev. 1, 26 (1956).

[65] Ohio ex rel. Eaton v. Price, 364 U.S. 263, 275 (1960) (dissenting from the judgment of an equally divided Court).

[66] See, e.g., People v. DenUyl, 318 Mich. 645, 651, 29 N.W.2d 284, 287 (1947), in which the Supreme Court of Michigan applied the state privilege against self-incrimination to exonerate from disclosure whenever there is a probability of prosecution in state or federal jurisdictions. "It seems like a travesty on verity to say that one is not subjected to self-incrimination when compelled to give testimony in a State judicial proceeding which testimony may forthwith be used against him in a Federal criminal prosecution." But see, as to the

federal privilege under the Fifth Amendment, United States v. Murdock, 284 U.S. 141 (1931).

See also Tex. Code Crim. Proc. art. 494 (Supp. 1960): "Whenever it is made known to the court at an arraignment or any other time that an accused charged with a felony is too poor to employ a counsel, the court shall appoint one (1) or more practicing attorneys to defend him."

And see proposed Ark. H.B. 111, introduced January 17, 1961. The conviction or acquittal of an offense against the United States, under this bill, would constitute a bar to Arkansas prosecution for the same offense. Cf. Bartkus v. Illinois, 359 U.S. 121 (1959), which itself has been overruled by an Illinois statute, Ill. Ann. Stat. ch. 38, § 601.1 (Smith-Hurd Supp. 1960), passed shortly after the Court's decision. This statute provides, "Whenever on the trial of an accused person for the violation of any criminal law of this State it is shown that he has previously been tried and convicted or acquitted under the laws of the Federal government, which former trial was based on the act or omission for which he is being tried in this State, it is a sufficient defense."

[67] See Douglas, "Vagrancy and Arrest on Suspicion," 70 Yale L.J. 1 (1960).

[68] 1 Annals of Cong. 432 (1789).

FELIX FRANKFURTER

Self-Willed Judges and the
Judicial Function

In the debate over the proper degree of intervention for the
Supreme Court in cases involving fundamental liberties, Justice
Frankfurter wrote lengthy and unambiguous opinions expressing his judgment. In his speeches off the bench, Frankfurter
tended to weave these themes into a larger fabric of historical
or biographical discussion, not only as a matter of his view of
the proprieties but because he felt such commentary was
strengthened for being anchored in those contexts and not
other, more "current" frameworks. The selection printed here
was the second part of a speech opening a three-day conference on "Government Under Law," held at Harvard Law
School in September of 1955 on the two hundredth anniversary of John Marshall's birth. The first part of the speech discussed Marshall's influence on the shaping of the "virgin
document" of the Constitution, and argued that American
history would have been "markedly different" if he had not
led the Court from 1801–1835. Then Justice Frankfurter moved
on to some additional comments, in what he called the tradition
of "the Greek chorus."

Source: "John Marshall and the Judicial Function," in
Arthur E. Sutherland (ed.) *Government Under Law* (Cambridge: Harvard University Press, 1956), 6–31.

Marshall's significance could not be more fittingly celebrated than by scrutinizing, which is the aim of this conference, the state of "government under law," more particularly under the legal system to which Marshall so heavily contributed, a hundred and twenty years after he wrote his last opinion. Could he listen to these proceedings, nothing would be bound to strike him more than the enlarged scope of law since his day. He would, of course, think of law as legally enforceable rights. For, while he occasionally referred to "natural law," it was not much more than literary garniture, even as in our own day, and not a guiding means for adjudication. He would have sympathized, as other judges have, with Sir Frederick Pollock's remark: "In the Middle Ages natural law was regarded as the senior branch of divine law and therefore had to be treated as infallible (but there was no infallible way of knowing what it was)." (I *Holmes-Pollock Letters* [Howe ed., 1941], p. 275.) Marshall would be amazed by the interpenetration of law in government, because during his whole era he was concerned with the Constitution as an instrument predominantly regulating the machinery of government, and more particularly, distributing powers between the central government and the States. The Constitution was not thought of as the repository of the supreme law limiting all government, with a court wielding the deepest-cutting power of deciding whether there is any authority in government at all to do what is sought to be done.

Thus, the gravamen of the attack in the Virginia and Kentucky Resolutions against the Alien and Sedition Acts of 1798 was that they infringed on the rights of the States and were promotive of "a general consolidated government." It deserves to be recalled that even Jefferson attributed to the States the power which he denied to the Federal Government. "Nor does the opinion of the unconstitutionality and consequent nullity of that law [the Sedition Act]," he wrote to Abigail Adams, "remove all restraint from the overwhelming torrent of slander which is confounding all vice and virtue, all truth and falsehood in the U.S. The power to do that is fully possessed by the several state legislatures. . . . While we deny that Congress have a right to controul the freedom of the press, we have ever asserted the right of the states, and their exclusive right, to do so. . . ."

The only two Marshallian constitutional opinions that concern individual rights as such, *Fletcher* v. *Peck*, 6 Cranch 87 (1810), and the *Dartmouth College Case*, 4 Wheat. 518 (1819), rather than the delimitation of power between two governments, are, in the perspective of time, not of great importance. This came to pass partly because of easy legislative correction, partly because the doctrine of strict construction devised in the *Charles River Bridge Case*, 11 Pet. 420 (1837), took the sting out of the decision of the *Dartmouth College Case*. Moreover, insofar as the latter case forbade legislative transfer of the property of the college to the trustees, it is a safe assumption that the Due Process Clauses would condemn such an attempt. . . .

The vast change in the scope of law between Marshall's time and ours is at bottom a reflection of the vast change in the circumstances of society. The range of business covered by Marshall's Court, though operating under a written Constitution, was in the main not very different from the concerns of the English courts, except that the latter dealt much more with property settlements. The vast enveloping present-day role of law is not the design of a statesman nor attributable to the influence of some great thinker. It is a reflection of the great technological revolution which brought in its train what a quiet writer in *The Economist* could call "the tornado of economic and social change of the last century." Law has been an essential accompaniment of the shift from "watch-dog government"—the phrase is George Kennan's—to the service state. For government has become a service state, whatever the tint of the party in power and whatever time-honored slogans it may use to enforce and promote measures that hardly vindicate the slogans. Profound social changes continue to be in the making, due to movements of industrialization, urbanization, and permeating egalitarian ideas.

With crude accuracy I have just summarized the situation in the countries of the English-speaking world, about which alone I may speak. But when these transforming economic and social forces got under full swing in the United States, lawyers and courts found available in the Fourteenth Amendment resources for curbing legislative responses to new pressures. The Amendment was gradually invoked against the substance of legislation and not merely to support claims based on traditionally fair procedure.

I have thus reached the slippery slope of due process. But not even to take a glance at it in a reconnaissance, however sketchy, of government under law, would indeed be to play *Hamlet* without Hamlet.

It has been frequently stated that when a question arises in due course of a litigation, whether a constitutional provision has been infringed, the established courts of justice "must of necessity determine that question." See Lord Selborne in *The Queen* v. *Burah*, 3 A.C. 889, 904 (1878), quoted approvingly by Lord Wright in *James* v. *Commonwealth*, [1936] A.C. 578, 613; and see also *Swart, N.O. and Nicol, N.O.* v. *de Kock and Garner*, 1951 (3) S.A. 589, 601–02 and 611. This is only qualifiedly true regarding our Constitution. Thus, the explicit provision requiring one State to surrender to another a fugitive from justice (Art. IV, § 2, cl. 2) is "merely declaratory of a moral duty" and is not, because of the subject matter, enforceable in the courts. *Kentucky* v. *Dennison*, 24 How. 66 (1861). Likewise, the "guarantee to every state" of "a Republican Form of Government," must, because of the subject-matter, look elsewhere than to the courts for observance. *Pacific States Tel. & Tel. Co.* v. *Oregon*, 223 U.S. 118 (1912). There are not a few other instances in which judicial relief was barred because "political questions" were deemed to be involved.

It is not for me to find the common denominator of these judicial abstentions, or to give the contour and content of what questions are "political," in the sense of precluding judicial examination. But I do venture to believe that no judge charged with the duty of enforcing the Due Process Clauses of the Fifth and Fourteenth Amendments, and the Equal Protection of the Laws Clause of the Fourteenth Amendment, can free himself from the disquietude that the line is often very thin between the cases in which the Court felt compelled to abstain from adjudication because of their "political" nature, and the cases that so frequently arise in applying the concepts of "liberty" and "equality."

In his First Inaugural Jefferson spoke of the "sacred principle" that "the will of the majority is in all cases to prevail." [1] Jefferson himself hardly meant all by "all." (See Jefferson's answers to Démeunier's first queries, reprinted in 10 *The Papers of Thomas Jefferson* [Boyd ed., 1954], p. 18.) In any event, one need not give full adherence to his view to be deeply mindful of the fact that judicial review is a deliberate check upon democracy through an organ of government not subject to popular control. In relation to the judiciary's task in the type of cases I am now discussing, I am raising difficulties which I think must in all good conscience be faced, unless perchance the Court is expected to register a particular view and unless the profession that the judiciary is the disinterested guardian of our Constitution be pretense.

It may be that responsibility for decision dulls the capacity of discernment. The fact is that one sometimes envies the certitude of outsiders regarding the compulsions to be drawn from vague and admonitory constitutional provisions. Only for those who have not the responsibility of decision can it be easy to decide the grave and complex problems they raise, especially in controversies that excite public interest. This is so because they too often present legal issues inextricably and deeply bound up in emotional reactions to sharply conflicting economic, social, and political views. It is not the duty of judges to express their personal attitudes on such issues, deep as their individual convictions may be. The opposite is the truth; it is their duty not to act on merely personal views. But "due process," once we go beyond its strictly procedural aspect, and the "equal protection of the laws" enshrined in the Constitution, are precisely defined neither by history nor in terms. It deserves to be noted that so far as gaining light from pertinent data on the intention of Congress on specific issues in formulating the Fourteenth Amendment, the Supreme Court found that "[a]t best, they are inconclusive." *Brown* v. *Board of Education*, 347 U.S. 483, 489 (1954). This finding of darkness was reached not for want of searching inquiry by Court and counsel.

No doubt, these provisions of the Constitution were not calculated to give permanent legal sanction merely to the social arrangements and beliefs of a particular epoch. Like all legal provisions without a fixed technical meaning, they are ambulant, adaptable to the changes of time. That is their strength; that also makes dubious their appropriateness for judicial enforcement—dubious because their vagueness readily lends itself to make of the Court a third chamber with drastic veto power. This danger has been pointed out by our greatest judges too often to be dismissed as a bogey. Holding democracy in judicial tutelage is not the most promising way to foster disciplined responsibility in a people. See *AFL* v. *American Sash & Door Co.*, 335 U.S. 538, 555–557 (1949) (concurring opinion).

It is, of course, no longer to be questioned that claims under the Fourteenth Amendment are subject to judicial judgment. This makes it all the more important to realize what is involved in the discharge of this function of the Court, particularly since this is probably the largest source of the Court's business. It is important, that is, fully to appreciate the intrinsic nature of the issues when the Court is called upon to determine whether the legislature or the executive has regulated "liberty" or "property" "without due process of law" or has denied "equal protection of the laws"; to appreciate the difficulties in making a judgment upon such issues, difficulties of a different order from those normally imposed upon jural tribunals; and, not least, to appreciate the qualifications requisite for those who exercise this extraordinary authority, demanding as it does a breadth of outlook and an invincible disinterestedness rooted in temperament and confirmed by discipline. Of course, individual judgment and feeling cannot be wholly shut out of the judicial process. But if they dominate, the judicial process becomes a dangerous sham. The conception by a judge of the scope and limits of his function may exert an intellectual and moral force as much as responsiveness to a particular audience or congenial environment.

We are dealing with constitutional provisions the nature of which can be best conveyed compendiously by Judge Learned Hand's phrase that they "represent a mood rather than a command, that sense of moderation, of fair play, of mutual forbearance, without which states become the prey of faction." *Daniel Reeves, Inc.* v. *Anderson,* 43 F. 2d 679, 682 (1930). Alert search for enduring standards by which the judiciary is to exercise its duty in enforcing those provisions of the Constitution that are expressed in what Ruskin called "chameleon words," needs the indispensable counterpoise of sturdy doubt that one has found those standards. Yesterday the active area in this field was concerned with "property." Today it is "civil liberties." Tomorrow it may again be "property." Who can say that in a society with a mixed economy, like ours, these two areas are sharply separated, and that certain freedoms in relation to property may not again be deemed, as they were in the past, aspects of individual freedom?

Let me sharpen these difficulties by concreteness. In *Plessy* v. *Ferguson,* 163 U.S. 537, 559 (1896), Mr. Justice Harlan floated an oft-quoted epigram, but in a few short years he did not apply it, proving once more that sonorous abstractions do not solve problems with intractable variables. See *Cumming* v. *Richmond County Board of Education*, 175 U.S. 528 (1899), and its influence on *Gong Lum* v. *Rice*, 275 U.S. 78, 85 (1927). Thinking of "equality" in abstract terms led Mr. Justice Harlan to be blind to the meaning of "yellow-dog contracts" as a serious curtailment of liberty in the context of anti-union strategy, *Adair* v. *United States*, 208 U.S. 161 (1908); Richard Olney, "Discrimination against Union Labor," 42 *Am. L. Rev.* 161 (1908), and to be equally blind to the fact that important differences between industry and agriculture may justify differentiation in legislation. See *Connolly* v. *Union Sewer Pipe Co.*, 184 U.S. 540 (1902), and compare with *Tigner* v. *Texas*, 310 U.S. 141 (1940).

Take the other side of the medal. It is too easy to attribute judicial review resulting in condemnation of restrictions on activities pertaining to property to "economic predilection" of particular judges. The Due Process Clauses extend to triune interests—life, liberty and property—and "property" cannot be deleted by judicial fiat rendering it nugatory regarding legislation touching property. Moreover, protection of property interests may, as already indicated, quite fairly be deemed, in appropriate circumstances, an aspect of liberty. Regulation of property may be struck down on assumptions or beliefs other than narrow economic views. And so we find that Justices who were the most tolerant of legislative power dealing with economic interests have found in due process a protection even against an exercise of the so-called police power. It was true of Mr. Justice Holmes in *Pennsylvania Coal Co.* v. *Mahon*, 260 U.S. 393 (1922), and of Mr. Justice Brandeis in *Thompson* v. *Consolidated Gas Utilities Corp.*, 300 U.S. 55 (1937).

Let us turn to the much-mooted "clear and present danger" doctrine. It is at least interesting that that phrase originated in one (*Schenck* v. *United States*, 249 U.S. 47, 52 [1919]) of a series of cases in which convictions for heavy sentences were sustained against defendants who had invoked the right of free speech in circumstances which led Mr. Justice Holmes to characterize them as "poor fools whom I should have been inclined to pass over if I could." (2 *Holmes-Pollock Letters*, [Howe ed., 1941], p. 11.) "Clear and present danger" thus had a compulsion for Mr. Justice Holmes against recognizing Debs's freedom to an utterance that in retrospect hardly seems horrendous. *Debs* v.

United States, 249 U.S. 211 (1919). Would it carry equal compulsion with other judges? One can be confident, in any event, that Mr. Justice Holmes would not have deemed his doctrine a bar to the power of a State to safeguard the fair conduct of a trial for a capital offense from being thwarted by intrusion of utterances from without. See *Maryland* v. *Baltimore Radio Show Inc.*, 338 U.S. 912 (1950), denying certiorari to 193 Md. 300, 67 A. 2d 497 (1949). There is the best of reasons for believing that Mr. Justice Brandeis would not have carried his natural devotion to the place of freedom of speech in a democracy to such a doctrinaire denial of an equally indispensable need of a free society—trial in court, not outside it.

Concerned as I am with the evolution of social policy by way of judicial application of Delphic provisions of the Constitution, recession of judicial doctrine is as pertinent as its expansion. The history of the constitutional position of the right to strike affords an illuminating instance. After invalidating a law withdrawing the use of the injunction against strikes, *Truax* v. *Corrigan*, 257 U.S. 312 (1921), the Court came to conceive of the conduct of a strike as an aspect of the constitutionally protected freedom of discussion, *Thornhill* v. *Alabama*, 310 U.S. 88 (1940), but soon retreated from this position and recognized that picketing, as the weapon of strikes, is not merely a means of communication, *Giboney* v. *Empire Storage & Ice Co.*, 336 U.S. 490 (1949). No matter how often the Court insists that it is not passing on policy when determining constitutionality, the emphasis on constitutionality and its fascination for the American public seriously confound problems of constitutionality with the merits of a policy. Industrial relations are not alone in presenting problems that suffer in their solution from having public opinion too readily assume that because some measure is found to be constitutional it is wise and right, and, contrariwise, because it is found unconstitutional it is intrinsically wrong. That such miseducation of public opinion, with its effect upon action, has been an important consequence of committing to the Court the enforcement of "the mood" represented by these vague constitutional provisions, can hardly be gainsaid by any student of their history.

Much as the constitution-makers of other countries have drawn upon our experience, it is precisely because they have drawn upon it that they have, one and all, abstained from including a "due process" clause. They have rejected it in conspicuous instances after thorough consideration of our judicial history of "due process." See Wallace Mendelson, "Foreign Reactions to American Experience with 'Due Process of Law,'" 41 *Va. L. Rev.* 493 (1955). It is particularly noteworthy that such was the course of events in framing the constitution of India. Sir. B. N. Rau, one of the most penetrating legal minds of our time, had a major share in its drafting, and for the purpose he made a deep study of the workings of the Due Process Clause during an extensive stay here.

Is it the tenor of these remarks that courts should have no concern with other than material interests, that they must be unmindful of the imponderable rights and dignities of the individual which are, I am sure I shall have your agreement in saying, the ideals which the Western world holds most high? Of course not. Recognition of them should permeate the law, and it does so effectively even in courts that do not have veto power over legislation. They constitute presuppositions where parliaments have not spoken unequivocally and courts are left with the jural task of construction in its fair sense.

Thus, while the Chief Justice of Canada could say: "We have not a Bill of Rights such as is contained in the United States Constitution and decisions on that part of the latter are of no assistance," he reached the same result in *Saumur* v. *City of Quebec* [1953], 2 S.C.R. 299, as a matter of construction, that was reached under the Due Process Clause in *Lovell* v. *City of Griffin*, 303 U.S. 444 (1938). Again, only the other day the Supreme Court of Canada rejected the view that the mere claim of immunity by a minister of the Crown from producing in court a document relevant to its proceeding is conclusive. It deemed such a claim "not in harmony with the basic conceptions of our policy." The reason given by Mr. Justice Rand deserves to be quoted: "What is secured by attributing to the courts this preliminary determination of possible prejudice is protection against executive encroachments upon the administration of justice; and in the present trend of government little can be more essential to the maintenance of individual security. In this important matter, to relegate the courts to such a subserviency as is suggested would be to withdraw from them the confidence of independence and judicial appraisal that so far appear to have served well the organization of which we are the heirs." *Regina* v. *Snider* [1954], S.C.R. 479, 485, 486. So, likewise, the Appellate Division of the Supreme Court of South Africa ruled that when an Act conferred autocratic powers upon a minister—it was the Suppression of Communism Act—it must, in the absence of explicit direction by Parliament, be construed with the least interference with the liberty of the subject. *R. v. Ngwevela*, 1954 (1) S.A. 123.

While the subjection to parliamentary criticism is the only remedy for much in Great Britain that with us becomes the stuff of lawsuits, the English executive is amenable to challenge in court for exceeding statutorily defined legal powers. In construing such authority, English courts enforce the right to a hearing as a presupposition of English law, unless Parliament has clearly enough indicated the contrary. See S.A. de Smith, "The Right to a Hearing in English Administrative Law," 68 *Harv. L. Rev.* 569 (1955); so, likewise in Canada, *L'Alliance des Professeurs Catholiques* v. *Labour Relations Board* [1953], 2 S.C.R. 140; and in New Zealand, *New Zealand Dairy Board* v. *Okitu Co-operative Dairy Co.* [1953], N.Z.L.R. 366. The English courts have also been resourceful, through the use they make of *certiorari*, in setting aside executive action when based on reasons not justifiable in law. For application of this principle in the United States see *Perkins* v. *Elg*, 307 U.S. 325 (1939), and *Securities and Exchange Commission* v. *Chenery Corp.*, 318 U.S. 80 (1943). This increasing tendency of courts to scrutinize the legal grounds given by administrative agencies for their actions may well promote greater responsibility in the agencies' exercise of authority and in their justification of that exercise.

If government under law were confined to what is judicially enforced, law in government would be very restricted, no matter how latitudinarian one's conception of what is fitting for judicial examination of governmental action. For one thing, courts have a strong tendency to abstain from constitutional controversies. *E.g.*, *Peters* v. *Hobby*, 349 U.S. 331 (1955). Thereby, they may avoid conflict, at least prematurely if not permanently, with the other branches of the government and they may avoid also the determination of conflict between the Nation and the States. Moreover, settlement of complicated public issues, particularly on the basis of constitutional provisions conveying indeterminate standards, is subject to the inherent limitations and contingencies of the judicial process. For constitutional adjudications involve adjustment of vast and incommensurable public interests through episodic instances, upon evidence and information limited by the narrow rules of litigation, shaped and intellectually influenced by the fortuitous choice of particular counsel.

Mr. Justice Brandeis made a fair estimate in saying that by applying its restrictive canons for adjudication, the Court has in the course of its history "avoided passing upon a large part of all the constitutional questions pressed upon it for decision." *Ashwander* v. *Tennessee Valley Authority*, 297 U.S. 288, 346 (1936). This is true not only of our Supreme Court, which cannot render advisory opinions however compelling the appeal for legal guidance even at times of national emergency. (See Chief Justice Jay's reply to President Washington's inquiry, conveyed by Thomas Jefferson, in 3 *The Correspondence and Public Papers of John Jay* [Johnston ed., 1891], pp. 486–89.) Insistence on an immediate, substantial, and threatened interest in raising such constitutional issues is a characteristic of all high courts with power to pass upon them. See the recent Australian case, *Australian Boot Trade Employees' Federation* v. *Commonwealth* (1954), 90 C.L.R. 24; see also *Musgrove* v. *Chun Teeong Toy* [1891], A.C. 272, 283. But even where advisory opinions are constitutionally authorized, tribunals are reluctant to pronounce in situations that are hypothetical or abstract or otherwise not conducive to judicial disposition. See Lord Haldane, in *Attorney General for British Columbia* v. *Attorney General for Canada* [1914], A.C. 153, 162; Lord Sankey, in *In re the Regulation and Control of Aeronautics* [1932], A.C. 54, 66. It is, I believe, not inaccurate to say that most of the occasions when the Supreme Court has come into virulent conflict with public opinion were those in which the Court disregarded its settled tradition against needlessly pronouncing on constitutional issues. (The *Dred Scott Case*, 19 How. 393 [1857], does not stand alone; see the *Income Tax Cases*, 157 U.S. 429 and 158 U.S. 601 [1895], controlling until the Sixteenth Amendment of February 25, 1913; *Adkins* v. *Children's Hospital*, 261 U.S. 525, 543 [1923], overruled by *West Coast Hotel Co.* v. *Parrish*, 300 U.S. 379 [1937].)

The confining limits within which courts thus move in expounding law is not the most important reason for a conception of government under law far transcending merely law that is enforced in the courts. The day has long gone by when Austin's notions exhaust the content of law. Law is not set above the government. It defines its orbit. But government is not law except insofar as law infuses government. This is not word-playing. Also indispensable to government is ample scope for individual insight and imaginative origination by those entrusted with the public interest. If society is not to remain stagnant, there is need of action beyond uniformities found recurring in instances which sustain a generalization and demand its application. But law is not a code of fettering restraints, a litany of prohibitions and permissions. It is an enveloping and permeating habituation of behavior, reflecting the counsels of reason on the part of those entrusted with power in reconciling the pressures of conflicting interests. Once we conceive of "the rule of law" as embracing the whole range of presuppositions on which government is conducted and not as a technical doctrine of judicial authority, the relevant question is not, has it been achieved, but, is it conscientiously and systematically pursued.[2]

What matters most is whether the standards of reason and fair dealing are bred in the bones of people. Hyde Park represents a devotion to free speech far more dependable in its assurances, though unprotected by formal constitutional requirement, than reliance upon the litigious process for its enjoyment. Again, widespread popular intolerance of the third degree, such as manifested itself in the well-known Savidge affair, reflects a more deeply grounded rule of law than is disclosed by the painful story of our continuing judicial endeavor to root out this evil through decisions in occasional dramatic cases. (For the Savidge case, see 220 *Hans. Deb.* [Commons], cols. 5, 805 *et seq.* [July 20, 1928]; Inquiry in regard to the Interrogation by the Police of Miss Savidge [1928, Cmd. 3147]. As to our experience, see, *e.g.*, "Report on the Third Degree" by Chafee, Pollak and Stern in 4 *National Commission on Law Observance and Enforcement, Reports,* p. 13 [1931], and the series of well-known cases in the Supreme Court Reports.) Let me give another illustration. "Crichel Down" will, in its way, serve to summarize the duty of obedience to standards of fair dealing and avoidance even of the appearance of official arbitrariness. As such it will affect the future conduct of English government as much as some of the leading cases which have been important factors in the development of a democratic society. See Public Inquiry ordered by the Ministry of Agriculture into the disposal of land at Crichel Down (1954, Cmd. 9176); R. Douglas Brown, *The Battle of Crichel Down.* You will note that the instances I have given of manifestations of law responsive to the deep feelings of a people are drawn from a nation that does not rely on a written constitution. I need not add that the distinctive historical development in Great Britain, in the context of its progressive cultural and economic homogeneity, has made possible accommodation between stability and change, defining the powers of government and the limits within which due regard for individual rights require it to be kept, without embodying it in a single legal document enforceable in courts of law.

I hope, however, that you will not deem me unduly romantic in deriving comfort from the undertaking given the other day by the Kabaka, as a condition of his return to his people in Buganda, when he promised that he "will well and truly govern Buganda according to law" (*The* [London] *Times*, Aug. 13, 1955, p. 6, col. 5). I find reason for my comfort in the fascinating account by Professor Max Gluckman of Manchester University of the extent to which law permeates the lives of the Barotse tribes of Northern Rhodesia, law in the sense in which this conference is discussing it and not something religious in nature. (Gluckman, *The Judicial Process among the Barotse of Northern Rhodesia* [1955].)

If what I have brought you, in my endeavor to give you as frankly as I may the distillation of sixteen years of reflection from within the tribunal peculiarly concerned with government under law, is charged with being an old-fashioned liberal's view of government and law, I plead guilty. For the charge implies allegiance to the humane and gradualist tradition in dealing with refractory social and political problems, recognizing them to be fractious because of their complexity and not amenable to quick and propitious solutions without resort to methods which deny law as the instrument and offspring of reason.

I have not been able to submit to you large generalizations that illumine or harmoniously assimilate discrete instances. Still less have I been able to fashion criteria for easier adjudication of the specific cases that will trouble future judges. They are bound to be troubled, whether they will be faced with variant aspects of old problems—old conflicts between liberty and authority, between the central government and its constituent members—or new problems inevitably thrown up by the everlasting flux of life.

Believing it still important to do so, I have tried to dispel the age-old illusion that the conflicts to which the energy and ambition and imagination of the restless human spirit give rise can be subdued, even if not settled, by giving the endeavors of reason we call law a mechanical or automatic or enduring configuration. Law cannot be confined within any such mold because life cannot be so confined. Man's most piercing discernment of the future cannot see very far beyond his day, even when guided by the prophet's insight and the compassionate humility of a Lincoln. And I am the last to claim that judges are apt to be endowed with these gifts. But a fair appraisal of Anglo-American judicial history ought to leave us not without encouragement that modest goals, uncompromisingly pursued, may promote what I hope you will let me call civilized ends without the need of defining them.

In what I have been saying you have no doubt heard undertones of a judge's perplexities—particularly of a judge who has to construe, as it is called, vague and admonitory constitutional provisions. But I am very far from meaning to imply a shriveled conception of government under law. Quite the contrary. The intention of my emphasis has been not on the limited scope of judicial enforcement of laws. My concern is an affirmation—my plea is for the pervasiveness throughout the whole range of government of the spirit of law, at least in the sense of excluding arbitrary official action. But however limited the area of adjudication may be, the standards of what is fair and just set by courts in controversies appropriate for their adjudication are perhaps the single most powerful influence in promoting the spirit of law throughout government. These standards also help shape the dominant civic habits and attitudes which ultimately determine the ethos of a society.

In exercising their technical jurisdiction, courts thus release contagious consequences. Nothing is farther from my mind than to suggest that judges should exceed the professional demands of a particular decision. If judges want to be preachers, they should dedicate themselves to the pulpit; if judges want to be primary shapers of policy, the legislature is their place. Self-willed judges are the least defensible offenders against government under law. But since the grounds of decisions and their general direction suffuse the public mind and the operations of government, judges cannot free themselves from the responsibility of the inevitable effect of their opinions in constricting or promoting the force of law throughout government. Upon no functionaries is there a greater duty to promote law.

FOOTNOTES

[1] The following is the sentence in which the quoted phrase occurs: "All, too, will bear in mind this sacred principle, that though the will of the majority is in all cases to prevail, that will to be rightful must be reasonable; that the minority possess their equal rights, which equal law must protect, and to violate would be oppression." A little later in that address Jefferson included in what he deemed "the essential principles of our Government," "absolute acquiescence in the decisions of the majority, the vital principle of republics, from which is no appeal but to force, the vital principle and immediate parent of despotism. . . ." 1 *Messages and Papers of the Presidents* (Richardson ed., 1899), pp. 322, 323.

[2] In what I have said of course I do not mean to give the remotest support to the notion that the law is "a brooding omnipresence in the sky." I reject it as completely as did Mr. Justice Holmes in *Southern Pacific Co.* v. *Jensen,* 244, U.S. 205, 222 (1917) (dissenting opinion). It might further avoid confusion to restrict the term "law," particularly in a judge's mouth, to the commands of society which it is the duty of courts to enforce, and not apply it to those decencies of conduct which should control other branches of government but are without judicial sanction. But perhaps law has so established itself as a portmanteau word that clarity does not require too pedantically restrictive a use of it as long as no doubt is left regarding the circumscribed scope of the judiciary's function.

EARL WARREN

The Cold War, Judicial Review, and the Military

When called upon to deliver the third annual James Madison Lecture at New York University Law School in 1962, Chief Justice Earl Warren chose to discuss the impact on civil liberties of the American military response to the cold-war challenge. Partly, this involved bringing up to date the debates and case-law involving the basic concept of civilian control of the military establishment, and indicating how this principle has been faring in an age of global disposition of American military forces, expansion of the peacetime military role and standing forces, and the entry of military questions in matters of economic and political decision-making in crises short of war. At the same time, the Chief Justice put within the boundaries of his discussion the broader issues posed by our military situation and our military response, from loyalty-security programs to problems of balancing what President Eisenhower referred to as the pressures of a "military-industrial complex." In all these issues, of course, Chief Justice Warren's central inquiry was the relation of Constitutional limitations to government power and military authority, and the place of the Supreme Court in asserting these limitations and making them stick.

Source: *The Bill of Rights and the Military*, 37 New York University Law Review 181 (1962).

Determining the proper role to be assigned to the military in a democratic society has been a troublesome problem for every nation that has aspired to a free political life. The military establishment is, of course, a necessary organ of government; but the reach of its power must be carefully limited lest the delicate balance between freedom and order be upset. The maintenance of the balance is made more difficult by the fact that while the military serves the vital function of preserving the existence of the nation, it is, at the same time, the one element of government that exercises a type of authority not easily assimilated in a free society.

The critical importance of achieving a proper accommodation is apparent when one considers the corrosive effect upon liberty of exaggerated military power. In the last analysis, it is the military—or at least a militant organization of power—that dominates life in totalitarian countries regardless of their nominal political arrangements. This is true, moreover, not only with respect to Iron Curtain countries, but also with respect to many countries that have all of the formal trappings of constitutional democracy.

Not infrequently in the course of its history the Supreme Court has been called upon to decide issues that bear directly upon the relationship between action taken in the name of the military and the protected freedoms of the Bill of Rights. I would like to discuss here some of the principal factors that have shaped the Court's response. From a broad perspective, it may be said that the questions raised in these cases are all variants of the same fundamental problem: Whether the disputed exercise of power is compatible with preservation of the freedoms intended to be insulated by the Bill of Rights.

I believe it is reasonably clear that the Court, in cases involving a substantial claim that protected freedoms have been infringed in the name of military requirements, has consistently recognized the relevance of a basic group of principles. For one, of course, the Court has adhered to its mandate to safeguard freedom from excessive encroachment by governmental authority. In these cases, the Court's approach is reinforced by the American tradition of the separation of the military establishment from, and its subordination to, civil authority. On the other hand, the action in question is generally defended in the name of military necessity, or, to put it another way, in the name of national survival. I suggest that it is possible to discern in the Court's decisions a reasonably consistent pattern for the resolution of these competing claims, and more, that this pattern furnishes a sound guide for the future. Moreover, these decisions reveal, I believe, that while the judiciary plays an important role in this area, it is subject to certain significant limitations, with the result that other organs of government and the people themselves must bear a most heavy responsibility.

Before turning to some of the keystone decisions of the Court, I think it desirable to consider for a moment the principle of separation and subordination of the military establishment, for it is this principle that contributes in a vital way to a resolution of the problems engendered by the existence of a military establishment in a free society.

It is significant that in our own hemisphere only our neighbor, Canada, and we ourselves have avoided rule by the military throughout our national existences. This is not merely happenstance. A tradition has been bred into us that the perpetuation of free government depends upon the continued supremacy of the civilian representatives of the people. To maintain this supremacy has always been a preoccupation of all three branches of our government. To strangers this might seem odd, since our country was born in war. It was the military that, under almost unbearable conditions, carried the burden of the Revolution and made possible our existence as a Nation.

But the people of the colonies had long been subjected to the intemperance of military power. Among the grievous wrongs of which they complained in the Declaration of Independence were that the King had subordinated the civil power to the military, that he had quartered troops among them in times of peace, and that through his mercenaries he had committed other cruelties. Our War of the Revolution was, in good measure, fought as a protest against standing armies. Moreover, it was fought largely with a civilian army, the militia, and its great Commander-in-Chief was a civilian at heart. After the war, he resigned his commission and returned to civilian life. In an emotion-filled appearance before the Congress, his resignation was accepted by its President, Thomas Mifflin, who, in a brief speech, emphasized Washington's qualities of leadership and, above all, his abiding respect for civil authority.[1] This trait was probably best epitomized when, just prior to the war's end, some of his officers urged Washington to establish a monarchy, with himself at its head. He not only turned a deaf ear to their blandishments, but his reply, called by historian Edward Channing "possibly, the grandest single thing in his whole career," [2] stated that nothing had given him more painful sensations than the information that such notions existed in the army, and that he thought their proposal "big with the greatest mischiefs that can befall my Country." [3]

Such thoughts were uppermost in the minds of the Founding Fathers when they drafted the Constitution. Distrust of a standing army was expressed by many. Recognition of the danger from Indians and foreign nations caused them to authorize a national armed force begrudgingly. Their viewpoint is well summarized in the language of James Madison, . . .

The veteran legions of Rome were an overmatch for the undisciplined valor of all other nations, and rendered her the mistress of the world. Not the less true is it, that the liberties of Rome proved the final victim of her military triumphs; and that the liberties of Europe, as far as they ever existed, have, with few exceptions, been the price of her military establishments. A standing force, therefore, is a dangerous, at the same time that it may be a necessary, provision. On the smallest scale it has its inconveniences. On an extensive scale its consequences may be fatal. On any scale it is an object of laudable circumspection and precaution. A wise nation will combine all these considerations; and, whilst it does not rashly preclude itself from any resource which may become essential to its safety, will exert all its prudence in diminishing both the necessity and the danger of resorting to one which may be inauspicious to its liberties. [4]

Their apprehensions found expression in the diffusion of the war powers granted the Government by the Constitution. The President was made the Commander-in-Chief of the armed forces. But Congress was given the power to provide for the common defense, to declare war, to make rules for the Government and regulation of the land and naval forces, and to raise and support armies, with the added precaution that no appropriation could be made for the latter purpose for longer than two years at a time—as an antidote to a standing army. Further, provision was made for organizing and calling forth the state militia to execute the laws of the Nation in times of emergency.

Despite these safeguards, the people were still troubled by the recollection of the conditions that prompted the charge of the Declaration of Independence that the King had "effected to render the military independent and superior to the civil power." They were reluctant to ratify the Constitution without further assurances, and thus we find in the Bill of Rights Amendments 2 and 3, specifically authorizing a decentralized militia, guaranteeing the right of the people to keep and bear arms, and prohibiting the quartering of troops in any house in time of peace without the consent of the owner. Other Amendments guarantee the right of the people to assemble, to be secure in their homes against unreasonable searches and seizures, and in criminal cases to be accorded a speedy and public trial by an impartial jury after indictment in the district and state wherein the crime was committed. The only exceptions made to these civilian trial procedures are for cases arising in the land and naval forces. Although there is undoubtedly room for argument based on the frequently conflicting sources of history, it is not unreasonable to believe that our Founders' determination to guarantee the preeminence of civil over military power was an important element that prompted adoption of the Constitutional Amendments we call the Bill of Rights.[5]

Civil supremacy has consistently been the goal of our Government from colonial days to these. As late as 1947, when the Department of Defense was established, Congress specifically provided for a civilian chief officer. And when President Truman asked the Congress for an amendment to make an exception for a soldier and statesman as great as the late George C. Marshall, serious debate followed before the Act was modified to enable him to become Secretary of Defense, and then only by a small majority of the total membership of the House and less than half of the Senate.[6] Those who opposed the amendment often expressed their high regard for General Marshall, but made known their fears concerning any deviation, even though temporary, from our traditional subordination of military to civil power.[7]

The history of our country does not indicate that there has ever been a widespread desire to change the relationship between the civil government and the military; and it can be fairly said that, with minor exceptions, military men throughout our history have not only recognized and accepted this relationship in the spirit of the Constitution, but that they have also cheerfully cooperated in preserving it.

Thus it is plain that the axiom of subordination of the military to the civil is not an anachronism. Rather, it is so deeply rooted in our national experience that it must be regarded as an essential constituent of the fabric of our political life.

But sometimes competing with this principle—and with the "Thou Shalt Nots" of the Bill of Rights—is the claim of military necessity. Where such a conflict is asserted before the Court, the basic problem has been, as I have indicated, to determine whether and how these competing claims may be resolved in the framework of a lawsuit.

Cases of this nature appear to me to be divisible into three broad categories. The first involves questions concerning the military establishment's treatment of persons who are concededly subject to military authority—what may be termed the vertical reach of the Bill of Rights within the military. These questions have been dealt with quite differently than the second category of disputes, involving what may be called the horizontal reach of the Bill of Rights. Cases of this type pose principally the question whether the complaining party is a proper subject of military authority. Finally, there are cases which do not, strictly speaking, involve the action of the military, but rather the action of other government agencies taken in the name of military necessity.

So far as the relationship of the military to its own personnel is concerned, the basic attitude of the Court has been that the latter's jurisdiction is most limited. Thus, the Supreme Court has adhered consistently to the 1863 holding of *Ex parte Vallandigham*[8] that it lacks jurisdiction to review by certiorari the decisions of military courts. The cases in which the Court has ordered the release of persons convicted by courts-martial have, to date, been limited to instances in which it found lack of military jurisdiction over the person so tried, using the term "jurisdiction" in its narrowest sense. That is, they were all cases in which the defendant was found to be such that he was not constitutionally, or statutorily, amenable to military justice. Such was the classic formulation of the relation between civil courts and courts-martial as expressed in *Dynes* v. *Hoover*,[9] decided in 1857.

This "hands off" attitude has strong historical support, of course.

While I cannot here explore the matter completely, there is also no necessity to do so, since it is indisputable that the tradition of our country, from the time of the Revolution until now, has supported the military establishment's broad power to deal with its own personnel. The most obvious reason is that courts are ill-equipped to determine the impact upon discipline that any particular intrusion upon military authority might have. Many of the problems of the military society are, in a sense, alien to the problems with which the judiciary is trained to deal.

However, the obvious reason is not always the most important one. I suppose it cannot be said that the courts of today are more knowledgeable about the requirements of military discipline than the courts in the early days of the Republic. Nevertheless, events quite unrelated to the expertise of the judiciary have required a modification in the traditional theory of the autonomy of military authority.

These events can be expressed very simply in numerical terms. A few months after Washington's first inauguration, our army numbered a mere 672 of the 840 authorized by Congress.[10] Today, in dramatic contrast, the situation is this: Our armed forces number two and a half million;[11] every resident male is a potential member of the peacetime armed forces; such service may occupy a minimum of four per cent of the adult life of the average American male reaching draft age; reserve obligations extend over ten per cent of such a person's life;[12] and veterans are numbered in excess of twenty-two and a half million.[13] When the authority of the military has such a sweeping capacity for affecting the lives of our citizenry, the wisdom of treating the military establishment as an enclave beyond the reach of the civilian courts almost inevitably is drawn into question.

Thus it was hardly surprising to find that, in 1953, the Supreme Court indicated in *Burns* v. *Wilson*[14] that court-martial proceedings could be challenged through habeas corpus actions brought in civil courts, if those proceedings had denied the defendant fundamental rights. The various opinions of the members of the Court in *Burns* are not, perhaps, as clear on this point as they might be. Nevertheless, I believe they do constitute recognition of the proposition that our citizens in uniform may not be stripped of basic rights simply because they have doffed their civilian clothes.

Despite *Burns*, however, it could hardly be expected that the regular federal judiciary would play a large role in regulating the military's treatment of its own personnel. The considerations militating against such intervention remain strong. Consequently, more important than *Burns* from a practical point of view was the action in 1951 of another guardian of the Bill of Rights, Congress, in enacting the Uniform Code of Military Justice and in establishing the Court of Military Appeals as a sort of civilian "Supreme Court" of the military.[15] The Code represents a diligent effort by Congress to insure that military justice is administered in accord with the demands of due process. Attesting to its success is the fact that since 1951 the number of habeas corpus petitions alleging a lack of fairness in courts-martial has been quite insubstantial.[16] Moreover, I know of no case since the adoption of the Code in which a civil court has issued the writ on the basis of such a claim. This development is undoubtedly due in good part to the supervision of military justice by the Court of Military Appeals. Chief Judge Quinn of that Court has recently stated:

> [M]ilitary due process begins with the basic rights and privileges defined in the federal constitution. It does not stop there. The letter and the background of the Uniform Code add their weighty demands to the requirements of a fair trial. Military due process is, thus, not synonymous with federal civilian due process. It is basically that, but something more, and something different.[17]

And the Court of Military Appeals has, itself, said unequivocally that "the protections in the Bill of Rights, except those which are expressly or by necessary implication inapplicable, are available to members of our armed forces." [18]

Thus our recent experience has shown, I believe, that the Court of Military Appeals can be an effective guarantor of our citizens' rights to due process when they are subjected to trial by court-martial. Moreover, the establishment of a special court to review these cases obviates, at least to some extent, the objection of lack of familiarity by the reviewing tribunal with the special problems of the military. In this connection, I think it significant that, despite the expanded application of our civilian concepts of fair play to military justice, the Chairman of the Joint Chiefs of Staff, General Lemnitzer, declared not long ago:

> I believe the Army and the American people can take pride in the positive strides that have been made in the application of military

law under the Uniform Code of Military Justice. The Army today has achieved the highest state of discipline and good order in its history.[19]

These developments support my conviction that the guarantees of our Bill of Rights need not be considered antithetical to the maintenance of our defenses.

Nevertheless, we cannot fail to recognize how our burgeoning army has posed difficult and unique problems for the Court in the application of constitutional principles. Thus, you may recall the case of Specialist Girard,[20] who, having been sent to Japan by the Army, contended that the Constitution entitled him to a trial by an American court-martial for an offense committed on an American army reservation in Japan against a Japanese national. The surrender of Girard to Japanese authorities was consonant with well-established rules of international law, and the Court's opinion cited, as its authority, the decision of Chief Justice Marshall in *The Schooner Exchange*,[21] written in 1812. But the case brought to light some problems we should consider in the light of developments unforeseen at the time the Constitution was written: the world-wide deployment of our citizens, called to duty and sent to foreign lands for extended tours of service, who may, by administrative decision of American authorities, be delivered to foreign governments for trial.[22] We are fortunate that our experience in this area has generally been a happy one,[23] and thus, to date, these constitutional problems have been largely submerged.

However, unique constitutional questions are, at times, presented for decision, which questions are, in part, an outgrowth of our expanded military forces. One of the most recent of these arose in *Trop v. Dulles*,[24] decided in 1958. In that case the Court considered a provision of our law that acted automatically to denationalize a citizen convicted of wartime desertion by a court-martial. Under this provision, over 7,000 men who had served in the Army alone, in World War II, were rendered stateless. It was the decision of the Court that, by this Act, Congress had exceeded its constitutional powers by depriving citizens of their birthright. Four members of the Court, of which I was one, expressed the view that this law, effectively denying the person's rights to have rights, was a cruel and unusual punishment proscribed by the Eighth Amendment. The need for military discipline was considered an inadequate foundation for expatriation.

The *Trop* case was [not?] an example, really, of how the Court has generally dealt with problems apart from the authority of the military in dealing with "its own." Rather, it was in the line of decisions dealing with attempts of our civilian Government to extend military authority into other areas. In these cases we find factors different from those the Court must consider persuasive in review of a soldier's disciplinary conviction by court-martial. The contending parties still advance the same general argument: protected liberties versus military necessity. Here, however, the tradition of exclusive authority of the military over its uniformed personnel is generally not directly relevant. Here, the Court has usually been of the view that it can and should make its own judgment, at least to some degree, concerning the weight a claim of military necessity is to be given.

The landmark decision in this field was, of course, *Ex parte Milligan*,[25] decided in 1866. It established firmly the principle that when civil courts are open and operating, resort to military tribunals for the prosecution of civilians is impermissible. The events giving rise to the *Milligan* case occurred while we were in the throes of a great war. However, the military activities of that war had been confined to a certain section of the country; in the remainder, the civil government operated normally. In passing upon the validity of a military conviction returned against Milligan outside the theater of actual combat, the Court recognized that no "graver question" was ever previously before it. And yet the Court, speaking through Mr. Justice Davis, reminded us that

> by the protection of the law human rights are secured; withdraw that protection, and they are at the mercy of wicked rulers, or the clamor of an excited people. If there was law to justify . . . [Milligan's] military trial, it is not our province to interfere; if there was not, it is our duty to declare the nullity of the whole proceedings.[26]

I do not propose to discuss in detail other cases that have been decided in a wartime context, for the risk is too great that they lie outside the mainstream of American judicial thought. War is, of course, a pathological condition for our Nation. Military judgments sometimes breed action that, in more stable times, would be regarded as abhorrent. Judges cannot detach themselves from such judgments, although by hindsight, from the vantage point of more tranquil times, they might conclude that some actions advanced in the name of national survival had in fact overidden the strictures of due process.[27]

Obviously such a charge could not be made against the Court in the *Milligan* case. However, some have pointed to cases like the companion decisions of *Hirabayashi* v. *United States* [28] and *Korematsu* v. *United States* [29] as aberrational. There, you will recall, the Court sustained the program under which, shortly after the attack on Pearl Harbor, over 100,000 Japanese nationals and citizens of that ancestry living in the western United States were, under Executive Order, with congressional sanction, placed under curfew and later excluded from areas within 750 miles of the Pacific Coast or confined in government detention camps.

Whatever may be the correct view of the specific holding of those cases, their importance for present purposes lies in a more general consideration. These decisions demonstrate dramatically that there are some circumstances in which the Court will, in effect, conclude that it is simply not in a position to reject descriptions by the Executive of the degree of military necessity. Thus, in a case like *Hirabayashi*, only the Executive is qualified to determine whether, for example, an invasion is imminent. In such a situation, where time is of the essence, if the Court is to deny the asserted right of the military authorities, it must be on the theory that the claimed justification, though factually unassailable, is insufficient. Doubtless cases might arise in which such a response would be the only permissible one. After all, the truism that the end does not justify the means has at least as respectable a lineage as the dictum that the power to wage war is the power to wage war successfully.[30] But such cases would be extraordinary indeed.

The consequence of the limitations under which the Court must sometimes operate in this area is that other agencies of government must bear the primary responsibility for determining whether specific actions they are taking are consonant with our Constitution. To put it another way, the fact that the Court rules in a case like *Hirabayashi* that a given program is constitutional, does not necessarily answer the question whether, in a broader sense, it actually is.

There is still another lesson to be learned from cases like *Hirabayashi*. Where the circumstances are such that the Court must accept uncritically the Government's description of the magnitude of the military need, actions may be permitted that restrict individual liberty in a grievous manner. Consequently, if judicial review is to constitute a meaningful restraint upon unwarranted encroachments upon freedom in the name of military necessity, situations in which the judiciary refrains from examining the merit of the claim of necessity must be kept to an absolute minimum. In this connection, it is instructive to compare the result in *Hirabayashi* with the result in cases that have been decided outside the context of war.

In times of peace, the factors leading to an extraordinary deference to claims of military necessity have naturally not been as weighty. This has been true even in the all too imperfect peace that has been our lot for the past fifteen years—and quite rightly so, in my judgment. It is instructive to recall that our Nation at the time of the Constitutional Convention was also faced with formidable problems. The English, the French, the Spanish, and various tribes of hostile Indians were all ready and eager to subvert or occupy the fledgling Republic. Nevertheless, in that environment, our Founding Fathers conceived a Constitution and Bill of Rights replete with provisions indicating their determination to protect human rights. There was no call for a garrison state in those times of precarious peace. We should heed no such call now. If we were to fail in these days to enforce the freedom that until now has been the American citizen's birthright, we would be abandoning for the foreseeable future the constitutional balance of powers and rights in whose name we arm.

Moreover, most of the cases the Court has decided during this period indicate that such a capitulation to the claim of military necessity would be a needless sacrifice. These cases have not been argued or decided in an emergency context comparable to the early 1940's. There has been time, and time provides a margin of safety. There has been time for the Government to be put to the proof with respect to its claim of necessity; there has been time for reflection; there has been time for the Government to adjust to any adverse decision. The consequence is that the claim of necessity has generally not been put to the Court in the stark terms of a *Hirabayashi* case.[31]

An excellent example of the approach adopted by the Court in the recent years of peacetime tension is its disposition of the various cases raising the question of court-martial jurisdiction over civilian dependents and employees of the armed forces overseas. Such jurisdiction was explicitly granted by the Uniform Code of Military Justice, and hence the issue was whether the statutory provision was constitutional.

In what the Court came to recognize as a hasty decision, this exercise of jurisdiction was at first sustained in the most striking of the cases presenting the problem—the trial of the wife of an American soldier for a capital offense. During the summer following that decision, a rehearing was considered and finally ordered. The next June, the rewritten, landmark decision of *Reid* v. *Covert* [32] struck down this exercise of military jurisdiction as an unconstitutional expansion of Congress' power to provide for the government of the armed forces. In 1960, *Reid* v. *Covert* was followed by the Court in similarly invalidating court-martial convictions of civilians accompanying and those employed by our services overseas, whether or not the offenses for which they had been convicted were punishable by death.[33]

Several features of these cases are worthy of note. First of all, the urgency of wartime was absent. Extended analysis and deliberation on the part of the parties and the Court were possible. Secondly, while, of course, the Government rested heavily upon a claim of military necessity, that claim could not be pressed with the same force that it was in *Hirabayashi*. Alternative methods of dealing with the military's problems could be considered. Indeed, the Court itself suggested a possible alternative in one of its opinions—the creation of a military service akin to the Seabees to secure the services theretofore performed by civilians. And finally, the extension of military jurisdiction for which the Government contended was extraordinarily broad. At that time, there were 450,000 dependents and 25,000 civilian employees overseas.[34] We could not safely deal with such a problem on the basis of what General Anthony Wayne did or did not do to camp followers at frontier forts in the last decade of the eighteenth century. In short, as in the case of trials of persons who are concededly part of the military, the burgeoning of our military establishment produced a situation so radically different from what the country had known in its distant past that the Court was required to return to first principles in coming to its judgment.

Another decision of the Court that is of significance in connection with the considerations I have been discussing was *Toth* v. *Quarles*.[35] There the Court held that a veteran holding an honorable discharge could not be recalled to active duty for the sole purpose of subjecting

him to a court-martial prosecution for offenses committed prior to
his discharge. The question was of enormous significance in the context of present-day circumstances, for the ranks of our veterans are
estimated to number more than 22,500,000. Thus a decision adverse to
the petitioner would have left millions of former servicemen helpless
before some latter-day revival of old military charges. So far as the
claim of military necessity was concerned, the facts were such that the
Court regarded itself as competent to deal with the problem directly.
Mr. Justice Black, speaking for the Court, said:

> It is impossible to think that the discipline of the Army is going to
> be disrupted, its morale impaired, or its orderly processes disturbed,
> by giving ex-servicemen the benefits of a civilian court trial when
> they are actually civilians. . . . Free countries of the world have
> tried to restrict military tribunals to the narrowest jurisdiction
> deemed absolutely essential to maintaining discipline among troops
> in active service.[36]

Attempts at extension of military control have not, of course, been
confined to the field of criminal justice, nor have all of them been
decided on constitutional grounds. *Harmon* v. *Brucker* [37] brought to
the Court the Army's claim that it had the authority to issue to a
draftee a discharge less than honorable on the basis of certain activities
in which the soldier was said to have engaged prior to his induction,
and which the Army thought made him a security risk. Again, the
gravity of the constitutional issues raised was underscored by the
existence of our system of peacetime conscription, for the sustaining
of the Army's claim would have affirmed its authority to affect the
pre-service political activities of every young American. A notable
feature of the case was that the Solicitor General conceded that, if
the Court had jurisdiction to rule upon the action of the Secretary
of the Army, his action should be held to be unconstitutional. Thus
the Government's case was placed entirely upon the asserted necessity for, and tradition of, the exclusive authority of the Secretary to
act with unreviewable discretion in cases of this nature. The Court,
however, found it unnecessary to reach constitutional issues. It disposed of the case on the non-constitutional ground that the Secretary
lacked statutory authority to condition the type of discharge he issued
upon any behavior other than that in which the soldier engaged dur-

ing his period of service. Such emphasis upon proper directives by Congress with respect to these problems, may be regarded as, in part, a further reflection of the principle of subordination of the military establishment to civil authority.

I cannot, of course, discuss more than a handful of the Supreme Court decisions bearing upon the military establishment's efforts to extend the scope of its authority in one way or another beyond service members. The cases I have dealt with, however, disclose what I regard as the basic elements of the approach the Court has followed with reasonable consistency. There are many other decisions that echo that approach, and there are some, to be sure, that seem inconsistent with it. But I would point to *Duncan* v. *Kahanamoku*,[38] in which the Court held, in the spirit of *Milligan*, although on non-constitutional grounds, that, after the Pearl Harbor attack, civilians in the Hawaiian Islands were subject to trial only in civilian courts, once those courts were open. And, of course, there have been a number of cases that, like *Harmon* v. *Brucker*, emphasize the Court's view that the military, like any other organ of government, must adhere strictly to its legislative mandate.[39]

On the whole, it seems to me plain that the Court has viewed the separation and subordination of the military establishment as a compelling principle. When this principle supports an assertion of substantial violation of a precept of the Bill of Rights, a most extraordinary showing of military necessity in defense of the Nation has been required for the Court to conclude that the challenged action in fact squared with the injunctions of the Constitution. While situations may arise in which deference by the Court is compelling, the cases in which this has occurred demonstrate that such a restriction upon the scope of review is pregnant with danger to individual freedom. Fortunately, the Court has generally been in a position to apply an exacting standard. Thus, although the dangers inherent in the existence of a huge military establishment may well continue to grow, we need have no feeling of hopelessness. Our tradition of liberty has remained strong through recurring crises. We need only remain true to it.

The last phase of the problem of the military in our society—the relationship of the military to civil government and affairs—is much more complex, and also perhaps much more important, than the subjects I have just discussed.

This relationship of the military to the rest of us raises issues that are less graphic, less tangible, less amenable to review or control by the courts. This aspect of the problem encompasses not only actions taken by our civil government in the name of defense that may impinge upon individual rights, but also matters such as the influence exerted on the civil government by uniformed personnel and the suppliers of arms. Such problems are not always clearly visible. Nor is the impact of our enormous financial, human and resource commitment to the needs of defense easy to measure.[40] Moreover, these problems often do not arise in a factual context suitable for a lawsuit and judicial review. Still, "cases and controversies" have occasionally arisen in recent years that suggest the magnitude of the difficulties we face.

Looking first at perhaps the broadest aspect of the problems generated by our defense needs, we could consider the question whether the industries basic to our defense are in all respects to be treated as "private" industry. In wartime, the total mobilization of our economy with its rationing, allocation of materials and manpower, and price and wage controls are acceptable restrictions for a free society locked in combat. The just compensation and due process provisions of the Constitution may be strained at such times. Are they to receive similar diminished deference in these days of "cold war"? This alone is a subject worthy of the most extended discussion. I can do no more here than suggest its pertinency. But it has been thrust upon the Court with a requirement for prompt decision in recent years.

You will recall the case of *Youngstown Sheet & Tube* v. *Sawyer*,[41] in which, in the midst of our military operations in Korea, the Court held that the President lacked the power, without specific Congressional sanction, to seize and operate the Nation's steel industry following its shutdown by a nation-wide strike. The numerous and lengthy opinions of the various members of the Court reveal the tremendous complexity of the issues such a case presents. And on what may the courts rely in such litigation? Consider these words from Mr. Justice Jackson's concurring opinion:

> A judge . . . may be surprised at the poverty of really useful and unambiguous authority applicable to concrete problems . . . as they actually present themselves. Just what our forefathers did

envision, or would have envisioned had they foreseen modern conditions, must be divined from materials almost as enigmatic as the dreams Joseph was called upon to interpret for Pharaoh. A century and a half of partisan debate and scholarly speculation yields no net result but only supplies more or less apt quotations from respected sources on each side of any question. They largely cancel each other. And court decisions are indecisive because of the judicial practice of dealing with the largest questions in the most narrow way.[42]

The result in the *Youngstown* case may be compared to the decision seven years later in *United Steelworkers of America* v. *United States*,[43] a decision reached during a time that no actual armed conflict engaged this country. There, the Court upheld a finding that since one per cent of the Nation's steel industry output was needed for defense purposes, the President had the authority, under the Taft-Hartley Act, to enjoin the union from continuing its strike, at least for eighty days. The critical factor upon which the injunction was based and sustained was a determination that even the temporary unavailability of one per cent of the industry's output might imperil the Nation's safety. Considerations that the injunction might infringe upon the workers' constitutional rights of free association, or perhaps the right *not* to work, fell, at least temporarily, before these findings. Should Congressional intervention—the difference between the *Youngstown* and *Steelworkers* cases—be so decisive? Would recourse to Taft-Hartley or other legislation by President Truman in 1952 have avoided the issues that made the *Youngstown* case so difficult? We need not, indeed cannot, answer that now. However, these cases illustrate the extent to which public and private interests merge and clash in controversies so vitally affecting the security of the Nation. The resolution of such cases is made no more simple or certain by the multitude of considerations that, while indisputably relevant, are outside the records before the courts.

On a less grand scale than the steel industry litigation, but perhaps no less significant, are the cases that have stemmed from the competition between the claims of national security and personal rights. The bulk of the many recent decisions concerning the contempt power of Congressional committees provides a graphic illustration. Some believe that these cases may be disposed of by the Court's balancing of the security of the Nation against the freedom of the individual litigant. If these are the appropriate weights to put in the scales, it is not surprising that the balance is usually struck against the individual. If balance we must, I wonder whether on the individual's side we might not also place the importance of our survival as a free nation. The issue, as I see it, is not the individual against society; it is rather the wise accommodation of the necessities of physical survival with the requirements of spiritual survival. Lincoln once asked, "[Is] it possible to lose the nation and yet preserve the Constitution?" [44] His rhetorical question called for a negative answer no less than its corollary: "Is it possible to lose the Constitution and yet preserve the Nation?" Our Constitution and Nation are one. Neither can exist without the other. It is with this thought in mind that we should gauge the claims of those who assert that national security requires what our Constitution appears to condemn.

Naturally the radiations of security requirements have come before the Court in contexts other than Congressional investigations. Even more closely connected with the defense effort have been the decisions concerning the right to employment in government and industry.

One may compare, for example, the 1959 case of *Greene* v. *McElroy* [45] with last Term's decision in *Cafeteria Workers* v. *McElroy*.[46] In the former, a serious constitutional issue was raised by the Navy's action in denying, on questionable grounds, security clearance to a privately employed aeronautical engineer. This, in turn, effectively precluded him from pursuing his occupation. The Court was able, however, to dispose of the case on the non-constitutional ground that requirements of confrontation prescribed by existing law had wrongfully been ignored.[47] In *Cafeteria Workers*, on the other hand, where a short-order cook employed by a concessionaire on a military base was summarily refused further security clearance without hearing, explanation, or opportunity to rebut, the Court reached the constitutional question and, by a five-to-four vote, decided it against the employee. I joined Mr. Justice Brennan's dissent, which took the position that the Court, while conceding petitioner's right not to be injured arbitrarily by the Government, in fact made that right non-enforceable by refusing to accord petitioner any procedural protection.

One of the principal difficulties presented by these "security risk" cases is that the claim of necessity takes the form of an assertion of the right of secrecy. Thus, the claim, by its very nature, tends to restrict the ability of the Court to evaluate its merit. This in turn impairs the efficacy of judicial review as an instrument for preserving the guarantees of the Bill of Rights. While the dilemma is in some cases serious, *Cafeteria Workers*, the most recent expression of the Court's views on the subject, does not, in my judgment, represent a satisfactory guidepost for resolution of the problem.

Our enormous national commitment of defense will, of course, pose still additional, difficult problems for the courts. We have, in the past considered,[48] and will probably be called upon in the future to review, cases arising out of the effort to accord our large number of veterans special compensation or preferences in return for their service to the country. While recognizing the need for such programs, we are also asked to consider to what extent such preferences impinge on opportunities of other citizens, whose public service and welfare are no less deserving of recognition. Questions concerning the review of military procurement, in the light of claims of emergency need, expert judgment and secrecy of information are still largely unresolved. The problem of the extent to which members of the armed forces may properly express their political views to other troops, particularly subordinates in the chain of command, and to the public at large, are subjects of controversy. Questions of the right of the people to know what their government is doing, their right to travel, speak, congregate, believe, and dissent will arise again and again. It is to the courts that the task of adjudicating many of these rights is delegated. I am one who believes firmly that the Court must be vigilant against neglect of the requirements of our Bill of Rights and the personal rights that document was intended to guarantee for all time. Legislative or executive action eroding our citizens' rights in the name of security cannot be placed on a scale that weighs the public's interest against that of the individual in a sort of "count the heads" fashion. Democracy under our Constitution calls for judicial deference to the coordinate branches of the Government and their judgment of what is essential to the protection of the Nation. But it calls no less for a steadfast protection of those fundamentals imbedded in the Constitution, so incorporated for the express purpose of insulating them from possible excesses of the moment. Our history has demonstrated that we must be as much on guard against the diminution of our rights through excessive fears for our security and a reliance on military solutions for our problems by the civil government, as we are against the usurpation of civil authority by the army. That is the important lesson of the Court cases, most of which have arisen not through the initiative of the military seeking power for itself, but rather through governmental authorization for intervention of military considerations in affairs properly reserved to our civilian institutions.

In concluding, I must say that I have, of course, not touched upon every type of situation having some relation to our military establishment which the Court considers. Those to which I have pointed might suggest to some that the Court has at times exceeded its role in this area. My view of the matter is the opposite. I see how limited is the role that the courts can truly play in protecting the heritage of our people against military supremacy. In our democracy it is still the Legislature and the elected Executive who have the primary responsibility for fashioning and executing policy consistent with the Constitution. Only an occasional aberration from norms of operation is brought before the Court by some zealous litigant. Thus we are sometimes provided with opportunities for reiterating the fundamental principles on which our country was founded and has grown mighty. But the day-to-day job of upholding the Constitution really lies elsewhere. It rests, realistically, on the shoulders of every citizen.

President Eisenhower, as he left the White House [in 1960], urged the American people to be alert to the changes that come about by reason of the coalescence of military and industrial power. His words were these:

> [T]his conjunction of an immense military establishment and a large arms industry is new in the American experience. The total influence —economic, political, even spiritual—is felt in every city, every state house, every office of the Federal Government. . . . [W]e must not fail to comprehend . . . [the] grave implications. Our toil, resources and livelihood are all involved; so is the very structure of our society.

> [W]e must guard against the acquisition of unwarranted influence . . . by the military-industrial complex. . . .

We must never let the weight of this combination endanger our liberties or democratic processes. We should take nothing for granted. Only an alert and knowledgeable citizenry can compel the proper meshing of the . . . machinery of defense with our peaceful methods and goals, so that security and liberty may prosper together.[49]

Coming from one who was our great Field Commander in World War II and for eight years Commander-in-Chief as President of the United States, these words should find lodgment in the mind of every American. It is also significant that both his predecessor and his successor have conveyed the same thought in slightly different words.[50] I am sure that none of them thought for a moment that anyone was deliberately trying to change the relationship between the military and the civil government. But they realized, as we all must, that our freedoms must be protected not only against deliberate destruction but also against unwitting erosion.

We may happily note that the Constitution has remarkably weathered a variety of crises. Some were as acute as those we face today. Today, as always, the people, no less than their courts, must remain vigilant to preserve the principles of our Bill of Rights, lest in our desire to be secure we lose our ability to be free.

FOOTNOTES

[1] 5 Freeman, George Washington 477 (1952).

[2] 3 Channing, A History of the United States 376 (1912).

[3] 24 Writings of Washington 272 (Fitzpatrick ed. 1938).

[4] The Federalist No. 41, at 251 (Lodge ed. 1888) (Madison).

[5] See, e.g., Pinkney's recommendations to the Federal Convention, 2 Records of the Federal Convention 341 (Farrand ed. 1911), and the discussion by Mason and Madison, id. at 617; Resolutions on Ratification of the Constitution by the States of Massachusetts, New Hampshire, New York and Virginia, reprinted in Documents Illustrative of Formation of the Union of American States, H.R. Doc. No. 398, 69th Cong., 1st Sess. 1018–20, 1024–44 (1927).

[6] The vote in the House was for: 220, against: 105, not voting: 104. In the Senate the vote was for: 47, against: 21, not voting: 28. 96 Cong. Rec. 14931, 14973 (1950).

[7] See, e.g., Remarks of Representatives Wolverton and Hoffman and Senators Watkins and Cain, 96 Cong. Rec. 14835, 14919, 15177, A6561 (1950).

[8] 68 U.S. (1 Wall.) 243 (1863).

[9] 61 U.S. (20 How.) 65 (1857).

[10] Report of Secretary of War Knox to the Congress on the Military Force in 1789, communicated to the Senate on August 10, 1789, 1 American State Papers—Military Affairs No. 1. At the time of the Constitutional Convention, consideration was given to limiting the size of the National Army for all time to a few thousand men, through express constitutional provision. 2 Records of the Federal Convention 323, 329, 330, 616–17 (Farrand ed. 1911).

[11] Total strength of the armed forces on November 30, 1961, was estimated to be 2,780,975 by the Directorate of Statistical Services, Office of the Secretary of Defense, Pamphlet 22.1 (Dec. 20, 1961).

[12] The Universal Military Training and Service Act of 1951, §§ 4(b), (d), establishes an active duty tour of two years and a reserve obligation of six years thereafter, as the norm for all persons subject to the Act. 65 Stat. 78 (1951), as amended, 50 U.S.C. App. §§ 454(b),(d) (1958). In statistics compiled in 1959, the American male between 20 and 25 had a life expectancy of another 49.5 years Nat'l Office of Vital Statistics, Life Tables § 5–5 (Dep't of Health, Educ., & Welfare 1959).

[13] On June 30, 1960, the Veterans Administration counted 22,534,000 veterans of all armed forces then living. 1960 Adm'r of Veterans Affairs Ann. Rep. 6–7 (1961).

[14] 346 U.S. 137 (1953).

[15] See Uniform Code of Military Justice, 10 U.S.C. §§ 867, 876 (1958).

[16] Similarly, since the adoption of the Uniform Code of Military Justice, the Court of Claims has not granted relief in the form of back pay to claimants alleging wrongful dismissal from government service through court-martial proceedings lacking fundamental fairness. Compare Shapiro v. United States, 69 F. Supp. 205 (Ct. Cl. 1947).

[17] Quinn, The United States Court of Military Appeals and Military Due Process, 35 St. John's L. Rev. 225, 232 (1961). In an early opinion, the Court of Military Appeals said, "If, because of the peculiarities of the military service, a variation from civilian practice is necessary to assure a fair trial, we should unhesitatingly adopt the procedure best suited to the administration of military justice, even though by so doing we may bring about a departure from a prior service rule." United States v. Hemp, 1 U.S.C.M.A. 280, 286, 3 C.M.R. 14, 20 (1952). Compare the evolution of the court's approach to "military due process" in United States v. Clay, 1 U.S.C.M.A. 74, 1 C.M.R. 74 (1951), with United States v. Jacoby, 11 U.S.C.M.A. 428, 29 C.M.R. 244 (1960).

[18] United States v. Jacoby, supra, note 19, at 430–31, 29 C.M.R. at 246–47.

[19] Dep't of the Army Pamphlet No. 27-101-18 (Oct. 7, 1959), reprinted in 1960 U.S.C.M.A. Ann. Rep. 4. Similar views have been expressed by ranking officers of the Army and Navy. See Army Chief of Staff General Decker, id., and Navy Judge Advocate General Admiral Mott, An Appraisal of Proposed Changes in the Uniform Code of Military Justice, 35 St. John's L. Rev. 300 (1961).

[20] Wilson v. Girard, 354 U.S. 524 (1957).

[21] The Schooner Exchange v. McFaddon, 11 U.S. (7 Cranch) 116 (1812).

[22] A recent survey by the Department of Defense lists 19 countries with which the United States has entered Status of Forces Agreements similar to the one with which the Court dealt in Girard. In addition, this country is signatory

to agreements with 56 nations (15 the same as SOFA signatories) in which military missions (as distinguished from troop deployments) have virtual diplomatic immunity. See also U.S. Dep't of State, Treaties in Force (Jan. 1, 1962).

23 See Senate Comm. on Armed Services, Operation of Article VII, NATO Status of Forces Treaty, S. Rep. No. 1041, 87th Cong., 1st Sess. 2 (1961).

24 356 U.S. 86 (1958).

25 71 U.S. (4 Wall.) 2 (1866).

26 Id. at 119.

27 In times of stress, the Court is not only vulnerable, to some extent, to the emotions of our people, but also to action by Congress in restricting what that body may consider judicial interference with the needs of security and defense. Following the Civil War, Congress actually exercised its constitutional powers to provide for the rules governing the appellate jurisdiction of the Supreme Court, for this very purpose. See Ex parte McCardle, 73 U.S. (6 Wall.) 318 (1867); 74 U.S. (7 Wall.) 506 (1868).

28 320 U.S. 81 (1943).

29 323 U.S. 214 (1944).

30 Chief Justice Hughes, speaking for the Court in Home Bldg. & Loan Ass'n v. Blaisdell, 290 U.S. 398, 426 (1934).

31 In this connection, we might also consider and compare the cases of Ex parte Quirin, 317 U.S. 1 (1942), and Abel v. United States, 362 U.S. 217 (1960). The former came before the Court at the outset of World War II, at a time when the outlook for the survival of the free world was dim. On the floor of Congress, fears were expressed that Hitler could subdue the country even without an invasion, through the use of "fifth columnists" and German allies thought to exist in every State of the Union. See 87 Cong. Rec. 555 (1941). When a small group of Nazi saboteurs was discovered on our shores, they were brought before a military tribunal——not our civilian courts. They were treated as wartime belligerents and spies, and ordered executed. The Supreme Court denied an application for a writ of habeas corpus, sustaining the military's jurisdiction.

However, when, in June 1957, Rudolph Abel was apprehended in his New York hotel room and identified as a colonel in the Russian army, he was not brought before a court-martial. A full civilian trial, with all the safeguards of our Bill of Rights, was accorded this agent of our adversary. Abel brought his case to the Supreme Court claiming the protection of our Constitution. I was among those who dissented from the Court's judgment that he had not been the subject of a constitutionally proscribed search and seizure. But all of the opinions reiterated our fundamental approach—that neither the nature of the case nor the notoriety of the defendant could influence our decision on the constitutional issue presented.

Cf. In re Yamashita, 327 U.S. 1 (1946), in which the Court denied habeas corpus relief to an officer of the enemy vanquished in a war fought in the cause of the Constitution, but who, for his wartime actions, was subjected to an American military court whose procedures were questionably squared with the spirit of due process.

32 354 U.S. 1 (1957), withdrawing 351 U.S. 487 (1956).

33 McElroy v. United States ex rel. Guagliardo, 361 U.S. 281 (1960) (employee—noncapital offense); Grisham v. Hagan, 361 U.S. 278 (1960) (employee

—capital offense); Kinsella v. United States ex rel. Singleton, 361 U.S. 234 (1960) (dependent—noncapital offense).

34 Brief for Petitioner, the Secretary of Defense, pp. 12, 71, 110–11, McElroy v. United States ex rel. Guagliardo, 361 U.S. 281 (1960).

35 United States ex rel. Toth v. Quarles, 350 U.S. 11 (1955).

36 Id. at 22.

37 355 U.S. 579 (1958).

38 327 U.S. 304 (1946). Cf. Madsen v. Kinsella, 343 U.S. 341 (1952).

39 For example, in Bell v. United States, 366 U.S. 393 (1961), the Army was challenged for declining to pay former soldiers who, during the Korean War, and while prisoners of war of the enemy, had betrayed some fellow prisoners and had refused initial opportunities for repatriation. Despite the absence of any authority for withholding the pay earned and accrued by these men to the dates of their well-deserved dishonorable discharges, the Army refused to make payment. As the situation was summarized by the dissenting judge in the Court of Claims, "Finding nothing in the law books to justify its refusal to pay these men, it threw the books away and just refused to pay them. It could have set before these confused young men a better example of government by law." 181 F. Supp. 668, 675 (Ct. Cl. 1960). We agreed.

In similar vein have been the series of decisions concerning the conscription procedures of the Selective Service System. For example, this Term we have again had occasion to consider a conviction based on an alleged failure of a registrant to notify his draft board of a change of address. After three unsuccessful prosecutions for draft evasion, the Government secured a belated indictment, conviction and three-year prison sentence for the young man's questionable failure to notify his board promptly of a change of address. But, from the record, it seemed clear that it was the registrant's annoying persistence in pursuing appellate rights to secure an exemption from active duty on a claim of being a minister of Jehovah's Witnesses that underlay the course of prosecution. Venus v. United States, 368 U.S. 345 (1961) (mem.). In 1955, in Gonzales v. United States, 348 U.S. 407 (1955), we were faced with a conviction for draft evasion, in which the draftee had not been accorded the simple right of examining a Department of Justice memorandum contesting his claims that he was a conscientious objector, and which memorandum had been presented to a Selective Service appeal board in reviewing Gonzales' classification. Understandably, we held that although the needs of the Army were great, it had to be fair in abiding by the law under which it sought conscripts. An additional factor of importance about these cases is that under the Selective Service law, violation of the call to military duty is a civil offense, punishable only in the civilian courts.

40 The Defense Department now spends over 50% of the total federal budget, a sum almost 10% of our gross national product. It is estimated that 10% of the entire national labor force is, in some manner, employed in defense industries or the defense establishment itself. See N.Y. Times, May 21, 1961, p. 48, cols. 4–5; U.S. Dept. of Commerce, Statistical Abstract of the United States 235, 301 (1961).

41 343 U.S. 579 (1952).

42 Id. at 634–35.

43 361 U.S. 39 (1959).

[44] 10 Complete Works of Abraham Lincoln 66 (Nicolay and Hay ed. 1894).

[45] 360 U.S. 474 (1959).

[46] 367 U.S. 886 (1961).

[47] For decisions in a comparable vein, see Cole v. Young, 351 U.S. 536 (1956), limiting, through interpretation to those in "sensitive" positions, the power of the Executive summarily to dismiss government employees in the interest of "national security"; Vitarelli v. Seaton, 359 U.S. 535 (1959), requiring government agencies dismissing employees in nonsensitive positions on security grounds, to afford the employees an opportunity to see the charges against them and to confront adverse witnesses; Kent v. Dulles, 357 U.S. 116 (1958), upholding the right of citizens to travel freely in the absence of compelling restrictions clearly to be found in Congressional action.

[48] See, e.g., McKinney v. Missouri-K.-T.R.R., 357 U.S. 265 (1958); Hyland v. Watson, 287 F.2d 884 (6th Cir.), cert. denied, 368 U.S. 876 (1961). Cf. the recent decision of Australia's highest court invalidating a far-reaching veteran's preference statute on the ground that with the World War II emergency past, the war power justification for such laws, under the Australian Constitution, had ceased. Illawarra District County Council v. Wickham, 101 Commw. L.R. 467 (Austl. 1959).

[49] N.Y. Times, Jan. 18, 1961, p. 22, cols. 5, 6.

[50] President Kennedy, in his special message to Congress on the defense budget delivered shortly after taking office, declared, "Neither our strategy nor our psychology as a nation—and certainly not our economy—must become dependent upon our . . . maintenance of a large military establishment. . . . Our arms must be subject to ultimate civilian control and command at all times. . . ." N.Y. Times, March 29, 1961, p. 16, cols. 1, 2.

Similarly, President Truman, on such occasions as his message to Congress urging the creation of a single Department of Defense, over which a civilian would preside, and his removal of General MacArthur as Commander of United Nations forces in Korea, reiterated these beliefs. 1945 Public Papers of the Presidents of the United States: Harry S. Truman 554–55, 558 (1961); 2 Truman Memoirs 449 (1956).